SOCIAL WELFARE

SOCIAL WELFARE
A History of the
American Response To Need

SECOND EDITION

June Axinn

Herman Levin
University of Pennsylvania

HARPER & ROW, PUBLISHERS, New York
Cambridge, Philadelphia, San Francisco,
London, Mexico City, São Paulo, Sydney

1817

Sponsoring Editor: Alan McClare
Project Editor: Pamela Landau
Designer: Robert Sugar
Production Manager: Jeanie Berke
Compositor: Lexigraphics Inc.
Printer and Binder: The Murray Printing Company

Social Welfare: A History of the American Response to Need, Second Edition
Copyright © 1982 by Harper & Row, Publishers, Inc.

Library of Congress Cataloging in Publication Data

Axinn, June.
  Social welfare.

  Includes bibliographical references and index.
    1. Public welfare—United States—History.   2. Public
welfare—United States—History—Sources.   I. Levin,
Herman, 1920–   II. Title.
HV91.A94   1982   361.6'0973   81-13503
ISBN 0-06-040399-3   AACR2

For Mildred
For Sidney

Contents

6   The Depression and the New Deal: 1930–1940   175

7   War and Prosperity: 1940–1970   231

8   Social Change and Economic Stagnation: The 1970s and 1980s   281

Preface
to the First Edition

This book has gone through many stages. Initially, the volume was planned as a collection of historical documents with brief introductory statements. The documents were to be materials pertinent to an understanding of the development of social welfare policies and programs in the United States. As our work progressed, we discovered the documents did not always support long-established interpretations found in popular secondary sources. The introductory statements got longer and longer as we became more intrigued with what we found. Three years later, the core of the book is the historical narrative. The documents included have been chosen to illuminate the history.

Successive drafts have been used by our students at the School of Social Work, University of Pennsylvania. They questioned, argued, and pushed us to further exploration. We thank them all for sharing our enthusiasm and for their valuable contributions to the substance of the book. Particularly, we wish to acknowledge the help of Carl Barnes, Thomas Carlton, Michael Cenci, James Chavis, Najma Davis, Gerald Fisher, Eudice Glassberg, Edward Kuhlman, Toba Schwaber, and Arthur Silbergeld. We owe a special debt to our colleague Dr. Sherman Labovitz, who read and criticized several chapters.

Our gratitude to Ms. Evelyn Butler, Chief Librarian, and Ms. Mary Sparhawk, Reference Librarian, at the university's School of Social Work. They were patient beyond measure with our many questions. They should be thanked, too, for making the library so rich a resource.

We want to thank all the secretaries who worked on the book. A special statement of appreciation is reserved for Ms. Alberta Orr, our secretarial assistant and typist for the final manuscript. We are most grateful for her thoughtful comments and caring attention to details.

A final word for Mildred and Sidney. Never were wife and husband more understanding of husband and wife.

JUNE AXINN
HERMAN LEVIN

Preface
to the Second Edition

The new edition of *Social Welfare: A History of the American Response to Need* represents a continuation of a process of learning and writing about the evolution of social welfare in the United States. The format of the original edition, historical analysis with supporting documents, remains in place with this edition. Numerous correspondents have attested to its value as a teaching base and it has lent itself to revision as current social welfare events raised new questions about old happenings. Thus, the use of documents as "turning points" in history is maintained in this edition. None have been deleted, but two have been added—one at the start of the book to demonstrate the powerful influence of the English heritage on American social welfare and the other at its close to suggest future directions. In regard to the narrative itself, an extensive amount of material has been added to highlight the role of women in social welfare.

The book (and the revisions) has continued to be used with our students at the School of Social Work, both in the master's and doctoral programs. We thank them all for their many helpful questions and comments. We are particularly appreciative of the contributions of Mark Kirszner, Jerry Kopelman, Ronald Myers, Mark Rodgers, and Kirk Seibert. We thank, too, the numerous persons who, having read and used the book, made verbal or written comment for enhancing its usefulness. Among them are Ralph Dolgoff at Adelphi University, Corinne Muldoon at Bloomsburg State College, and Mark Stern of our own faculty at the University of Pennsylvania.

We again extend our thanks to Ms. Evelyn Butler, Chief Librarian, and Ms. Mary Sparhawk, Reference Librarian, at the University of Pennsylvania's School of Social Work, and to the secretarial staff who were so helpful in their work on the book.

And, finally, a word of appreciation for Mildred and Sidney. Their delight in the success of our book makes the reality of this revision all the more a happy occurrence.

JUNE AXINN
HERMAN LEVIN

Chapter 1
Introduction

This volume is a history of social welfare in the United States. Its special concern is the American response to the needs of the poor and the oppressed. Values and attitudes are explored, as well as the political and economic forces that have brought about particular social welfare policies and programs at any one time.

The goals of social welfare programs for the poor derive from the goals of the larger society for itself and from the view that society holds of itself and of its various members. In turn, decisions about who is needy and how the needy are to be helped bear upon economic development, political organization, social stability, and family integrity. Social welfare programs involve a redistribution of resources—from the "haves" to the "have nots." This nation has been reluctant to do that, holding instead to a faith in laissez faire and individualism. The country has valued the private economy over the public and individual choice over collective choices.

Because social welfare goals touch a core of ideologies, they tend to polarize Americans. Priorities for funding programs for old people or children, for example, vie with programs meant to encourage work among employables. Similarly, priorities regarding old people or children may conflict with traditions of self-help among family members and consequently lead to programs that discourage acceptance of needed help.

Decisions need to be made about the nature of social welfare programs. Should help be offered in cash, in "kind,"—that is, as goods—or in services? Money, food, or advice? Rent supplements or public housing? Should cash

1

transfers be tied to work incentive programs? Are money payments to be joined to counseling services? Is help in one's own family or community preferable to institutional care? Need the extension of health care benefits be tied to insurance mechanisms? Simultaneously, decisions about benefit levels and, equally important, terms of entitlement must relate closely to the purposes for which programs have been devised. The extent to which potential beneficiaries are viewed as claimants, recipients, or clients suggest not only the intent of the program but also the extent to which eligibility factors will be deterrent or invitational.

Additional decisions are inherent in efforts to implement social welfare programs and to establish a coherent welfare system. The sheer land size of the United States, the size of its population, and the number of religious, racial, and ethnic groups that compose it—as well as legal and social traditions related to volunteerism, to separation of church and state, to states' rights, and to local responsibility—all complicate legislative and administrative decisions in social welfare matters. Which programs should be government funded and administered and at which level of government? Which programs should be both funded and administered by voluntary and/or proprietary organizations? What should be the degree of consumer participation in program design and service delivery? The list of policy and program decisions to be made is not yet complete.

The history of social welfare is paralleled by and enmeshed with the growing professionalism of those who administer social services—that is, with the history of the social work profession. The early development of the public and voluntary sectors of social welfare was accompanied by the development of purveyors of service seemingly appropriate to the purposes of each: both the overseer of the poor and the lady bountiful. Historical evolution has led to professionalization in both the public and the private sectors. In both sectors there have been and still are philosophical differences leading to quite different program positions and social strategies. Those social workers who emphasize societal causation of social problems seek programs establishing governmental responsibility for meeting needs and develop coalitions for reform and institutional change. On the other hand, those who emphasize individual causation of social problems have moved to the development and use of psychological theory and to a therapeutic approach to helping. Historical cleavages continue to divide social welfare generally and social work in particular.

This book emphasizes the meaning of social welfare for the family as a unit and for family members as individuals. The assumption is that the family is the basic organizing device of modern society and that all social policy decisions impinge on family well-being. In this sense, then, social policy and family policy are essentially one. The fact that the United States has no governmental family policy, no social policy that overtly supports family integrity as a goal in itself, highlights the discrepancies and dilemmas that have marked the American approach to social welfare. Society's interest in the family has not resulted in a stated, widely accepted, goal for family welfare. Efforts to clarify such a goal through the calling of a White House Conference on Families were marked by confusion, dissension, and delays. The family remains an essentially private venture.

From the beginning, a separate channeling of "family" welfare and child welfare, originating with English Poor Laws, and, therefore, at one with the fabric of an English colonial milieu, divided social welfare responses for the worthy, impotent poor — the disabled and children — from those for the unworthy — the ablebodied poor. The incorporation of the English Poor Law into the legislative framework of American colonial governments differentiated those who were unable to work from those who were potentially employable. Poor Law programs were vitally concerned with those who were employed and who might be in danger of "falling into pauperism." The family was effective to the degree that it maintained the social order and the economic viability of its individual members. To a considerable extent, social welfare programs for poor people in the twentieth century are characterized by this same orientation.

The essential worthiness of children and the importance of nurturing their potential for social and economic contribution led to stated, public concern for their well-being as members of families and eventually to grudging recognition of the needs of families. The twentieth century was proclaimed the Century of the Child, and pressures to make the label stick resulted in the calling of the first White House Conference on Children in 1909, and to a positive statement of public policy in regard to child care. Home and family life were declared to be society's goal for children, an enunciation of the rights of children. Economic necessity, many felt, should not require that a mother leave her child care responsibilities for work outside the home. Time and reality have demonstrated ambivalence of policy and practice in child welfare. Today there is sharpened conflict about the policy itself.

Now, as in the past, welfare programs are fragmented and disparate. Efforts to develop a holistic family policy and an integrated income maintenance system have foundered. Budgetary constraints and concern with the recent growth in the number of single-parent families are part of the reluctance to "reform" and possibly, thereby, to expand, public welfare and social services. Additionally, the increased labor force participation of all women — single and married, mothers and the childless — weakens the argument for governmental support of mothers as homemakers. Throughout this volume, attention is given to the place of women in the contemporary social and economic structure. The process by which the ablebodied poor — a label applied to poor men of the eighteenth and nineteenth centuries — came, in our own time, to signify poor women is traced.

The social welfare needs of two groups, veterans and blacks, are given special analysis to demonstrate two extremes in social policy in the United States. History shows the assignment of veterans to special consideration for social welfare benefits as a result of their unique social and economic contribution through service in the armed forces. So much value has been placed on this contribution that benefits initiated for veterans have tended to set precedents for benefits later extended to others.

For minority populations — blacks, Hispanics, American Indians, and Asian-Americans, for example — a very different picture emerges. Our attention is focused primarily on the largest of these groups, the black population. Blacks have suffered the dual difficulties of color and class, of racial discrimination and poverty. They have been assigned a social and economic role that has assured their vulnerability to the risks of industrial society and to extended need. Simultaneously, the assignment of that peculiar economic and social role has been used to rationalize the denial of economic and social justice that might have enabled them to meet their needs. Being black and female is to live with double jeopardy.

It should be noted that the assignment of special roles to veterans and to minorities has been based on considerable agreement in the general population. Interestingly, most of the poor have concurred with the special treatment of these groups and with the general expectation that families support themselves.

Over the years these principles have been implemented in accordance with the country's economic realities. As the country became richer, social welfare programs have expanded. The range of treatment of different groups persists, but policies have become more generous for all.

The low level of individual economic output relative to the level of production needed during the colonial period permitted little choice in regard to ability or willingness to work. The well-being, the very existence, of the colonies depended upon the maximum contribution of each of the colonists. Such dependence, supported by a view of human beings as inherently evil and easily seduced into idleness and pauperism, resulted in a policy of coercive alternatives to relief—the workhouse, indenture, apprenticeship, contracting out, and so on.

In contrast, the affluence of our own times presents a situation in which technological advance makes for a potential surplus of goods. Our industrial society has now achieved a stage of development in which there is more labor than needed for simple maintenance, and therefore more choice is possible in formulating policy and devising programs for those who are less productive. The growth of social welfare expenditures in the twentieth century reflects the rising ability of society to meet the social welfare needs created by the industrial process and its impact on family structure. The greater freedom to choose notably appears in the separation of money payments to public assistance recipients from socially controlling services. Nevertheless, recurring periods of recession and inflation make it clear that the ability to finance welfare programs is finite, that the economy continues to require an allocation of "scarce" productive resources among competitive uses. And to the extent that this is true, the goals of money payment programs will continue to influence the choice of benefits offered and the terms of entitlement to these services.

An examination of the history of the American response to dependency gives evidence that morality and ideology follow upon technological and economic reality. The colonial perception of work as moral and idleness as immoral is challenged, in an affluent society, by a concept of entitlement to protection from society's hazards and by a view of poverty as immoral. The resistance to change suggests the strength of the ideological overlay inherited from an earlier economy of severe scarcity, as well as the need to resolve value conflicts, if policy and program decisions relevant to today's various families are to be made.

Even a cursory historical review of social welfare policies and programs demonstrates that political decisions about family welfare have been economically based. Overall, the family has been seen as a unit to be supported, if such support achieves eventual economic independence for its members. When the family seems unlikely as an appropriate model, when it is not socially approved—that is, work-oriented—conventional political wisdom has resided in the denial of public support. The hypothesis that family welfare policies and programs are economically based suggests again the numerous questions to be answered before benefits can be determined.

No exact formula is available for achieving an integrated response to the questions. Nevertheless, this volume assumes that decisions leading to the formulation of social policies and programs for families result from the interaction of four factors:

1. The level of output
2. The view of society itself, that is, the view of the effectiveness with which "the system" is operating
3. The view of human nature
4. The historical heritage

The level of productivity, of output, of a particular society lends obvious constraints to choices about the uses of that output. These constraints are quite real. High levels of output and affluence increase the possibilities for choice; and the degree of equality in a society can, and indeed often does, increase as national income rises. At the same time that wealth makes some redistribution possible, it also makes it psychologically necessary; our concept of what might be a tolerable level of poverty varies with gross national product. Still the United States has not been a generous or equalitarian nation. Far beyond the demands of economic reality, the nonproductive have been subjected to poverty programs that in the end maintain the poor only minimally.

The view that is held of the effectiveness of society's functioning strongly influences the initiation and development of social welfare programs. If society believes itself to be operating effectively, and if most people feel they do well within the system, then those who find it hard to survive can be looked upon as individual failures. In such circumstances, the approach to the poor and to poverty issues is by way of remedial, residual programs aimed at uplifting the failures, at changing them to look like the rest of us. On the other hand, when society is considered to be operating ineffectively, the demand is for institutional change. The response to the severe, localized unrest of the 1960s was the War on Poverty, which consisted of educational, employment, legal, and social services aimed at helping individuals to become more effective participants in the labor market. In contrast, government responded to the widespread unemployment crisis of the Great Depression with the permanent social insurance programs of the Social Security Act, which altered the income distribution system and helped it become more effective in meeting the needs of individuals and families.

The commonly held view of human nature unquestionably contributes to the nature of the response to human need. A belief in the superiority of any group in the population—indeed, any racial, ethnic, religious, or sexual hierarchical ordering—becomes a basis for discrimination and exploitation. Certainly, the history of social welfare in the United States reflects this in its insistence on "blaming the victims." In the nineteenth century, Americans used Social Darwinism to rationalize greed; more recently, sociobiology has filled the same function.

If people are seen as basically lazy, as shiftless, even sinful, then social welfare programs are devised to deter. A nineteenth-century listing of the causes of dependency highlighted individual character flaws and argued that the help given the poor by organized charity aggravated the problem. The dominant nineteenth-century response to dependency was the organization of friendly services aimed at pushing the poor individual, and by extension the family, above the need for relief. Alternatively, if people are considered essentially good (that is, ambitious), the response to need is more likely to be guided by the offer of incentives and the development of programs that provide opportunity for self-advancement.

Historically, both views of the human condition, as reflected in the treatment of the poor, have been held. The poor have been considered both blessed and condemned by God, both virtuous and sinful, both lazy and ambitious. And these contrasting views have been held simultaneously. In connection with the family, for example, the prevailing nineteenth-century view of Charity Organization Society leaders that family members had to be deterred from a base, inherited instinct for pauperism was countered by Settlement House Movement leaders' conviction about the constructive force of human aspiration. To the former, pauperism — its effects upon the individual, the family, and society — was a disease worse than death; and hunger and starvation were to be endured for its exorcism. To the latter, poverty resulted from the denial of opportunity, and pressure was exerted for legislative reform designed to affirm and expand an inherent core of human dignity.

The need for resolution of value conflicts seems especially clear as we move toward revisions in our welfare system. The federalization of adult categories of public assistance—Old Age Assistance, Aid to the Needy Blind, and Aid to the Permanently and Totally Disabled—on January 1, 1974, and the rejection by Congress of proposals by Presidents Nixon and Carter to replace the Aid to Families with Dependent Children category of public assistance, demonstrate enduring, contradictory views of human nature and the force of history on the shape of social welfare. Public acceptance of the Supplemental Security Income Program for the worthy, adult, nonworking poor highlights, by contrast, the suspicion with which we continue to view the needy family with employable members.

The rejection of Nixon's Family Assistance Plan and Carter's Better Jobs and Income Proposal was especially significant considering their obeisance to the belief in the therapeutic value of work. The fact that the proposals were steeped in adherence to the work ethic did not dispel the fear that adding the "working poor" to the welfare rolls would lead to widespread moral debilitation. The linkage between work and the receipt of income security benefits was not strong enough to dispel the threat to our economic system that Congress saw in a guaranteed annual income—no matter how low that income was.

The impact of cultural bias is clear throughout our history. The Poor Laws, as they developed in England during the longtime move away from agriculture to factory production, were an effort to deal with disjuncture and the conflict in that society between feudal lords and an emerging industrialism. The adoption of the Poor Laws for use by the American colonies represented the imposition of laws that were culturally appealing but in some aspects inappropriate to the American territorial and agricultural scene. The renewed vigor with which the Poor Laws were administered during the post–Civil War period demonstrates again the significance of historical heritage. The reliance upon family responsibility and local settlement as requirements for financial relief was detrimental not only to industrial expansion but also to family welfare. The importance of mobility and of the nuclear family to successful urbanization and industrialization went unheeded, and the country was bemused by welfare measures that eased but did not eliminate the hazards of the new society. The racially discriminatory application of the Poor Law principles to the freed slaves was touted as a base for helping blacks achieve the independent status of fellow American citizens.

The significance of history to an understanding of social welfare policies and programs can be demonstrated further by the pattern of administration devised for their operation. Federal, state, and local relationships have varied from program to program in accordance with concepts of local responsibility and states' rights. Even now, when the financial problems of the various states, the discrepancies among state-administered welfare programs, and the outcry against racial and ethnic discrimination have created a demand for new social welfare measures, Congress has moved with due regard to the inherited restraints of federal–state and public–voluntary agency relationships. True, the federal government now funds and administers new Supplemental Security Income benefits and may eventually fund and administer some new family assistance program. Social services, however, are left with the separate states, which are now enabled and, indeed, encouraged to purchase services from voluntary agencies. The federal government's move away from grant-in-aid programs to a system of block grants to states for social welfare purposes — for education, social services, urban development, for example — while providing more flexibility, still leaves services fragmented and noninclusive. Consumers of services have not necessarily gained when renewed deference to states' rights and to voluntarism replaces federal standard-setting guidelines.

In summation, the congruence of technology and the level of output, the view of society, the view of human nature, and the historical heritage will determine the kinds of social policy decisions reached. This does not mean that these four factors contribute equally at any given moment. The very fact that the family, from the point of view of public policy, has been considered primarily an economic unit suggests that the degree to which each factor will exert influence on policy will depend upon existing economic conditions. The response to human need during the 1930s was remarkably different from the response to need during the high employment era of the 1960s. And yet both were periods during which need per se was widely recognized and civil disorder threatened. The past and the present must be understood in order to make any predictions for the future.

This volume is organized around historical time periods and gives a description of the economic, political, and cultural situation for each. When necessary, geographic differences are described. Social welfare programs and institutions are examined through the use of legislative documents, judicial decisions, administrative rulings, and statements of public and voluntary social welfare leaders. Reference is made to these documents in the text; documents that represent historical turning points are given in original form.

DOCUMENT

The document that accompanies this introductory chapter is an Act for the Relief of the Poor, better known as the Poor Laws of 1601, passed by the English Parliament during the forty-third year of the reign of Queen Elizabeth. It is the only document in this book not derived from the American experience. Its inclusion is based on the tremendous and lasting influence that the Poor Laws have had upon social welfare policy and programs first in the American colonies, and subsequently in the United States.

Underlying the provisions of the Act for the Relief of the Poor are those features that have been identified as Poor Law principles: first, individual and family responsibility; then public responsibility for the poor, at the local level. The act sets forth the qualifications for the selection of overseers of the poor, their duties and accountability. In addition, the act details the provisions to be made for various categories of poor persons and the ways in which benefits are to be funded and administered. All in all, the act deals with social policy decisions still required of social policy analysts and program planners. More striking is the fact that the American response to need continues to reflect principles devised for another country and another time.

THE

STATUTES AT LARGE,

From The

Thirty-ninth Year of Q. Elizabeth,

TO THE

Twelfth Year of K. Charles II. inclusive.

To which is prefixed,

TABLE containing the TITLES of all the STATUTES during that Period.

VOL. VII.

DANBY PICKERING, of Gray's Inn, Esq;

Reader of the Law Lecture to that Honourable Society.

Edited by Joseph Bentham, CAMBRIDGE, Printer to the University; Charles Bathurst, at the Cross-Keys, opposite St. Dunstan's Church in Fleet-Street, London 1763.

CUM PRIVILEGIO.

An Act for the Relief of the Poor, 43 Elizabeth, 1601

Be it enacted by the authority of this present parliament, That the church-wardens of every parish, and four, three or two substantial householders there, as shall be thought meet, having respect to the proportion and greatness of the same parish and parishes, to be nominated yearly in *Easter* Week, or within one month after *Easter*, under the hand and seal of two or more justices of the peace in the same county, whereof one to be of the *quorum*, dwelling in or near the same parish or division where the same parish doth lie, shall be called overseers of the poor of the same parish: and they, or the greater part of them, shall take order from time to time, by and with the consent of two or more such justices of peace as is aforesaid, for setting to work the children of all such whose parents shall not by the said church-wardens and overseers, or the greater part of them, be thought able to keep and maintain their children; and also for setting to work all such persons, married or unmarried, having no means to maintain them, and use no ordinary and daily trade of life to get their living by: and also to raise weekly or otherwise (by taxation of every inhabitant, parson, vicar and other, and of every occupier of lands, houses, tithes impropriate, propriations of tithes, coal-mines, or saleable underwoods in the said parish, in such competent sum and sums of money as they shall think fit) a convenient stock of flax, hemp, wool, thread, iron and other necessary ware and stuff, to set the poor on work: and also competent sums of money for and towards the necessary relief of the lame, impotent, old, blind, and such other among them, being poor and not able to work, and also for the putting out of such children to be apprentices. . . .

• • •

III. And be it also enacted, That if the said justices of peace do perceive, that the inhabitants of any parish are not able to levy among themselves sufficient sums of money for the purposes aforesaid; That then the said two justices shall and may tax, rate and assess as aforesaid, any other of other parishes, or out of any parish, within the hundred where the said parish is, to pay such sum and sums of money to the church-wardens and overseers of the said poor parish for the said purposes, as the said justices shall think fit, according to the intent of this law: (2) and if the said hundred shall not be thought to the said justices able and fit to relieve the said several parishes not able to provide for themselves as aforesaid; Then the justices of peace at their general quarter-sessions, or the greater number of them, shall rate and assess as aforesaid, any other of other parishes, or out of any parish, within the said county for the purposes aforesaid, as in their discretion shall seem fit.

• • •

IV. And that it shall be lawful, as well for the present as subsequent church-wardens and overseers, or any of them by warrant from any two such justices of peace, as is aforesaid, to levy as well the said sums of money, and all arrearages, of every one that shall refuse to contribute according as they shall be assessed, by distress and sale of the offender's goods, as the sums of money or stock shall be behind upon any account to be made as aforesaid, rendering to the parties the overplus; (2) and in defect of such distress, it shall be lawful for any such two justices of the peace to commit him or them to the common goal of the county, there to remain without bail or mainprize until payment of the said sum, arrearages and stock: (3) and the said justices of peace, or any one of them, to send to the house of correction or common goal, such as shall not employ themselves to work, being appointed thereunto, as aforesaid: (4) and also any such two justices of peace to commit to the said prison every one of the said church-wardens and overseers which shall refuse to account, there to remain without bail or mainprize until he have made a true account, and satisfied and paid so much as upon the said account shall be remaining in his hands.

• • •

V. And be it further enacted, That it shall be lawful for the said church-wardens and overseers, or the greater part of them, by the assent of any two justices of the peace aforesaid, to bind any such children, as aforesaid, to be apprentices, where they shall see convenient, till such man-child shall come to the age of four and twenty years, and such woman-child to the age of one and twenty years, or the time of her marriage; the same to be as effectual to all purposes, as if such child were of full age, and by indenture of convenant bound him or her self. (2) And to the intent that necessary places of habitation may more conveniently be provided for such poor impotent people; (3) be it enacted by the authority aforesaid, That it shall and may be lawful for the said church-wardens and overseers, or the greater part of them by the leave of the lord or lords of the manor, whereof any waste or common within their parish is or shall be parcel, and upon agreement before with him or them made in writing, under the hands and seals of the said lord or lords, or otherwise, according to any order to be set down by the justices of peace of the said county at their general quarter-sessions, or the greater part of them, by like leave and agreement of the said lord or lords in writing under his or their hands and seals, to erect, build, and set up in fit and convenient places of habitation in such waste or common, at the general charges of the parish, or otherwise of the hundred or county, as aforesaid, to be taxed, rated and gathered in manner before expressed, convenient houses of dwelling for the said impotent poor; (4) and also to place inmates, or more families than one in one cottage or house; one act made in the one and thirtieth year of her Majesty's reign, intituled, *an act against the erecting and maintaining of cottages,* or anything therein contained to the contrary notwithstanding: (5) which cottages and places for inmates shall not at any time after be used or employed to or for any other habitation, but only for impotent and poor of the same parish, that shall be there placed from time to time by the church-wardens and overseers of the poor of the same parish, or the most part of them, upon the pains and forfeitures contained in the said former act made in the said one and thirtieth year of her Majesty's reign.

• • •

VII. And be it further enacted, That the father and grandfather, and the mother and grandmother, and the children of very poor, old, blind, lame and impotent person, or other poor person not able to work, being of a sufficient ability, shall, at their own charges, relieve and maintain every such poor person in that manner, and according to that rate, as by the justices of peace of that county where such sufficient persons dwell, or the greater number of them, at their general quarter-sessions shall be assessed; (2) upon pain that every one of them shall forfeit twenty shillings for every month which they shall fail therein.

• • •

VIII. And be it further enacted, That the mayors, baliffs, or other head officers of every town and place corporate and city within this realm, being justice or justices of peace, shall have the same authority by virtue of this act, within the limits and precincts of their jurisdictions, as well out of sessions, as at their sessions, if they hold any, as is herein limited, prescribed and appointed to justices to the peace of the county, or any two or more of them, or to the justices of peace in their quarter-sessions, to do and execute for all the uses and purposes in this act prescribed, and no other justices of peace to enter or meddle there: (2) and that every alderman of the city of *London* within his ward, shall and may do and execute in every respect so much as is appointed and allowed by this act to be done and executed by one or two justices of peace of any county within this realm.

• • •

X. And further be it enacted by the authority aforesaid, That if in any place within this realm there happen to be hereafter no such nomination of overseers yearly, as if before appointed, That then every justice of peace of the county, dwelling within the division where such default of nomination shall happen, and every mayor, alderman and head officer of city, town or place corporate where such default shall happen, shall lose and forfeit for every such default five pounds, to be employed towards the relief of the poor of the said parish or place corporate, and to be levied, as aforesaid, of their goods, by warrant from the general sessions of the peace of the said county, or of the same city, town or place corporate, if they keep sessions.

• • •

XI. And be it also enacted by the authority aforesaid, That all penalties and forfeitures before-mentioned in this act to be forfeited by any person or persons, shall go and be employed to the use of the poor of the same parish, and towards a stock and habitation for them, and other necessary uses and relief, as before in this act are mentioned and expressed; (2) and shall be levied by the said church-wardens and overseers, or one of them, by warrant from any two such justices of peace, or mayor, alderman, or head officer of city, town or place corporate respectively within their several limits, by distress and sale thereof, as aforesaid; (3) or in defect thereof, it shall be lawful for any two such justices of peace, and the said alderman and head officers within their several limits, to commit the offender to the said prison, there to remain without bail or mainprize till the said forfeitures shall be satisfied and paid.

• • •

XII. And be it further enacted by the authority aforesaid, That the justices of peace of every county or place corporate, or the more part of them, in their general sessions to be holden next after the feast of *Easter* next, and so yearly as often as they shall think meet, shall rate every parish to such a weekly sum of money as they shall think convenient; (2) so as no parish be rated above the sum of six-pence, nor under the sum of a half-peny, weekly to be paid, and so as the total sum of such taxation of the parishes in every county amount not above the rate of two-pence for every parish within the said county: (3) which sums so taxed shall be yearly assessed by the agreement of the parishioners within themselves, or in default thereof, by the church-wardens and petty constables of the same parish, or the more part of them: or in default of their agreement, by the order of such justice or justices of peace as shall dwell in the same parish or (if none be there dwelling) in the parts next adjoining.

• • •

XV. And be it further enacted, That all the surplusage of money which shall be remaining in the said stock of any county, shall be discretion of the more part of the justices of peace in their quarter-sessions, be ordered, distributed and bestowed for the relief of the poor hospitals of that county, and of those that shall sustain losses by fire, water, the sea or other casualties, and to such other charitable purposes, for the relief of the poor, as to the more part of the said justices of peace shall seem convenient.

• • •

XVI. And be it further enacted, That if any treasurer elected shall willfully refuse to take upon him the said office of treasurership, or refuse to distribute and give relief, or to account, according to such form as shall be appointed by the more part of the said justices of peace; That then it shall be lawful for the justices of peace in their quarter-sessions, or in their default, for the justices of assize at their assizes to be holden in the same county, to fine the same treasurer by their discretion; (2) the same fine not to be under three pounds, and to be levied by sale of his goods, and to be prosecuted by any two of the said justices of peace whom they shall authorize. (3) Provided always, That this act shall not take effect until the feast of *Easter* next.

• • •

XVII. And be it enacted, That the statute made in the nine and thirtieth year of her Majesty's reign, intituled, *An act for the relief of the poor*, shall continue and stand in force until the feast of *Easter* next; (2) and that all taxations heretofore imposed and not paid, nor that shall be paid before the said feast of *Easter* next, and that all taxes hereafter before the said feast to be taxed by virtue of the said former act, which shall not be paid before the said feast of *Easter*, shall and may after the said feast of *Easter* be levied by the overseers and other persons in this act respectively appointed to levy taxations, by distress, and by such warrant in every respect, as if they had been taxed and imposed by virtue of this act, and were not paid. . . .

Chapter 2
The Colonial Period: 1647–1776

English colonists coming to America in the seventeenth century brought with them the entire fabric of English customs, including the Poor Laws. As early as 1647, at the first session of its colonial legislature, Rhode Island announced the Elizabethan Poor Law principles that stressed, most importantly, public responsibility for the poor:

> It is agreed and ordered by this present Assembly, that each towne shall provide carefully for the relief of the poor, to maintain the impotent, and to employ the able, and shall appoint an overseer for the same purpose. Sec. 43 Eliz. 2[1]

Considering the severe economic and physical privations of the early settlers, it is not surprising that public responsibility for relief should have been buttressed by those other principles of English Poor Law: local responsibility, family responsibility, and the residency requirement of legal settlement. These principles had been evolving in England for some 200 years and had been codified in 1601 in the most famous of all pieces of poor relief legislation, An Act for the Relief of the Poor, 43 Elizabeth.[2]

The principle of local responsibility made public aid the domain of small units of government. Family responsibility originally denoted the legal obligation of support that adults had for their minor children and grandchildren and for their aged parents. Settlement, added in 1662, made a designated period of residence a requirement for the receipt of assistance. "43 Elizabeth" represented for the English people and the English government the climax of a process of change. The protections and "knowns" of an agricultural, feudal society had begun to give way to an expanding woolen industry with its demands for sheep raising and the production of woolen products. As titled lands were converted and enclosed for pasture, as farming itself was commercialized, tenant farmers were forced off the land. Very naturally they moved toward the towns where industrial development gave promise of employment, if not security. Unfortunately, even with mining added to the manufacture of woolens as a major industrial pursuit, the new industries could not absorb the growing labor supply, and bands of the unemployed wandered the English countryside as vagrants and beggars. These sturdy vagabonds, the beggars, the unemployed poor, whose numbers and potential for civil disorder loomed frighteningly large, were people caught in the middle of forces beyond their control. They were people in need; and the Poor Laws, in providing public relief, were designed to meet their needs.

The terms upon which relief was offered reflected much more than the interests of the poor. Parliament was subject to the crunch of conflicting pressures. The owners of large farms wanted to assure the availability of local low-cost seasonal workers; the emerging industrialists needed to encourage the migration of factory labor; town officials wanted to minimize the need to levy taxes to support the homeless. The decision of Parliament to make local settlement an eligibility condition for relief reflected the power of the landed gentry. In supporting this interest the government provided incentive for labor to remain on the farms—the risk of leaving was clear. At the same time, they were able to satisfy the towns' concern for minimizing local costs. Furthermore, by limiting the mobility of the poor, government could respond to the interest of landowners and of industrialists in maintaining law and order.

In accordance with the Act of Settlement of 1662 a newcomer could be returned to his place of legal residence even though he had not actually applied for assistance.

> That it shall and may be lawful upon complaint made by the churchwardens or overseers of the Poor of any Parish . . . for any two Justices of the Peace . . . where any Person or Persons are likely to be chargeable to the Parish shall come to inhabit . . . to remove and convey such Person or Persons to such Parish where he or they were last legally settled. . . .[3]

By 1795 power had shifted. There had been marked industrialization during the eighteenth century. Now the Poor Laws were amended and the penalties for vagrancy eased. No one could be removed until an application for assistance had been made. The amendment represented the maturing of industrial need and a victory of industrial over farming interests.

The Poor Laws in the Colonies

Although the long-time evolution of the Poor Laws in England served both as a hindrance and an aid to an inexorable process of industrialization, that evolution was always concentrated on the availability of masses of workers. The climate of the American colonies was strikingly different, however. There was no persistent unemployment problem; no mass of employables had been pushed off the land; no industries existed to pull workers into towns; no pool of workers awaited hiring. Initially there was neither an economic reason nor a law-and-order reason to reduce mobility; and, in fact, since land was abundantly and fully available, economic interest—societal and individual—might have encouraged movement. The rationale for the adoption of the Poor Laws rested on other grounds.

In the main, those colonists who were potential recipients of relief were the sick, the disabled, widows with children—all essentially unemployable—and the seasonally unemployed.

Frequent wars with the Indians; recurring epidemics of small pox, dysentery, measles, and yellow fever; major uncontrollable fires; high childbirth mortality rates; the hazards of fishing and the consequent loss of life at sea—all gave rise to economic need. These risks to which the colonists were subject were ones for which all held common concern. The colonists were small bands of individuals joined together in enterprises whose success depended upon the contribution and well-being of each. The smallness of their numbers made it possible to keep friendly, public watch over individual misfortunes. Their isolation made this public watch over community affairs a matter of individual self-interest. The Poor Laws assured individual and public protection. Those known to be in need through no fault of their own could be helped with cash relief in their own homes or in the homes of neighbors. Relief for people in home—that is, family—settings was well regarded because of the order and stability such settings promised for the community as a whole.

Concomitantly, the restraints of the Poor Laws served an economic purpose growing out of the fact that the colonial economy was one of extreme scarcity requiring that there be a minimum number of people not working. The low level of productivity meant that there was no excess of common wealth available for relief purposes. The situation was aggravated by the paucity of organized charities able to take on a major part of the burden of relieving the poor.

Slowly, as population increased and towns developed, voluntary societies to meet special welfare needs were formed. The Scots Charitable Society was established in Boston as early as 1657.[4] In 1713 the Friends Almshouse was established in Philadelphia to provide relief for poor Quakers.[5] In 1724 the Boston Episcopal Society was formed,[6] and in 1767 the Society of House Carpenters was organized in New York.[7]

These societies were an early representation of the variety of religious and ethnic groups resulting from an increasing flow of immigrants, as well as a representation of the commercial interests of the colonists. But as might be expected, the resources of these societies were very limited. Other resources were similarly hindered. The church, a helpful force in England, was too poor—and too congregationally fragmented—to take on very much in the colonies. Thus, in many respects, the Poor Laws seemed a rational approach to a severe problem. The laws offered some support to the disabled, but they also served as a deterrent to the ablebodied who might consider not working. The specific provisions regarding settlement and family responsibility limited the number of inhabitants for whose relief the town might be called upon to accept responsibility.

In a situation of such economic scarcity and of such threatening welfare measures, the family (and its structure) was a central force for maintaining economic, social, and political stability. Even at the close of the seventeenth century, 90 percent of the colonists were farmers; and their farms isolated, small, and poorly equipped. For the most part, then, these farming families had to supply their own food, clothing, and equipment, as well as their own education, entertainment, and health care. Family governance was hierarchical—generally with the husband in command. Within this structure all persons made valued contributions. Men and boys cleared fields, farmed, cut wood, and trapped. Women and girls spun thread, engaged in weaving, turned cloth into clothes, and took responsibility for a myriad of internal household chores. Men and women together worked to produce and to improve whatever implements, utensils, furniture, and weapons were needed for self-sufficiency. Since large families were a necessity, childbearing was viewed as a productive contribution to the family economy. If the husband were killed or disabled, the wife moved naturally into the family and economic role he had held. Women in the colonial period could—and did—hold property, run small businesses, and work for wages.

During the eighteenth century, even as the colonies became more firmly established and the colonists benefited from improved technology, from expanding commercial activities and shipbuilding, home manufactures continued to flourish. Their pursuit was increasingly encouraged by official efforts to maintain colonial independence and to ward off the economic stringencies of trade restrictions and embargoes imposed as disputes between the colonies and London grew in intensity. Improvements in the spinning wheel—particularly after 1765,* when the invention of the spinning jenny made it possible for a person to spin 8 to 10 yarns simultaneously—made possible some home production for market sale. With men continuing to concentrate on farming, the newly oriented home manufacturing fell largely to women. In effect, women—and children—began to expand a function that had long been theirs, and did so in their own homes so that their work was easily integrated into family life. Contemporary dependence upon, and respect for, women's work is demonstrated in a number of occurrences. In 1750, Boston opened a group of spinning schools for female children. In 1751, the Society for Encouraging Industry and Employing the Poor was founded to promote the manufacture of woolen

---

*Interestingly, 1765 was also the year in which the English Parliament passed the Stamp Act, that major stimulus to conflict between the colonists and England.

cloth and to employ "our own women and children who are now in great measure idle."[8] The Massachusetts Province Laws of 1753–1754 supported the manufacturing of linen, again with the employment of women and children in mind:

> The number of poor is greatly increased . . . and many persons, especially women and children, are destitute of employment and in danger of becoming a public charge.[9]

The colonies welcomed home manufacturing and the employment it provided. Poor rates could be lessened, and employment could be offered to women and children who might otherwise be "useless, if not burdensome, to society."[10] Shortages resulting from the gathering revolutionary storm could be diminished.

The dire language of the Poor Laws and of subsequent legislation designed to assure their rigorous administration rested on cultural as well as economic factors. The popularity of spinning schools and the enthusiastic attendance at and participation in spinning bees sponsored by New England townships in the years preceding the Revolutionary War suggest the extent to which the essential isolation of the colonists had "produced a home-bred, home-living, and a home-loving people—a people who found both their employment and their pleasure in their own and their near neighbor's home."[11] Involved was the internalization of pleasure in work which would later be labeled "the work ethic." A fuller explanation of the meaning and operation of the Poor Laws must take account of the moral underpinnings provided by Puritan Calvinism.

The New England colonists had emigrated in order to escape religious persecution and to seek freedom to worship in accordance with their own religious beliefs. The result was a unity of church and "state" peculiarly suited to New World conditions. The stark need for labor in New England necessarily required that the colonists operate with regard for the common store of wealth, that is, for profit in their joint enterprise; but they also operated out of religious necessity with regard for individual, private control of resources. With individual status and economic reward a manifestation of predestined grace, the Puritan work ethic was a conceptually useful tool for minimizing what was publicly, communally available in order to maximize individual and family wealth and well-being. Although poverty could not be equated with unworthiness, it could suggest—especially if public relief was necessary—a character and moral flaw that dared not be pampered for the common welfare and for the individual's state of grace. Giving, within reason, was encouraged; but charity reflected a concern for the salvation of the rich—the stewards of God's wealth—more than a concern for the poor. Despite the family's usefulness, the impetus to maximize individual and family well-being did not center on the individual as a family member or on the individual family as a unit. When a family was in trouble, the concern was to save its potentially productive members. Hence, there developed such social welfare measures as farming out, indenture, and apprenticeship, which provided a family structure for governance and a means for productivity.

Poor Law provisions for public aid took no cognizance of the family as a social entity to be helped. Indeed, the provisions for relief established categories of individuals—the young, the old, the disabled, and the able-bodied. By implication the family consisted of a number of individuals living together for the purpose of assuring self-support and, by extension, avoiding the necessity for support by taxpayers. Hindsight would suggest that the term "family responsibility" is a misinterpretation of Poor Law intent; for the laws designated relative, rather than family, responsibility for support. Such designation was perhaps quite purposeful at a time when financial independence, worthiness, and divine reward were perceived as facets of individually achieved success. In this context, the family that could not maintain financial independence was not simply unsuccessful but actually dangerous, both economically and morally. Such families could not by example, precept, or education be expected to prepare the young for adult, independent living. The colonists, therefore, provided for the binding out of children as apprentices for "better educateing of youth in honest and profitable trades and manufactures, as also to avoyd sloath and idleness wherewith such young children are easily corrupted"[12] and required that in addition to a trade, children learn to "read and understand the principles of religion & the capitall lawes of this country."[13] These were preventive measures designed to protect children from the contagion of parental failures.

Unattached, neglected, or dependent children could be placed with persons willing to take responsibility for their care and who would educate and train them for a useful calling. Persons assuming such responsibility for children were expected to recoup their expenses from the child's work. Thus, indenture and apprenticeship were preventions against the danger of pauperism and ensured that children were immediately and potentially profitable to themselves and to the community.

Apprenticeship reflected colonial society's concern with the home life, the work life, and the religious life of the child. Ideally, each child would grow up "under some orderly family government"[14] that provided support and an opportunity for learning both for economic and religious salvation. When the natural family did not provide these essentials, apprenticeship to a contracted family was an alternative that often eased the burden on the public treasury.

> If after warning and admonition given by any of the Deputies; or Select-men, unto such Parents or Masters, they shall still remain negligent in their duty, in any the particulars aforementioned, whereby Children or Servants may be in danger to grow Barberous, Rude or Stubborn, and so prove Pests instead of Blessings to the Country; That then a fine of ten shillings shall be levied on the

Goods of such negligent Parent or Master, to the Towns use, except extreme poverty call for mitigation of the said fine.

And if in three months after that, there be no due care taken . . . then a fine of twenty shillings to be levied. . . .

And Lastly, if in three months after that, there be no due Reformation of the said neglect, then the said Selectmen with the help of two Magistrates, shall take such children and servants from them, and place them with some Masters for year, (boyes till they come to twenty-one, and girls eighteen years of age) which will more strictly educate and govern them according to the rules of this Order.[15]

The counterpart of the systems of indenture and apprenticeship for children were the systems of indenture contracting or farming out for adults. In accordance with colonial welfare legislation, overseers of the poor were empowered "to take effectual care that . . . persons of able body living within the same town or precincts thereof (not having estates otherwise to maintain themselves) do not live idly or misspend their time loitering, but that they be brought up or employed in some honest calling, which may be profitable unto themselves and the public."[16]

To the end that individuals be profitable to themselves and to the common wealth, indenture contracts enforced labor by sentencing potential paupers to servitude, sometimes to a master of their own choosing and sometimes to an assigned master. Under farming out, the adult poor could be turned over to the bidder willing to contract, at the lowest charge to the community, to take on the care of paupers and to put them to work. Such care might permit the individual relieved to remain home. As centers of population and wealth developed, it often meant commitment to a privately owned workhouse, a publicly owned house of correction, a poor farm, or an almshouse where care or "proper" punishment and hard labor could more easily be administered. The first almshouse was established in Rensselaerswyck, New York, in 1657. Plymouth ordered the construction of an almshouse in 1658, and Boston did the same two years later.

The early development of workhouses and almshouses—welfare mechanisms that were both sophisticated and expensive—is indicative of the rapid population growth experienced by the colonies and of the increased financing ability to be found in some colonies. Occasionally, where towns could not afford such institutions, private philanthropists made contributions to the public effort.[17]

The indenture contract, in retrospect, was indicative of a society still in transition from feudalism. Seventeenth-century England and colonial America—both in New England and the South—no longer offered the security of work and assistance guaranteed by the feudal manor system. The responsibility for this security, that is, for mutual aid for children and for adults, had shifted to the family. The small farm of early colonial New England and the later cottage industries affirmed the necessity for mutual aid. Consequently, the Poor Laws in all their regard for family responsibility

(A) The Manager's Apartment   (B) The House of Employment

The Bettering House. This is a view of the House of Employment, the Almshouse, and the Pennsylvania Hospital which were built in 1766–67 in Philadelphia. The three buildings comprised a complex devoted to the problems of the poor. The Manager's apartment strategically separated the workhouse from the poorhouse.
Courtesy of the Historical Society of Pennsylvania

and the obligation of local residence also clarified where people belonged and what their rights were in regard to each other.

Colonial welfare legislation stressed the provision of indoor relief, that is, care offered in homes other than one's own and, in time, in institutions. Nevertheless, the seasonally unemployed might benefit from tax remissions, and the overseers of the poor could legally provide outdoor relief, money payments to persons permitted to remain in their own homes because their poverty resulted from physical disability, widowhood, or old age. Taxes were collected for the latter purpose. Frequent wars coupled with postwar recessions created increased demands for help. In crises, private philanthropy supported the practice of outdoor relief by the provision of such items

(C) The Almshouse   (D) The Pennsylvania Hospital

as blankets and stockings. During the severe winter of 1761–1762, the Quakers in Philadelphia distributed fuel stamps—"tickets of recommendation"—to be redeemed for wood.[18]

The worthiness denoted by the receipt of outdoor relief was not, however, tantamount to protection from the stigma of pauperism. In 1718, a statute of the Province of Pennsylvania made it obligatory that every person receiving public relief "upon the shoulder of the right sleeve . . . in open and visible manner, wear . . . a large Roman P. together with the first letter of the name of the county, city or place whereof such poor person is an inhabitant, cut either in red or blue cloth, as by the overseers of the poor, it shall be directed and appointed."[19] In New York, relief recipients were required to wear badges enscribed with the large letters "N.Y."[20]

The coercive work features of the Poor Laws and the meagerness of relief provisions were indirectly, as well as directly, deterring. Not only did the laws spell out the kinds of care that might be made available to those who applied, but they also directed the overseers to seek out those whose situations or ways of living portended financial burden for the community.

23

Direct deterrence was enhanced by the Poor Law principle of family responsibility requiring that "the father and grandfather and the mother and grandmother and the children of every poor, old, blind, lame, and impotent person, or other poor·person not able to work . . . shall at their own charges relieve and maintain every such poor person as the justices of the peace . . . shall order and direct."[21] The overt demand that relatives support each other in time of need was covertly strengthened by the general awareness of the alternatives.

The Poor Laws were designed to protect those who held legal claim to settlement in particular localities. They offered protection against strangers who threatened the stability—namely, the morality and physical safety—of a society singularly concerned with order. In regard to strangers the Poor Laws demonstrated most clearly their law-and-order nature. The requirement of settlement for public assistance—for example, 40 days in New York, three months in Massachusetts, a year in North Carolina—clarified the absence of local responsibility for outsiders. Beyond that, internal protection was attempted through such preventive measures as "warning out." Strangers were carefully screened. Those few who could assure their financial independence and future contribution to the community were permitted to remain and to acquire settlement. More frequently they were escorted beyond local geographical jurisdictions. The colonists were realistically concerned with the threat to economic survival posed by possible drains on the public treasury resulting from the potentially poor and sick outsider. This fear often outweighed the value of labor skills the stranger might bring.

Additional evidence that the protection of society, rather than the care of the poor, dictated the writing of the colonial Poor Laws is offered by the fact that the laws contain no expression of concern for the poor beyond the concise statements of provision for their care. The laws do, however, make explicit the rights and duties of the overseers of the poor and spell out in detail methods for selecting and appointing overseers, their taxing powers, their responsibilities, their accountability—as well as the penalties to which they were subject if they peformed improperly. The laws indicate that the tasks of the overseers were considered onerous. In Pennsylvania, for example, the overseers were appointed to a one-year term of office, but, on penalty of having to serve a second year or pay a heavy fine, were required to set forth the names of their successors.[22]

Population Growth: Immigration and Slavery

In New England the township became the unit of colonial Poor Law administration, and, as might be expected, the major thrusts of administrative practice implementing welfare legislation were toward work coercion and toward adherence to religion. Although they were adapted to local conditions and to variations of religious tenets, colonies outside of New England also took over the poor relief system of England. This is not surprising when one considers that colonization as a base for exploiting the resources of the New World was primarily an English thrust. The colonists, whether Anglican, as in Virginia, Puritan, as at Plymouth and Massachusetts Bay, or Catholic, as in Maryland, were English in their political and social heritage.* The English character of these colonial enterprises were enhanced by the fact that they were essentially private enterprises. All were financed through private capital raised by such investment organizations as the London and Massachusetts Bay companies or, as in the case of Maryland, by individual landowners ready to risk their own fortunes. In either instance, royal support was given in the form of charters or, again as in the case of Maryland, in the form of land grants. Colonization was a reflection of England's long-time process of democratization, industrialization, and commercialization forged within the military and political struggles of older powers. Their success derived from a combination of patriotism, profit seeking, and religious fervor.

Furthermore, the colonists shared a common experience of hardship and scarcity in America. The severity of the New England winter, the "horrid snow" described by Cotton Mather,[24] was counterpart to the unexpected, unbearable heat that brought death to one half of the Virginia settlers during their first summer in America. Captain John Smith, a leader of the Virginia Company, wrote, "Nothing can be expected thence, but by labor."[25] In the South, as in the North, the Poor Laws seemed a reasonable response to a situation in which financial disaster and death seemed imminent and which, in fact, did produce social and physical disabilities.

The fact that the colonists did not yield to early misfortune and return to England is attributable, first of all, to the quickly found availability of the profit-making resources they had come to seek—tobacco in Virginia, fur trading in New England. However, in view of the dangers from natural causes and, in addition, from Indian raids, profit making would not have sufficed had not Europe—and, in particular, England—continued to be wracked by political, religious, and military upheaval. The intent of the original colonists to settle permanently in the New World was strengthened by the rapid addition of new settlers and new settlements. The English revolution that led to the overthrow of King Charles I in 1649, the establishment of the Puritan Commonwealth, and the restoration of the Monarchy in 1660 spurred emigration, especially of those who were seeking freedom and purity of religion. The emigrants to New England were of all classes of English society and consisted of whole families and individuals ready to establish homes and families in the new country.

The Restoration, and the emigration of Puritans it sparked, foreshadowed the dominance of Puritanism in colonial America. Protestant

---

*The Dutch settled New Amsterdam in 1609 and set up a church system of poor relief. By 1664, however, New Amsterdam came under English rule, and with its new English name, New York's relief efforts were changed to a public, Poor Law, system.[23]

Puritan domination was assured by the influx of French Huguenots and Scotch Calvinists into Carolina as a result of religious persecution and trade restrictions respectively. The possibilities for religious and political freedom and for economic stability brought additional settlers—Welsh, Jews, Swiss—and the colonial population soared. By 1640 more than 27,000 Englishmen were scattered through Massachusetts, Connecticut, Rhode Island, New Hampshire, Maine, Maryland, and Virginia. In 1690 there were 200,000 inhabitants; by 1710 there were 350,000; and in 1760, 1.5 million people lived in the thirteen colonies, representing many parts of Europe and Africa. The numbers of blacks had grown from the original 20 brought in 1619 to 16,700 in 1690, to 44,900 in 1710, and to 325,000—22 percent of the population—in 1760.[26]

Population growth in the New England colonies was controlled by the factors that led to their founding. The colonists were bound by a common set of religious and ethical motivations and, for the most part, had underwritten the expenses of their passage and of supplies through the purchase of shares in a joint enterprise. The New England colonies, despite official ties to England, were essentially independent and used their independence to accept and reject immigrants on the basis of religious beliefs and potential for economic self-sufficiency. A predominantly free labor system developed.

A different pattern evolved in the South, reflecting the different base for settlement and the different economic base that developed. Virginia was settled solely as a commercial enterprise. A large number of its early settlers were working-class Englishmen who paid for their passage through indenture contracts a four- to seven-year commitment to work. In 1625, 487 people—almost 40 percent of Virginia's population—were indentured servants.[27] The South grew as it developed tobacco and prospered with the establishment of large plantations. The first blacks to come to Virginia came as indentured workers. As servants and as freemen, they had much in common with their white counterparts in terms of status and problems. By 1661, however, slavery was institutionalized, and by the eighteenth century slaves were the base of the labor force.

With New England practicing selectivity in the acceptance of immigrants and the South relying increasingly upon the use of slave labor, immigrants were quite naturally funneled into the Middle Atlantic colonies. Large numbers were unable to pay for their passage and came under contracts of indenture. It is estimated that two-thirds of the settlers in Pennsylvania came under such provisions of servitude. German and Scotch-Irish families who arrived during the eighteenth century came as "redemptioners," people who had made a down payment on passage and who used the promise of work as collateral for the balance. Indentured servitude resulted for those who defaulted.

By the close of the colonial period, the colonies had prospered greatly. When Georgia was declared a crown colony in 1752, all the 13 American colonies were formal geographic and political entities. Between 1700 and

S I R,

THE efforts made by the legiflative of this provincein their laft feffions to free themfelves from flavery, gave us, who are in that deplorable ftate, a high degree of fatisfaction. We expect great things from men who have made fuch a noble ftand againft the defigns of their *fellow-men* to enflave them. We cannot but wifh and hope Sir, that you will have the fame grand object, we mean civil and religious liberty, in view in your next feffion. The divine fpirit of *freedom*, feems to fire every humane breaft on this continent, except fuch as are bribed to affift in executing the execrable plan. ·

We are very fenfible that it would be highly detrimental to our prefent mafters, if we were allowed to demand all that of *right* belongs to us for paft fervices ; this we difclaim. Even the *Spaniards*, who have not thofe fublime ideas of freedom that Englifh men have, are confcious that they have no right to all the fervices of their fellow-men, we mean the *Africans*, whom they have purchafed with their money ; therefore they allow them one day in a week to work for themfelve, to enable them to earn money to purchafe the refidue of their time, which they have a right to demand in fuch portions as they are able to pay for (a due appraizment of their fervices being firft made, which always ftands at the purchafe money.) We do not pretend to dictate to you Sir, or to the honorable Affembly, of which you are a member : We acknowledge our obligations to you for what you have already done, but as the people of this province feem to be actuated by the principles of equity and juftice, we cannot but expect your houfe will again take our deplorable cafe into ferious confideration, and give us that ample relief which, *as men*, we have a natural right to.

But fince the wife and righteous governor of the univerfe, has permitted our fellow men to make us flaves, we bow in fubmiffion to him, and determine to behave in fuch a manner, as that w may have reafon to expect the divine approbation of, and affiftance in, our peaceable nd lawful attempts to gain our freedom.

We are willing to fubmit to fuch regulations and laws, as may be made relative to us, until we leave the province, which we determine to do as foon as we can from our joynt labours procure money to tranfport ourfelves to fome part of the coaft of *Africa*, where we propofe a fettlement. We are very defirous that you fhould have inftructions relative to us, from your town, therefore we pray you to communicate this letter to them, and afk this favor for us.

In behalf of our fellow flaves in this province, And by order of their Committee.

Pᴇᴛᴇʀ Bᴇsᴛᴇs,
Sᴀᴍʙᴏ Fʀᴇᴇᴍᴀɴ,
Fᴇʟɪx Hᴏʟʙʀᴏᴏᴋ,
Cʜᴇsᴛᴇʀ Jᴏɪᴇ.

For the Rᴇᴘʀᴇsᴇɴᴛᴀᴛɪᴠᴇ of the town of *Thompfon*

Broadside Letter from 4 Negroes, asking to return to Africa, 1773, Boston.
Courtesy of the New York Historical Society, New York City

1776, a great deal of cultural, social, political, and economic change occurred. Population growth had occurred not only by natural increase but also by way of immigration. The resulting intermingling of various religious, ethnic, and racial groups lent a cosmopolitan air to such identifiable urban centers—all busy ports of trade and entry—as Boston, New York, Philadelphia, and Baltimore. The regular plying of sailing vessels between North

America and the European continent brought not only economic returns to all but also, to the upper classes, the latest turns of fashion in dress, belles lettres, and social amenities. The establishment of active legal and political ties between the separate colonies and London and the frequent exchange of representatives this required lent additional encouragement to the maintenance of continental social graces, at the same time that the separation of the American and European continents presented the colonies with opportunity for self-government.

Nor was education neglected, particularly in New England where the Puritan legacy of religious authority based on biblical precepts encouraged knowledge of reading and writing. A college—soon to be called Harvard— was established at Cambridge in the Massachusetts Bay Colony as early as 1636. By the mid-eighteenth century, William and Mary, Yale, The University of Pennsylvania, Princeton, Brown, Rutgers, and Dartmouth were all established. The ties of communication among the colonies were fostered by a flood of printed materials and broadsides and the practice of letter writing. Newspapers proliferated, and the instituting of a mail service, carried regularly by 1732 between Massachusetts and Virginia, was additionally encouraging to writings of all kinds.

The many changes that marked colonial life at the end of the period were made apparent in the emergence of sharpened class differences. By the time of the American Revolution many colonials were already third- and fourth-generation Americans. A wealthy, leisured, even aristocratic, class had evolved—for the most part, Protestant. Beneath this class existed a group, again largely Protestant, of middle-class farmers, artisans, small tradesmen, and laborers in the fledgling manufacturing establishments. Alongside and below this group existed another large group—non-English, frequently non-Protestant, sometimes nonwhite, and almost always without property.

Different bases for prosperity for the North and South resulted in different views of people and of their need for social welfare programs. New England and the Middle Atlantic colonies shifted from sole dependence upon farming and fishing to home manufacturing, shipbuilding, and trading. These colonies were sufficiently urbanized to add the risks of a market economy to those of colonial frontier life. Problems of dependency increased with the influx of poorly paid immigrants and with the growing numbers of disabled men resulting from the wars of European powers in America and from wars with Indians. Particularly stark were the needs of elderly and disabled blacks who had been freed as a way of avoiding their care in old age.[28] These factors, combined with an economy of scarcity and with a growing population, made the enforcement of the Poor Laws attractive to town governments.

In the South the introduction of slavery and the continued reliance upon a farm economy prevented the development of a large free laboring class. If the large plantation holdings of Virginia contrasted sharply with small tenant farmer holdings of Carolina, the two were, nevertheless, joined in a feudal system that created less in the way of economic insecurity. The milder climate, the availability of fertile land, the mixture of less austere religious sects fostered a warmer, more favorable view of the free man. As early as 1728, William Byrd, a prosperous and educated gentleman who served on a commission set up to run the dividing line between Virginia and North Carolina, observed the way of life in North Carolina:

> Surely there is no place in the World where the inhabitants live with less labour . . . by the great felicity of the Climate, the easiness of raising Provisions. . . . Indian Corn is of so great increase, that a little Pains will Subsist a very large Family with Bread, and then they may have meat without any pains at all, by the Help of the Low Grounds, and the great Variety of Mast that grows on the Highland.[29]

While such ease of living might have led to laziness and an "Aversion to Labor," as Byrd feared, the fact was that it also led to greater tolerance of human misfortune—again for free men. By the middle of the seventeenth century, Virginia had adopted both the Poor Laws and apprenticeship to provide for poor free men: white and black, orphans, illegitimate children, and mulatto children of white women. There was no recognition of any social welfare needs that slaves or indentured servants might have, and it was left to these groups themselves to develop their own informal self-help mechanisms.

Challenge to the Poor Laws

The Poor Law principle of public responsibility for the relief of dependency did not go unchallenged. So influential a person as Benjamin Franklin argued for abolition of the Poor Laws. As Franklin saw it, the cause of poverty was of the individual's own making; the social system worked well, the growing wealth of the upper classes was justified, and an assumption of social responsibility would inevitably aggravate the problem by fostering further dependency.

> I have sometimes doubted whether the laws peculiar to England, which *compel the rich to maintain the poor*, have not given the latter a dependence, that very much lessens the care of providing against the wants of old age.
> I have heard it remarked that the *poor* In *Protestant* countries, on the continent of Europe, are generally more industrious than those of *Popish* countries. May not the more numerous foundations in the latter for relief of the poor have some effect towards rendering them less provident? To relieve the misfortunes of our fellow creatures is concurring with the Deity; it is godlike; but, if we provide encouragement for laziness, and supports for folly, may we not be fighting against the order of God and Nature, which perhaps has appointed want and misery as the proper punishments for, and cautions against, as well as necessary consequences of, idleness and extravagance? . . .
> However, as matters now stand with us, care and industry seem absolutely

necessary to our well-being. They should therefore have every encouragement we can invent, and not one motive to diligence be subtracted; and the support of the poor should not be by maintaining them in idleness, but by employing them in some kind of labour suited to their abilities of body, as I am informed begins to be of late the practice in many parts of England, where workhouses are erected for that purpose. If these were general, I should think the poor would be more careful, and work voluntarily to lay up something for themselves against a rainy day, rather than run the risk of being obliged to work at the pleasure of others for a bare subsistence, and that too under confinement.[30]

Franklin's view highlights a belief in the responsibility of people for their own welfare in an ordered society that rewards industry and thrift. Franklin rationalized poverty and inequality in income distribution:

Much malignant censure have some writers bestowed upon the rich for their luxury and expensive living, while the poor are starving, & c.; not considering that what the rich expend, the labouring poor receive in payment for their labour. It may seem a paradox if I should assert, that our labouring poor do in every year recieve *the whole revenue of the nation;* I mean not only the public revenue, but also the revenue or clear income of all private estates, or a sum equivalent to the whole. . . .

In support of this position I reason thus. The rich do not work for one another. Their habitations, furniture, cloathing, carriages, food, ornaments, and every-thing in short, that they or their families use and consume, is the work or produce of the labouring poor, who are, and must be continually, paid for their labour in producing the same.[31]

Some went so far as to argue that, for the market economy to function, individual earned income should never be supplemented. This would compel labor force participation and assure a supply of workers willing to perform menial, difficult, and unpleasant tasks.

It seems to be a law of nature, that the poor should be to a certain degree improvident, that there may always be some to fulfil the most servile, the most sordid, and the most ignoble offices in the community. The stock of human happiness is thereby much increased, whilst the more delicate are not only relieved from drudgery, and freed from those occasional employments which would make them miserable, but are left at liberty, without interruption, to pursue those callings which are suited to their various dispositions, and most useful to the state. As for the lowest of the poor, by custom they are reconciled to the meanest occupations, to the most laborious works, and to the most hazardous pursuits; whilst the hope of their reward makes them cheerful in the midst of all their dangers and their toils.[32]

Societal responsibility as institutionalized in colonial welfare legislation and in program administration by the end of the colonial period was concerned with the dangerous excesses of charitable impulses and the frightening consequences of falling back upon public support. Concern about poverty was not to be construed as sympathy for the poor, who were viewed as having to be coerced to work and deterred from pauperism.

Veterans: A Special Class

Welfare measures for veterans, however, differed from those applied to the general population. The English "Acte for Reliefes of Souldiours" of 1593 set the tone for colonial legislation. It had recognized both the special services and special needs of disabled soldiers and sailors and provided relief for this group *as a right* on the basis of disability, with payments scaled to military pay. As early as 1624 the colony of Virginia passed similar legislation. In 1636 Plymouth Colony declared that any soldier injured in defense of the colony was entitled to support.

> That in case necessity require to send forces abroade, and there be not volunteers sufficient offered for the service, then it be lawfull for the Governor and [his] assistants to presse [men into service] in his Majesties name . . . provided that if any that shall goe returne mamed & hurt, he shall be mayntayned completely by the Colony duringe his life.[33]

Other colonies followed the precedent, and by 1777 all but Connecticut had made special provisions for veterans. The entitlement to these provisions did not carry the onus of pauperism and, equally important for the future, carried no requirement of local settlement. Colonies, not towns, were responsible for financing and administration. The pattern was so well accepted that the Continental Congress in 1776 adopted a report of the Committee on Disabled Soldiers and Sailors recommending to the states pensions for invalid and disabled veterans.[34] This special attention to veterans and, in some instances to other persons identified as the "unsettled poor," broke ground for eventual contributions by the states and by the federal government to social welfare.

Of more immediate interest, however, is the logic by which the colonies selected veterans for preferential treatment—domiciliary care, pensions, for elderly and disabled veterans, and outdoor relief for widows and children of veterans. This selection for special treatment was, after all, consistent with the colonial view of humanity. Veterans had participated in an unusual kind of work. In doing so, they had made an extraordinary contribution to the common wealth, at the same time that they had made visible their own individual worth. Certainly such work and such worthiness were not to be deterred in a society where their special services were so badly needed.

DOCUMENTS
The Colonial Period

The two documents selected to illustrate the thrust of social welfare during the colonial era are *An Act of Supplement to the Acts Referring to the Poor* (Massachusetts Bay, 1692) and the contract of indenture entitled *The Binding of Moses Love* (1747). The documents illustrate legislative and judicial actions taken to achieve societal stability and individual well-being. For society and the individual the actions were protective and preventive and called upon a family unit to perform the functions of a social welfare institution. Where no natural family existed to support members in need, a substitute family was found. The number of colonists was very small and the community itself functioned in part as an extended family.

An Act of Supplement expresses governmental concern for all the inhabitants of Massachusetts Bay. The act explicitly states that its provisions extend beyond those who receive public alms; its intent is to assure that all single persons under the age of 21 years live "under some orderly family government." The significance of such an assurance stems from the nature of a society in which government and family mirrored one another in their responsibility to fulfill God's plan that people work and produce. Both were organized in a fixed hierarchical structure to which each individual had been called to an assigned place. Fulfilling one's responsibility within the structure was a duty to oneself, to the community, to God. Family government was protective of the individual who might be tempted to fall away from that responsibility and protective of the community that would bear the cost of such a fall. The family model reinforced the Puritan values of work and frugality as religious observances. In a society of scarcity, such a joining of religious and secular concerns was particularly felicitous.

The Binding of Moses Love demonstrates that the colonists observed the human condition with a certain solicitousness. Moses Love was bound out when only two years and eight months of age. The indenture contract is concerned not only with the child's learning a trade, but also with his being provided with food, clothing, and lodging "both in sickness and in health" and with an education. All in all, the rights and responsibilities bestowed on Moses Love's master are those of a parent. As indicated in the *Act of Supplement,* this discharge of governmental and familial responsibilities toward children generally endeavored "to defend them from any wrongs or injuries" and to prepare them for economic self-sufficiency in adulthood.

The ACTS AND RESOLVES, Public and Private

of the

PROVINCE OF THE MASSACHUSETTS BAY:

CHAPTER 14.

AN ACT OF SUPPLEMENT TO THE ACTS REFERRING TO THE POOR,

&c.

1692-3, ch. 28,&7.

WHEREAS the law for the binding out poor children apprentice is misconstrued by some to extend only to such children whose parents receive almes; for explanation whereof—

Be it declared and enacted by His Excellency the Governour, Council and Representatives in General Court assembled, and by the authority of the same,

Selectmen or overseers of the poor to bind out poor children, &c.;

[SECT. 1.] That the selectmen or overseers of the poor in any town or district within this province, or the greater part of them, shall take, order and are hereby impowred from time to time, by and with the assent of two justices of the peace, to set to work, or bind out apprentice, as they shall think convenient, all such children whose parents shall, by the selectmen or overseers of the poor, or the greater part of them, be thought unable to maintain them, (whither they receive almes or are chargeable to the place or not), so as that they be not sessed to publick taxes or assessments, for the province or town charges; male children till they come to the age of twenty-one years, and females till they come to the age of eighteen years, or time of marriage: which shall be as good and effectual in law, to all intents and purposes, as if any such child were of full age, and by indenture of covenant had bound him or herself, or that their parents were consenting there [un] to: provision therein to be made for the instructing of children so bound out, to read and write, as they may be capable.

—to inquire into the usage of such as they bind out.

And the selectmen or overseers of the poor shall inquire into the usage of children bound out by themselves or their predecessors, and endeavour to defend them from any wrongs or injuries.

And, for the better preventing of idleness, and loose or disorderly living,—

Be it further declared and enacted by the authority aforesaid,

Selectmen or overseers of the poor to set to work idle persons.

[SECT. 2]That the selectmen or overseers of the poor, or the greater part of them, be and are further impowred, by and with the assent of two justices of the peace, to set to work all such persons, married or unmarried, able of body, having no means to maintain them, that live idlely and use or exercise no ordinary and daily lawful trade or business to get their living by. And no single person of either sex, under the age of twenty-one years, shall be suffered to live at their own hand, but under some orderly family government; nor shall any woman of ill fame, married or unmarried, be suffered to receive or entertain lodgers in her house. And the selectmen or overseers of the poor, constables and tythingmen, are hereby ordered to see to the due observance of this act, and to complain and inform against any transgressions thereof to one or more justices of the peace, or the court of general sessions of the peace, who are hereby respectively required and impowred, upon due conviction of the offender or offenders for living idely or disorderly, contrary to the true intent of this act, to commit or send such offenders to the house of correction or work-house, there to remain and be kept to labour, until they be discharged by order of the court of general sessions of the peace, unless such person or persons so complained of shall give reasonable caution or assurance, to the satisfaction of the justice or court, that they will reform: *provided*, this act shall not be construed to extend to hinder any single woman of good repute from the exercise of any lawful trade or imployment, for a livelihood, whereto she shall have the allowance and approbation of the selectmen or overseers of the poor, or the greater part of them, any law, usage or custom to the contrary notwithstanding: *provided*,—

> No single person under twenty-one years old to live out of family government.

[SECT.3.] This act shall continue in force for the space of three years next coming, and to the end of the session of the general assembly next after. [*Passed November 27; published December 3.*]

Volume I. Boston: Wright & Potter, Printers to the State, 1869.

• • •

THE BINDING OF MOSES LOVE

This Indenture made the fourteenth day of September Anno domini 1747 by and between Luke Lincoln, Benja Tuckor, Nathall Goodspeed and John Whittemor all of Leicester in the Covnty of Worcester selectmen of sd Leicester on the one part, Matthew Scott of Leicester aforesaid yeoman on the other part Wittnesseth that the above sd selectmen by virtue of the Law of this province them Impowering & with the assent of two of the Majesties Justices of the Peace for sd Covnty hereto annexed to put and bind out to the sd Matthew Scott & to his heirs Execvtors & Adminrs as an Apprentice Moses Love a Minor aged two years and Eeight Months with him & them to

Live and dwell with as an apprentice dureing the term of Eighteen years and fovr months (viz) untill he shall arrive to the age of twenty-one years—he being a poor Child & his parants not being well able to support it. Dureing all which the sd apprentice his sd Master his heirs Execvtors & Adminrs shall faithfully serve at such Lawfull imployment & labovr as he shall from time to time Dureing sd term be Capable of doing and performing & not absent himself from his or their service without Leave & In all things behave himself as a good & faithfull apprentice ought to do and the sd Matthew Scott for himself his heirs Execvtors & Adminrs do Couenant promise and grant to & with the above sd selectmen of Leicester aforsaid & with their successors in the office or trust of selectmen of Leicester aforsaid & Inbehalf of sd apprentice that he the sd Matthew Scott his heirs Execvtors & Adminrss shall & will Dureing the term aforsd find and provide for the sd apprentice sufficient Cloathing meet drink Warshing and Lodging both in Sickness & in health & that he will teach him or cavse him to be tavght to read & write & siffer fiting his degree if he be Capable of Learning and at the Expiration of the term to Dismiss him with two suits of apparril one to be fitt for Lords days In Wittness where of the partyes to these present Indentvrs haue Interchangably set their hands & seals the day and year first written. Signed sealed & Delivered in presence of

Steward Southgate
John Brown

Luke Lincoln (seal)
Benja Tucker (seal)
John Whittemor (seal)

New England Historical and Geneological Register, Boston, 1880, Vol. XXXIV, p. 311.

Chapter 3
The Pre-Civil War
Period: 1777–1860

With their declaration of independence from England and the beginning of the Revolutionary War, the now independent states established a loose confederation for governance. But the Articles of Confederation gave the new central government little power. James Madison, predicting its failure, cited the Confederation as "nothing more than a treaty of amity of commerce and of alliance between . . . . independent and Sovereign States."[1] It was too weak to deal with the political and economic crises of the early postwar years.

The Articles of Confederation had promised a "perpetual union" of the states, but post–Revolutionary War disorganization and disruption highlighted the need for even closer and more effective political ties. The Federal Convention, which sat at Philadelphia from May 25 to September 17, 1787, drafted a new constitution for the states and the United States government began to function on March 4, 1789, with the commencement of the first presidential term.

The Preamble of the Constitution of the United States cited the promotion of "the general welfare" as one of the reasons for forming the new government. Nevertheless, there was no mention of social welfare concerns among the carefully enumerated powers of the government's legislative body, the Congress. Since the Constitution specifically reserved to the states such powers as had not been delegated to the central government, providing for the social welfare needs of families and individuals remained the responsibility of the separate states, much as it had been the responsibility of the separate colonies. Still further, the Poor Law tradition of reluctant governmental intervention meant that individual succor largely remained the province of voluntary, charitable endeavor.

The years between the operationalizing of the Constitution of the United States and the outbreak of the Civil War were years of major political, economic, and social changes. These changes were accompanied by and in turn furthered rapid population growth, enormous geographical expansion, mechanization of farm and factory, and heated political and ideological struggles. By the turn of the century, the country had already lost the mark of a colonial dependent; by 1860 the country could be considered a world power. The pre-Civil War period was one of excitement and turmoil, expansion and recession, opportunity and frustration, exhilaration and discontent. It was a period of rapid change necessarily affecting the welfare of individuals and families.

Population growth, composition, and movement comprise one aspect of the pre-Civil War transformation.[2] In 1790, the year of the first United States census, the total population of the country numbered 3,929,000. By 1800 the population had risen by 34 percent to about 5,297,000, of whom 1,002,000—19 percent—were nonwhite and 322,000—6 percent—lived in urban areas. By 1830, on the eve of massive migrations, especially from Ireland and Germany, the total population stood at 12,901,000. By 1840 the population reached 17,120,000; in 1850 it was 23,261,000 and in 1860 it was 31,513,000. Thus, from 1800 to 1860 the population had multiplied six times, and almost 20 percent now lived in urban areas. The percentage of the nonwhite population had dropped to about 14 percent, 4,521,000 persons, of whom 3,954,000 were slaves.

Population growth had been the result of a number of factors, including native births and the purchase, annexation, and cession of populated territories. Probably the most important cause of the population explosion, however, was the extraordinary wave of migration beginning during the 1830s when 538,381 immigrants arrived in the United States. Immigration rose to 1,427,337 during the 1840s and peaked during the 1850s with the arrival of 2,814,554 individuals. Interestingly, the 1860s, which encompassed the war years, showed only slight decline, with 2,084,201 persons arriving.

Of the total of 1,427,337 immigrants to the United States during the decade 1840—1849, 1,170,351 came from Ireland and Germany—874,917 and 395,434 respectively. Spurred by famine in the former and political repression in the latter, immigration from those two countries continued at extremely high levels during the 1850s, when together they accounted for 87 percent of the aliens entering the country. Almost all the immigrants landed at entry points between Baltimore and Boston, and almost all remained in the northern section of the country, where they congregated in cities. The Irish, coming primarily from a background of peasant farming, with little education, moved into canal and railroad construction, domestic service, and the developing textile industry. The Germans, political refugees, were for the most part skilled artisans and intellectuals and moved into industrial and commercial pursuits.

Whether from Ireland or Germany, the immigrants represented a threat to native Americans. They were foreign and Catholic in an essentially Protestant country. Moreover, they came at a time of initial industrial conflict. The sudden availability of workers ready to take employment at lower than generally accepted wages and the introduction, by German immigrants especially, of radical political philosophies upset American labor and industry alike. Further, many of the immigrants arrived in need of immediate employment or emergency financial aid. The addition of newcomers to the rolls of public charges added to opposition and agitation against them.

Although population growth between 1790 and 1860 was most spectacular in the northern areas of the country—east as well as west—growth occurred in the South as well. In 1850 the population of the 15 states (Delaware, Maryland, Virginia, North Carolina, South Carolina, Georgia, Florida, Alabama, Mississippi, Louisiana, Tennessee, Kentucky, Missouri, Arkansas, and Texas) was about 10 million, of whom 3 million were slaves. This slave population was an increase from the 1.5 million counted in 1820. During the years between 1820 and 1850 the number of free blacks had increased from 234,000 to 434,000. From 1850 to 1860, the number of free blacks had increased by only 58,000, and the number of slaves by 750,000. The continuing increase in the slave population was due primarily to native births, since opposition to slavery had succeeded in cutting off slave trade. As early as 1774 the Continental Congress had prohibited further importation of slaves into the colonies after December 1, 1775. This prohibition was not entirely successful, and the question was again debated at the Federal Convention of 1787, where, as part of the compromises reached in forming the United States and writing the Constitution, it was agreed that the further importation of slaves would cease after January 1, 1808. Although slavery had no effect on institutional public or voluntary social welfare measures, its effect upon the well-being of the country, as reflected in economic and social reform activity, was enormous.

Population growth prior to the Civil War was matched by territorial expansion. Territorial additions included the Northwest Territory secured by treaty with Great Britain in 1783, the Louisiana Purchase from France in 1803, the Florida Purchase from Spain in 1819, the Texas Annexation in 1845, the Oregon and Mexican Territories secured by treaties with Great Britain and Mexico in 1846 and 1848 respectively, and the Gadsden Purchase from Mexico in 1853. Thus, by 1860 the country's land area reached to the Pacific Ocean, and its northern and southern borders were fixed. The 13 original states had increased to 33. In 1790 the original 13 states contained 94 percent of the total population. Only 250,000 of a total population of 4 million persons lived in the land west of the boundaries of these states. In 1860 half of the population lived in trans-Appalachian regions,[3] despite the heavy European immigration into the Northeast. The rapid increase in the number of states admitted to the Union was due not only to the existence of already populated centers in territories acquired by the young country, but also to the intense, deliberate development of the territories as part of the struggle between proponents and opponents of slavery.

Although the Western expansion and development was encouraged on ideological grounds, political decisions concerning it were determined by economic reality. The invention of the cotton gin in 1793 had made cotton production a base of the Southern economy and slavery the most profitable form of labor. The economy of New England was shaped by the introduction of the spinning jenny and the power loom, bringing together the processes of spinning and weaving under one roof and requiring a larger scale of operation than the cottage. Cotton land in the South was held by plantation landlords who controlled extensive acreage, and a large permanent labor supply could be used profitably year-round. The textile factories of the North were smaller operations; their need for labor, more seasonal. As a group these industrialists required the availability of a large, but free labor force, a group for which they need feel no responsibility during off-seasons or periods of recession.

The New England and Southern states quite naturally moved to opposing sides on questions related to territorial expansion and to the acceptance of new states into the Union. The cultivation of cotton lent itself not only to the use of slave labor but also to the creation of large plantations, essentially an enclosure system in the tradition of the English manor. Ever larger enclosures were desired, and the search for improved climate and fertility led westward. The assumption of the South was that Western lands would be needed for cotton planting and, therefore, that these lands must, as far as possible, be open to the use of slave labor. New England, with its concern for a large, readily available supply of free labor, was initially opposed to territorial expansion because of the threat such expansion represented to the retention of an adequate labor pool in New England.

Labor requirements led New England and the South—that is, the industrialists and plantation owners who controlled the economic destinies of the areas—to opposing views on other issues. The matter of land grants constituted one such issue. The federal government's policy in regard to selling public lands became increasingly flexible and generous during the pre-Civil War period. Originally, the government's policy was to sell only large tracts of land, a policy that was favorable to large landholders. In 1800 and again in 1820 the government reduced the minimum number of acres required for purchase. This policy, which encouraged small landholders, was further liberalized in 1832 with recognition of the "right of preemption," a right that permitted squatters to take possession of land without a cash down payment and to pay for it later.

The period of recession that followed the War of 1812 helped to encourage migration to the West. This migration, seemingly about to reduce the population of the Northeast at the very beginning of its era of industrial revolution, led to a conservative approach to the homestead question. As industrialization proceeded, however, and as the inflow of immigrants dissipated concern about the labor supply, the region's interest shifted to securing Western lands as free lands to be purchased easily by workers who were discontented with the conditions of the factory system or by workers who were unemployed during industrial crises. The fact that the shift was pressured by the self-interest of laborers highlighted the free man versus slave aspect of this North-South controversy.

The tariff question was also one that found New England and the South pitted against each other. The Northern manufacturing states were in severe competition, with Great Britain in particular, to buy their raw material, cotton, and to sell their products, textiles. Understandably, the North sought high-tariff protections against the importation of foreign-made goods. The South, on the other hand, seeking high prices for raw cotton and low prices for finished products, favored low tariffs and competition among industries, domestic and foreign. The tariff struggle continued until the outbreak of the Civil War; and to the extent that it led to the Doctrine of Nullification—the right to nullification by a state of federal tariff legislation—was a significant cause of the outbreak of hostilities.

The mechanization of cotton production in the South and the industrialization of the production of cotton goods in the New England states were the base of expansion for all sections of the country.

In 1792, the year before the invention of the cotton gin, the annual production of cotton was about 6,000 bales. In 1794, the year after the cotton gin's invention, production rose to 17,000 bales. By 1800, 73,000 bales were being produced; and by 1860, 3,841,000 bales.[4] Just as the South's production of raw cotton outstripped the country's production of all other agricultural products, New England's production of finished cotton goods outstripped the country's manufacture of all other goods. The value of cotton products, which stood at $46 million in 1840, rose to $116 million in 1860.[5] Simultaneously, the needs of these two areas spurred the development of the Middle Atlantic states, which produced farm commodities, meat and dairy products, lumber, and other necessities. In addition, the Middle Atlantic states became the shipping and banking centers for the country. Truly, the South, New England, and the Middle Atlantic states were closely joined, and the tie that bound was made of cotton. The digging of canals and building of railroads opened the West, an important factor in its own right, but additionally so in view of the way in which its resources served to strengthen the dependence of the other areas, one upon the other.

Labor and Economic Security

The economic realities that led the South and New England to different solutions to the questions of labor supply had inevitable consequences for the social well-being of their workers. To speak of workers in the South is to speak largely of slaves and, therefore, to speak of no public social welfare programs. Free blacks were left to help themselves. Self-help among the slaves was practiced also; but the very fact of being owned left with the owner the responsibility for maintaining his property in working order. An apologist for slavery defined it as a "system of labor which exchanges subsistence for work."[6]

> Slavery makes all work, and it insures homes, food and clothing for all. It permits no idleness, and it provides for sickness, infancy, and old age. It allows no tramping or skulking, and it knows no pauperism.[7]

Outside the plantation, there were stretches of territory cultivated by small farmers without slave labor. The "hardy yeomen" occupied areas generally not suitable to growing cotton, but quite suitable for raising cattle and for cultivating corn and wheat. As a class, they were prosperous and independent. There remained only the poor whites, also farmers; but because they were landless or owned the most worthless worn-out land, their subsistence was most precarious. Nevertheless, they were not directly subject to the economic fluctuations created by the mechanization of agriculture.

Despite the overall picture of self-sufficiency, there were Southerners who found themselves in need. The poor whites, although generally capable of independence, were one such group. But in developing Southern towns there were others—abandoned and orphaned children, mulattoes, freed slaves. A warmer, more accepting approach to need carried over from colonial days. In a situation of relatively little need, the approach to such need as did arise was characterized by noblesse oblige.

Destitution in the North during the pre-Civil War period was more directly related to urbanization, industrialization, and the development of the factory system. In 1791, the year of Hamilton's *Report of Manufacture*, household manufacture of wool and cotton cloth was occurring in all of the states and could still be characterized as "a vast scene."[8] The first successful cotton mill, using the principle of the spinning jenny, had already been put into operation in Pawtucket, Rhode Island, and by 1809 there were 62 mills operating in New England with 25 more in the process of construction.[9] New England had thus become the textile manufacturing center of the country. The introduction of the power loom in the factory at Waltham, Massachusetts, was the impetus for further development.

The large-scale production of cotton textiles required, first of all, the construction of factories so expensive that their costs had to be borne by absentee owner-investors. Operation of the factories required the recruitment of large numbers of workers to towns. In New England, the workers recruited during the early years of industrialization were young women from farm families living in surrounding areas. In order to attract these young women, the factory owners erected dormitories or saw to the development of boarding homes, where social, religious, and educational activities for workers could be planned and supervised. The combined offer of work, religion, and learning was peculiarly a New England tradition and was an enormously successful recruitment device.[10]

The growing ease with which young women were recruited for factory work paralleled farm mechanization, the decline of the household manufacturing of cloth, and the transfer to the market of services formerly performed at home. The reality of large families as a liability could, for the moment, be mitigated by the fact that girls could earn wages for use in an increasingly monied society. Harriet Martineau, a traveler to the United States in 1835, reported her visit to "the corporate factory-establishment at Waltham":

> Most of the girls live in houses provided by the corporation, which accommodate from six to eight each. When sisters come to the mill, it is a common practice for them to bring their mother to keep house for them and some of their companions, in a dwelling built by their own earnings. In this case, they save enough out of their board to clothe themselves, and have their two or three dollars a week to spare. Some have thus cleared off mortgages from their father's farms; others have educated the hope of the family at college; and many are rapidly accumulating an independence.[11]

These young recruits were white, Protestant, and native-born. Later, as immigration swelled the ranks of job seekers, they would be replaced by women, men, and children—whole families—of "foreign" and Catholic extraction. At that point, native-born women moved into such occupations as teaching. If financially able, they moved into a new genteel ethos of homemaking. A major social welfare shift had occurred. The first laborers in the textile industry had homes to which they might return in times of need; for the new textile labor force, recession and unemployment were a disaster.[12]

The success of the textile factories fostered the development of other manufactures required for the maintenance of that industry and that industry's employees. The "factory system" was applied to other industries and spread rapidly throughout the New England and Middle Atlantic states, with the result that centers of considerable size, offering employment to males as well as females, to skilled as well as unskilled laborers, developed. Whereas 202,000 persons lived in urban centers in 1790, 6.2 million were living in cities in 1860. The growth of older cities demonstrates what was happening. For example, the census of 1790 recorded the largest urban centers as having populations numbering 25,000 to 50,000. The census of 1860 showed the largest centers to have populations numbering 500,000 to 1 million.[13] New York City's population grew from 123,000 in 1820 to 805,000 in 1860; Philadelphia's jumped from 112,000 in 1820 to 562,000 in 1860; Boston's went from 43,000 to 177,000 and Baltimore's from 62,000 to 212,000 during the same years.[14] In addition, many new cities sprang up, not only in New England and the Middle Atlantic states, but also in the West and the South. Pre-Civil War population growth, industrialization, and urbanization were precursors of post-Civil War developments that would shift the country from an agricultural to an industrial economy.

Industrialization and urbanization led to many problems for which social welfare measures—particularly financial aid—were necessary. Mobility and the finding and holding of wage-paying jobs increasingly became requirements for family solvency. With extended kinship ties frequently broken by distance and with adults away from home at work, families were more and more subject to forces beyond their control and more and more dependent upon services supplied from outside the family unit. The hazards of the developing market economy in which families depended on money wages and in which industrial competition, domestic and foreign, kept wages marginal and employment uncertain, were aggravated by the occurrence of a series of economic depressions—one, 1815 to 1821; another, 1837 to 1843; still another, 1857 to 1859. Only the years 1850 to 1856 showed vigorous, sustained recovery. The long stretch between 1815 and 1859 was a difficult time for individuals and families who were not physically or psychologically free to move to the open lands and opportunities of the West. These people included immigrant families physically and financially exhausted by their journey; old people; children who had been orphaned or abandoned; disabled veterans of the War of 1812, the Mexican War, and the Indian Wars; the sick.

The existence of a debilitating handicap was not the only reason westward migration did not occur. Pulling up stakes, even for the ablebodied was risky. The newer agricultural states of the West were poorer than the eastern industrial states and subject to budget constraints. They feared an influx of dependents and were slow to ease residency requirements for public aid. Their maintenance of settlement laws in effect deterred mobility. The frontier existed, but it had only a limited ability to absorb the poverty population of the East.

The Reform Movements

Much of the response to unemployment and inequality of income distribution took the path of "reform" activities. Such activities supported a view of the basic soundness of the economic order at the same time that they demonstrated new convictions about the potential for change of individuals and of aspects of the social structure. As early as 1827, with the formation of the Mechanics' Union Trade Association in Philadelphia, an effort was made to organize all skilled artisans. Although attempts at a combined national association failed, labor entered the depression starting in 1837 with at least five national trade unions: cordwainers, comb makers, carpenters, weavers, and printers.[15] These unions, and the workers' political parties that developed during the 1830s, demanded action in regard to a number of reform and protection issues:[16]

1. Equal and universal free education

2. The availability of public lands for settlement
3. The deprecation of child labor and apprenticeship abuses
4. Restrictions on competitive prison labor
5. Better working conditions for women
6. Establishment of a ten-hour day without any decreases in wages
7. Governmental control of currency
8. The right to organize
9. Provision of jobs for the unemployed in public works programs

They did not demand a change in basic property relationships, but they did demand a larger share of the product of the existing economic system.

By the beginning of the Civil War, the labor movement had generally collapsed. To some extent this failure was due to the fact that labor's success in achieving a liberal land policy meant that frustrated employees could, in sufficient numbers, leave behind their reasons for discontent. Failure to unionize workers was also due to organized corporate and judicial opposition. Most American workers saw a greedy, powerful few employers as the problem and did not generalize a class interest.

Whatever hardships labor suffered, the promise of a new world for common people seemed real enough. Industrialization had fostered the development of a middle class—skilled workers and artisans, merchants, owners of small manufacturing enterprises, professional and service entrepreneurs. Similarly, westward migration had produced large numbers of small independent landowners. It appeared to native-born Americans and immigrants alike that the country's economic growth and geographic expansion were of their own making, that their own toil and adventuresomeness had produced a situation in which dreams could come true. Thus, what developed was a view of humanity as flawed but, nevertheless, as self-determining and perfectable. The colonial view of man as predestined to condemnation and needing to be coerced to forgo evil ways gave way to a view of people as having the power to change, if properly led. The easing of economic pressures was accompanied, therefore, by an easing of Calvinistic determinism. The new age of reason meant that individuals could respond to the godliness of their own nature and could control their own destinies, including economic and social welfare.

The election of Andrew Jackson to the presidency in 1828 and the launching of Jacksonian democracy symbolized the change that had swept the country. The victory of a man popularly believed to have been born in a log cabin was proof of the possibility of egalitarianism and a spur to its further achievement. Reform of individuals was the process by which the achievable was to be achieved.

Areas of reform activity included the extension of suffrage, temperance, more effective poor relief, humane treatment for the insane, rehabilitation of criminals, child saving, and, of course, the drive for the abolition of slavery. A large part of the reform effort centered on free public education as a weapon in the battle for egalitarianism, for democracy. Horace Mann labeled education "the great equalizer of the conditions of men—the balance-wheel of the social machinery."[17] Only through education could the rich and poor be brought together.

> Now surely nothing but universal education can counterwork this tendency to the domination of capital and the servility of labor. . . . But, if education be equally diffused, it will draw property after it by the strongest of all attractions: for such a thing never did happen, and never can happen, as that an intelligent and practical body of men should be permanently poor. Property and labor in different classes are essentially antagonistic; but property and labor in the same class are essentially fraternal.[18]

There was widespread agreement that "universal and complete" education" would do more than all things else to obliterate factitious distinctions in society." Democracy could be real, if the poor could be made the equal of the rich. Education could instill the means and will to make it so.

This drive for education was left to the states for development and moved from New England to the West, where Jacksonian political democracy was most advanced. The Middle Atlantic states—New York, Pennsylvania, New Jersey, and Delaware—experienced more difficulty, but by midcentury these states had permissive statutes allowing for the establishment of schools by localities. In the South no statewide systems of public education were in operation prior to the Civil War. For the country as a whole, however, an "educational consciousness" had been achieved.

The opening of the West must be credited with the rapid advance of white male suffrage.

> As people went westward and formed new states, they made new constitutions. In the western country there were few great differences in wealth . . . much the same state of poverty and hope. Naturally, under such conditions . . . all were equally capable of bearing the responsibility of voting or governing. The new states of the days after the War of 1812, Indiana, Illinois, Alabama, and Missouri, provided white manhood suffrage though Mississippi clung to a tax provision.[19]

In the East, where urbanization was bringing large numbers of people together for effective, collective action, demands for the vote were heard. Connecticut liberalized its suffrage qualifications in 1818. Massachusetts followed in 1820. In 1821 New York legislated universal male suffrage, even for free blacks if they owned property. Other states followed and "male political democracy" became a reality. Women did not achieve legal and political equality with men, but the reform period was the beginning of a long campaign for women's rights. In 1848 a first Women's Rights Convention was held in Seneca Falls, New York, at which suffrage was demanded and a Declaration of Independence adopted.

Not so clearly recognized was the effect of industrialization and urbanization upon the economic structure of the family. The technological revolution, which gained such momentum during the pre-Civil War period, spelled the beginning of a decline in farming as a chief means of support and the virtual end of the family system of manufacturing. Not only had wages, per se, become a basic means of family support, but these wages were being earned in factory employment—away from home. Out of this economic reality evolved separate worlds for men and women. All that went on outside the home—particularly in the areas of work and politics—was the world of men. For the middle class the world of women centered in the home, the family, and the church. The pastoral letter read on July 28, 1837, from the pulpit of all Congregational Churches in New England described a proper woman operating in her "proper sphere."

> The appropriate duties and influence of women . . . are unobtrusive and private. . . . When the mild, dependent, softening influence of women upon the sternness of man's opinion is fully exercised, society feels the effects of it in a thousand forms. The power of woman is in her dependence, flowing from . . . that weakness which God has given her for her protection, and which keeps her in those departments of life that form the character of individuals and of the nation.[20]

Women became involved in reform movements—temperance, suffrage, and the abolition of slavery. They moved from a concern for the rooting out of individual imperfections that would lead to unhappy family living to a demand for explicit political recognition and power, and then to larger social issues.

The American Society for the Promotion of Temperance was founded in 1826 and engaged in widespread propaganda against intemperance. The Temperance Movement involved itself in social and political activities, and by 1860 it boasted a membership of a number of formal social groups and more than a million individuals. One state (Maine) had voted for prohibition. The Temperance Movement would become more vocal and politically stronger after the Civil War, but the attention given to the problem during the prewar period was evidence of a growing concern about the relation of drinking to unemployment and to pauperism. Thus temperance issues presented an immediate reality problem.

Spurred by the growth in corn production by the pioneer farmers of the Ohio River Valley and the burgeoning distilling industry of the East, whiskey became abundant and cheap—and whiskey drinking something of a national pastime for men, women, and children.[21] During the first three decades of the nineteenth century, annual per capita consumption increased to more than five gallons. After 1830, as a result of the Temperance Movement and of stiff federal taxation, it dropped to less than two gallons per capita.[22] Before that, however, the proliferation of unregulated taverns that encouraged drinking, particularly on the part of male laborers, aggravated perceptions of social chaos and disorder in the lower class, especially immigrants. The loss of time from work because of drunkenness on the part of the male breadwinner and the habit of spending time at the saloon on payday were real threats to family well-being. The unavailability of adequate jobs for women made them dependent upon men for the family's support. The physical abuse that often accompanied the drinking added to the urgency of temperance as "a matter of women's rights as well as a religious and humanitarian reform."[23]

During the 1830s and 1840s, thousands of local and state temperance societies were formed with the intention of regulating or prohibiting the sale of liquor. While these societies generally had women's auxiliaries appended, an independent women's gesture was made when Amelia Bloomer founded the newspaper, *The Lily*. In her first editorial, Amelia Bloomer wrote:

> It is WOMAN that speaks through the LILY. It is upon an important subject, too, that she comes before the public to be heard. Intemperance is the great foe to her peace and happiness.[24]

Tales of victimized women, of victimized families, led Mrs. Bloomer and *The Lily* to an alliance with those more specifically focused on women's rights.

The Temperance Movement addressed itself to the economic costs of drinking and also served as a reflection of the crusading, religious spirit of the era, the striving of the era for perfection and beauty as a response to the reality and harshness of a changing society. The democratic, educated, temperate, spiritual individual was the ideal; and reform activity was an acknowledgment of human perfectability as well as a spur to the accomplishment of aspirations. For some, the reality of the larger world seemed too oppressive and they withdrew to such utopias as Brook Farm or Walden Pond or to the intellectual and metaphysical world of Transcendentalism. For others, the reform of people, and of institutions that dampened their progress, was cause for the good fight.

The assurance of opportunity and liberation to fulfill human and societal potential underlay the zeal of adherents to particular causes and comprised the moral force that brought Quakers, Transcendentalists, free blacks, activist women, and reformers of all types together in the abolitionist cause. The new religious humanitarianism, the growing democratic thrust, the moral force surrounding black uprisings in behalf of freedom, made abolition the central and urgent core of the Northern reform movement. Concurrently, in the South, the principles of Jeffersonian democracy and its apologetic approach to slavery lost out to an aggressive ideological defense. The egalitarianism and humanistic spirit of the North and West were rejected. Leadership passed from the moderate Virginians to the extremists of South Carolina, and eventually the aristocratic view representing the interests of a small group of planters prevailed. The white South united in an effort to maintain and extend slavery.

The intensity of the struggle around slavery was a vital element in the differences represented by the economic systems of the North and South. In the North, labor's efforts to organize were sometimes supported by comparing the laborers' situation to that of the slaves. For the most part, however, workers appeared to reject the idea that laborers in the industrial North were "white slaves" in the toil of an "oppressing, enslaving industrial system." Questions of morality were centered on Southern black slavery. The moral, social, and economic issues in the struggle around slavery were so intense that a major war was needed to resolve them. The Northern war effort was accompanied by an increasingly vociferous demand for a proclamation of freedom for slaves, and in the end the abolition movement procured the most basic systemic social welfare reform of the era.

Institutions, Almshouses, and Paupers

For the most part, reform during the pre-Civil War period was geared to the reform of individuals—not to reform of systems—and the effort was to find an environment in which individual changes might be encouraged. The memorials written by pioneer reformer Dorthea L. Dix to encourage provisions for the construction of hospitals for the insane exemplified contemporary efforts to help people fulfill their potential through the use of specialized facilities. Institutions for the insane, for children, for the disabled, for the poor, were particularly important in this regard, since they offered attention to classified needs and surcease from worldly instability. Miss Dix wrote about "the mischiefs which result alike from religious, social, civil, and revolutionary excitements,"[25] excitements that characterized the pre-Civil War period and that were deemed responsible for the increase in mental illness. In the same vein, society was held responsible for an increase in crime and pauperism. The economic growth, geographic expansion, and extension of political democracy that had created a world of opportunity had also created a world of change, insecurity, and temptation. A society making claim to a belief in human perfectability but given to the creation of environmental and human disorders must provide order—and cure—for both. Institutions were thought to do just that.

During the pre-Civil War period, 32 hospitals for the insane were built. The expectation that they and other specialized institutions cure both human and societal ills was burdensome indeed. Speaking particularly of the insane, Miss Dix said:

> To confine the insane to persons whose education and habits do not qualify them for this charge, is to condemn them to mental death. . . .
> Under well-directed hospital care, *recovery is the rule—incurable* permanent insanity the exception. . . .
> But cure alone . . . is not the sole object of hospital care. . . . Of vast importance is the secure and comfortable provision for . . . the incurable insane. Their condition . . . is susceptible of amelioration, and of elevation to a state of comparative comfort and usefulness.[26]

Professional and humane treatment could cure, especially if that treatment were offered in an ordered, stable milieu, a milieu that provided the sick individual relief from excitement and a sense of dignity. At the least, it would ameliorate symptoms. In either case, the conviction that individuals were capable of self-perfection required that they be treated as though they might perfect themselves. The institution became the answer to the individual's ailment and, simultaneously, in its exemplification of needed reform, the answer for society's ills.

Local, state, and federal governmental participation in reform was solicited. Dorthea Dix's Memorial to Congress in 1848 asking that 5 million acres of public land be given to the building of institutions for the insane was a challenge to the federal government to support reform. In time, Congress passed a bill allocating 10 million acres, taking cognizance of the needs not only of the insane, but also of the blind and the deaf. President Pierce's veto in 1854 denied the federal government's responsibility for the social welfare of the country. In so doing, however, the veto upheld the historic responsibility of the states in matters of social welfare, when people could not sustain their own social well-being through self-endeavor or private charity.

> I readily and, I trust, feelingly acknowledge the duty incumbent on us all as men and citizens, and as among the highest and holiest of our duties, to provide for those who, in the mysterious order of Providence, are subject to want and to disuse of body or mind; but I can not find any authority in the Constitution for making the Federal Government the great almoner of public charity throughout the United States. . . . And if it were admissable . . . I can not avoid the belief that it would in the end be prejudicial . . . to the noble offices of charity. . . .
>
> If the several States, many of which have already laid the foundation of munificent establishments of local beneficence, and nearly all of which are proceeding to establish them, shall be led to suppose . . . that congress is to make provision for such objects, the fountains of charity will be dried up at home. . . .[27]

The Pierce veto reinforced the pattern of state responsibility and of private charity dominance in social welfare. Only in regard to veterans did the federal government maintain direct responsibility for a group of disabled citizens. By 1790 Congress had taken over financial support for disabled veterans, veterans' widows, and orphans of veterans. Pensions were established for those groups during the Revolutionary War and were extended without serious questioning to participants of the War of 1812, the Seminole Indian Wars, and the Mexican War of 1846–1848. Benefits to ablebodied veterans of each war were eventually granted. The pensions were small and the numbers of veterans covered were few because of the time that had elapsed between each war's end and congressional action. Nevertheless the precedent of some benefits regardless of economic need was established.

For most people, however, economic need continued to be viewed as an individual aberration. The view of poverty and of the plight of families in need changed very little from that of the colonial period. Welfare legislation passed by the founding states had represented the carrying over of colonial,

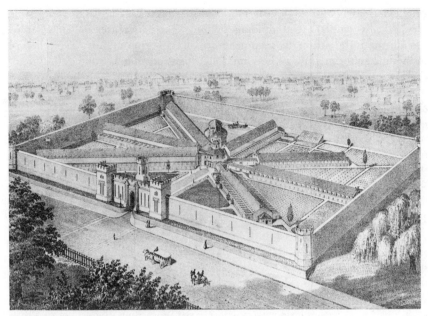

The State Penitentiary for the Eastern District of Pennsylvania.
Courtesy of the Pennsylvania Prison Society

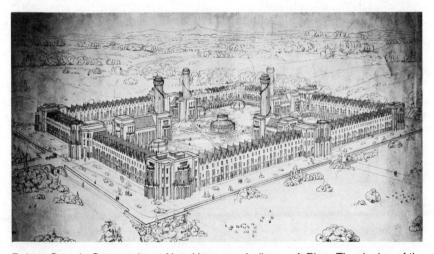

Robert Owen's Community at New Harmony, Indiana—A Plan. The design of the Eastern State Penitentiary and of Robert Owen's New Harmony in Indiana are remarkably similar. Both reflected the era's belief in the value of the well ordered environment. The design for the New Harmony community was never realized; the penitentiary, however, was occupied in 1829—the last inmate removed in 1971.
Courtesy of the Indiana Historical Society Library

provincial law; welfare legislation of subsequently admitted states was ideologically similar. Unemployment and sharp increases in relief roles reconfirmed the ultimate responsibility of government for the relief of individual suffering but, at the same time, fostered an expanded definition of the responsibility of relatives, one for the other. In most Northeastern and North Central states, grandchildren were added to the list of legally responsible relatives; in many states, brothers and sisters were added. The humane conviction that the poor were an inescapable obligation meant the provision of minimal, survival relief. But, more than ever, the view was that relief should be unnecessary and that government was obligated to minimize the cost to the taxpayer for the care of the poor. Only the legislation of the Southern and Western states tempered this view with any concern for the "comfort of the poor" or with legislation less restrictive than that of New England.

The more restrictive approach of the Northeastern and North Central states seems quite natural taking into account the fact that the crises in unemployment and the rise in relief expenditures were chiefly felt there. In his 1824 report on the relief and settlement of the poor, John V. N. Yates, secretary for New York State, wrote that "populous places have at all times, been burdened with a larger proportion of paupers, than places where a thin or scattered population is found."[28] At the time of the report, well over half the population of the country was still living on the Atlantic Coast. The beginning influx of immigrants, who tended to remain in Eastern cities, aggravated the reaction to public outdoor relief giving, since they frequently were among the unemployed. Indeed, what appears to be an overreaction to public outdoor relief giving—New York City, for example, with a population of 203,000—had expended only $16,000 in 1830[29] might really have been a veiled stance against immigrants. Similarly, the influx of foreigners strengthened the argument that relief giving be left to benevolent societies and to the rich. The uncertainty of private charity was in itself considered a virtue, for it instilled in the newcomer that most American of all values, independence. Furthermore, private charity preserved a Puritan value—the need of the rich to give charity.

The fact that there is little indication in the mainstream of pre-Civil War law or literature that the economic system was considered in any way responsible for poverty and the creation of a poor class does not mean that there was no challenge to this view. Thomas Paine as early as 1792 and Mathew Carey in 1833 both saw poverty as related to the malfunctioning of the economic system. Paine urged the abolition of the Poor Laws and the establishment of a system of pensions, family allowances, subsidized education, and guaranteed employment.

> By the operation of this plan, the poor laws, those instruments of civil torture, will be superseded, and wasteful expense of litigation prevented. The hearts of the humane will not be shocked by ragged and hungry children, and the persons

of seventy or eighty years of age, begging for bread. The dying poor will not be dragged from place to place to breathe their last, as a reprisal of parish upon parish. Widows will have a maintenance for their children, and not be carted away, on the death of their husbands, like culprits and criminals; and children will no longer be considered as increasing the distresses of their parents. The haunts of the wretched will be known, because it will be to their advantage, and the number of petty crimes, the offspring of distress and poverty, will be lessened. *The poor, as well as the rich, will then be interested in the support of government, and the cause and apprehension of riots and tumults will cease.*[30]

Mathew Carey, a renowned pamphleteer on political and economic matters, responded to the charge that the poor rates and the aid of private philanthropy demoralize the poor and lead to corruption of pride in independence. His "appeal to the wealthy of the land" was written to refute "certain pernicious errors" that prevailed respecting the situation of the poor:

1. That every man, woman, and grown child, able and willing to work may find employment.
2. That the poor, by industry, prudence, and economy, may at all times support themselves comfortably, without depending on eleemosynary aid. . . .
3. That their suffering and distresses chiefly, if not wholly arise from their idleness, their dissipation, and their extravagance.
4. That taxes for the support of the poor, and aid . . . by charitable individuals . . . are pernicious, as . . . they foster their idleness and improvidence, and thus produce, or at least increase, the poverty and distress they are intended to relieve.[31]

Through comparisons of average annual wages and subsistence expenses for workers in selected occupations, Carey demonstrated the inevitable gaps between income and need—the necessity for financial supplementation. He demonstrated further that only 549 paupers had been supported with outdoor relief—that most suspected form of relief—in Philadelphia in 1830, and that the aid granted had averaged 46¼ cents per week—less than 7 cents per day. Pointing up how many of those supported were either families with children, the disabled, or the aged, Carey argued that the poor rates and the aid of benevolent societies "far from producing the pernicious effects ascribed to them are imperiously necessary." Rather than look to the poor as the cause for the rise in poor rates, he concluded that one must look to the workings of a market economy in a society becoming increasingly dependent upon machines "for the low rate of wages is the root of mischief."

A cause has been steadily and powerfully operating to increase the poor rates. . . . I mean the rapid and oppressive reduction of wages, consequent on the wonderful improvements in machinery. Manual labour succumbs in the conflict with steam and water power; and everything that supersedes the demand for that labour must increase competition, lower wages; produce distress and . . . increase the poor rates.[32]

The arguments of Paine and Carey did little to improve programs for the poor. They did, however, help to prevent the abolition of public relief despite the powerful forces aligned against it. The retention of the Poor Laws was rationalized on the basis of humaneness, even by some who believed them to be unnecessary. So distinguished a leader as Josiah Quincy— congressman, mayor of Boston, and chairman of a state committee to study the pauper laws—considered the Poor Laws, "too deeply rivetted in the affections, or the moral sentiment of our people to be loosened by theories, however plausible."[33]

The physically disabled aside, public and private sources generally agreed that the causes of poverty were to be found in individual character flaws and in organizations that encouraged and promoted dependency. The New York Society for the Prevention of Pauperism was founded "to investigate and as far as possible to remove the causes of mendicity; to devise plans for ameliorating the condition of the poor and wretched, and to secure their successful operation."[34] The Society successfully petitioned the Corporation of the City to appoint five members of that body to the Board of Managers of the Society, thus encouraging the Board "to calculate upon municipal countenance and aid." The first annual report (1818) of the Society listed the causes of poverty as ignorance, idleness, intemperance, and imprudence (especially to marry). The report listed the following as tending to aggravate the causes of poverty: lotteries, pawnbrokers, houses of ill fame, and the numerous charitable institutions. Although public relief and private benevolence did admittedly relieve some misery and suffering, the long view of the Society, as expressed by its president and its chairman of the Committee to Prepare a Report on the Subject of Pauperism, was that giving and taking help encouraged the tendency to idleness and extravagance on the part of the poor, relaxed their need for industry, and eventually diminished that "wholesome anxiety to provide for the wants of a distant day, which alone can save . . . from a state of absolute dependence, and from becoming a burden to the community."[35]

New York City had already erected "buildings for eleemosynary purposes, at an expense of half a million dollars, and . . . [was being called upon] for the annual distribution of 90,000 dollars more."[36] Failure to find a solution to the burgeoning expense of supporting an increasing number of paupers was frightening:

> Without a radical change in the principles upon which public alms have been usually distributed, helplessness and poverty would continue to multiply— demands for relief would become more and more importunate, the numerical difference between those who are able to bestow charity and those who sue for it, would gradually diminish, until the present system must fall under its own irresistible pressure, prostrating, perhaps, in its ruin, some of the pillars of the social order.[37]

The agreement that pauperism could be prevented and cured only by erecting "barriers against the encroachments of moral degeneracy" fostered a review of contemporary relief practices and a search for barriers that could, at one and the same time, save the poor from pauperism and the rich from taxation. Voluntary organizations, such as the New York Society for the Prevention of Pauperism and the Associations for Improving the Condition of the Poor that developed later in several large cities, sought "to remove the various causes of mendicity" primarily through friendly advice. These efforts at personalized attention—foreshadowing the more persistent operations of the Charity Organization Societies (COS)—were aimed at raising the needy above the need for relief by bringing about a change in character. But, also like the COS, these early voluntary organizations attempted to effectuate governmental provisions for bettering the circumstances of the poor and thus to lend encouragement to individual and familial effort. The New York Society's Sub-Committee on Ignorance was charged as follows:

> This Committee shall report the number of children who do not attend any school; the number of adults who cannot read; the number of families and individuals who do not attend public worship; and the causes which prevent.[38]

Equalization of opportunity and the betterment of human beings were, of course, cornerstones of the morality underlying the era's reform efforts.

Dissatisfaction with public outdoor relief, especially of the ablebodied, focused on its effectiveness in relieving or preventing poverty. There was considerable belief that cash assistance promoted the very opposite of its intended purpose. So strongly was this view held that the State of Delaware prohibited local outdoor relief. Philadelphia abolished it from 1827 to 1839 and Chicago from 1848 to 1858. As for farming out and indenture, their abuses were notorious; and for some, indoor relief was no less suspect. Discussion was most intense where the problem was most serious, in the East. A series of state reviews of public relief giving developed, the most widely publicized of which were those of Massachusetts, New York, New Hampshire, and Pennsylvania.

In 1821 Josiah Quincy's "Report of the Committee to whom was Referred the Consideration of the Pauper Laws of this Commonwealth" placed in "strong light the objections to the entire principle of our existing pauper laws" but despaired of the laws being abolished. Among the Committee's recommended principles for the operation of a relief system, two were particularly important:

> 1. That of all modes of providing for the poor, the most wasteful, the most expensive, and most injurious to their morals and destructive of their industrious habits is that of supply in their own families.
> 2. That the most economical mode is that of Alms Houses; having the character of Work Houses, or Houses of Industry, in which work is provided for every degree of ability in the pauper; and thus the able poor made to provide, partially at least for their own support, and also to the support, or at least the comfort of the impotent poor.[39]

In summary, the Report stressed the responsibility of society to diminish pauperism and recommended the use of a single administrative mechanism, the almshouse, for doing so—"denying for the most part all supply from public provision, except on condition of admission into the public institution."[40]

In 1823, in response to rising costs of relief, the Senate and Assembly of the State of New York resolved that the secretary of state study and report on the expenses and operation of the Poor Laws in New York as well as in other states, for the purpose of suggesting improvements in the New York welfare system. Secretary Yates's report, submitted in February 1824, divided the poor of the state into "the permanent poor," that is, those who received support regularly during the year studied, and "the occasional poor," that is, those who received help during part of the year (perhaps briefly during the autumn and winter months). Of the first group, he found 6,896; and of the second, 15,215. Of the total of 6,896 permanent poor, only 1,789, "though not in the vigor of life," could be considered capable of earning their subsistence. Among the permanent poor not capable of earning their subsistence were 2,604 children under 14 years of age. Yates did not specify the number of families represented by the 6,896 individuals classified as permanent poor, but he did assert that 1,585 of the total were men who had been reduced to that state by drinking and "of consequence, that their families . . . were reduced to the same penury and want."[41]

In connection with the operation of the relief system in New York, the secretary reported four major findings: (1) that the poor, when farmed out, were frequently treated with barbarity and neglect; (2) that the education and morals of the children of paupers were almost wholly neglected; (3) that there was no adequate provision for the employment of the poor for the inculcation of industrious habits; and (4) that there was little attention being given to the disbursement of public funds appropriated for the support of the poor. As a single, total remedy for all these evils, Yates recommended the adoption of the "poorhouse plan" for every county of the state. In accordance with the plan, the one or more poorhouses to be erected in each county would be houses of employment where paupers might be "maintained and employed . . . in some healthful labor, chiefly agricultural, their children to be carefully instructed, and at suitable age, to be put out to some useful business or trade." As for sturdy beggars or vagrants—most likely the occasional poor—they were to be confined to penitentiaries connected to the poorhouses and subjected to a regimen of discipline consisting of "a rigid diet, hard labor, employment at the stepping mill, or some treatment equally efficacious in restraining their vicious appetites and pursuits."

The recommendations of the Yates report called for a separation of the worthy and unworthy poor; long-term care in houses of employment for the former and short-term penitentiary or workhouse confinement for the latter. The two types of houses were to be physically joined to form a system of almshouse care for the poor.

> Until a system . . . can be devised, which with economy and humanity, will administer relief to the indigent and infirm, incapable of labor, provide

employment for the idle, and impart instruction to the young and ignorant, little hope can be entertained of meliorating the condition of our poor or relieving the community from the growing evils of pauperism.[42]

Thus the almshouse would be that particular institution given to the creation of an environment in which concern for the worthy poor and attention to their needs would militate against the development of pauperism in the individual and, by extension, in society. The unworthy occasional poor were to be handled quite differently, but not without attention to what they seemed to need, if they were to be saved from themselves.

Historically, the Yates report is significant, since it gained widespread attention and established indoor almshouse care as the major approach to the relief of the poor in the United States. In 1824 Yates reported the existence of 30 almshouses in New York State. In 1857 a state Select Senate Committee to Visit Charitable and Penal Institutions reported the existence of 55 almshouses, exclusive of the almshouses and poorhouses in New York and Kings counties.[43] Massachusetts listed 83 almshouses in 1824; there were 219 in 1860. By 1860 Pennsylvania had 31 county, in addition to local, almshouses. By 1860 Maryland had almshouses in all but one county, and that county was permitted use of the facility in Baltimore.[44]

As the Civil War approached, almshouse care was being used extensively throughout the United States. But condemnation of the "catchall almshouse" had begun. The condemnation might be traced to a failure to put into practice Yates's concepts of humane treatment and classification of the poor. In 1824, however, the almshouse seemed the obvious answer for all who deviated (or might deviate) from those who could support themselves—the impotent elderly or disabled, the potent ablebodied, and the eventually "potent" child. The emphasis in the Yates report upon saving the poor from pauperism and upon deterring the ablebodied from accepting relief, despite statistical evidence that the overwhelming numbers of the poor had been brought to their state by social and physical disabilities beyond their control, showed an inability to think beyond individual salvation to family welfare. Nowhere is this more evident than in the childsaving activities of the era.

Child Saving

Stirrings of dissatisfaction with almshouse care, especially for children, developed soon after the Yates report appeared. This dissatisfaction was based in part on the reform, crusading interests of the era. The period was one of growth of democratic concepts, of increased concern for individual self-realization. In child welfare this meant a beginning awareness of children as children—young people who must grow into adults able to participate in a democratic government. It seemed to the reformers that neither the undifferentiated almshouse nor the environment provided by the family—particularly the poor family—would provide the requisite discipline and education for children.

The "mischief" and "excitements" attributable to urbanization had led to social change and unrest. Self-realization and individual freedom were not to be confused with license and self-indulgence. Democracy was not to be extended to family life and the relaxation of parental authority. Fear of permissiveness in the care of children was aggravated by the growing presence of immigrants, who, it was thought, were unaware of traditional American child-rearing practices. The goal for a reformed American society was the return to the well-ordered "institutions" of the colonial era; for if children were to save the country for democracy, they must first be saved themselves.

Again the institution—this time with specialized concern for dependent, neglected, and delinquent children—offered an approach that appeared to be both humane and salving for the individual, as well as a visible example of disciplined living for all families. That the children's institution, except as it attempted the achievement of order and stability, was not a model of colonial family life somehow went unobserved.

Institutions for children had appeared early on the American scene but were few in number until the nineteenth century. The first American institution for children was founded in 1729. This was a private institution for girls established in New Orleans by the Ursuline Sisters. The Bethesda House for Boys, founded in 1740 near Savannah, Georgia, was also privately supported. The first governmentally supported institution was established in 1790 in Charleston, South Carolina, and remained the only publicly funded institution for children until the turn of the century. The Charleston Orphan House was founded for the "Purpose of Supporting and Educating Poor Orphan Children, and Those of Poor, Distressed and Disabled Parents, Who are Unable to Support and Maintain Them."[45]

During the first half of the nineteenth century, the number of children's institutions increased rapidly, so that by 1851 there were 77. An additional 47 were built prior to 1860.[46] Most of these institutions were orphan asylums or simply asylums for dependent children; some were houses of refuge, reformatories for delinquent children. Most were privately controlled by religious, social, or foreign-born national groups, but many were the beneficiaries of state subsidies. The first private institution to receive a state subsidy was the Orphan Asylum of New York, which was granted a subsidy by an act of the state legislature in 1811. Similar grants were made in other states. The New York (City) House of Refuge and the Philadelphia House of Refuge were opened in 1825 and 1828 respectively. Both were supported by a combination of city appropriations, state subsidies, and voluntary contributions. During the so-called child-saving era, 1840–1860, the system of state subsidies was greatly extended. Institutions wholly supported by public funds were also developed, generally to meet the needs of special classes of children. The Boston House of Reformation established in 1826 was the first reformatory for juveniles funded by a municipality. The first state reform school, The House of Refuge for Delinquent Boys, was established in Massachusetts in 1847. A School for Idiots, under the superintendency of Dr. Samuel Gridley Howe, was opened in 1848, also in Massachusetts. Similar publicly funded schools were opened in the next decade in Albany, New York, in Columbus, Ohio, and in Lakeville, Connecticut.

Institutional child care, as provided during the pre-Civil War period, gravitated toward an undemocratic and antifamily approach. Starting with distrust for contemporary child-rearing practices and with a sense of crisis that required a demonstration of proper child care, superintendents of children's institutions discouraged visits by parents except under severely restricting conditions. As for the actual care provided, in both orphan asylums and institutions for delinquents, the goal was submission and obedience on the part of the child. The Charleston orphan asylum saw itself as educating boys to become disciplined workers and citizens. The erection of houses of refuge for delinquent children spoke most pointedly to pre-Civil War concerns about the care of children. The delinquent child highlighted the "vicious tempers and habits" that could develop in an environment where authority and governance did not exact obedience and submission. How easily the willful, offending child could become the adult criminal, the contributor to societal breakdown! The movement for institutions devoted to delinquent children was begun by the New York Society for the Prevention of Pauperism in 1819; and the New York House of Refuge opened in 1826. By 1857 the number of such institutions had grown sufficiently to warrant a national convention of refuge superintendents.

Houses of refuge, like institutions for dependent, homeless children, offered a model for family home care, a combination of shelter, routine, and discipline. Isolated and shielded from outside, particularly from own-family influences, delinquent children were subjected to a "vigorous course of moral and corporal discipline" with the intent that they "be made tractable and obedient"[47] and, ultimately, good citizens. As indicated by the report of the investigation of the Philadelphia House of Refuge in 1835, the success of such an institution was thought to be measured by the extent to which its practices were a demonstration of parenting and parental responsibilities fulfilled.

> The inmates present a healthy appearance; their clothing is comfortable, and their fare is abundant and wholesome. Their labour is suited to their age and capacity—regular, but not severe. Their government . . . is parental.—They have their regular hours of labour, and instruction; while every attention is paid to induce habits of industry, the greatest possible care is had for their intellectual improvement. . . .
>
> To this unfortunate class, the advantages of this institution are peculiarly adopted. Here then vicious tempers and habits are restrained—their minds improved—principles of virtue inculcated; and not a few, who were on the broad road to ruin, have been rescued from destruction and prepared for usefulness. . . .[48]

The model of "home life" offered by the house of refuge and by other child-caring institutions was semimilitary, characterized by discipline, training, and rehabilitation. The model was one in which the design of the institution and the imposition of a controlled, regulated environment were in themselves to effect needed reformation. Thus, the realization of the goal of child saving through institutionalization meant mass, as opposed to individualized, care for children.

Despite the increase in special institutions for children, the unquestioned acceptance of institutional child care declined during the 1850s. This decline resulted partly from an inability to build specialized institutions in sufficient numbers to absorb the growing number of dependent, homeless, orphaned, and delinquent children. Economic uncertainty was increasing, and for adults without economic resources, there was little capacity to withstand these uncertainties and to support their children. In New York City alone, according to a police report in 1852, "there were an estimated 10,000 abandoned, orphaned, runaway children roaming the streets."[49] The catchall almhouse, rather than the specialized institution, remained the most available form of care for children.

Other factors contributed to a less positive view of institutional child care; the rise of public education and the decline of opportunities for legal indenture and apprenticeship were two. The pattern of child-caring institutions had included a relatively short period of institutional housing during which education and reeducation for orderly living were provided. Having satisfactorily completed this period of rehabilitation, the male child was placed out by the institution as an apprentice in a particular trade or occupation; the female child was indentured as a domestic servant. The spread of public, increasingly compulsory, education made the educational efforts of child-caring institutions inadequate and unnecessary and, moreover, took the child back into the very community from which he was to have been saved. Similarly, the gradual disappearance of cottage industries not only meant the disappearance of work opportunities that could be selected and put under surveillance by the institution but also the disappearance of family care as an aspect of indentured apprenticeship. Simultaneously, increasingly heavy migrations from Europe combined with stretches of economic recession to make for a surplus of adult workers, rendering contracted child labor less profitable.

> As the apprenticeship system . . . passed away with the profound changes that occurred in industrial conditions, the indenturing of children underwent a change for the worse. The value of the instruction received from the "masters" became less, and the value of the services rendered by the children increased.[50]

A new system of child care was required.

The Children's Aid Society of New York was founded in 1853 by Charles Loring Brace for the purpose of effecting a new approach to child care. The circular announcing the formation of the Society expressed the urgency of the task ahead.

> But a small part of the vagrant population can be shut up in our asylums. . . .
> The class increases. Immigration is pouring its multitudes of poor foreigners,
> who . . . leave young outcasts everywhere abandoned in our midst. For the
> most part . . . [they] grow up utterly by themselves. No one cares for them, and
> they care for no one. . . . Every cunning faculty is intensely stimulated. They
> are shrewd and old in vice when other children are in leading-strings.[51]

Conceptually, Brace was bent on saving children through the provision of
education and shelter and, where necessary, through separation of children
from parents.

Efforts to secure adequate and proper shelter for dependent children
led Brace to the notion of foster home care:

> The workers . . . in this movement [foster home placement] felt from the
> beginning that "asylum-life" is not the best training for outcast children in
> preparing them for practical life. In large buildings, where a multitude of
> children are gathered together, the bad corrupt the good, and the good are not
> educated in the virtues of real life. The machinery, too, which is so necessary in
> such large institutions, unfits a poor boy or girl for practical handwork.[52]

Brace became convinced that foster home placement in an environment
totally different from that of New York City was the only possible solution.
That totally different environment turned out to be the West, where "the
best of all Asylums for the outcast child . . . [would be] the farmer's
home."[53] The fact that farm labor was in demand in the West and, therefore,
that large numbers of children could be absorbed fit neatly with a romantic
conception of country life. During the 12-year period, 1853–1864, the
Children's Aid Society of New York placed 4,614 children with Western
farmers. An even larger number were placed during the decade following
the Civil War.[54]

The apparent success of the Children's Aid Society led to the organiza-
tion of other child-saving agencies employing similar placement methods—
that is, removing dependent children from city environs, sometimes to the
West, sometimes simply to the rural areas of a home state. The Church
Home Society was founded in Boston in 1855; the Henry Watson Children's
Aid Society, in Baltimore in 1860; and the Home for Little Wanderers also in
New York in 1861. With their emphasis upon child saving, these organizations, like institutions and almshouses, offered programs that did not
individualize the child.

Retreat from the Almshouse

After the Civil War, the practices of the Children's Aid Society were brought
under scrutiny and criticism. Prior to the war, however, it was almshouse
care that was subjected to a process of reevaluation. In New York, the state
Select Senate Committee to Visit Charitable and Penal Institutions made its
report in 1857. The committee had been appointed

to visit . . . all charitable institutions supported or assisted by the State, and all city and country poor and work houses and jails . . . to examine into the conditions of the said establishments, their . . . government, treatment, and management of the inmates, the conduct of the trustees, directors, and other officers . . . and all other matters whatever pertaining to their usefulness and good government.[55]

The Committee made its visits during the summer and autumn months when the "average number in the poor house is twenty-five percent less than in the winter" and made the following overall statement about what was found:

> The poor houses throughout the State may be generally described as badly constructed, ill-arranged, ill-warmed, and ill-ventilated. The rooms are crowded with inmates; and the air, particularly in the sleeping apartments, is very noxious, and to casual visitors, almost insufferable.[56]

Still further:

> The evidence taken by the committee exhibits such a filth, nakedness, licentiousness, general bad morals, and disregard of religion and the most common religious observances, as well as of gross neglect of the most ordinary comforts and decencies of life, as if published in detail would disgrace the State and shock humanity.[57]

The Committee recalled that almshouses had been originally designed to be "comfortable asylums for worthy indigence" and gave examples of how they had been permitted to become "unsuitable refuge for the virtuous poor, and mainly places of confinement for the degraded."[58]

The care of old people, of worthy adults who were suffering temporary reverses, of the insane, and of children was found to be especially outrageous. The Committee recommended outdoor relief for worthy adults and specialized institutional care for children and the insane, the object being the removal of these classes from the almshouses.

> A . . . more efficient and economic auxiliary in supporting the poor, and the prevention of absolute pauperism, consists . . . in the proper and systematic distribution of *outdoor* relief. Worthy indigent persons should . . . be kept from the degradation of the poor house, by reasonable supplies of provisions . . . at their own homes.[59]

As for children:

> It is a great public reproach that they should ever be suffered to enter or remain in the poor houses as they are now mismanaged.
>
> The Committee most earnestly recommend[s] the establishment of special institutions for the purpose of maintaining and educating them by themselves, apart from the contaminations which now surround and vitiate them.[60]

It was recommended that the insane be removed to state asylums.

In Massachusetts, too, almshouse care was found wanting. A special committee was appointed in 1858 to "investigate the whole system of public charitable institutions of the Commonwealth." The committee found the system of state almshouses to have "grave disadvantages."

> For example: (1) partisan administration, (2) tendency of breaking up families to perpetuate dependency, (3) greater difficulty in placing children, (4) or finding work, (5) increased costs of transportation, (a) involved extra school and church facilities, (b) increased risks from fire and from moral and social contamination.[61]

The Committee recommended that the almshouse system be abandoned at the earliest convenience.

Neither direct criticism of almshouse care, as in the New York and Massachusetts reports, nor indirect criticism, as implied in beginning efforts to remove special classes of indigents, produced an immediate retreat from such care. The eruption of the Civil War was, certainly, a prime factor for the hiatus. Perhaps the nature of the population of inmates is even more telling. Although estimates vary widely, there is general agreement that more than half the inmates were foreign-born.[62] The probability is that most people agreed with Brace that these were "dangerous classes" and that fear rather than concern was the mark of public opinion. Almshouse care remained the dominant form of care for the poor until the Progressive Era of the late nineteenth century.

DOCUMENTS
The Pre-Civil War Period

Three documents have been selected to illustrate the tenor of social welfare during the pre-Civil War period: The *First Annual Report of the Society for the Prevention of Pauperism in New York City* (1816); *The Constitution and By-Laws of the Female Orphan Asylum of Portland, Maine* (1828) and President Franklin Pierce's *Veto of The Ten-Million Acre Bill,* the act granting public lands to the various states for the benefit of indigent persons (1854). The documents demonstrate several major themes:

1. That the causes of poverty are outside the economic system, and that poverty can be abolished through the reform of individuals.
2. That institutions can serve as mechanisms for the rehabilitation of individuals and of the social order.
3. That the development and administration of social welfare programs are local public and voluntary social welfare concerns, rather than a responsibility of the federal government.

The managers of the Society for the Prevention of Pauperism in their First Annual Report give evidence of the change that had occurred in society's view of people. The Puritan doctrine of a fixed, preordained, predestined societal structure gave way to one in which achievement was limited only by failure to fulfill individual potential. It was the age of reason, and the will of God yielded to free will. The rational man could reach perfectability, if he willed to do so. The problem for social welfare then, as for all institutions, was to create an environment in which individual reform and perfectability were encouraged and could take place. The managers of the Society were particularly frightened by the growth of pauperism, a condition they thought was easily fostered in a rapidly changing society if various internal and external forces went unheeded. The feared result was not only a detraction from individual potential, but from the fullest accomplishments of a whole society obviously on the path to perfection. The report of the managers demonstrates the extent to which rational human beings, freed of heavenly strictures, could rationalize the harsh treatment of the poor.

During the pre-Civil War era, institutions were founded to provide and demonstrate the well-ordered environmental setting in which human perfectability could flourish. Children's institutions were particularly important in this regard, since the future of the country quite literally depended upon the kind of adults that children became. The Female Orphan Asylum of Portland, Maine, was established to "carry into effect *means* for the support, instruction and employment of female children, from three to ten years of age." The By-Laws of the Asylum demonstrate the premium placed upon stability and regularity in the daily lives of children. Their clothing, their fare, their instruction, and their activities are proscribed in rules and regulations so as to inculcate "habits of *order, neatness,* and *industry.*" Of equal importance was the prevention of parental interference "in the management of the children." Indeed, parents could not visit except in the presence of the Asylum's governess. To be preferred was the parent's relinquishing all claim to the child, thus freeing the institution for its work. At the age of 11, the children were generally "placed out" with virtuous families; and the Asylum followed their conduct and circumstances until they had reached eighteen.

President Pierce vetoed "the 10 million acre bill" in the belief that the bill would eventuate in the "transfer to the Federal Government the charge of all the poor in all the States." His decision to veto was based on the constitutional guarantee that those powers not specifically delegated to the United States by the Constitution were reserved for the states. Since he could find no specific delegation of authority for social welfare, the president interpreted the Constitution to mean that social welfare matters involved issues of states' rights and, therefore, required the exercise by each state of its own "police power" to provide for the welfare of its inhabitants. In addition to the constitutional question of states' rights, the president's decision was steeped in historical precedent by which programs to meet social welfare needs had long been the province of local and voluntary organizations. The veto was to sustain the tradition until the depression of the 1930s.

The First Annual Report of the Managers of the Society

for the Prevention of Pauperism in the City of New York

Read and Accepted October 26, 1818

To which is added:

A REPORT ON THE SUBJECT OF PAUPERISM,

dated February 4, 1818

THE Managers of the Society for the Prevention of Pauperism in the city of New York, REPORT:

That their anticipation of the importance and difficulty of their duties has been fully realized. Their first efforts were necessarily directed to the development of the objects which they were appointed to consider. Though these objects were specified as far as practicable; though the nature of the duty allotted to the Board was pointed out, as well as the general aspect of the plan, such as the Managers should have in view, yet the basis only was laid, and it was their work to erect the superstructure. They were not at a loss for materials. These were more and more exhibited to them in the multifarious ramifications of their labours. But it was not an easy task to arrange them in proper order, and to dispose of them to advantage; it therefore required time, deliberation, and assiduity, to digest an effectual plan, and to take measures for rendering it subservient to the momentous purposes of the Society.

In order to investigate, and as far as possible to remove the various causes of mendicity; to devise plans for meliorating the condition of the poor and wretched, and to secure their successful operation, the Managers, immediately after their appointment, respectfully solicited the Corporation of this city to appoint five Managers from that body, agreeably to the 6th article of the constitution. The favourable result of this application warrants the Board to calculate upon municipal countenance and aid.

The 3d article of the By-laws declares that "each attending Committee shall consist of as many members of the Society as the Board may think necessary. They shall make rules, or by-laws, to govern themselves; keep a book, wherein they shall enter their proceedings, and report to the Board at every stated meeting, a summary of their proceedings, with their opinions on the most adviseable course for the Board to pursue relative thereto."

Nine Standing Committees were accordingly appointed, to carry into effect the views of the Managers, as stated in the following extract from the minutes:—

DISTRICTING COMMITTEE.

This Committee shall consist of as many members of this Board as there are wards in the city, who shall form a general plan of operations;—and as soon after as possible each person shall, in his respective ward, associate with as many members of the Society as may be thought adviseable, who shall divide the ward into as many districts as they may think proper. These sub-committees shall embrace in their operations the duties specified on the 12th and 13th pages of the printed Report on the subject of Pauperism.

IDLENESS AND SOURCES OF EMPLOYMENT.

The object of this Committee shall be to devise means for the employment of the poor.

INTEMPERANCE.

This Committee shall inform the Board as to the number of places where ardent spirits are retailed in small quantities;—what quantity is drunk, with an estimate of its cost, and the class of citizens most subject to the vice of intemperance.

The Committee shall give opinions at large on every thing connected with this subject, including the law, police regulations, officers, &c. &c.

LOTTERIES.

This Committee shall report the number of lottery offices in the city; the amount of money annually expended; the probable waste of time occasioned by lotteries; the usual percent advance on tickets; the extent of the evil arising from the insuring of tickets; how far the restraining laws are enforced, &c. &c.

HOUSES OF ILL FAME.

This Committee shall report the probable number of houses of this description; families that live by prostitution; and in what particular the police regulations on the subject may be amended.

PAWN-BROKERS.

This Committee shall report the number of pawn-brokers, their manner of doing business, and the best mode of correcting the evils arising therefrom.

CHARITABLE INSTITUTIONS.

This Committee shall inform the Board as to the number in the city; the gross and annual amount of their funds, and the mode respectively adopted by them, in the distribution of charity to the poor.

GAMBLING.

This Committee shall report the number and kinds of gambling houses, and their opinion as to the best mode of diminishing or suppressing them.

IGNORANCE.

This Committee shall report the number of children who do not attend any school; the number of adults who cannot read; the number of families and individuals who do not attend public worship; and the causes which prevent. . . .

In the years 1788–1789, there were under the old system,

```
Paupers .............................7391
        In the Hospital  ............... 894
        ——Penitentiary  .............. 446
        ——Orphan House  ............1000
                                        ————
                        Total 9757
```

In the year 1798-1799, when the new system was in operation, there were

```
Paupers .............................3090
        In the Hospital  ............... 894
        ——Penitentiary  .............. 147
        ——Orphan House  ............ 600
                                        ————
                        Total 4731
```

Exhibiting a decrease in *one city* of 5026.

It is evident, therefore, that the object of the New-York Society for Preventing Pauperism is such as cannot, in the nature of things, be speedily accomplished. Habits and vices, which take their rise from the worst passions and propensities of men, however deplorable in their effects upon individuals and society, will yield to no sudden remedies. They must be supplanted gradually by the influence of appropriate agencies, by the assiduities of patient and persevering labour, by the constant and meliorating operations of benevolence. The measures pointed out in the document appended to this Report, are adapted ultimately to remove those evils which so much afflict society, and which the severest enactments of civil authority have been found unable to repress. Let the moral sense be awakened, and a moral influence be established in the minds of the improvident, the unfortunate, and the depraved; let them be approached with kindness and an ingenuous concern for their welfare; inspire them with self-respect, and encourage their industry and economy: in short, enlighten their minds, and teach them to care for themselves. These are the methods of doing them real and permanent good, and relieving the community from the pecuniary exactions, the multiplied embarrassments, and threatening dangers of which they are the authors. Happily, the object proposed by this institution is one which may be aided by every individual, whatever be his circumstances; though it prospectively demands the concurrence and patronage of all. The public is called upon not so much for pecuniary subscriptions and benefactions, as for friendly advice, for vigilant attention to the common good, for the adoption of wholesome opinions, and the exertion of a salutary influence. They who experience the ill effects of pauperism and its attendant evils, are urged, not to make fresh sacrifices and incur additional embarrassments, but to act upon the defensive, to employ the means of prevention, to check an inundation which threatens to overwhelm them. They are invited to adopt measures which cannot possibly be hurtful in any instance; which seem alone adapted to the end in view, which are required by the necessity of the case, and sanctioned by the results of experience.

The Managers consider the information which they have thus laid before the Society, of sufficient moment to encourage every member, and to stimulate the citizens generally, to give their utmost sanction and support to this truly benevolent institution, whose aim is to improve the temporal and moral condition of a considerable portion of this community.

Conscientiously engaged in so good a cause, let *all* rely on the blessing of that Almighty Father who "maketh his sun to rise on the evil and the good, and sendeth rain on the just and on the unjust."

MATTHEW CLARKSON, *President*

JOSEPH CURTIS, *Sec'y, pro tem.*
New-York, Oct. 26, 1818.

New York: Printed by J. Seymour, 49 John-Street, 1818.

• • •

REPORT

ON THE

SUBJECT OF PAUPERISM.

To the "New-York Society for the prevention of Pauperism."

THE Committee appointed to prepare a Constitution for the government of the Society, and a statement of the prevailing causes of pauperism, with suggestions relative to the most suitable and efficient remedies, Report,

That we entered upon the duties assigned us, under a strong conviction of the great importance of the subject of Pauperism. We were persuaded that on the judicious management of this subject depend, in a high degree, the comfort, the tranquility, and the freedom of communities.

We were not insensible of the serious and alarming evils that have resulted, in various places, from misguided benevolence, and imprudent systems of relief. We knew that in Europe and America, where the greatest efforts have been made to provide for the sufferings of the poor, by high and even enormous taxation, those sufferings were increasing in a ratio much greater than the population, and were evidently augmented by the very means taken to subdue them.

We were fully prepared to believe, that without a radical change in the principles upon which public alms have been usually distributed, helplessness and poverty would continue to multiply—demands for relief would become more and more importunate, the numerical difference between those who are able to bestow charity and those who sue for it, would gradually diminish, until the present system must fall under its own irresistible pressure, prostrating perhaps, in its ruin, some of the pillars of social order.

It might be long indeed before such a catastrophe would be extensively felt in this free and happy country. Yet it is really to be feared, as we apprehend, that it would not be long before some of the proximate evils of such a state of things would be perceived in our public cities, and in none, perhaps, sooner than in New-York. Although these consequences are but too apparent from the numerous facts which recent investigations have brought to light, particularly in Great Britain, and in some parts of the United States, yet we are very sensible of the difficulties attendant upon every attempt to provide an adequate remedy for poverty, and its concomitant wretchedness.

The evil lies deep in the foundation of our social and moral institutions; and we cannot but consider it as one of the most obscure and perplexing, and at the same time, interesting and imposing departments of political economy.

While there exists so great a disparity in the physical and intellectual capacitites of men, there must be, in every government, where a division of property is recognized by law and usage, a wide difference in the means of support. Such, too, is the complication of human affairs, the numerous connexions, and close dependencies of one part upon another, it is scarcely to be presumed, and it would be extravagant to expect, that under the most moral, and the wisest civil regulation to which human society is susceptible of attaining, partial indigence and distress will not be experienced to an amount that will ever demand the exercise of Christian benevolence.

The great and leading principles, therefore, of every system of charity, ought to be, *First*, amply to relieve the unavoidable necessities of the poor; and, *Secondly*, to lay the powerful hand of moral and legal restriction upon every thing that contributes, directly and necessarily, to introduce an artificial extent of suffering; and to diminish, in any class of the community, a reliance upon its own powers of body and mind for an independent and virtuous support. That to the influence of those extraneous, debilitating causes, may be ascribed nine tenths of the poverty which actually prevails, we trust none will doubt, who are extensively acquainted with facts in relation to this subject.

The indirect causes of poverty are as numerous as the frailties and vices of men. They vary with constitution, with character, and with national and local habits. Some of them lie so deeply entrenched in the weakness and depravity of human nature, as to be altogether unassailable by mere political regulation. They can be reached in no other way, than by awakening the dormant and secret energies of moral feeling.

But with a view to bring the subject committed to our charge more definitely before the Society, we have thought it right, distinctly to enumerate the more prominent of those causes of poverty which prevail within this city; subjoining such remarks as may appear needful.

1st. IGNORANCE. Arising either from inherent dullness, or from want of opportunities for improvement. This operates as a restraint upon the physical powers, preventing that exercise and cultivation of the bodily faculties by which skill is obtained, and the means of support increased. The influence of this cause, it is believed, is particularly great among the foreign poor that annually accumulate in this city.

2d. IDLENESS. A tendency to this evil may be more or less inherent. It is greatly increased by other causes, and when it becomes habitual, it is the occasion of much suffering in families, and augments to a great amount the burden of the industrious portions of society.

3d. INTEMPERANCE IN DRINKING. This most prolific source of mischief and misery drags in its train almost every species of suffering which afflicts the poor. This evil, in relation to poverty and vice, may be emphatically styled the *Cause of Causes*. The box of Pandora is realized in each of the kegs of ardent spirits that stand upon the counters of the 1600* licensed grocers of this city. At a moderate computation, the money spent in the purchase of spirituous liquors would be more than sufficient to keep the whole city constantly supplied with bread. Viewing the enormous devastations of this evil upon the minds and morals of the people, we cannot but regard it as the crying and increasing sin of the nation, and as loudly demanding the solemn deliberation of our legislative assemblies.

4th. WANT OF ECONOMY. Prodigality is comparative. Among the poor it prevails to a great extent, in an inattention to those small but frequent savings when labour is plentiful, which may go to meet the privations of unfavourable seasons.

---

*Since this Report was written, the number of licenses has been very considerably reduced by the present chief magistrate of the city.

5th. IMPRUDENT AND HASTY MARRIAGES. This, it is believed, is a fertile source of trial and poverty.

6th. LOTTERIES. The depraving nature and tendency of these allurements to hazard money, is generally admitted by those who have been most attentive to their effects. The time spent in inquiries relative to lotteries, in frequent attendance on lottery offices, the feverish anxiety which prevails relative to the success of tickets, the associations to which it leads, all contribute to divert the labourer from his employment, to weaken the tone of his morals, to consume his earnings, and consequently to increase his poverty. But objectionable and injurious to society as we believe lotteries to be, we regard as more destructive to morals, and ruinous to all character and comfort, the numerous self-erected lottery insurances, at which the young and the old are invited to spend their money in such small pittances, as the poorest labourer is frequently able to command, under the delusive expectation of a gain, the chance of which is as low, perhaps, as it is possible to conceive. The poor are thus cheated out of their money and their time, and too often left a prey to the feelings of desperation: or, they are impelled by those feelings to seek a refuge in the temporary, but fatal oblivion of intoxication.

7th. PAWNBROKERS. The establishment of these offices is considered as very unfavourable to the independence and welfare of the middling and inferior classes. The artifices which are often practised to deceive the expectation of those who are induced, through actual distress, or by positive allurement, to trust their goods at these places, not to mention the facilities which they afford to the commission of theft, and the encouragement they give to a dependence on stratagem and cunning, rather than on the profits of honest industry, fairly entitle them, in the opinion of the Committee, to a place among the *causes of Poverty*.

8th. HOUSES OF ILL FAME. The direful effects of those sinks of iniquity upon the habits and morals of a numerous class of young men, especially of sailors and apprentices, are visible throughout the city. Open abandonment of character, vulgarity, profanity, &c. are among the inevitable consequences, as it respects our own sex, of those places of infamous resort. The effects upon the several thousands of females within this city, who are ingulphed in those abodes of all that is vile, and all that is shocking to virtuous thought, upon the miserable victims, many of them of decent families, who are here subjected to the most cruel tyranny of their inhuman masters—upon the females, who, hardened in crime, are nightly sent from those dens of corruption to roam through the city "seeking whom they may devour," we have not the inclination, nor is it our duty, to describe. Among "the causes of poverty," those houses, where all the base-born passions are engendered—where the vilest profligacy receives a forced culture, must hold an eminent rank.

9th. THE NUMEROUS CHARITABLE INSTITUTIONS OF THE CITY. The Commitee by no means intends to cast an indiscriminate censure upon these institutions, nor to implicate the motives, nor even to deny the usefulness, in a certain degree, of any of them. They have unquestionably had their foundation in motives of true philanthropy; they have contributed to cultivate the feelings of Christian charity, and to keep alive its salutary influence upon the minds of our fellow-citizens; and they have doubtless relieved thousands from the pressure of the most pinching want, from cold, from hunger, and probably, in many cases, from untimely death.

But, in relation to these societies, a question of no ordinary moment presents itself to the considerate and real philanthropist. Is not the partial and temporary good which they accomplish, how acute soever the miseries they relieve, and whatever the number they may rescue from sufferings or death, more than counterbalanced, by the evils that flow from the expectations they necessarily excite; by the relaxation of industry, which such a display of benevolence tends to produce; by that reliance upon charitable aid, in case of unfavourable times, which must unavoidably tend to diminish, in the minds of the labouring classes, that wholesome anxiety to provide for the wants of a distant day, which alone can save them from a state of absolute dependence, and from becoming a burden to the community?

In the opinion of your Committee, and in the opinion, we believe, of the greater number of the best writers, of the wisest economists, and of the most experienced philanthropists, which the interesting subject of Pauperism has recently called into action; the balance of good and evil is unfavourable to the existence of societies for gratuitous relief:—that efforts of this nature, with whatever zeal they may be conducted, never can effect the removal of poverty, nor lessen its general amount; but that indigence and helplessness will multiply nearly in the ratio of those measures which are ostensibly taken to prevent them.

Such are the consequences of every avowal on the part of the public of a determination to support the indigent by the administration of alms. And in no cases are measures of this kind more prolific in evil, than where they are accompanied by the display of large funds for the purposes of charity; or where the poor are conscious of the existence of such funds, raised by taxation, and of course, as they will allege, drawn chiefly from the coffers of the rich.

How far these evils are remediable, without an entire dereliction of the great Christian duty of charity, is a problem of difficult solution. The principle of taxation is so interwoven with our habits and customs, it would, perhaps, in the present state of things, be impossible to dispense with it. But while our poor continue to be thus supported, to prevent the misapplication and abuse of the public charity, demands the utmost vigilance, the wisest precaution, and the most elaborate system of inspection and oversight.

To what extent abuses upon our present system of alms are practised, and how far the evils which accompany it are susceptible of remedy, we should not at present feel warranted in attempting to state. The pauperism of the city is under the management of five Commissioners, who, we doubt not, are well qualified to fulfil the trust reposed in them, and altogether disposed to discharge it with fidelity. But we cannot withhold the opinion, that without a far more extended, minute, and energetic scheme of management than it is possible for any five men to keep in constant operation, abuses will be practised, and to a great extent, upon the public bounty; taxes must be increased, and vice and suffering perpetuated.

LASTLY. Your Committee would mention WAR, during its prevalence, as one of the most abundant sources of poverty and vice, which the list of human corruptions comprehends. But as this evil lies out of the immediate reach of local regulation, and as we are now happily blessed with a peace which we hope will be durable, it is deemed unnecessary further to notice it.

Such are the causes which are considered as the more prominent and operative in producing that amount of indigence and suffering, which awakens the charity of this city, and which has occasioned the erection of buildings for eleemosynary purposes, at an expense of half a million of dollars, and which calls for the annual distribution of 90,000 dollars more. But, if the payment of this sum were the only inconvenience to be endured—trifling, indeed, in comparison would be the evils which claim our attention. Of the mass of affliction and wretchedness actually sustained, how small a portion is thus relieved! Of the quantity of misery and vice, which the causes we have enumerated, with others we have not named, bring upon the city, how trifling the portion actually removed, by public or by private benevolence! Nor do we conceive it possible to remove this load of distress, by all the alms-doing of which the city is capable, while the causes remain in full and active operation.

Effectually to relieve the poor, is therefore a task far more comprehensive in its nature, than simply to clothe the naked and to feed the hungry. It is, to erect barriers against the encroachments of moral degeneracy;—it is to heal the diseases of the mind;—it is to furnish that aliment to the intellectual system which will tend to preserve it in healthful operation.

But can a task of this nature come within the reach of any public or any social regulation? We answer, that to a certain, and to a very valuable extent, we believe it can. When any measure for the promotion of public good, or the prevention of public evil, founded upon equitable principles, is supported by a sufficient weight of social authority, it may gradually pass into full and complete operation, and become established upon a basis as firm as a law of legislative enactment. And in matters of private practice, reformation which positive statute could never accomplish, social and moral influence may thoroughly effect. . . .

To conclude, the committee has by no means intended, in the freedom with which it has thus examined the causes of pauperism, and suggested remedies, to encourage the expectation that the whole of these remedies can be speedily brought within the power and control of the society. A work of so much importance to the public welfare cannot be the business of a day; but we nevertheless entertain the hope, that if the principles and design of this Society shall, upon mature examination and reflection, receive the approbation of the great body of our intelligent fellow-citizens, and the number of its members be augmented accordingly, it will be able gradually to bring within its operation all the important measures suggested in this report. By what particular mode these measures shall be encountered, whether through the agency of large and efficient Committees of this Society, or by auxiliary societies, each established, for a specific purpose, under the patronage of the parent institution, and subordinate to its general principles, we leave to the wisdom and future decision of the Society.

On behalf of the Committee,

JOHN GRISCOM, *Chairman.*

New-York, Second month 4, 1818.

• • •

CONSTITUTION, BY-Laws, &c., of the

Female Orphan Asylum of Portland, Maine

ACT incorporating the Female Orphan Asylum
of Portland

STATE OF MAINE

In the year of our Lord one thousand eight hundred and twenty-eight.

AN ACT to incorporate the Female Orphan Asylum of Portland.

SECTION 1. *Be it enacted by the Senate and House of Representatives, in Legislature assembled,* That Sally M. Smith, Thankful Hussey, Mary B. Storer, Charlotte Andrews, Mary Radford, Mary B. Merrill, Elizabeth L. Fox, Elizabeth G. Atwood, Susan Richardson, Nancy Cushman, Marcia Hill, Alice Ilsley, Lowis W. Dana, Susan E. Wood, and Eliza L. Goddard, their associates and successors be, and they hereby are, constituted a body politic and corporate by the name of the Female Orphan Asylum of Portland, with power to prosecute and defend suits at law; to have and use a common seal, to make and establish any by-laws for the management of their affairs, not repugnant to the laws of the State; to take and hold any estate, real or personal, for the purpose of supporting, instructing and employing female children, the first attention to be given to orphans; and to give, grant, bargain or sell the same; and with all the powers and privileges usually granted to other societies instituted for purposes of charity and beneficence.—*Provided,* that the value of the real estate of said corporation, shall never exceed forty thousand dollars, and the annual income of the whole estate of said corporation shall not exceed twenty thousand dollars.

SECTION 2. *Be it further enacted,* That the first meeting of said corporation shall be holden at such time and place, and be notified in such manner, as a majority of the persons named in this act shall direct.

SECTION 3. *Be it further enacted,* That the powers granted by this Act, may be enlarged, restricted, or annulled at the pleasure of the Legislature.

In the House of Representatives, February 16, 1828. This Bill, having had three several readings, passed to be enacted.

JOHN RUGGLES, *Speaker.*

In Senate, February 18, 1828. This Bill, having had two several readings, passed to be enacted.

ROBERT P. DUNLAP, *President*

February 18, 1828, Approved.

ENOCH LINCOLN.

STATE OF MAINE
Secretary of State's Office,
Portland, February 20, 1828.

I hereby certify, that the foregoing is a true copy of the original, deposited in this Office.

ATTEST, A. NICHOLS, *Secy. of State.*

Shirley and Hyde, Printers

• • •

CONSTITUTION

OF THE

Female Orphan Asylum

OF PORTLAND

ARTICLE 1. This Society shall be called The Female Orphan Asylum of Portland, and being strictly a charitable Institution, no article shall be admitted into this Constitution, which shall recognize the peculiar sentiments of any particular denomination of Christians, but all shall be considered as enjoying equal rights and privileges.

ART. 2. The *object* of this Institution shall be to provide and carry into effect, *means* for the support, instruction and employment of female children, from three to ten years of age: the first attention to be paid to Orphans.

ART. 3. Any lady who shall subscribe and pay a sum not less than *two* dollars annually, shall become a member of said Society; her membership however to cease, whenever she shall refuse or neglect to pay said annual subscription.

ART. 4. The Society shall meet on the second Tuesday in September annually, for the purpose of electing by *ballot* a Treasurer, and a board to consist of fifteen managers: which board shall choose from among themselves a first and second Directress, a Secretary, and an Assistant Secretary if necessary: and they shall have power to fill their own vacancies.—Not *less* than *five* shall constitute a quorum for transacting business.

ART. 5. The Managers shall superintend the concerns of the Society, enact their own rules and by-laws; shall have the entire direction of the children committed to them; shall provide for them a suitable Governess; shall see that they are properly clothed, fed and instructed; shall determine where they shall be placed when their age and acquirements are such, as to render it proper for them to leave the Asylum; and in all respects, exercise over them a *maternal care*.

ART. 6. The first Directress shall preside at all meetings, and in case of equal division give the casting vote. Upon any urgent occasion the first or second Directress, or in their absence the Secretary, or when requested in writing by twenty members of the Society, *any five* of the Managers shall call a special meeting of the Society, which shall be duly notified.

ART. 7. The Secretary shall register the names of the members; shall notify the meetings of the Society, by causing to be published in one or more of our newspapers the time and place of said meeting, at least seven days previous thereto; and shall record their transactions. She shall also meet with and record the proceedings of the Board. She shall receive all the *dues* of the Society, pay them over to the Treasurer, and at each stated meeting of the board, render an account of the sums thus received and paid over, and of such as still remain due.

ART. 8. The Treasurer shall always be a single woman of the age of twenty-one years or upwards; and shall give a bond with sufficient sureties. She shall meet with the Managers when necessary, and shall render to them and to the Society, a statement of its property, with her receipts and payments whenever requested.

ART. 9. All donations shall be reserved as a fund for *building,* and after that object is accomplished, shall go to the establishment of a *permanent fund.*

All subscriptions and the interest on donations, shall be appropriated to defray the annual expenses of the Society.

ART. 10. The Governess shall board the children committed to her care by the Managers, and instruct them in Reading, Writing, and Sewing, with the various branches of domestic employment, and shall make report of their conduct and improvement to the Managers, whenever requested.

ART. 11. The children shall be dressed in a plain manner and treated with kindness, If sick, they shall be visited by a regular physician, whose services shall be paid by the Society, when not rendered gratuitously.

ART. 12. The yearly *tax* shall be accounted *due* at the annual meetings of the Society.

ART. 13. Any alteration of this *Constitution,* not subversive of the *original object* of the Institution, may be made at any special meeting of the Society, called by the Managers for that purpose, by a vote of *two thirds* of the members present.

OFFICERS AND BOARD OF MANAGERS

For the year ending Sept. 1828

Mrs. Sally M. Smith, *First Directress,*
Mrs. Thankful Hussey, *Second Do.*
Mrs. Mary B. Storer, *Sec'ry.*
Mrs. Elizabeth L. Fox,
Mrs. Alice Ilsley,
Mrs. Eliza L. Goddard,
Mrs. Lois W. Dana,
Mrs. Susan Wood, } *Managers.*
Mrs. Charlotte Andrews,
Mrs. Marcia Hill,
Mrs. Elizabeth G. Atwood,
Mrs. Mary S. B. Merrill,
Mrs. Mary Radford,
Mrs. Susan Richardson,
Mrs. Nancy Cushman,
Miss Lucretia Frothingham, *Treasurer.*

BY-LAWS

ESTABLISHED BY THE BOARD OF MANAGERS

APRIL 1828

1. Regular Meetings of the Board of Managers shall be held on the first Tuesday in every month, for the purpose of attending to the concerns of the Society. These meetings shall be opened with prayer.

2. The first Directress shall preside at all meetings of the Board; and in case of equal division give the casting vote. In her absence the second

Directress shall preside; and in the absence of both, a Moderator shall be chosen for the meeting.

The first Directress shall have power to call special meetings of the Board whenever necessary; and in her absence, the second Directress; and in the absence of both, the Secretary shall call a special meeting whenever requested by *three* Managers.

The special meetings of the Board shall be notified by the Secretary.

3. A collecting Committee shall be appointed annually by the Board of Managers, whose duty shall be to collect all the annual subscriptions to the Society, and pay them over to the Secretary.

This Committee shall consist of such a number as the Board shall from time to time think necessary.

4. When the Treasurer is required to attend any meeting of the Board, she shall be notified by the Secretary, four days previous thereto; and at every such meeting, she shall render an account of monies received, and paid out, and remaining in her hands. And at the end of every six months, she shall settle her accounts with a Committee to be appointed for that purpose by the Board.

5. All accounts against the Society, shall be laid before the Board of Managers, and if allowed, an order shall be drawn by the Secretary on the Treasurer for payment of the same; and no monies shall be paid without such an order, drawn in pursuance of a vote of the Board.

6. A Committee consisting of three Managers shall be chosen every quarter, whose duty it shall be, to examine into the circumstances of children proposed for admission into the Asylum; and also to inquire respecting those persons who may apply to take a child out of the Asylum; and they shall make report to the Board of Managers.

7. It shall be the duty of the Secretary, to place in the Managers' Room in the Asylum, the names of this Committee, with their places of residence.

8. A list of such children as are approved by the Board for admission into the Asylum, shall be kept by the Secretary; priority of application shall give right to admission, unless in the opinion of a majority of the managers at a regular meeting, the circumstances of a child shall require immediate relief.

9. No child shall be received into, or dismissed from the Asylum, or placed in any family, without a vote of the Board at a regular meeting.

10. No child shall be received into the Asylum, until its parents or relatives have relinquished all claim to it. Should, however, any child under the protection of the Society, be claimed by her connexions, she shall be returned to them, whenever all expenses incurred on her account are reimbursed.

11. No relative or friend shall interfere in the management of the children in the Asylum; or visit them except in the presence of the Governess; nor at any time, when their visits are disapproved by the Board.

12. At a suitable age, the children shall be placed in virtuous families, until the age of Eighteen, or marriage within that age; unless some other way for their gaining a livelihood should offer, which the Managers shall deem more eligible.

No child shall be placed out of the Asylum before she has attained to the age of *eleven* years, unless some special circumstance shall render it expedient.

13. In putting out the children, subscribers shall always have the preference. Every child on her leaving the Asylum, shall be supplied by the Society, with one suit of every day wearing apparel. And any person on taking a child, must provide all other clothing necessary for her.

14. A Committee shall be chosen from time to time, whose duty shall be, to make inquiry respecting the conduct and circumstances of the children placed out by the Managers; particularly to ascertain whether they are properly instructed, and treated with kindness; and report to the Board.

15. A Committee of two Ladies shall be chosen every month to provide for the house; to procure and attend to the clothes of the children, and to examine into their improvement; inquire respecting their treatment, and report at every meeting of the Board.

16. A sample of the Bread, meat, and other provisions used in the Asylum, shall be produced to the Board or monthly Committee, whenever required.

17. In case of sickness, the children shall be committed to the care of such Physicians as the Board shall direct.

18. Twenty-five subscribers in any town adjacent to Portland, shall be entitled to place a child in the Asylum, for so long a time as they pay their annual subscription.

19. The Governess shall always be a woman of piety. She shall be chosen by ballot; and a majority of the whole Board shall be necessary to constitute a choice.

20. No alteration in, or addition to, these By-Laws shall be made, unless two thirds of the whole Board of Managers shall concur, at a special meeting notified for that purpose four days previous thereto.

RULES AND REGULATIONS

FOR THE GOVERNMENT OF CHILDREN IN THE ASYLUM

1. All the children on the Sabbath, shall, if the weather permit, regularly attend public worship with the Governess, at such place as the Board shall direct; and during the intervals of worship, they shall read in the Bible and other religious books. They shall also attend the Sabbath School attached to the Society with which they worship.

It shall be the duty of the Governess to pay particular attention to their observance of the Sabbath, teaching them by precept and example, to reverence and keep it holy.

2. The Governess shall read a chapter in the Bible, and pray with the children every morning. She shall attend them at their meals, see that proper order is observed, and that grace is said before and after. She shall teach them to pay a sacred regard to truth, and to the performance of every moral duty; and shall give them such religious instruction as is suited to their age and capacity.

3. The Governess shall instruct the children in reading, writing, arithmetic, plain needle work and knitting.

Those who are old enough, shall mend their own clothes, and assist by weekly rotation, in the domestic business of the family. The Governess shall be particularly careful to educate them in habits of *order, neatness,* and *industry.*

4. The Governess shall not be absent a night from the Asylum, without permission from one of the Board.

She shall visit the children's rooms every night before going to bed. She shall not suffer any of the children to be absent from the Asylum, without special permission in writing from one of the Managers.

GENERAL DIRECTIONS

From the first of April to the first of October, the Children shall rise at six o'clock, say their Prayers, wash themselves, comb their hair, make their beds, and clean their chambers; breakfast at seven; play or work in the garden until nine, when the governess shall read a chapter in the Bible and pray with them; attend school until twelve, dine at one, play until two, attend school until five, after which, play one hour. In the evening say their Prayers, go to bed at eight, wash their feet every night.

From the first of October to the first of April, the Children shall rise at seven o'clock, say their Prayers, wash themselves, comb their hair, make their beds and clean their chambers;—breakfast at eight, attend prayers, school and play hours as before. In the evening, say their Prayers; go to bed at Seven; and wash their feet once a week.

BILL OF FARE

BREAKFAST

Sunday and Thursday mornings, tea, coffee, chocolate or shells, with bread. All other mornings, milk or milk-porridge and bread.

SUPPERS

Sunday nights, tea with bread and butter. All other nights bread, hastypudding, or rice with milk.

DINNERS

Fresh meat, salt beef and pork, salt fish, fresh fish, dried beans and peas, vegetables, and puddings.

CLOTHING

Factory Gingham or Calico for Summer, Bombazette for Winter.

The Society commenced their operations the first of April.

Their House is situated on the corner of Free and South Streets.

Mrs. ABIGAIL RICH, *Governess.*

Miss SARAH RICH, *Assistant.*

The present number of Children belonging to the Asylum, is ten.

At a late meeting of the Board of Managers it was *voted,* "that it is expected, no person will visit the Asylum except in company with one of the Managers, or without a written permission from one of them."

The necessity of such a regulation it is presumed, will be obvious to all; and the Managers take this opportunity to inform all interested in the Institution, that the House is open to inspection, and they will be happy to wait on those who wish to visit it.

FORM OF OBLIGATION

To be signed by a Parent or Guardian on surrendering a child or ward to the protection of the Female Orphan Asylum of Portland.

I, the Subscriber, do hereby surrender my daughter (or Ward) to the Managers of the Female Orphan Asylum of Portland, and to their successors in Office, and to their sole and exclusive care, guardianship and direction, to be by them exercised according to the Rules and Regulations of the Society aforesaid, until my said daughter (or Ward) shall have arrived at the age of eighteen years.

In witness, whereof, I have hereunto set my hand and seal, this day of   in the year of our Lord, one thousand eight hundred and

SIGNED, SEALED AND DELIVERED IN
PRESENCE OF US,

• • •

PRESIDENT FRANKLIN PIERCE: VETO MESSAGE

An Act Making A Grant of Public Lands

to the Several States

for the Benefit of Indigent Insane Persons
Washington, *May 3, 1854*

To the Senate of the United States:

The bill entitled "An act making a grant of public lands to the several States for the benefit of indigent insane persons," which was presented to the Senate, the House in which it originated, with a statement of the objections which have required me to withhold from it my approval.

In the performance of this duty, prescribed by the Constitution, I have been compelled to resist the deep sympathies of my own heart in favor of the humane purpose sought to be accomplished and to overcome the reluctance with which I dissent from the conclusions of the two Houses of Congress, and present my own opinions in opposition to the action of a coordinate branch of the Government which possesses so fully my confidence and respect.

If in presenting my objections to this bill I should say more than strictly belongs to the measure or is required for the discharge of my official obligation, let it be attributed to a sincere desire to justify my act before those whose good opinion I so highly value and to that earnestness which springs from my deliberate conviction that a strict adherence to the terms and purposes of the federal compact offers the best, if not the only, security for the preservation of our blessed inheritance of representative liberty.

The bill provides in substance:

First. That 10,000,000 acres of land be granted to the several States, to be apportioned among them in the compound ratio of the geographical area and representation of said States in the House of Representatives.

Second. That wherever there are public lands in a State subject to sale at the regular price of private entry, the proportion of said 10,000,000 acres falling to such State shall be selected from such lands within it, and that to the States in which there are no such public lands land scrip shall be issued to the amount of their distributive shares, respectively, said scrip not to be entered by said States, but to be sold by them and subject to entry by their assignees: *Provided,* That none of it shall be sold at less than $1 per acre, under penalty of forfeiture of the same to the United States.

Third. That the expenses of the management and superintendence of said lands and of the moneys received therefrom shall be paid by the States to which they may belong out of the treasury of said States.

Fourth. That the gross proceeds of the sales of such lands or land scrip so granted shall be invested by the several States in safe stocks, to constitute a perpetual fund, the principal of which shall remain forever undiminished, and the interest to be appropriated to the maintenance of the indigent insane within the several States.

Fifth. That annual returns of lands or scrip sold shall be made by the States to the Secretary of the Interior, and the whole grant be subject to certain conditions and limitations prescribed in the bill, to be assented to by legislative acts of said States.

This bill therefore proposes that the Federal Government shall make provision to the amount of the value of 10,000,000 acres of land for an eleemosynary object within the several States, to be administered by the political authority of the same; and it presents at the threshold the question whether any such act on the part of the Federal Government is warranted and sanctioned by the Constitution, the provisions and principles of which are to be protected and sustained as a first and paramount duty.

It can not be questioned that if Congress has power to make provision for the indigent insane without the limits of this District it has the same power to provide for the indigent who are not insane, and thus to transfer to the Federal Government the charge of all the poor in all the States. It has the same power to provide hospitals and other local establishments for the care and cure of every species of human infirmity, and thus to assume all that duty of either public philanthropy or public necessity to the dependent, the orphan, the sick, or the needy which is now discharged by the States themselves or by corporate institutions or private endowments existing under the legislation of the States. The whole field of public beneficence is thrown open to the care and culture of the Federal Government. Generous impulses no longer encounter the limitations and control of our imperious fundamental law; for however worthy may be the present object in itself, it is only one of a class. It is not exclusively worthy of benevolent regard.

Whatever considerations dictate sympathy for this particular object apply in like manner, if not in the same degree, to idiocy, to physical disease, to extreme destitution. If Congress may and ought to provide for any one of these objects, it may and ought to provide for them all. And if it be done in this case, what answer shall be given when Congress shall be called upon, as it doubtless will be, to pursue a similar course of legislation in the others? It will obviously be vain to reply that the object is worthy, but that the application has taken a wrong direction. The power will have been deliberately assumed, the general obligation will by this act have been acknowledged, and the question of means and expediency will alone be left for consideration. The decision upon the principle in any one case determines it for the whole class. The question presented, therefore, clearly is upon the constitutionality and propriety of the Federal Government assuming to enter into a novel and vast field of legislation, namely, that of providing for the care and support of all those among the people of the United States who by any form of calamity become fit objects of public philanthropy.

I readily and, I trust, feelingly acknowledge the duty incumbent on us all as men and citizens, and as among the highest and holiest of our duties, to provide for those who, in the mysterious order of Providence, are subject to want and to disease of body or mind; but I can not find any authority in the Constitution for making the Federal Government the great almoner of public charity throughout the United States. To do so would, in my judgment, be contrary to the letter and spirit of the Constitution and subversive of the whole theory upon which the Union of these States is founded. And if it were admissible to contemplate the exercise of this power for any object whatever, I can not avoid the belief that it would in the end be prejudicial rather than beneficial in the noble office of charity to have the charge of them transferred from the States to the Federal Government. Are we not too prone to forget that the Federal Union is the creature of the States, not they of the Federal Union? We were the inhabitants of colonies distinct in local government one from the other before the Revolution. By that Revolution the colonies each became an independent State. They achieved that independence and secured its recognition by the agency of a consulting body, which, from being an assembly of the ministers of distinct sovereignties instructed to agree to no form of government which did not leave the domestic concerns of each State to itself, was appropriately denominated a Congress. When, having tried the experiment of the Confederation, they resolved to change that for the present Federal Union, and thus to confer on the Federal Government more ample authority, they scrupulously measured such of the functions of their cherished sovereignty as they chose to delegate to the General Government. With this aim and to this end the fathers of the Republic framed the Constitution, in and by which the independent and sovereign States united themselves for certain specified objects and purposes, and for those only, leaving all powers not therein set forth as conferred on one or another of the three great departments—the legislative, the executive, and the judicial—indubitably with the States. And when the people of the several States had in their State conventions, and thus alone, given effect and force to the Constitution, not content that any doubt should in future arise as to the scope and character of this act, they ingrafted thereon the explicit declaration that "the powers not delegated to the United States by the Constitution nor prohibited by it to the States are reserved to the States respectively or to the people." Can it be controverted that the great mass of the business of Government—that involved in the social relations, the internal arrangements of the body politic, the mental and moral culture of men, the development of local resources of wealth, the punishment of crimes in general, the preservation of order, the relief of the needy or otherwise unfortunate members of society—did in practice remain with the States; that none of these objects of local concern are by the Constitution expressly or impliedly prohibited to the States, and that none of them are by any express language of the Constitution transferred to the United States? Can it be claimed that any of these functions of local administration and legislation are vested in the Federal Government by any implication? I have never found anything in the Constitution which is susceptible of such a construction. No one of the enumerated powers touches the subject or has even a remote analogy to it. The powers conferred upon the United States have reference to federal relations, or to the means of accomplishing or executing things of federal relation. So also of the same character are the powers taken away from the States by enumeration. In either case the powers granted and the powers restricted were so granted or so restricted only where it was requisite for the maintenance of peace and harmony between the States or for the purpose of protecting their common interests and defending their common sovereignty against aggression from abroad or insurrection at home.

I shall not discuss at length the question of power sometimes claimed for the General Government under the clause of the eighth section of the Constitution, which gives Congress the power "to lay and collect taxes, duties, imposts, and excises, to pay debts and provide for the common defense and general welfare of the United States," because if it has not already been settled upon sound reason and authority it never will be. I take the received and just construction of that article, as if written to lay and collect taxes, duties, imposts, and excises *in order* to pay the debts and *in order* to provide for the common defense and general welfare. It is not a substantive general power to provide for the welfare of the United States, but is a limitation on the grant of power to raise money by taxes, duties, and imposts. If it were otherwise, all the rest of the Constitution, consisting of carefully enumerated and cautiously guarded grants of specific powers, would have been useless, if not delusive. It would be impossible in that view to escape from the conclusion that these were inserted only to mislead for the present, and, instead of enlightening and defining the pathway of the future, to involve its action in the mazes of doubtful construction. Such a conclusion the character of the men who framed that sacred instrument will never permit us to form. Indeed, to suppose it susceptible of any other construction would be to consign all the rights of the States and of the people of the States to the mere discretion of Congress, and thus to clothe the Federal Government with authority to control the sovereign States, by which they would have been dwarfed into provinces or departments and all sovereignty vested in an absolute consolidated central power, against which the spirit of liberty has so often and in so many countries struggled in vain. In my judgment you can not by tributes to humanity make any adequate compensation for the wrong you would inflict by removing the sources of power and political action from those who are to be thereby affected. If the time shall ever arrive when, for an object appealing, however strongly, to our sympathies, the dignity of the States shall bow to the dictation of Congress by conforming their legislation thereto, when the power and majesty and honor of those who created shall become subordinate to the thing of their creation, I but feebly utter my apprehensions when I express my firm conviction that we shall see "the beginning of the end."

It is a marked point of the history of the Constitution that when it was proposed to empower Congress to establish a university the proposition was confined to the District intended for the future seat of Government of the United States, and that even that proposed clause was omitted in consideration of the exclusive powers conferred on Congress to legislate for that District. Could a more decisive indication of the true construction and the spirit of the Constitution in regard to all matters of this nature have been given? It proves that such objects were considered by the Convention as appertaining to local legislation only; that they were not comprehended, either expressly or by implication, in the grant of general power to Congress, and that consequently they remained with the several States.

The general result at which I have arrived is the necessary consequence of those views of the relative rights, powers, and duties of the States and of the Federal Government which I have long entertained and often expressed and in reference to which my convictions do but increase in force with time and experience.

I have thus discharged the unwelcome duty of respectfully stating my objections to this bill, with which I cheerfully submit the whole subject to the wisdom of Congress.

FRANKLIN PIERCE

Chapter 4
The Civil War And
After: 1860–1900

The years following the Civil War were a time of rapid economic growth, political unification, and peace with foreign nations. At the same time they were years in which poverty problems intensified, regional sectionalism accelerated, and increasing polarization of economic classes occurred.

The period was one in which science and invention progressed rapidly and created a base for growth in all phases of the economy—transportation, communication, agriculture, mining, and manufacturing. Population increase, the discovery of additional natural resources, the extension of transportation, the development of new means of communication, the appearance of hundreds of new industries, the evolution of new forms of business organization, the growth of credit institutions, the further concentration of economic power, the beginning of effective organization of a free labor class were all components of the new wealth. Population doubled during the last 30 years of the century; gross national product rose from about $6.7 billion to an estimated $16.8 billion—about two-and-a-half times—which meant a substantial increase in per capita income.[1] All groups of the population, all sectors of the economy, and all sections of the country shared this growth. But growth did not proceed uniformly, nor was it distributed equally, among industries, among regions of the country, or among population groups.

The war and the industrial development it hastened had laid the base for the acquisition of major fortunes; and the postwar railroad boom fostered the accumulation of individual wealth. Soon the formation of industrial corporations and trusts and the expansion of the stock market made it possible to extend and exploit the technological gains and inventions of the period. And along with the development of oil, steel, aluminum, and meat packing came the rise of a class of millionaires. The open display of affluence, of wild speculation and ruthlessness in business, and of widespread political immorality highlighted the precariousness of the lives of factory workers and tenant farmers and made the misery of the lives of the poor more bitter. Moreover, cyclical fluctuations brought panic, depression, and severe unemployment during the years 1873–1878 and 1893–1898. Population growth, the normal hazards of an increasingly industrial and urban society, and the recurring periods of economic depression resulted in expanding relief rolls. Obvious reality aside, the country at large looked with envy and fascination upon the success of the rich and with despair and disapproval upon the failure of the poor.

For the North the war had meant prosperity. The increased output of war goods and rising prices for food and clothing had stimulated the process of industrialization. Demand for labor was high; and the need for workers to fill newly created jobs, as well as the old ones left vacant by men away at war, meant continuing encouragement of immigration and steady expansion of the size of cities. The end of the Civil War and the return to civilian production furthered the process of industrialization and economic growth.

The war was a catalyst for Northern growth, but for the South it meant devastation of land, property, transportation facilities, and credit institutions. While the Northeast and Midwest saw increasing concentration of property and wealth, the South saw some breaking up of plantations and a decentralization of land ownership. While jobs were plentiful in the North, workers in the South—white and black—struggled to find employment and a means of self-support. The process of Southern reconstruction eventually led to the beginnings of industrialization and, of even more significance for the eventual shape of the Southern economy, to the simultaneous reestablishment of agricultural interests and the rise of tenant farming. The pattern that was to evolve was one of recovery and of growth, but of a growth rate much slower than the rest of the nation.

For the development of the West in the postwar period, the most important factors were the settlement and differential utilization of previously acquired Western territories. Dissatisfaction with the urbanization and industrialization of Northeastern states, and with the commercialization and tenant farm structure of agriculture in Southern states, led to the westward movement of population. As grazing was displaced by agriculture, cultivation of Western land increased. The westward trek was particularly responsive to periods of economic recession and labor unrest and to the pressures of integrating returning veterans and a constantly swelling number of immigrants into the population. In 1860 the five states immediately west of the Mississippi—Texas, Arkansas, Missouri, Iowa, and Minnesota—had only 15.3 million acres in improved farmlands. By 1880 these same five states had increased improved farmlands to 50 million acres; by 1910, to 87 million acres. The rate of Western expansion is highlighted by the fact that the closing of the frontier was noted as early as 1890, when the superintendent of the census wrote: "Up to and including 1880 the country had a frontier settlement but at present the unsettled area has been so broken into isolated bodies of settlement that there can hardly be said to be a frontier line."[2] Beyond that is the fact that the number of states west of the Mississippi had increased from 7 in 1860 to 18 in 1900. For the country as a whole, the number of states had increased from 37 in 1860 to 45 in 1900.

Territorial expansion and industrial and agricultural growth went hand in hand with growth and shifts in population. The country's overall population grew from 36 million in 1865 to 76 million in 1900, an increase of 40 million, or 113 percent.[3] The proportion of blacks in the total population remained comparatively stable—13 percent in 1865 and 12 percent in 1900. The number of immigrants to the United States between 1865 and 1900 totaled 13 million, which constituted 32 percent of the increase in population during those years.[4] They came largely from Great Britain (including Ireland), Scandinavia, and Germany. Whereas the Scandinavians and Germans tended to move to the West, the Irish—for the most part unskilled and unlettered—tended to remain in the East. In industrial areas especially, the immigrants posed a threat to the existing labor force. They were mainly young adults, so they were employable.* Furthermore, the fact that they had come with little resources meant not only that they had to have employment but also that they were likely to be willing to work for lower wages. Finally, they were Catholic and were expected to have large families, which raised the fear that their becoming dependent upon public support might burden the general population for extended periods.

At the same time that the center of population moved westward, the overall density increased. Between 1870 and 1900 the center of population moved 162 miles westward, while the density increased from 13.4 persons per square mile to 25.6.[6] Despite the westward movement, however, the region of densest population remained the older portion of the country, more than ever a region of manufacturing and commerce. The population of the Northeast had risen from less than 11 million in 1860 to 21 million in 1900.

The increase in the number of cities with populations of more than 100,000 showed the Midwest to be keeping pace with the rest of the nation. In 1860 there had been eight cities with populations over 100,000—four in the East, three in the Midwest, and one in the South. By 1900 there were 33 cities over 100,000—17 in the East, 13 in the Midwest, three in the South, and

---

*The influx of unskilled Irish labor was particularly devastating for free black males struggling to find jobs in Northern urban areas. This may be a partial explanation of the imbalance in the male/female population ratios in the cities. In Philadelphia, for example, in 1870 there were 1,360 females for every 1,000 males, and in 1890 there were 1,127 females per 1,000 males, reflecting the poor employment opportunities for black men.[5]

now three in the Far West.[7] Unquestionably, the process of urbanization had made great strides. In 1860, 20 percent of the country's territory had been defined as urban; by 1900, 40 percent. But this very fact emphasizes that in 1900 the country was, for the most part, still rural.[8]

The structure of rural life in the post-Civil War period changed in response to shifts in the organization of agriculture. The major crop of the prewar South was cotton, with some land devoted to tobacco and sugar. Ownership and control had been lodged primarily in a plantation system with slave labor. The postwar period saw the development of tenant farming, sharecropping, and some independent ownership of small farms. The average size of a farm in the South Atlantic states dropped from 352.8 acres in 1860 to 108.4 in 1900. Almost half the farms were tenant operated.[9] The average size of a farm operated by blacks, 75 percent of whom were tenants, was only 51.2 acres, recalling the postwar proposal that large plantations be seized and "40 acres and a mule" be distributed to poor whites and freed blacks.[10] This dramatically smaller size of farms made economically marginal black tenant farmers in the South Atlantic states extremely vulnerable to scientific and technological changes that, after the turn of the century, were to require large farms and expensive farm equipment.

The postwar South saw some diversification of products, especially the development of corn as a cash crop and of fruit orchards. But this was small and largely confined to a group of independent white farmers. Cotton remained the staple. Familiarity, ready marketability, and most critically, the dependence for capital on conservative credit sources prevented further diversification. Output of cotton was 4.5 million bales in 1861, 300,000 in 1864, and 4.4 million in 1870; by 1877 output was above prewar levels.[11] Recovery in cotton production both paralleled and limited the postwar recovery of the Southern economy.

The West, too, saw major structural shifts. As in the South, the average size of a farm decreased; unlike the South, this was a response to a major change in output. The vast Western lands provided first an opportunity for cattle and sheep raising and, sequentially, for growing wheat and corn. The availability of land resources for exploitation and for settling was particularly opportune at the close of the Civil War when the disjuncture created by unemployment due to necessary changeovers in war industries, troop demobilization, and continuing immigration could all be eased by movement westward. Additionally, this migration reflected a continuation of the attraction provided by the Homestead Act passed by Congress in 1864. The act was meant to attract immigrants, who were exempted from war duty, to settle in the West on farms, and thereby relieve citizens for army service. The act's offer of free public lands had widespread appeal.

Migration was given further impetus by the completion of the first transcontinental railroad in 1869. Subsequently, through the use of land grants, Congress chartered the construction of the Northern Pacific to connect the Great Lakes with Puget Sound, the Southern Pacific and Santa Fe to tie the Mississippi Valley with the Pacific Coast, and the Denver and Rio Grande to slice through the mountains of Colorado to Salt Lake City. The building of state-supported rival lines and of branch lines served to connect the states of the West with each other and the West with the East. In addition to their being direct transportation links with Eastern markets, the railroads stimulated trade carried on ships operating out of the Great Lakes and connecting with ports in New York State and in foreign countries. Grazing moved westward as more land came under cultivation.

Western crop acreage increased and, with the introduction of fertilizers, productivity rose. As a result, the country's production of wheat had jumped from 173 million bushels in 1859 to 600 million in 1900; the production of corn rose from 839 million bushels in 1859 to 2.7 billion in 1900.[12] With the value of wheat and corn exports up to $73 million and $85 million respectively by 1900, the West, in addition to being the breadbasket of the United States, had also become a substantial supplier of foreign need.[13]

The opening of the West was speeded, too, by the discovery of and search for precious metals—gold, silver, and zinc—and soon by the realization of the existence of vast supplies of other extractives—copper, coal, iron ore, petroleum. The rise in the value of mining from 1 percent of the nation's total output on the eve of the Civil War to 5 percent in the last year of the century was a mark of advancing Western enterprise as well as a base for Eastern industrialization.[14]

The recovery of the South and the settling and development of the West cannot be understood without awareness of their ultimate dependence upon the growth of manufacturing, particularly of Eastern manufacturing. In the country as a whole, the number of manufacturing establishments grew from 140,000 in 1860 to 208,000 in 1900. Between those same years, the number of employees grew from 1 million to 4.7 million—a 370 percent increase; the value of manufactured products from $1.8 billion to $11 billion—a 505 percent increase. Capitalization grew by 789 percent during these years. Manufacturing had become more capital-intensive, necessitating the eventual move toward larger units of manufacturing and decreased competition.[15] The value of manufacturing output rose by 515 percent from the period immediately preceding the Civil War to the end of the century. The value of agricultural output rose by 127 percent during the same period. Although both had increased in value, they had reversed positions in relative importance.[16]

The dominance of the East in manufacturing is demonstrated by the fact that 67.3 percent of the country's manufacturing establishments were located in New England and the Middle Atlantic States in 1859. Although manufacturing grew in the Western states, the New England and Middle Atlantic states continued to account for 52.4 percent of all manufacturing enterprises at the end of the century.[17]

The Welfare of Soldiers and Veterans

During and immediately after the Civil War, in all sections of the country, the social welfare needs of soldiers and their families demanded attention. During the war years 2.3 million served in the Union forces, of whom 719,000 died and 280,000 were wounded—a casualty rate of 43 percent. Participants in the Confederate forces totaled 781,000, of whom 307,000 died and 100,000 were wounded—a casualty rate of 52 percent.[18] Whether for medical care, domiciliary care, or financial support, the needs of veterans were considered apart from the needs of the civilian population and as deserving of state and federal governmental support.

Federal legislation affording benefits to soldiers and veterans was passed first by Congress for the Union forces and, later, was confined to veterans of the Union. In July 1862, Congress enacted a pension system covering individuals disabled in the line of duty, as well as widows, children, and dependent relations of those who were killed. Efforts to encourage enlistment, such as the Enrollment Act of 1863, stated each citizen's obligation to defend the country and the right of the federal government to impose that obligation.[19] But the enactment of additional legislation in the veteran's behalf clarified the reciprocal nature of the obligation—the necessity for taking care of "our battered heroes . . . in such a way as to maintain the military spirit and the national pride . . . and to keep in the eye of the Nation the price of its liberties."[20]

The United States Sanitary Commission was established in 1861 by the secretary of war in response to a recommendation by the Women's Central Relief Association of New York. The Association represented the joined forces of the women comprising the Women's Central Association of Relief for the Sick and Wounded of the Army, the Advisory Committee of the Boards of Physicians and Surgeons of the Hospitals of New York, and the New York Medical Association for furnishing hospital supplies in aid of the army. Pointing to "the spontaneous and earnest efforts" of women in many parts of the Union to perform volunteer service in behalf of an essentially volunteer army, the Association called for a governmental body responsible "to keep the women of the loyal states everywhere informed how their efforts may be most wisely and economically employed."[21]

The New York Association, like its counterparts in many other localities, was aware of the recent experience with sanitary science in the Crimean War, particularly as publicized through the testimony of Florence Nightingale in parliamentary hearings. The need, as set forth in an address to the secretary of war on May 18, 1861, was for preventive services, such as the supervision of the diet and hygiene of the troops, and, in addition, the furnishing of medical and nursing personnel and supplies, of financial relief, and of personal services.

The acting surgeon-general of the United States acquiesced and, on June 13, 1861, President Lincoln approved the appointment of a Commission of Inquiry and Advice in respect of the Sanitary Interests of the United States Forces.

The "voluntary" nature of the Commission—its dependence upon contributions of money and labor—is reflected in its original and popular title, the People's Commission of Sanitary Inquiry and Advice.[22] Once appointed, the Commission "prepared to go to work without a dollar in its treasury." Subsequently, "the irrepressible determination of the American people to manifest . . . their direct personal interest in the soldier" led to "countless forms of popular sympathy" demonstrated in "clamorous and persistent . . . offers of relief as the war went on."[23] The Commission became the channel for directing this national outpouring of contributions toward the relief and comfort of the Union forces.

The nine officially appointed members of the Commission were men, despite the fact that women's groups funded and implemented its programs. The work of overlooking the welfare of the military was performed in the belief that the country could "never half repay them for the sacrifices they have made or half balance our debt of gratitude."[24] From the start, these groups supported the Sanitary Commission's promotion of national concern for the care veterans would receive once the war was over.

On March 3, 1865, President Lincoln signed an act to incorporate a national military and naval asylum for the relief of totally disabled officers and men of the voluntary forces of the United States. Subsequently, this enabling legislation was strengthened by the provision of funds to make possible the building and operation of a group of national homes, first for Union veterans suffering economic distress due to wartime disabilities and, later, for economically distressed veterans whose disabilities were not service connected. The country's view of the needy Union veteran as "worthy" was illustrated in an 1871 report of a congressional committee that had investigated the conditions of the early national homes:

> Liberal expenditures have been made to provide . . . facilities for recreation and for intellectual and moral culture, as well as . . . good quarters, food, clothing, and hospital attendance. The constant and proper aim of the management is . . . that the asylums were in no sense almshouses . . . but homes which the disabled soldiers have earned for themselves. . . .[25]

During the Civil War and for the 25 years following it, the federal government liberalized the terms of entitlement to pensions and raised the level of benefits. In 1866, one year after the war's end, annual federal expenditures for Union veterans' pensions totaled $15 million; by 1882 this doubled; and by 1889, it reached $86 million.[26] In 1890, pushed by pension claims agents and the GAR, and responding to the large number of disabled and destitute veterans, Congress acted to keep veterans from almshouses and from dependency on "the frigid bosom of public charity." The Dependent Pension Act of 1890 dropped the requirement that disability be service connected and instead provided pensions for veterans (and their wives) who had served at least 90 days and who were unable to earn a living by physical labor. By 1898, expenditures tripled and the number of veterans covered jumped from under 420,000 to over 745,000.[27]

By 1900 federal as well as state responsibility for the care of needy and disabled veterans and their dependents was well established. Cash payments, medical services, and domiciliary care were all parts of a system that viewed the social welfare of veterans and their families as a special obligation of the society as a whole. The obligation was being met through legislative provisions that, for their time, were generous and that were couched in language meant to protect the beneficiary's right to help and to avoid a pauper's label. New York State, for example, in 1887 went so far as to prohibit "sending indigent soldiers, sailors, and marines (or their families, or the families of those deceased), to any almshouse (or orphan asylum) without the full concurrence and consent of the commander and relief committees of the post of the Grand Army of the Republic."[28] The founding of the Grand Army of the Republic, a veterans' organization, in 1866 had provided an organized constituency able to push for progressive liberalization of benefits and, when danger threatened, to secure those benefits against attack.

Federal largesse did not extend to Confederate veterans. In national homes established at Kecoughtan, Virginia, and Johnson City, Tennessee, only those Southerners who had served on the Union side were welcome. The Pension Act of 1890 limited benefits to veterans of the Union army. During the war and the postwar period, such benefits as did accrue to veterans of the Confederate army were provided on a local and state level. As with Northern veterans, aid for Southern soldiers and their families was outside the stigma of poor relief laws. Families of Confederate soldiers became the "new poor" and Southern localities enacted special legislation, including special taxes, to provide emergency assistance. As the war progressed, responsibility shifted from voluntary agencies, to local government, and then to state governments and the Confederate Congress. The Confederate veteran was considered by his government and his neighbors to be as worthy as his Northern counterpart. Resources were so limited, however, that relief efforts were meager.

Social Welfare: The Rural South

During the war the Southern states had experienced widespread destruction as well as severe curtailment of agricultural economic activity. Cessation of hostilities highlighted a general situation of dire need. Wounded veterans and their families, widows and orphans of slain soldiers, large numbers of freed, homeless blacks, and a civilian population were all made needy by the war itself. Near famine resulted from drought and lack of organized manpower to get the economy moving. The situation was worse for lack of an extensive prewar public or private welfare system to draw upon.

In the immediate postwar period, the individual states gave first attention to the needs of veterans and their dependents for artificial limbs and cash pensions. Concern for the orphans of Confederate soldiers led to the establishment of orphanages and of apprenticeship procedures. As for the general white population, most Southern states set up central public welfare stations for the distribution of food and clothing. The states moved to deal with the freed black population through attempts to reinstitute a system of control of the labor market.

Black codes designed to regulate the lives of ex-slaves were passed in all the former Confederate states but Tennessee. The codes limited property rights, forbade working as artisans and mechanics, and otherwise specified the kinds of economic activities in which freed blacks could engage. The codes of Georgia, for example, stated that "all persons strolling about in idleness would be put in chain gangs and contracted out to employers."[29] In effect, the codes used the old Poor Law provisions in regard to vagrancy to secure state revenues while simultaneously organizing manpower to be used in reconstruction and industrial pursuits. Vagrants were rounded up, labeled criminal, and subjected to leases as long as 10 to 20 years in duration.[30]

Black children were similarly handled. In 1865, for example, Mississippi declared all blacks under 18 who were orphans, or whose parents could no support them, available for apprenticing. Former masters were given preference. Black children were not afforded such guarantees in regard to food, clothing, and education as were written into indentureship agreements for white children. Thus, a solution to black dependency and a means for building a slavelike labor force went hand in hand.

The excesses of "white reconstruction" led Congress in March of 1867 to require the Confederate states to call state conventions for the purpose of creating more representative state governments and for ratifying the Fourteenth Amendment to the Constitution as a prerequisite for readmission into the Union. By 1870 all the Southern states had complied. No redistribution of land had been required and little was achieved. There was an enlargement of the role of state government in matters of expenditures for social welfare and education for blacks and for whites. A pattern of separate institutions for blacks and whites evolved. Despite much discussion of state responsibility, however, no comprehensive programs of state welfare emerged. Orphanages, mental hospitals, and almshouses were built, but each state followed its own limited design, and local responsibility, especially for relief, was endemic.

All in all, the Southern social welfare scene was dominated by the federal government through the activities of the Freedmen's Bureau.[31] Even before the close of the war, it was evident that Northern effort would be required to bring the South relief from destitution. The Port Royal Experiment of 1862 represented one such effort and became precursor to the Freedmen's Bureau. When, in the face of the Union army's advance into South Carolina, whites abandoned the plantations of the Port Royal area, 10,000 slaves were left to fend for themselves. Their distress led the president to authorize (but not fund) an experimental relief and rehabilitation program. Two volunteer organizations, the National Freedmen's Relief Association of New York and the Boston Education Commission, supplied most of the funding and labor. Several hundred volunteers saw to the distribution of food and clothing and the rehabilitation of abandoned and pillaged homes. In addition, they established schools for black children and attempted to use free labor in large-scale cotton cultivation.

For all the experiment's success, the needs of the South were beyond the resources of volunteer organizations, and the Bureau of Refugees, Freedmen, and Abandoned Lands—more familiarly known as the Freedmen's Bureau—was established by Congress in March 1865, two months before the end of the war. The Bureau was placed in the War Department; however, since no appropriations for relief purposes or salaries were made, the Bureau was dependent upon the military for whatever was distributed in the way of food, clothing, and medical supplies. In 1866 Congress extended the life of the Bureau for two years by overriding President Johnson's veto. The extension was fostered by the fact that the Bureau, faced with the extreme hunger and poverty of whites as well as blacks, had helped both; and both protested the threatened withdrawal of relief. The 1866 act provided the first direct appropriation—$6.9 million—for the Bureau's work; and in 1867, in response to the threat of famine, Congress authorized the use of funds for all destitute and helpless Southerners regardless of wartime loyalties.

Basically, the Bureau had been established to deal with transient, homeless blacks and with the management of abandoned and confiscated property. In time the Bureau took on the task of organizing freed blacks into a labor force. In connection with the last, the Bureau not only sought jobs and organized work opportunities for freed men but also drew up and supervised labor contracts for blacks in their relation with whites. General Howard, who carried responsibility for the operations of the Bureau, saw to the adjudication of labor disputes and to the prevention of reenslavement.

The Freedmen's Bureau was the first federal welfare agency and, between 1865 and 1869, the major source of public welfare in the South. During its existence the Bureau engaged in numerous social welfare activities. It provided transportation home for refugees and aided in reuniting families. In its first three years it distributed 18.3 million rations, about 5.2 million of which went to whites. By the end of its fourth year of existence, it had distributed 21 million rations, about 6 million having gone to whites. In addition to distributing medical supplies, the Bureau established 46 hospitals. It set up orphan asylums for children and participated in the establishment and running of 4,329 schools for black children. Among institutions of higher learning, it helped found or support Howard, Atlanta, and Fisk universities, Hampton Institute, and Talladega College.

The Bureau was subject to a good deal of criticism and question. There was, of course, the basic concern about large-scale federal aid to the needy.

The Freedman's Village, Hampton, Virginia, (From *Harper's Weekly*, September 30, 1865.) The sketch shows a typical rebuilt Freedman's Village. The communities were generally uniform in appearance with buildings built of rough barrel staves or split boards.

Courtesy of the New York Historical Society, New York City

This question was especially thorny when raised as one of redistribution of income from Northern to Southern states. Moreover, there was opposition from Southern planters and townspeople who, wanting the blacks to return to work on a more or less prewar basis, accused the Bureau of fostering idleness and pauperism. Indeed, this concern about pauperizing freed blacks led General Howard to retrench on direct relief giving and to break up camps that had been organized to provide government-created jobs. The many questions addressed to the Bureau's activities added to its personnel problems; and a growing view that it represented a radical movement led to its demise in 1872.

Social Welfare: Urban Problems

With the demise of federal responsibility, the domination of social welfare returned to private groups in the Northeast, where urban problems were multiplying. Since the war had been fought in the South, the North was not faced with the necessity for rebuilding. Industrialization to meet the needs of the war provided it with the organization and experience for further expansion at the war's close, when the needs of the South and of the rapidly developing West for manufactured items and for markets was pressing. A high protective tariff served to prevent domestic buyers from buying foreign-made goods. Not surprisingly, the East, as the industrial center of the country, became the center for credit, the center for economic and

The photo shows the headquarters of the Superintendent of the Poor. After the capture of New Berne a large amount of clothing fell into the hands of Federals which was stored at this point. Headquarters were established for its distribution among the needy inhabitants.

Courtesy of The National Archives

political power, and the center of labor unrest. The Reconstruction Period was one of expanding markets and rising prices but falling real wages. The recession of 1873–1878 was a period of serious unemployment. Concern with poverty and with pauperism led to different organizational responses from labor and from philanthropic groups.

During the Civil War the labor movement began to regain its strength as workers found that they were not sharing in the enormous profits accruing to business. Craft unions were organized in sufficient numbers to warrant the calling of the first National Labor Congress in 1866. The power of railroads and business increased during the postwar era as corporate forms appeared and as the development of pools, legal trusts, holding companies, and consolidations was accompanied by a decline in free market competition. Numerous corporate attempts to regulate production and prices within industries, quantity discounting and rebating, wild speculation—all occurred as struggles for monopoly and control took place between larger and larger units of operation. The unhappiness of workers was aggravated by the reality of impersonal employers sufficiently powerful to lower wages. The ability of industrial giants to manipulate labor was enhanced by the presence of a large reserve labor force willing to work for lower wages.

The financial problems of working people were aggravated by the conviction among leaders of organized charities that the purpose of modern philanthropy was to suppress pauperism rather than to aid the needy. In 1895, in the midst of widespread unemployment, the New York Association for the Improvement of Conditions among the Poor railed against longshoremen striking to prevent a cut in wages:

> Every man has a right to work or not . . . but no man has a right to refuse to support his family and himself when he is able to do it; and no one has a right to prevent others from working, as these strikers persistently attempted to do, while they are themselves idling about the streets and wharves and corner liquor shops.[32]

It came as no surprise, then, that union members viewed supporters of benevolent societies as being aligned against the interests of workers.

The problems posed by the emergence of powerful big businesses led to some federal and state efforts to regulate interstate and intrastate commerce and to a resurgence of union activity. The Interstate Commerce Act of 1887 was an effort to limit the ability of railroads to play one section of the country against another, one state against another, to their own advantage. By 1890 fourteen states and territories had antimonopoly provisions in their constitutions, and thirteen states had antitrust laws.[33] The ineffectiveness of these provisions and the necessity for some form of federal regulation led to the passage of the Sherman Antitrust Act. It, too, was largely ineffectual, but it declared the illegality of trusts or other combinations in restraint of trade.

The problems of farmers in interstate commerce were recognized in 1889, when the Department of Agriculture was raised to the rank of an executive department and its head made a secretary with cabinet status. Federal recognition of the challenge of labor led, in 1884, to the creation of the Bureau of Labor Statistics with authority "to collect information upon the subject of labor, its relation to capital, the hours of labor, and the earnings of laboring men and women, and the means of promoting their material, social, intellectual, and moral prosperity."[34]

Neither the Department of Agriculture nor the Bureau of Labor Statistics was sufficiently strong at the inception to ease the plight of its constituency. Of necessity each constituency resorted to organization— farmers into granges, laborers into larger and stronger unions. By 1875 some 30,000 local granges, with a combined membership of 2.5 million, were in existence.[35] Concerned originally with securing legal protections against railroads, the granges increasingly engaged in a broad range of political activities designed to strengthen farmers in their relation to corporate enterprise. In addition, the need for low-cost loans and reduced tariffs united the Southern and Western farming communities in political movements to combat the dominance of the East.

The potential of large-scale associations of laborers to counter the power of industry and to protect workers against the risks of industrial society had led in 1878 to the organization of the International Labor Union (ILU) and to the initial attempts of the Knights of Labor to consolidate many trade unions and grades of workers. With the demise of the ILU in 1882, the Knights began to grow. In 1883 membership stood at 50,000; in 1886 the membership skyrocketed to 700,000.[36]

Despite its phenomenal growth, the Knights of Labor was torn by internal dissension. There was a fundamental difference between the leadership, which persisted in the repudiation of the strike except as a weapon of last resort, and the membership, which was finding that strikes and boycotts could secure important gains. The leadership was convinced that strikes were futile, since "a strike cannot regulate the laws of supply and demand, for if it cuts off the supply, it also cuts off the demand by throwing consumers out of work, thereby curtailing their purchasing power.[37] The leadership argued that lasting victory could be attained only through the concept of self-employment epitomized in the creation of cooperatives. They looked to the development of a cooperative society that would take the place of the wage system. The decline of the Knights of Labor came swiftly. The reasons: failure to convince the membership that the road to riches lay in a recasting of the structure of the economy, failure to find a mechanism to preserve unity among factions, and the dissensions created by the violent strikes of 1886.

Leadership in the labor movement shifted to the American Federation of Labor, a federation of craft unions, which saw labor's advance, not in the abandonment of a capitalist mode of organization but in a reshuffling of the spoils of this arrangement. By 1900 labor became increasingly militant in achieving its ends. The battle of labor was, of course, for job protection and for a share in the country's growth. It was also a battle against poverty and against the country's view of the poor. This battle tied economic security to employment and separated union workers, who might occasionally be in need, from "dependent classes."

There were many aspects to the intensification of problems related to the poor. The reluctance to acknowledge social responsibility for poverty and to explore the meaning of being poor in a context of affluence was one. The continuing tide of immigrant workers and their threat to wage standards (already precariously low in many unorganized industries) and to the employment of the existing native labor force was another. Further, there was the sudden proliferation of sectarian and lay relief societies all struggling to exist as well as to meet the needs of their clientele. Finally, there was the frustration of not having been able to deal with poverty in a way consistent with what had become an American self-image, that is, with efficiency, economy, and progress.

The expectation of progress in eliminating poverty and the hope of decreased relief costs found a rationale in the analogy of the application of scientific knowledge to industrial advance. In addition to machines that revolutionized industrial and agricultural activities, achievements in the realm of applied science opened new fields of communications (the telegraph and telephone), transportation (air brakes, automobiles), and business machines (typewriters, for example). Research was pursued in biology, chemistry, physics, botany, eugenics, ethnology, geology, and astronomy. The rigor of the search and success with the organization of knowledge for practical use became a "dogmatic religion . . . whose notaries often behaved in the manner of theologians, pretending to possess the one true key to the riddle of the universe."[38] No wonder, then, that leaders in voluntary and public social welfare should look to science and to the organization of scientific knowledge for new approaches to the alleviation of poverty.

The Charity Organization Movement

In the public arena, the growing numbers of public institutions and the haphazard proliferation of private societies led to the creation of State Boards of Charities, whose overall function was to protect the poor and the public. In the private sector, the fear of control by state bodies and the competition and disarray among relief societies led to the creation, in Buffalo, in 1877, of the first citywide Charity Organization Society and to the emergence of a Charity Organization Movement strong enough to wrest leadership for charitable affairs from the hands of public officials. The National Conference of Charities and Corrections was first convened in 1874 by the leaders of the State Boards for their own professional purposes. Leaders of the private social welfare sector were invited to participate. Eventually, however, these private agencies took control of the Conference.

In large measure, the strength of the Charity Organization Movement was derived from its promise of a "scientific approach" to poverty and pauperism. The frequent intercourse and communications between American and European scientists had led to widespread knowledge of Darwinian theory and of Herbert Spencer's application of that work to social theory. The new religion preached the need for a laissez-faire economy in which the fittest would become the richest. It feared that social welfare measures that supported dependency and misfits would end in the weakening of mankind. The belief in the possibility of an evolution toward a more affluent society, combined with belief in the openness of that society to individual achievement, made the acquisition of personal wealth not only a sign of fitness, but a condition of moral superiority as well. Andrew Carnegie, the capitalist, and Amos. G. Warner, the economist and social welfare leader, could both agree with Russell Conwell, the educator and minister, who said:

> You ought to be rich . . . . When a man could have been rich just as well, and he is now weak because he is poor, he has done some great wrong; he has been untruthful to himself; he has been unkind to his fellowmen. We ought to get rich if we can by honorable and Christian methods, and these are the only methods that sweep us quickly toward the goal of riches.[39]

The Charity Organization Movement accepted Social Darwinism as its theoretical underpinning for helping—or not helping—the poor and called this process "scientific charity." Thus, the recognition that the times required a new orientation to social welfare matters eventuated in the application of "science" to the development of a delivery system that continued to place the individual, rather than the individual's environment, at the center of the problem. The situation was one in which the more obvious the social causes of poverty, the more insistence there was upon the personal aberration and immorality of paupers.

Interestingly, the stage was set for private sector domination of social welfare in the report to the First Conference of Charities and Corrections by its Department [Committee] of Social Economy. This report of pauperism in the city of New York, written in 1874 at a time of economic depression, condemned the giving of outdoor relief, whether in the form of public funds or publicly displayed soup kitchens, as inducing many to become paupers. The report contrasted the benevolence of the business community (in spite of its own temporarily embarrassing impoverishment) with the unwillingness of the poor (having become accustomed to depending upon the bounty of others) to accept work at markedly lower wages. The fact of the depression itself, the reality of need, was all the more reason for rigidly limiting—after careful house visitation—the giving of relief and, when given, for assuring its connection with work. Available statistics of pauperism showed "a condition of things . . . less alarming than had been supposed." This did not, however, mitigate the fear of the transmittability of pauperism from adult to child and from relief recipient to worker. Concern persisted that pauperism might degenerate the individual's physical and mental powers to final extinction.[40]

The growth in numbers and power of the Charity Organization Societies in all the major cities of the country assured the continuation of an anti-public welfare stance, as well as the stance, often receiving concurrence from public officials, as to the dangers and inheritability of pauperism. In 1890, at the seventeenth annual meeting of the National Conference of Charities and Corrections, Josephine Shaw Lowell, perhaps the leading advocate for the private sector, declared that public relief should be given only in cases of extreme distress, "when starvation is imminent." Since it is difficult to prove the imminence of starvation, conditions of deterrence must be maintained. The refuge from pauperism, according to Mrs. Lowell, was self-support or help provided by private sources presumably after investigation and determination of worthiness.[41] Even then, when contributors to the New York Charity Organization Society asked Mrs. Lowell, its president, how much of their contribution would go to the poor, she responded hopefully, "Not one cent."[42]

The harshness of view expressed by Mrs. Lowell must be seen in the context of contemporary beliefs about the corruptibility of human nature. This view of human nature, whose lineage extends to a doctrine of original sin, marked the religious origins as well as the sustained power of the private charity idea. If indeed human beings are flawed, they must be conscious of and guard against their potential for harm to themselves and to the species.

Puritan almsgiving for the salvation of the rich was replaced by scientific charity. Now, the poor were to be helped to find social and economic salvation through work. Clerics were replaced by social workers, and evangelism was replaced by therapy.

The sequence of events that led to the widespread institutionalization of private charity simultaneously justified the emergence of a leisure class. In a world in which the individual was seen as captain of his or her own fate, poverty and wealth were viewed as equally natural, if not equally desirable. Both the poor and the rich were threatened by the undermining, seductive influences of pauperism. The threat was to an economic system that was generally accepted as operationally and morally sound. Evidence of exploitation of the system by a power elite created no general alarm over the rules of the game.

The optimism of the American people in accepting the economic system as structurally viable, as offering endless potential for every individual willing to work and to participate in the American dream, was rooted in some reality. Despite recessions and bitter labor disputes, the view held that, for the most part, the economy *was* working successfully. Its moments of faltering were not equated with failure, especially on the Eastern seaboard where millions of immigrants could realistically compare present living conditions with those from which they fled. The thousands of Irish who had escaped the famine and great hunger resulting from the potato crop failures of 1845–1848 could give witness by their own changed circumstances. Immigrants from all over Europe—whose coming was slowed somewhat during the Civil War but resumed with the onset of peace—and immigrants from the Orient during the last decades of the century could point to their own comparative success and to their hope for the future. Their perception was supported by a rapidly rising gross national product, by the existence of national boundaries that quite literally provided lands for cultivation, and by the element of truth in the Horatio Alger myth. The steady movement of immigrants into commercially successful ventures and into politically powerful positions confirmed the view of class mobility. And there was always the example of a Carnegie or a Rockefeller to demonstrate how far a poor boy could go if he would take advantage of the opportunities the country offered.

Thus was established the view that the causes of pauperism lay with the individual. Empirical evidence was sought to sustain this position. Reverend Oscar C. McCulloch's Report to the Fifteenth Annual Conference of Charities and Corrections on the Tribe of Ishmael, a study of 250 related families, was viewed as a frightening example of social degradation brought on by the degeneracy of the inherited influences of pauperism.[43]

No less an authority than Amos G. Warner, the general agent for the Charity Organization Society of Baltimore, stressed deterioration of character as an immediate cause of poverty. He emphasized this despite his equal awareness of the relationship of the less immediate but perhaps more important contribution of objective environmental factors to poverty. Although in his famous work of 1894, *American Charities,* Warner found unemployment and illness to be the causes of almost half of the poverty cases, he included the following in his listing of objective causes of poverty: "evil associations" and "unwise philanthropy." The latter apparently fostered such subjective causes as "indolence," "lubricity," and a variety of "unhealthy appetites."[44]

In such an atmosphere, not only did public welfare seem unnecessary, but a positive consideration of a right to financial help could not be tolerated and, indeed, was feared. Exactly this fear was expressed in the report of the Department of Social Economy at the first National Conference of Charities and Corrections (1874) and, 20 years later, by Warner. The ideal of charity, then, was to help the individual, through example and precept, through the sympathy and encouragement of personal relations, to rise above the need for relief. The ideal of charity was service on the part of the well-to-do, service whereby the poor could learn self-respect and resolution, which would build character. This ideal was carried out by an army of Friendly Visitors recruited by the Charity Organization Societies and trained for the service.

The appeal of friendly visiting, balanced by the promise of scientific methodology in investigating the need for relief, led in some cities to turning over the responsibility for investigating applications for relief to the Charity Organization Society. In some cases, Charity Organization leaders were able to have public outdoor relief suspended and even abolished.

The overall purpose of the societies was the maintenance of virtuous families. Guidelines for establishing eligibility for relief often showed the virtue of a family to be derived from the virtue of the breadwinner. Thus, if the breadwinner were disabled or had died, then the widow and her children might be found eligible. Where poverty resulted from the breadwinner's drinking or from his having deserted his family, then the removal of the children for placement among more wholesome associates might be considered best. Unquestionably, the practice of friendly visiting was intended to make self-help the true cure for poverty.

Charity Organization leaders were, of course, not alone in their beliefs about inherited tendencies toward pauperism. Nor is it fair, with the wisdom of hindsight, to picture them as totally destructive in their work with families. Warner's statistically based delineation of objective environmental causes of poverty and the social fact-finding of other welfare leaders helped foster social legislation. Such legislation impelled changes in housing, in working conditions for women, in child labor practices, in sanitation—all of which were to improve the individual and the family's opportunity for self-betterment and success. An awakening interest in eugenics and Social Darwinism provided a framework for some support of social legislation, but it carried with it the position that there was no major defect in society itself. Quite simply, the inability to take advantage of enhanced opportunity was further evidence of individual weakness.

The vociferousness of Charity Organization leaders and the dominance of their view did not signify unanimity of opinion among social welfare leaders. Among public welfare leaders, especially, there were those ready to point up social causes of poverty and to assert society's responsibility for helping to meet individual and familial needs. At the thirteenth Conference of Charities and Corrections in 1886, Fred H. Wines questioned the use of statistics for the pseudoscientific purpose of proving individuals to be the cause of poverty and crime. He urged the Conference to look at the "three or four great facts" that characterized modern social life: the invention of laborsaving machinery, the aggregation of capital in the hands of large and wealthy corporations, the aggregation of population in great centers, and the emancipation of women. Taken together, he felt these characteristics had changed the relation of people to one another and might "account in some degree for the present measure and manifestations of pauperism" and other social ills.[45]

At the seventeenth Conference of Charities and Corrections in 1890, Franklin B. Sanborn spoke more specifically about family welfare and made a strong plea for outdoor relief, which he defined as "family aid." In analyzing the purposes for which "family aid" was expended in Massachusetts, he pointed out that reports of outlays for aid to the poor in their own families often overstated the sum actually expended by including payments for the sick in hospitals, burials, and so on. As for the ablebodied poor in almshouses, said Sanborn, "that mythical class . . . are scarcely found in this country in public establishments, except for a few months in the cold season, when the number of employments . . . is considerably reduced by Nature herself." The statement is reminiscent of the one made by John V. N. Yates in 1824; but unlike Yates, Sanborn concluded in favor of cash payments to families in their own homes. Asking that the poor be classified according to their real character and needs and not herded together in a common "receptacle" for all forms of poverty, Sanborn pointed out that "there are persons, be the number greater or less, who need public relief at their own homes, and who can receive it there with greater advantage both to themselves and to the public than anywhere else." In a telling argument— probably embarrassing for his listeners—he pointed out that outdoor relief must continue not only because it is less costly than indoor relief but also because there would never be "almshouses, workhouses, hospitals, and other places of indoor relief in sufficient number to contain all the poor at any season, or half of them in seasons of special destitution." In a final burst, Sanborn said that one reason cash relief had been distributed, even to the point of abuse, was "the desire to prevent the breaking up of families, the corruption of the young, and the unspeakable distress of the old and the virtuous, by throwing them into forced association with the dregs of mankind, in what was ironically termed a charitable establishment."[46] It was in response to and in disagreement with Sanborn that Josephine Shaw Lowell addressed the Conference on the demoralizing effects of public outdoor relief.

In time, hostility to the philosophy and methodology of charity organization became openly vocal and widespread. Charles D. Kellogg, chairman of the National Conference of Charities and Corrections' Committee on History of Charity Organization, reported in 1893:

> The very name of Charity Organization indicates a paramount purpose to bring about cooperation of those engaged in ministering to the poor. . . . Yet cooperation is one of the most difficult of attainments. . . . In some cities there exists a distinct hostility in the older charitable societies to Charity Organization. They resent the implication that their work may need amending. . . . [47]

These "older charitable societies" were understandably suspicious of Charity Organization's assumed authority for standard setting in a field in which they had long been functioning. They were particularly aroused by the threat to their autonomy in their being asked to "sustain [through cooperation] a society that is purely administrative,"[48] that is, a society to whom they would be accountable for their relief activities.

Still further, Charity Organization's emphasis upon the repression of fraud was taken to be the sole purpose of registering and investigating applicants for relief. Thus, charity organizers were accused of lumping the honest with the dishonest poor to the detriment of the former and the inhumane neglect of the latter.[49] In the words of a popular poem:

> The organized charity scrimped and iced
> In the name of a cautious, statistical Christ.[50]

Trade unions were particularly incensed during periods of recession and unemployment. They interpreted Charity Organization's investigatory methods and its stress upon the debilitating effects of relief as creating unnecessary suffering and as prolonging an "unfair social system as a result of which workers find themselves unemployed."[51]

Finally, the motives of the influential and wealthy leadership were suspect. Hostility toward charity organization societies grew out of the view that the societies might just be "devices for saving the taxpayer, and secured for them the title 'Society for the Suppression of Benevolence.' "[52]

The Social Welfare of Women

Mrs. Lowell's prominence in the Charity Organization movement, and in social welfare generally, reflects the extent to which women had ventured into public life during the post-Civil War era. The period held enormous consequences for women—particularly middle-class women. Expanded affluence offered independence and leisure, and women sought to establish for themselves a "proper sphere" more nearly equivalent in significance and power to that of men.

During the war, women had participated in the abolition movement, but the drive for women's rights had ceased as they became engaged in wartime tasks. As they did in the Sanitary Commission, women—in the

South, as well as in the North—took on war-related services for which the government had been unprepared. Women took jobs vacated by men going off to battle. They worked in industries and businesses, on farms and plantations, and in the professions. They worked "at the bench" and loom; they taught and nursed; they organized and managed. For some, this was seen as proof of equality with men and they were shocked by the passage and ratification of the Fourteenth Amendment, which, for the first time, explicitly defined voters as men. They felt another rebuff with the passage and ratification of the Fifteenth Amendment, which extended suffrage to include black men while excluding women.

In 1869, women in the suffrage movement split over the racial issue. The American Equal Rights Association, which had carried the fight for women's rights since 1866, was replaced by two contesting groups, the National Woman Suffrage Association, led by Susan B. Anthony and Elizabeth Cady Stanton, and the group that had supported the Fifteenth Amendment, the American Woman Suffrage Association. In 1890, they reunited as the National American Women Suffrage Association, having finally come to an agreement on the racial issue, which had brought about the rift. But the 20-year battle had been bitter.

The new Association suggested a trade-off: impose educational qualifications, but not sexual ones for voting. In effect, it promised an increase in "educated suffrage"—that is, the votes of middle-class white women for those of lower-class black and immigrant men.[53]

For all the publicity they engendered, the number of women formally associated with the national suffrage movement was small, probably never more than 10,000.[54] Nevertheless, large numbers of women did join organizations that represented more widespread and acceptable interests. The women's auxiliaries of the Patrons of Husbandry (the Grange), the General Federation of Women's Clubs, and especially, the National Women's Christian Temperance Union, for example, were organizations in which women found companionship as well as outlets for interests and energies in a limiting world.

The expectation that women quietly return home at the end of the war was thwarted by the very economic, industrial, and social advances which the war had stimulated. Indoor plumbing, electric lighting and household laborsaving devices, and the spread of commercial canning and baking were examples of technological innovations that reduced the hours of labor for housekeeping. The falling birthrate among middle-class families[55] as well as the availability of inexpensive immigrant and black domestic help furthered the process by which native-born, middle-class white women were released from work at home. The founding of women's colleges offered additional opportunities. Vassar was founded in 1865; Smith, in 1871; Bryn Mawr, in 1885. Finally, in an era whose purported ideal was the married woman in the home, there was an excess of females in most of the Northeastern states, those states whose women provided leadership for the feminist movement.[56]

Women's organizations and organizational activities were the result. The Temperance Movement was, perhaps, most symbolic of the situation.

The National Women's Christian Temperance Union was formed in 1874 and constituted a country-wide formalization of earlier local efforts to contain the manufacture and sale of alcoholic beverages. In the postwar era the intent of the movement was abstinence and prohibition. Within 20 years, the Union's membership totaled more than 200,000 women, representing "the most influential women's organization in the country."[57] Unlike the derision to which suffragists were subjected, members of the WTCU were recognized as active in a legitimate cause. Their concern about observed deleterious effects of alcoholism on the family and about the possible further deterioration of family life was considered well within the bounds of women's concerns, particularly since women were considered to possess moral superiority. The work of the WTCU was labeled "home protection"; and the Union's first president, Frances E. Willard, called upon all Christian women to join the crusade.[58]

The zeal with which women took up the cause of temperance is best understood in the context of contemporary social and cultural attitudes and beliefs—that is, in the context of changes that, in the social welfare arena, had led to the Charity Organization Movement and scientific philanthropy. As indicated by the adoption of Social Darwinism as an underlying approach to people, society's view of human nature had shifted from the prewar belief in the perfectibility of persons to a fear of their corruptibility. Postwar letdown was part of the shift. The uncertainties and dislocations of rapid industrial, economic, and social change were involved, as were the political scandals of the Johnson and Grant administrations. Added to this were the fears engendered by a developing dissatisfied poor (frequently unemployed) working class—white and black, male and female. A final factor was the hostile nativism aroused by additional waves of immigrants whose customs and manners seemed threateningly different. All in all, the American way and the American family seemed under attack and a crusade against drink and drinking, the most corrupting of influences, seemed logical. It was just as logical that women should lead this crusade against "snares that men have legalized"[59] and that threatened the economic stability of families, of homes, and of the society itself.

With moral superiority the foundation for a proper women's sphere and the home and family the appropriate locale of the operation, conflicts inevitably marked the wider women's movement. The publicness of any activity outside the home had to be rationalized. This was relatively easy in the matter of temperance. Even college education could be justified as "education for motherhood."[60] Friendly visiting for the Charity Organization Societies could be seen as instilling the virtues of independent American family life in the poor. But the right to vote, as demanded by suffragists, was another matter. The right to vote was a call for political power, and those few women who demanded it were suspect. Even when Mrs. Willard determined that the purpose of the WCTU could be achieved only by way of women's votes, her call was cloaked in the mantle of "home protection."[61] And, even then, the Union's resolution, passed at its national convention in 1877, called for women's voting in local elections and only on the question of prohibition.

For the middle class, the idea of working women represented a thorny issue. The ideal woman of the postwar era might work before marriage but not after. Thus, despite an expansion in the kinds of jobs women held,[62] many women found themselves increasingly "dependent on the money wages of their husbands or fathers, wages that they themselves did not earn."[63] The era's concept of "true womanhood" helped limit opportunities for economic and social independence.

Nevertheless, women did work. In 1890, 4 million women 14 years and older were employed—18 percent of the female population, 17 percent of the civilian labor force. By 1900, 5 million women—many of them married—were working outside the home.[64] Edith Abbott, in her study of women in industry, attributed the presence of married women and of older women in the job market largely to the employment of immigrants, children of immigrants, and blacks.[65]

Whatever the middle-class ideal, foreign-born and black women, along with many native-born white women, had to work in order to support the family economy, which was dependent on their wages along with the wages of their husbands. The double bind of lower-class women did not go unnoticed by Josephine Shaw Lowell:

> Of course there are women who can attend to home duties and also do outside work; but the average woman cannot do it; and the division of work between man and woman is discriminated by their natures,—he to do the outside work, the woman to do the inside work. . . . I think one of the causes of poverty is that we have adopted the theory for poor people—not for ourselves—that it is the business of women to help support the family. . . . When the husband dies, the double work that ought to be done by both father and mother, come to the widow.[66]

The Widow's/Mother's Pension Movement of the early decades of the twentieth century—a movement to provide cash support to widows with young children—was intended to deal with this deviation from ideal, true womanhood.

A New View of Child Welfare

By the turn of the century, the lines of disagreement between private and public welfare leaders were drawn. The private sector, despite contributions to social legislation, had opted for a professional service approach to people in need. Many in the public sector had moved away from the use of almshouses toward an income approach based upon the social necessity of giving and receiving cash relief.

The prominence of Northern social welfare leaders tended to obscure emerging efforts to meet needs in the South and West. As urban population centers grew in these areas, officials tended to follow the path of institutionalization developed 50 years earlier in the North Atlantic region. While the North argued the pros and cons of outdoor relief, the South and West started to build and expand almshouses, mental hospitals, orphan asylums, and correctional institutions. By now, however, their goal was custodial, not remedial, for by 1880 it was clear that institutions throughout the United States were not succeeding in providing an environment for the reconstruction of the lives of the residents, but were offering protection for the larger society against criminals, paupers, and the insane.

Society did not, however, feel it needed protection against children. Rather, the public good required that children be rescued from a life of dependency or criminality and helped to become productive citizens. A new view of child welfare developed; child care was to be separate and special.

The legal implications of this new approach were reflected in the enactment of the first juvenile court act in 1899, "An Act to Regulate the Treatment and Control of Dependent, Neglected, and Delinquent Children."[67] This act, which established separate treatment and control for children, was of major significance because it had common law derivations. Thus the newly established juvenile court moved child welfare away from an orientation of statutory criminal law, which had previously governed child welfare cases.

Children were to be removed from the adult correctional system and from the general welfare system. The optimistic hopes for poorhouse care expressed by Yates in 1824 had not come to pass, and for children especially, the almshouse had come to be recognized as a disaster. New York State was the first to remove children to foster family homes and to specialized institutions, and other states followed suit.

The eighth annual report of the New York State Board of Charities (submitted January 15, 1875) contained Commissioner William F. Letchworth's study of pauper and destitute children in the state's almshouses.[68] Despite a strenuous effort at removal, in 1874 there remained 593 children in almshouses (9 percent of all inmates), nearly 300 of whom were described as intelligent children, over two years of age, who needed proper training and care to fit them for useful stations in life. The slow pace of removing children from almshouses led to the Board's recommendation that "the commitment of children of intelligence over two years of age, to county poor-houses, be prohibited by statute," and on April 24, 1875 an Act to Provide for the Better Care of Pauper and Destitute Children was passed by the Senate and Assembly of the State of New York. It became unlawful for any child over 3 and under 16 years of age to be committed to a county poorhouse "unless such child be an unteachable idiot, an epileptic or paralytic, or . . . otherwise defective, diseased or deformed, so as to render it unfit for family care."[69] The latter children were presumably "unfit for family care" because they could not become self-supporting.

Much of the urgency for removing dependent and neglected children from the catchall almshouse was related to the current belief in inheritable tendencies toward pauperism, tendencies that could be enhanced by children's associations during their early life, and to the fear of creating generations of dependents. Institutional care as devised during the pre-Civil War period was intended to provide for the child a model of disciplined, organized, productive life as a substitute for disorganized family living. Instead, almshouse care was found to expose children to adult paupers, frequently the child's own parents, so that the model supported the very pattern it was intended to supplant. The removal of children would break up these families, by placing the children in "good," "humble" foster homes. In these homes, according to Anne B. Richardson, reporting to the thirteenth annual Conference of Charities and Corrections (1886) on the care of dependent and delinquent children in Massachusetts, the children are restored to conditions of family life where strains produce character.[70]

Warner reiterated the point in 1894:

> The child who is born in an almshouse and grows up there is almost always a pauper, because his bad heredity is reinforced by such an environment. . . .
> The child that grows up in an infant asylum or orphans' home has at most an imperfect opportunity for right development, and the original possibilities of its nature are but faintly reflected by its career. With a child boarded out in a private family, or given to foster parents while still an infant, the conditions are better and more might be inferred if we could compare its characteristics with those of its parents.[71]

Pauper families, perhaps, could not be saved; but all children could.

In Pennsylvania, as in New York and Massachusetts, anxiety existed about the retention of children in almshouses. The Report of the Commissioners of Public Charities for the Year 1882 expressed the dangers of permitting children to be in constant association with "these imbecile and debased paupers."

> It must be kept in view that they are one and all *involuntary* and *helpless* prisoners, not from any fault of their own, but too often inheriting the worst traits of a degraded parentage; and, if to this inborn nature is added the results of the society and example of the most degraded of our race, are we to expect anything better from them than their training will promise?[72]

The Commissioners recommended to the state legislature an act to prevent and forbid the detention of children between the ages of 2 and 16 years in poorhouses or almhouses. The act was passed in 1883.[73]

Reports from New York, Massachusetts, and Pennsylvania showed that the removal of children already resident in almshouses was slow. Charles S. Hoyt, secretary of the New York State Board of Charities, reporting on "The Causes of Pauperism" (1877) was shrill in denouncing "the practice of receiving parents and children into poor-houses together" and of retaining

Children's Aid Society of New York: Going West, 1886 (Last Party Sent Out by Mrs. John Jacob Astor Before Her Death). Charles Loring Brace, the leading proponent of the foster home movement for children, was the founder and executive of the Children's Aid Society of New York City. The agency's efforts to send children to the rural West continued well into the post Civil War period, reaching a peak in 1873.

Photograph by Jacob A. Riis, The Jacob A. Riis Collection, Museum of the City of New York

them there as families. His contention that heredity entered so largely in the problem of pauperism led him to assert unequivocally that it was against sound policy to keep pauper families, whether in or out of the almshouse, together; "in fact the sooner they can be broken up the better. . . . "[74] Certainly the fear of hereditary influences would lead to anxiety in regard to the slowness of the process of removal. At the same time, the threatened removal of children had an equally important, if less publicized, effect—that of deterring families from entering the poorhouse. Thus poor families who required public help were doubly deterred, for if they entered almshouses they would face deplorable living conditions as well as the possibility of family breakup.

A number of reasons underlay the slowness of reducing the number of children in almshouses. Oddly enough, one reason was simply that the laws against accepting children were not always known or understood by almshouse superintendents. During the next decade the movement to deinstitutionalize children lost ground and a concern for family togetherness developed. The 1883 Report of the Pennsylvania Board of Commissioners of Public Charities, for example, mentioned the acceptance of families in almshouses, especially bereaved and immigrant families who must have temporary help, but for whom outdoor relief was not available because of "mistaken notions of economy."[75] Such temporary use of the almshouses made it possible for families to stay together. The report urged the wider use of outdoor relief as even more efficacious in preventing the breaking up of homes.

Eventually the momentum for removing children from almshouses accelerated. Child welfare leaders began to state a rationale for individualizing the needs of children—a parallel reaction, perhaps, to the Charity Organization emphasis upon individualizing families. In his report for 1888, Charles W. Birtwell, General Agent of Boston's Children's Aid Society described the agency's changing practices:

> The aim will be in each instance to suit action to the real need—heeding the teachings of experience, still to study the conditions with a freedom from assumptions . . . as complete as though the case in hand stood absolutely alone.[76]

In his report for 1893, Birtwell made the logical connection between the individualized child and the individualized family.

> These children cannot be divorced from the natural relations of family life without loss . . . and therefore we must humbly set ourselves to learn the ways in which family ties may be strengthened and parental responsibilities maintained . . .[77]

The census of 1890 showed that the number of children in the country's almshouses had decreased by 36 percent during the previous decade, from 7,770 in 1880 to 4,987 in 1890.[78] A part of the decrease could be attributed to an interesting combination of positive concern for families and for individual character leading to the removal from almshouses of entire, intact families who were then sent to the West where employment and a "proper" moral climate were both generously available. The philosophy of Charles Loring Brace was now serving a larger purpose.

The Settlement House Movement

At the end of the nineteenth century, a second major movement developed in the voluntary sector of social welfare: the Settlement House Movement.

Inspired by the efforts of Canon Samuel Barnett's Toynbee Hall in London to bring the privileged and underprivileged together to overcome the effects of spiritual and social disintegration, Stanton Coit and Charles B. Stover founded the Neighborhood Guild of New York City in 1887. Their hope in opening this first American settlement house, where educated persons might live among the poor newcomers to the United States, was to bring about a sense of neighborliness that could lead to the making of good citizens. In 1889 Jane Addams established Hull House in Chicago and Vida Scudder founded the College Settlement in New York. Located in large cities, these settlement houses emphasized neighborhood services and community development. Although Charity Organizations in "socialized" circles at least, had captured "the family" as their area of functional expertise, settlements were no less concerned with family welfare. The groups differed, however, in their views of families, in their views of society, and, ultimately, in their views of social welfare as a helping mechanism.

Charity Organization Societies had come into being for the express purpose of organizing voluntary and public charities in order to direct toward worthy families the relief-giving services of others.[79] Their particular concern was with the poor, and especially with those individuals whose flawed character permitted them to sup at the public trough while contributing nothing to the public larder. Their investigations of applicants for relief—investigations that led eventually to the development of casework methodology and to the emergence of a social work profession—were meant to individualize each poor family so that particular flaws could be detected and overcome and independence could be regained. The Charity Organization Societies did make an effort to separate the "worthy" poor from the "unworthy" poor in order to help the former adequately, but the fear of encouraging pauperism led for the most part to a basic philosophy that deterred all from asking for help. In essence, the orientation of Charity Organizations toward relief was in line with the Poor Law tradition and led to competition with public officials for supremacy in handling relief matters. In many localities, Charity Organization Societies took on the job of investigating relief applicants for public agencies, a job they had assumed very early for private relief societies.[80]

Whereas Charity Organization Societies assumed a well-functioning society but with malfunctioning families as the starting point of their operation, Social Settlements assumed as their operational base the adequate functioning of the families they served. Much of the clientele and of the neighborhoods served by settlement houses consisted of migrants and immigrants whose problems quite clearly were associated with making the transition from rural to urban living and from a known to an unknown culture. Whatever their problems with the culture or the language, clients of settlement houses were viewed as able, normal, working-class families with whom the wealthier, upper classes were joined in mutual dependence. When such families could not cope, settlement leaders assumed that society itself was at fault and this assumption led quite naturally to a drive for societal reform.[81]

The Charity Organization and Settlement House movements in the early years were quite different in goals, in techniques, and in service programs. Charity Organizations were bent upon preventing pauperism. To aid in this process of reformation, Charity Organization Societies engaged heavily in "Repressive Work," the detection of fraud through the establishment of Confidential Exchanges, and in "Provident Work," the establishment or promotion of "various wellproved schemes for the encouragement of thrift and self help."[82] Settlement houses, on the other hand, from their inception moved toward the socialization of the normal, adequately functioning family, and their goal was reflected in the three strands of their program activities: neighborhood clubs providing recreational and educational opportunities, social research in regard to family and community needs, and, especially, social action leading to legislative and political change.

The Settlement Movement began with a belief in the normality of its family clientele and geared its program to an expansion of the idea of family to an ideal of communal living. When problems arose for the family unit, correction through societal change, through social reform, was sought. Jane Addams stated the difference between the Charity Organization Society and the Settlement:

> The settlement does stand for something unlike that which the charity visitor stands for. You are bound, when you are doing charitable work, to lay stress upon the industrial virtues. . . . Now the settlement . . . does not lay perpetual and continual stress upon them. It sees that a man may, perhaps, be a bit lazy, and still be a good man and an interesting person. . . . It does not lay so much stress upon one set of virtues, but views the man in his social aspects . . . . To adjust an individual to civilization as he finds it round him, to get him to the pitch which shall induce him to push up that civilization a little higher . . . is perhaps the chief function of a settlement.[83]

For all their differences, the Charity Organization and Settlement House Movements were both concerned with the well-being of families and would make outstanding contributions to family welfare during the Progressive Era. Their contributions would take the form of social welfare legislation and the development of the profession of social work dedicated to the individual needs of individual families.

The Civil War and After

Three documents are used to highlight the direction of social welfare developments from the close of the Civil War to the turn of the century. The documents include: President Andrew Johnson's *veto of the Extension of the Freedmen's Bureau* (1866), the State of New York's *Act to provide for the relief of indigent soldiers, sailors and marines, and the families of deceased military personnel* (1887), and an excerpt from Josephine Shaw Lowell's address, *The Economic and Moral Effects of Public Outdoor Relief,* delivered at the National Conference of Charities and Corrections (1890). Each deals with a major social welfare concern of the post-Civil War era.

The Freedmen's Bureau had been making a serious contribution to the welfare of Southerners caught in the path of the devastation and change brought about by the Civil War. For blacks, particularly, the Bureau meant emergency aid in the transition from slavery to freedom. Considering the state of affairs in the vanquished Southern states, a continuation of the life of the Bureau seemed certain. However, President Johnson vetoed the bill to extend the life of the Bureau, objecting on constitutional grounds to the act's seemingly unlimited extension of federal military jurisdiction "over all parts of the United States containing refugees and freedmen"—in effect, the entire country. He objected, too, to measures permitting broad administrative discretion, "without the intervention of a jury," to the Bureau's agents in their attempts to enforce the act's provisions.

Most significantly, President Johnson objected to the federal government's assumption of responsibility for social welfare. "A system for the support of indigent persons in the United States," he wrote, "was never contemplated by the authors of the Constitution. . . ." Ironically, he argued that the special circumstances of freed blacks made adherence to constitutional intention more important; for the intent had been that blacks, on becoming free, would automatically become a "self-sustaining population." In reasoning typical of the era, he placed responsibility for recovery from slavery on its victims. Legislation that delayed "a self-sustaining condition must have a tendency injurious alike to their character and their prospects." The veto was overridden and set a precedent for federal participation in social welfare during emergency periods.

New York's legislation to provide relief for indigent servicemen and their families is an example of one state's special attention to the claims of veterans. The legislation provides state funding for relief, a shift from strict adherence to local responsibility for relief giving and from the requirement of local residence. Need was to be determined and relief was to be administered by designated relief committees in each post of the Grand Army of the Republic, a veterans' organization. Placement of indigent servicemen or their families in an almshouse without the consent of the Grand Army of the Republic was prohibited. By definition, veterans were not "paupers" and not subject to the ordinary conditions prescribed for handling the needs of "the poor."

The excerpt from Josephine Shaw Lowell's address is significant for its demonstration of the current view of mankind and the poor. During the postwar era, an earlier view of man's perfectability gave way to a view of the corruptibility of the individual. Social Darwinism supported a theory of social evolution that permitted the abandonment of those who could not sustain themselves or add to the resources of society. Mrs. Lowell fell short of arguing for complete abandonment, admitting that some persons do "need relief (that is, *help*) in their own homes." What she could not accept was the use of public funds for relief giving, seeing no good in such giving for the community at large. In fact, she saw an "inverse ratio between the welfare of the mass of people and the distribution of (public) relief." The moral weakening of the individual who received public relief led to a weakening of people in the larger society.

Mrs. Lowell was a leader among those who sought to apply "scientific" methodology to philanthropy. She was a major supporter of a new delivery system, the Charity Organization Society, whose original intent was to use volunteer counseling services in an attempt to avoid the necessity for cash relief.

Mrs. Lowell's address sheds additional light on the significance of President Johnson's veto of the Freedmen's Bureau extension and of New York's provision for indigent servicemen. The fear of the transmittability of pauperism expressed by Social Darwinism was evident in the president's concern that freedmen not be made dependent on help. As for the veterans of the Civil War: they had already proved themselves. There was little risk in offering extra consideration for their contribution.

PRESIDENT ANDREW JOHNSON: VETO MESSAGE
The Freedmen's Bureau

To the Senate of the United States:

I have examined with care the bill which originated in the Senate and has been passed by the two Houses of Congress to amend an act entitled "An act to establish a Bureau for the Relief of Freedmen and Refugees," and for other purposes. Having, with much regret, come to the conclusion that it would not be consistent with the public welfare to give my approval to the measure, I return the bill to the Senate with my objections to its becoming a law.

I might call to mind in advance of these objections that there is no immediate necessity for the proposed measure. The act to establish a Bureau for the Relief of Freedmen and Refugees, which was approved in the month of March last, has not yet expired. It was thought stringent and extensive

The Congressional Globe, The Debates and Proceedings of the First Session, 39th Congress, 1866.

enough for the purpose in view in time of war. Before it ceases to have effect further experience may assist to guide us to a wise conclusion as to the policy to be adopted in time of peace.

I share with Congress the strongest desire to secure to the freedmen the full enjoyment of their freedom and property, and their entire independence and equality in making contracts for their labor; but the bill before me contains provisions which in my opinion are not warranted by the Constitution, and are not well suited to accomplish the end in view.

The bill proposes to establish, by authority of Congress, military jurisdiction over all parts of the United States containing refugees and freedmen. It would, by its very nature, apply with most force to those parts of the United States in which the freedmen most abound; and it expressly extends the existing temporary jurisdiction of the Freedmen's Bureau with greatly enlarged powers over those States "in which the ordinary course of judicial proceedings has been interrupted by the rebellion." The source from which this military jurisdiction is to emanate is none other than the President of the United States, acting through the War Department and the Commissioner of the Freedmen's Bureau. The agents to carry out this military jurisdiction are to be selected either from the Army or from civil life; the country is to be divided into districts and subdistricts; and the number of salaried agents to be employed may be equal to the number of counties or parishes in all the United States where freedmen and refugees are to be found.

The subjects over which this military jurisdiction is to extend in every part of the United States include protection to "all employes, agents, and officers in this bureau in the exercise of the duties imposed" upon them by the bill. In eleven States it is further to extend over all cases affecting freedmen and refugees discriminated against "by local law, custom, or prejudice." In those eleven States the bill subjects any white person who may be charged with depriving a freedman of "any civil rights or immunities belonging to white persons" to imprisonment or fine, or both, without, however, defining the "civil rights and immunities" which are thus to be secured to the freedmen by military law. This military jurisdiction also extends to all questions that may arise respecting contracts. The agent who is thus to exercise the office of a military judge may be a stranger, entirely ignorant of the laws of the place, and exposed to the errors of judgment to which all men are liable. The exercise of power, over which there is no legal supervision, by so vast a number of agents as is contemplated by the bill, must, by the very nature of man, be attended by acts of caprice, injustice, and passion.

The trials, having their origin under this bill, are to take place without the intervention of a jury, and without any fixed rules of law or evidence. The rules on which offenses are to be "heard and determined" by the numerous agents, are such rules and regulations as the President, through the War Department, shall prescribe. No previous presentment is required, nor any indictment charging the commission of a crime against the laws; but the trial must proceed on charges and specifications. The punishment will be, not what the law declares, but such as a courtmartial may think proper; and from these arbitrary tribunals there lies no appeal, no writ of error to any of the courts in which the Constitution of the United States vests exclusively the judicial power of the country.

While the territory and the classes of actions and offenses that are made subject to this measure are so extensive, the bill itself, should it become a law, will have no limitation in point of time, but will form a part of the permanent legislation of the country. I cannot reconcile a system of military jurisdiction of this kind with the words of the Constitution, which declare that "no person shall be held to answer for a capital or otherwise infamous crime unless upon a presentment or indictment of a grand jury, except in cases arising in the land and naval forces, or in the militia when in actual service in time of war or public danger"; and that "in all criminal prosecutions the accused shall enjoy the right to a speedy and public trial, by an impartial jury of the State or district, wherein the crime shall have been committed." The safeguards which the experience and wisdom of ages taught our fathers to establish as securities for the protection of the innocent, the punishment of the guilty, and the equal administration of justice, are to be set aside, and for the sake of a more vigorous interposition in behalf of justice, we are to take the risk of the many acts of injustice that would necessarily follow from an almost countless number of agents established in every parish or county in nearly a third of the States of the Union, over whose decisions there is to be no supervision or control by the Federal courts. The power that would be thus placed in the hands of the President is such as in time of peace certainly ought never to be intrusted to any one man.

If it be asked whether the creation of such a tribunal within a State is warranted as a measure of war, the question immediately presents itself whether we are still engaged in war. Let us not unnecessarily disturb the commerce and credit and industry of the country by declaring to the American people and to the world that the United States are still in a condition of civil war. At present there is no part of our country in which the authority of the United States is disputed. Offenses that may be committed by individuals should not work a forfeiture of the rights of whole communities. The country has returned or is returning to a state of peace and industry, and the rebellion is in fact at an end. The measure, therefore, seems to be as inconsistent with the actual condition of the country as it is at variance with the Constitution of the United States.

If, passing from general considerations, we examine the bill in detail, it is open to weighty objections.

In time of war it was eminently proper that we should provide for those who were passing suddenly from a condition of bondage to a state of freedom. But this bill proposes to make the Freedmen's Bureau, established by the act of 1865 as one of many great and extraordinary military measures to suppress a formidable rebellion, a permanent branch of the public administration, with its powers greatly enlarged. I have no reason to suppose, and I do not understand it to be alleged, that the act of March, 1865, has proved deficient for the purpose for which it was passed, although at that time, and for a considerable period thereafter, the Government of the United States remained unacknowledged in most of the States whose inhabitants had been involved in the rebellion. The institution of slavery, for the military destruction of which the Freedmen's Bureau was called into existence as an auxiliary, has been already effectually and finally abrogated throughout the whole country by an amendment of the Constitution of the United States, and practically its eradication has received the assent and concurrence of most of those States in which it at any time had an existence. I am not, therefore, able to discern, in the condition of the country, anything to justify an apprehension that the powers and agencies of the Freedmen's Bureau, which were effective for the protection of freedmen and refugees during the actual continuance of hostilities and of African servitude, will now, in a time of peace and after the abolition of slavery, prove inadequate to the same proper ends. If I am correct in these views, there can be no necessity for the enlargement of the powers of the bureau, for which provision is made in the bill.

The third section of the bill authorizes a general and unlimited grant of support to the destitute and suffering refugees and freedmen, their wives and children. Succeeding sections make provision for the rent or purchase of landed estates for freedmen, and for the erection for their benefit of suitable buildings for asylums and schools, the expenses to be defrayed from the Treasury of the whole people. The Congress of the United States has never heretofore thought itself empowered to establish asylums beyond the limits of the District of Columbia except for the benefit of our disabled soldiers and sailors. It has never founded schools for any class of our own people, not even for the orphans of those who have fallen in the defense of the Union, but has left the care of education to the much more competent and efficient control of the States, of communities, of private associations, and of individuals. It has never deemed itself authorized to expend the public money for the rent or purchase of homes for the thousands, not to say millions, of the white race, who are honestly toiling from day to day for their subsistence. A system for the support of indigent persons in the United States was never contemplated by the authors of the Constitution, nor can any good reason be advanced why, as a permanent establishment, it should be founded for one class or color of our people more than another. Pending the war, many refugees and freedmen received support from the Government, but it was never intended that they should thenceforth be fed, clothed, educated, and sheltered by the United States. The idea on which the slaves were assisted to freedom was that, on becoming free, they would be a self-sustaining population. Any legislation that shall imply that they are not expected to attain a self-sustaining condition must have a tendency injurious alike to their character and their prospects.

The appointment of an agent for every county and parish will create an immense patronage; and the expense of the numerous officers and their clerks, to be appointed by the President, will be great in the beginning, with a tendency steadily to increase. The appropriations asked by the Freedmen's Bureau, as now established, for the year 1866, amount to $11,745,000. It may be safely estimated that the cost to be incurred under the pending bill will require double that amount—more than the entire sum expended in any one year under the administration of the second Adams. If the presence of agents in every parish and country is to be considered as a war measure, opposition, or even resistance, might be provoked, so that, to give effect to their jurisdiction, troops would have to be stationed within reach of every one of them, and thus a large standing force be rendered necessary. Large appropriations would therefore be required to sustain and enforce military jurisdiction in every county or parish, from the Potomac to the Rio Grande. The condition of our fiscal affairs is encouraging; but in order to sustain the present measure of public confidence, it is necessary that we practice not merely customary economy, but, as far as possible, severe retrenchment.

In addition to the objections already stated, the fifth section of the bill proposes to take away land from its former owners without any legal proceedings being first had, contrary to that provision of the Constitution which declares that no person shall "be deprived of life, liberty, or property without due process of law." It does not appear that a part of the lands to which this section refers may not be owned by minors, or persons of unsound mind, or by those who have been faithful to all their obligations as citizens of the United States. If any portion of the land is held by such persons, it is not competent for any authority to deprive them of it. If, on the other hand, it be found that the property is liable to confiscation, even then it cannot be appropriated to public purposes until by due process of law it shall have been declared forfeited to the Government.

There is still further objection to the bill on grounds seriously affecting the class of persons to whom it is designed to bring relief. It will tend to keep the mind of the freedman in a state of uncertain expectation and restlessness, while to those among whom he lives it will be a source of constant and vague apprehension.

Undoubtedly the freedman should be protected, but he should be protected by the civil authorities, especially by the exercise of all the constitutional powers of the courts of the United States and of the States. His condition is not so exposed as may at first be imagined. He is in a portion of the country where his labor cannot well be spared. Competition for his services from planters, from those who are constructing or repairing railroads, and from capitalists in his vicinage or from other States, will enable him to command almost his own terms. He also possesses a perfect right to change his place of abode; and if, therefore, he does not find in one community or State a mode of life suited to his desires, or proper remuneration for his labor, he can move to another, where the labor is more esteemed and better rewarded. In truth, however, each State, induced by its own wants and interests, will do what is necessary and proper to retain within its borders all the labor that is needed for the development of its resources. The laws that regulate supply and demand will maintain their force, and the wages of the laborer will be regulated thereby. There is no danger that the exceedingly great demand for labor will not operate in favor of the laborer.

Neither is sufficient consideration given to the ability of the freedmen to protect and take care of themselves. It is no more than justice to them to believe that as they have received their freedom with moderation and forbearance, so they will distinguish themselves by their industry and thrift, and soon show the world that in a condition of freedom they are self-sustaining, capable of selecting their own employment and their own places of abode, of insisting, for themselves, on a proper remuneration, and of establishing and maintaining their own asylums and schools. It is earnestly hoped that instead of wasting away, they will, by their own efforts, establish for themselves a condition of respect, ability, and prosperity. It is certain that they can attain to that condition only through their own merits and exertions.

In this connection the query presents itself, whether the system proposed by the bill will not, when put into complete operation, practically transfer the entire care, support, and control of four million emancipated slaves to agents, overseers, or task-masters who, appointed at Washington, are to be located in every county and parish throughout the United States containing freedmen and refugees? Such a system would inevitably tend to a concentration of power in the Executive, which would enable him, if so disposed, to control the action of this numerous class and use them for the attainment of his own political ends.

I cannot but add another very grave objection to this bill. The Constitution imperatively declares, in connection with taxation, that each State shall have at least one Representative, and fixes the rule for the number to which in future times each State shall be composed of two Senators from each State, and adds with peculiar force, "that no State, without its consent, shall be deprived of its equal suffrage in the Senate." The original act was necessarily passed in the absence of the States chiefly to be affected, because their people were then contumaciously engaged in the rebellion. Now the case is changed, and some at least of those States are attending Congress by loyal Representatives, soliciting the allowance of the constitutional right of representation. At the time, however, of the consideration and the passing of this bill, there was no Senator or Representative in Congress from the eleven States which are to be mainly affected by its provisions. The very fact that reports were and are made against the good disposition of the people of that portion of the country is an additional reason why they need, and should have Representatives of their own in Congress to explain their condition, reply to accusations, and assist, by their local knowledge, in the perfecting of measures immediately affecting themselves. While the liberty of deliberation would then be free, and Congress would have full power to decide according to its judgment, there could be no objection urged that the States most interested had not been permitted to be heard. The principle is firmly fixed in the minds of the American people, that there should be no taxation without representation.

Great burdens have now to be borne by all the country, and we may best demand that they shall be borne without murmur when they are voted by a majority of the representatives of all the people. I would not interfere with the unquestionable right of Congress to judge, each House for itself, "of the elections, returns, and qualifications of its own members," but that authority cannot be construed as including the right to shut out, in time of peace, any State from the representation to which it is entitled by the Constitution. At present, all the people of eleven States are excluded—those who were most faithful during the war not less than others. The State of Tennessee, for instance, whose authorities engaged in rebellion, was restored to all her constitutional relations to the Union by the patriotism and energy of her injured and betrayed people. Before the war was brought to a termination they had placed themselves in relations with the General Government, had established a State government of their own; as they were not included in the emancipation proclamation, they by their own act had amended their constitution so as to abolish slavery within the limits of their State. I know no reason why the State of Tennessee, for example, should not fully enjoy "all her constitutional relations to the United States."

The President of the United States stands toward the country in a somewhat different attitude from that of any member of Congress. Each member of Congress is chosen from a single district or State; the President is chosen by the people of all the States. As eleven are not at this time represented in either branch of Congress, it would seem to be his duty, on all proper occasions, to present their just claims to Congress. There always will be differences of opinion in the community, and individuals may be guilty of transgressions of the law; but these do not constitute valid objections against the right of a State to representation. I would in nowise interfere with the discretion of Congress with regard to the qualifications of members; but I hold it my duty to recommend to you, in the interests of peace and in the interests of union, the admission of every State to its share in public legislation, when, however insubordinate, insurgent, or rebellious its people may have been, it presents itself not only in an attitude of loyalty and harmony, but in the persons of Representatives whose loyalty cannot be questioned under any existing constitutional or legal test.

It is plain that an indefinite or permanent exclusion of any part of the country from representation must be attended by a spirit of disquiet and complaint. It is unwise and dangerous to pursue a course of measures which will unite a very large section of the country against another section of the country, however much the latter may preponderate. The course of emigration, the development of industry and business, and natural causes will raise up at the South men as devoted to the Union as those of any other part of the land. But if they are all excluded from Congress, if, in a permanent statute, they are declared not to be in full constitutional relations to the country, they may think they have cause to become a unit in feeling and sentiment against the Government. Under the political education of the American people the idea is inherent and ineradicable that the consent of the majority of the whole people is necessary to secure a willing acquiescence in legislation.

The bill under consideration refers to certain of the States as though they had not "been fully restored in all their constitutional relations to the United States." If they have not, let us at once act together to secure that desirable end at the earliest possible moment. It is hardly necessary for me to inform Congress that, in my own judgment, most of these States, so far at least as depends upon their own action, have already been fully restored, and are to be deemed as entitled to enjoy their constitutional rights as members of the Union. Reasoning from the Constitution itself, and from the actual situation of the country, I feel not only entitled, but bound to assume that, with the Federal courts restored, and those of the several States in the full exercise of their functions, the rights and interests of all classes of the people will, with the aid of the military in cases of resistance to the laws, be essentially protected against unconstitutional infringement or violation. Should this expectation unhappily fail, which I do not anticipate, then the

Executive is already fully armed with the powers conferred by the act of March, 1865, establishing the Freedman's Bureau, and hereafter, as heretofore, he can employ the land and naval forces of the country to suppress insurrection or to overcome obstructions to the laws.

In accordance with the Constitution I return the bill to the Senate, in the earnest hope that a measure involving questions and interests so important to the country will not become a law unless, upon deliberate consideration by the people, it shall receive the sanction of an enlightened public judgment.

ANDREW JOHNSON.

The conclusion of the reading of the message was followed by loud applause and hisses in the galleries.

• • •

LAWS OF THE STATE OF NEW YORK

ONE HUNDRED AND TENTH SESSION

January 4 – May 26, 1887

Chap. 706

AN ACT to provide for the relief of indigent soldiers, sailors and marines, and the families of those decreased.

PASSED June 25, 1887; three-fifths being present.

The People of the State of New York, represented in Senate and Assembly, do enact as follows:

Town or city auditing boards may grant relief to indigent soldiers, etc.

SECTION 1. For the relief of indigent and suffering soldiers, sailors and marines, who served in the war of the rebellion, and their families, or the families of those deceased, who need assistance in any town or city in this State, the proper auditing board of such city or town may provide such sum or sums of money as may be necessary, to be drawn upon by the commander and quartermaster of any post of the Grand Army of the Republic in said city or town, upon the recommendation of the relief committee of said post, in the same manner as is now provided by law for the relief of the poor, provided said soldier, sailor and marine, or the families of those deceased, are and have been resident of the State for one year or more, and the orders of said commander and quartermaster shall be the proper vouchers for the expenditure of said sum or sums of money.

Expenditure, how supervised.

To whom, relief may be granted.

Relief committee in certain towns.

§ 2. In case there be no post of the Grand Army of the Republic in any town in which it is necessary that such relief, as provided for in section one, should be granted, the town board of said town shall accept and pay the orders drawn as hereinbefore provided, by the commander and quartermaster of any post of the Grand Army of the Republic, located in the nearest city or town, upon the recommendation of a relief committee, who shall be residents of the said town in which the relief may be furnished.

Notice to city or town clerk, of taking charge of relief.

§ 3. Upon the passage of this act the commander of any post of the Grand Army of the Republic, which shall undertake the relief of indigent veterans and their families, as hereinbefore provided, before the acts of said commander and quartermaster may become operative in any city or town, shall file with the city clerk of such city, or town clerk of such town, a notice that said post intends to undertake such relief as is provided by this act. Such notice shall contain the names of the relief committee of said post in such city or town, and of the commander and other officers of said post. And the commander of said post shall annually thereafter, during the month of October, file a similar notice with said city and town clerks, and also a detailed statement of the amount of relief furnished during the preceding year, with the names of all persons to whom such relief shall have been furnished, together with a brief statement in each case, from the relief committee upon whose recommendation the orders were drawn.

Annual statement as to relief, etc., how filed.

§ 4. The said auditing board of any city or town may require of the said commander and quartermaster of any post of the Grand Army of the Republic, undertaking such relief in said city or town, a bond with sufficient and satisfactory sureties for the faithful and honest discharge of their duties under this act.

Bond of relief committee.

§ 5. Superintendents and overseers of the poor are hereby prohibited from sending indigent soldiers, sailors, and marines, (or their families, or the families of those deceased), to any alms-house (or orphan asylum) without the full concurrence and consent of the commander and relief committee of the post of the Grand Army of the Republic, having jurisdiction as provided in sections one and two. Indigent veterans with families, and the families of deceased veterans, shall, whenever practicable, be provided for and relieved at their homes in such city or town in which they shall have a residence, in the manner provided in sections one and two of this act. Indigent or disabled veterans of the classes specified in section one, who are not insane, and who have no families or friends with whom they may be domiciled, may be sent to any soldiers' home. Any indigent veteran of either of the classes specified in section one, or any member of the family of any living or deceased veteran of said classes, who may be insane, shall, upon recommendation of the commander and relief committee of such post of the Grand Army of the Republic, within the jurisdiction of which the case may occur, be sent to any insane asylum, and cared for as provided for

Duties of overseers and superintendents of poor, as to committals to alms-house, etc.

Out-door or home relief, to be given when possible.

Soldiers' Home, relief at.

Care of indigent insane veterans.

indigent insane in section twenty-six of chapter one hundred and thirty-five of the laws of eighteen hundred and forty-two. § 6. This act shall take effect immediately.

• • •

PROCEEDINGS OF THE NATIONAL CONFERENCE OF CHARITIES AND CORRECTIONS

1890

THE ECONOMIC AND MORAL EFFECTS OF PUBLIC OUTDOOR RELIEF.

BY MRS. CHARLES RUSSELL LOWELL, OF NEW YORK.

I have not been able to assent to the report of the Chairman of the Committee on Indoor and Outdoor Relief, only because, as it seems to me, he does not draw the distinction which is necessary between public and private relief.

I admit, of course, that there are persons who need relief (that is, *help*) in their own homes, and that both Pitt's argument and Mr. Sanborn's argument apply to such: "Great care should be taken, in relieving their distresses, not to throw them into the great class of vagrant and homeless poor." Such people, however, are, to my mind, not proper subjects for public relief at all; for what is public relief, and upon what grounds is it to be justified? Public relief is money paid by the bulk of the community (every community is of course composed mainly of those who are working hard to obtain a livelihood) to certain members of the community, not, however, paid voluntarily or spontaneously by those interested in the individuals receiving it, but paid by public officers from money raised by taxation. The only justification for the expenditure of public money (money raised by taxation) is that it is necessary for the public good. That certain persons need certain things is no reason for supplying them with those things from the public funds. Before this can be rightly done, it is necessary to prove that it is good for the community at large that it should be done. . . .

The practice of any community in this particular is a matter of great importance, for there can be no question that there is an inverse ratio between the welfare of the mass of the people and the distribution of relief. What some one has called "the fatal ease of living without work and the terrible difficulty of living by work" are closely interrelated as cause and effect; and, if you will permit me, I will try to show by a short allegory what this relation is.

Once upon a time there lived in a valley, called the Valley of Industry, a people who were happy and industrious. All the goods of this life were supplied to them by exhaustless subterranean springs of water, which they pumped up into a great reservoir on the top of a neighboring hill, the Hill of Prosperity, from which it flowed down, each man receiving what he himself pumped up, by a small pipe which led into his own house, a moderate amount of pumping on the part of every one keeping the reservoir well filled.

Finally, a few of the inhabitants of the Valley, more keen than the rest, reflected that it was unnecessary to weary themselves with pumping, so long as every one else kept at work. The Hill of Prosperity looked very attractive; and they therefore mounted to a convenient point, and put a large pipe into the reservoir, through which they drew off copious supplies of water without further trouble. The number of those who gave up pumping and withdrew to the Hill was at first so small that the loss did not add very much to the work of the mass of the people, who still kept to their pumping, and it did not occur to them to complain; but those who could followed the others up the Hill until it was all occupied, and by this time, although those who remained in the Valley did find their pumping a good deal harder than it was when all who used the water joined in the work, yet every one had become so accustomed to some people using the reservoir water without doing any pumping that it had come to be considered all right, and still there were no complaints. Meanwhile, the people on the Hill of Prosperity having nothing to do but enjoy the prospect, some of them began to explore the neighboring country, and soon discovered another valley at the foot of the Hill, running parallel with the Valley of Industry, and called the Valley of Idleness, and in it were a few people who had wandered from the former Valley (for the two were connected at the farther end), and who were living in abject misery, with no water, and apparently no means of getting any, so long as they stayed where they were. The people from the Hill of Prosperity were very much shocked at the suffering they found. "What a shame!" they cried. "The poor things have no water! We have plenty and to spare, so let us lead a pipe from the reservoir down into their Valley." No sooner said than done: the pipe was carried into the Valley of Idleness, and the people were made more comfortable. But as soon as the news was brought into the Valley of Industry, some of the pumpers who were tired or weak, and some who were only lazy, left their pumping, and hastened into the neighboring Valley, to enjoy the "free" water; but the pipe was not very large, and soon there was want and suffering again, and the people from Prosperity Hill were much disturbed, and decided to lay down another small pipe, which they did. But the result was the same, for the new supply of water attracted more people from the Valley of Industry. And so it went on, new pipe, more people, new pipe, more people, until the inhabitants of Prosperity Hill were full of distress about it, and exclaimed, "It seems a hopeless task to try to make these people happy and comfortable!" And they would have given up in despair, but a new idea occurred to them; and they said, "They do not seem to know how to take very good care of their children, and we will therefore take their children from them, and teach them to be comfortable and happy." So they built large, fine houses for the children, and they carried water in large pipes into the houses. And some of them said, "Let us put faucets, so as to teach them to turn on the water when they need it." But others said: "Oh, no! How troublesome it is to have to turn a faucet when you need water! Let them have it as we do, free." And sometimes one or other would suggest that, perhaps, after all, it was not quite right to waste so much of the water from the reservoir, and that the large pipe itself, which supplied the Hill of

Prosperity, ought to have some means of checking the flow; but the answer was, "It is necessary and right that the water should be wasted; for otherwise the people in the Valley of Industry would have nothing to do, and they would starve." Usually, however, the Prosperity Hill people were too much engaged in taking care of the inhabitants of the Valley of Idleness to give much thought to those of the Valley of Industry; and their anxiety was quite justified, for they had to keep up a perpetual watchfulness, the people increasing so fast that it was necessary constantly to lay more pipe to keep them from the most abject suffering, and even this device never succeeded for very long, as I have said.

In fact, no one thought much about the Valley of Industry or its people. Those in the Valley of Idleness only thought of them long enough to reflect how silly they were to keep on pumping all the time and making their backs and arms ache, when they might have water without any exertion, by simply moving into their Valley. The children born in the Valley of Idleness did not even know there was a Valley of Industry, or any pumps, or any pumpers, or any reservoir: they thought the water grew in pipes, and ran out because it was its nature to. As for the people on the Hill of Prosperity, they were, as we have seen, rather confused in their views in this particular; and, besides thinking that their waste of the water from the reservoir was what kept the people in the Valley of Industry from starving, they used also to say sometimes: "How good it is for those people to have such nice, steady work to do! how strong it makes their back and arms! how it hardens their muscles! What a nice, independent set of people they are! and *what* a splendid quantity of pure, life-giving water they get out of our reservoir!"

Meanwhile, you can imagine, though they could not, that it was rather hard on the men in the Valley of Industry, not only to have the water they pumped up drawn off at the top to supply two other communities, but also to have their own ranks thinned and their work increased by the loss of those who were tempted into the Valley of Idleness, to live on what the Prosperity Hill people and the Valley of Idleness people like to call euphemistically "free water," because they got it free, though actually it was not free at all; for the Valley of Industry people paid for it with their blood and muscle.

I might go on to tell you how the situation was still further complicated and made harder for them, and indeed for almost everyone, when a few of them obtained control of the inexhaustible subterranean springs; but here, I think, the allegory may end for the purposes of this Conference, and it seems to me to teach a lesson which we may well heed.

Chapter 5
Progress and Reform: 1900–1930

The era of social welfare reform of the late 1890s culminated in the Progressive Era of economic, social, and political change of the early decades of the twentieth century. After World War I, however, reform and progress were superseded by a sense of prosperity and security and a belief in the nearness of "the final triumph over poverty."[1] The United States had become the richest country on earth—a world leader in farm and manufacturing output. By 1925 it was producing 55 percent of the world's iron ore, 66 percent of the steel, 62 percent of the petroleum, 52 percent of the timber, 60 percent of the cotton, 80 percent of the sulfur, and 95 percent of the automobiles.[2] Solutions to all economic problems seemed within the reach of rational individuals.

The entire continent had been spanned and the harnessing of resources—water, coal, steam, electricity, petroleum—made it possible to expand to the limits of the frontier while simultaneously annihilating the great distance between the coasts. The development of railroads and inland waterways continued apace. Even before World War I, the automobile had become a factor of daily living; and after the war a period of major highway construction ensued, which, along with the establishment of federal air mail routes, hastened unification of the country. Communications for personal and buisness purposes were additionally furthered by the ready availability and popular use of telephone and telegraph facilities. There were 1.4 million telephones in 1900, 10.5 million in 1915, and over 20 million by 1930. By that time, radio and motion pictures had moved the country toward cultural as well as economic unification.

Twentieth-century inventions and innovative managerial skills revolutionized industry and agriculture. The years following the depression ending in 1898 were for the most part prosperous years during which living standards rose for the majority of the people in most sectors of the country. Between 1899 and 1929 the total output of manufacturing increased 273 percent.[3] Growth occurred throughout the period but was particularly stimulated by the war, when new industries were developed to replace the previously imported German dyes, chemicals, and optical instruments. When European industries were left devastated by World War I, the United States became the leading world supplier of both manufactured and agricultural products.

The period from the turn of the century to the depression of the 1930s saw the development of new power supplies, greater mechanization, and enormous advances in "scientific management." Whereas in 1913 it had taken 14 hours to assemble a car, in 1914 the job was done in 93 minutes; and by 1925 Henry Ford was able to produce an automobile every 10 seconds.

In agriculture, too, mechanization and new sources of power joined with improved means of transportation to increase productivity and provide easier distribution. The value of agricultural output rose steadily, due almost entirely to the increase in crop yields per acre. As farming became mechanized, labor was freed to move into manufacturing. By the end of the period, although the United States had only 4 percent of the world's farmers and farm laborers, it was producing nearly 70 percent of the world's tobacco, 25 percent of the oats and hay, 20 percent of the wheat, 13 percent of the barley, and 7 percent of the potatoes.[4]

Technological progress and relatively steady employment levels resulted in a climbing gross national product, despite brief recessions. GNP stood at about $17 billion in 1900, and by 1929 it had reached $104 billion. Much of this, of course, was absorbed by the increase in population and by inflation. But even allowing for price changes, per capita GNP rose by 73 percent in the first 30 years of the century.[5]

The increase in GNP was based on the ability of the agricultural sector to support a larger and larger urban, industrial population. Between 1900 and 1930 the population of the United States increased by 46.8 million to reach 123 million. During those same years, the total number of persons living in urban areas increased by 38 million to a total of 69 million. Forty percent of the population lived in urban areas in 1900; this rose to 51 percent in 1920 and to 56 percent in 1930.[6] Much of the shift from an agricultural to a predominantly urban society was achieved by a steady migration from farm areas to the cities. This was true for both the black and white populations. For the United States as a whole, 27 percent of the black population and 49 percent of the white population lived in urban areas in 1910; in 1930, 44 percent of the black population and 58 percent of the white population lived in urban areas.[7] There was a heavy concentration of black population in rural areas of the South. In the northern and western parts of the country, blacks lived predominantly in urban areas. After 1915, as blacks were forced off the farms, they moved increasingly into the cities of both the North and the South.

A measure of the economy's strength during the 1900–1930 period was its ability to absorb the almost 20 million immigrants included in the population. By far the greatest bulk of this immigration occurred during the first 15 years of the century, when 14.5 million people came, many from southern and eastern Europe. Most—about 75 percent—stayed in the cities, where rapid population growth meant a period of booming construction.[8]

Between 1920 and 1930, some 6 million people moved from farms to cities, resulting for the first time in a net loss—of 1.2 million—in farm population. As cities grew, they became increasingly commercial and industrial in character; they became work cores surrounded by residential areas. The number of such urban centers with populations of at least 100,000 grew from 38 in 1900 to 83 in 1930.[9] The growth was haphazard, causing crowded, unsanitary, tenement living. Families, both from abroad and from rural areas, were naive in regard to urban living. Their social and economic vulnerability made them subject to political exploitation, to "bossism," and corruption. Political machines operated to manipulate the processes of democratic government, while the pressing need for housing, sanitation, fire protection, policing, traffic regulation, and educational facilities went unheeded.

Growth and change occurred in the organization of industry, as well as in its output. In 1897 about a dozen corporations other than railroads were capitalized at $10 million. By 1903 the number of such corporations had risen to 300, of which about 50 were capitalized at more than $50 million; 17 were capitalized at more than $100 million; and one, U.S. Steel, was capitalized at almost $1.5 billion. These were the years in which some of the largest trusts in America were formed: Standard Oil, Consolidated Tobacco, and American Smelting, in addition to U.S. Steel. The efforts of the federal government to enforce antitrust laws led to some slowdowns in the rate of growth of monopolies. Nevertheless, by 1914, supercorporations dominated anthracite coal, agricultural machinery, sugar, telephone and telegraph, and public utilities in addition to iron and steel, railroads, oil, tobacco, and copper. Control of American industry had shifted from individual owners to a professional managerial class responsible to a board of directors often controlled by a small and powerful group of investment bankers.[10]

Paralleling the concentration of corporate power was a concentration of wealth and income. As the nation prospered, the growth at the top far exceeded that of either the middle class or the working class. It was the era of the multimillionaire. Andrew Carnegie, for example, was said to have had an average annual income of over $10 million—not subject to any income tax—at the turn of the century. In 1899 the richest 1.6 percent of the population had received 10.8 percent of national income. By 1910 this had jumped to 19 percent. Rising wages and relatively steady employment meant that working-class incomes rose too, but at a much slower rate. A 1915 report by the Commission on Industrial Relations took the critical question of the era to be: "Have workers received a fair share of the enormous increase in wealth which has taken place in this country during the period, as a result largely of their labor?" Its response: "The answer is emphatically—No!"[11]

Poverty and the Working Class

The Commission's report pointed out that during the period 1890–1912 personal wealth had increased 188 percent; but the aggregate income of wage earners in manufacturing, mining, and transportation had risen only 95 percent. The wage earner's share of the net product in manufacturing had actually declined. The Commission estimated that to achieve a minimum decency level, an average family of 5.6 members required an annual income of $700. Since 79 percent of the country's fathers earned less than $700 a year, earnings from other family members were necessary to sustain the family. And, indeed, the Census Bureau reported that 1,750,000 children between 10 and 15 years of age were gainfully employed in 1900; by 1910, this number had dropped to 1,600,000. In 1930, however, the figure still stood as high as 667,000.[12]

The report of the Commission on Industrial Relations concluded that, despite the labor of wives and children, and despite the widespread practice of taking in boarders and lodgers, 50 to 66 percent of working-class families were poor and that a third lived in "abject poverty." Other estimates confirmed the judgment of poverty and risk. Robert Hunter, a social worker, writing in 1904, estimated the poverty population at 10 million.[13] Father John A. Ryan, ethical theorist and economist, writing in 1906, found that the average family needed an annual income of at least $600 and that 60 percent of all wage earners received less.[14] Within the ranks of the working class, and, as the AFL succeeded in unionizing some crafts, dissatisfaction was further aggravated by the notable difference in payments to skilled and unskilled workers. Each recession (1910–1911, 1914–1915, 1920–1921) meant increased unemployment and lowered wages, especially for unskilled workers—largely ex-farmhands, blacks, and immigrants. Indeed, by 1928–1929 social welfare agencies were reporting increased caseloads. Between the newly rich, with their extreme wealth, and the working class, with its extreme poverty, lay the large middle class—a group with adequate income but little to spare, a group that was dissatisfied because it could not keep pace with the rapidly rising standard of living of those at the top.

Concomitant with labor unrest and with the dissatisfaction of the middle class was a developing farm crisis. The pre-World War I period was one of prosperity marked by rising farm income. The closing of the frontier, however, meant rising land prices. This, combined with rising costs of mechanization, made easy access to low-cost credit to buy land and machinery a major issue for most farmers. For the marginal farmer, land became more and more difficult to acquire. As the average size of farms started to grow, farm tenancy, already prevalent in the South, began to spread to the Midwest. In 1900, 35 percent of the nation's farms were tenant operated; by 1930 this had risen to 42 percent. For black farmers in the South, the figure reached 79 percent in 1930. The demands of World War I had led to an overextension of agriculture; and in 1920 an agricultural depression occurred, and it continued intermittently throughout the decade. Farm income, even for large-farm owners, did not rise as rapidly as corporate profits; for small-farm owners the crunch was intolerable. Between 1919 and 1929 the number of farms actually declined.[15]

Thus the lowest income classes—unskilled laborers and tenant farmers—fared poorly in the early years of the twentieth century, despite the general prosperity. Within this group, the black population particularly failed to share in the nation's economic growth. The expectation that Northern victory in the Civil War and that the conditions imposed upon the Southern states for return to the Union would bring about changed relations between Southern whites and blacks had been subverted. The advances begun by the programs of the Freedmen's Bureau, the political and civil protections guaranteed by the Thirteenth, Fourteenth, and Fifteenth Amendments to the Constitution, and the enforcement of black rights during the brief period of "radical reconstruction" had come formally to an end with the withdrawal of federal troops from the South by President Hayes in 1877. Through a series of legal and illegal acts and court decisions, the Southern black—now a freed person and a citizen—was abandoned to the "oppressions of those who had formerly exercised unlimited domination over him."[16]

The extent of the abandonment of blacks to white supremacists was not limited to the North's concession to the Southern states of complete control over domestic affairs and institutions or to Northern tolerance of the epidemic of lynchings and the outrageous activities of the Ku Klux Klan. Of equal significance was that process by which the North took on the Southern view of the black as "an alien, a menial, and a probable reprobate."[17] Collusion in the segregation and suppression of blacks was given judicial respectability by the Supreme Court's approval in 1896 of the "separate but equal" doctrine.[18] Northern rationalization of the necessity for segregation and suppression was epitomized by the widespread acceptance of D. W. Griffith's 1915 film, *Birth of a Nation*, in which freed blacks were stereotyped as cruel, vengeful rulers over starving, helpless whites and as "racially incapable of understanding, sharing, or contributing to Americanism."[19] In this atmosphere, Booker T. Washington's espousal of progress by separate evolution for his people found support among whites who gained comfort and conviction from the seeming acquiescence of the country's outstanding

Negro leader—the founder of Tuskegee Institute—in policies of social segregation and political cooperation. Washington wrote:

> The wisest among my race understand that the agitation of questions of social equality is the extremest folly, and that progress in the enjoyment of all the privileges that will come to us must be the result of severe and constant struggle rather than of artificial forcing. No race that has anything to contribute to the markets of the world is long in any degree ostracized. It is important and right that all privileges of the law be ours, but it is vastly more important that we be prepared for the exercise of these privileges.[20]

Thus the Progressive Era was not one of progress as regards the economic, political, or social plight of blacks. Sunk in the tenancy-mortgage morass of the sharecropper and crop-lien systems and subjected to the lynchings and harassments of Klansmen, the black population began to migrate to urban areas, where they entered textile factories, steel mills, automobile plants, and packing houses. In 1900 there were only 2 million blacks living in cities. The largest single group was in Washington, D.C., and it totaled 86,702. Baltimore, New Orleans, Philadelphia, and New York each had more than 60,000 black residents.[21] Increasingly, the migration was to the North. Net migration of blacks to Northern states amounted to only 426,000 between 1910 and 1920, but it jumped to 713,000 during the next decade.[22]

The beginning of the flight from the South coincided with a period of dramatically increased labor productivity, as mass production techniques and assembly lines were introduced. From 1919 to 1929 manufacturing output increased by 53 percent, while the number of wage earners in manufacturing remained stable.[23] Annual real earnings rose and the length of the workweek fell, so that for those employed it was a prosperous period. But for blacks forced off the farms and trying to gain entry into the labor market, it was a difficult time. Although there were not enough black migrants in the cities for them to have political or economic clout, their numbers were sufficient to foster Northern hostility, both because of their competition with whites for jobs and because of their being used, along with immigrants, as strikebreakers in labor disputes. Discrimination dominated white-black relations, and blacks were successfully excluded from the ranks of both organized and unorganized labor. This pattern of exclusion allayed the fears of Southerners over the possible loss to Northern cities of a captive, cheap labor force for Southern farms and nascent textile industries.

The black population was generally unaffected by reform activities and the social welfare benefits that resulted from them. In an era marked by economic progress and social mobility, this group remained poor and powerless. More social legislation aiding and protecting the working class was passed during the Progressive Era than had been passed in any previous century. For the most part, however, legislation affecting the labor of women and children, workmen's compensation, regulation of hours and wages, and industrial safety all applied to industries in which black participation was minimal. This fact eluded social welfare reformers who tended to view the problems of all minorities as coextensive with the problems of immigrants. Despite periodic race riots, the relatively small number of blacks in the cities of the North (where most agitation for social reform was concentrated) and their segregation from the mainstream of economic, political, and social life made it possible to ignore their special problems.

Coalitions for Reform

The Progressive reform movement took shape as separate attacks upon political, economic, and social conditions. Reforms were demanded to protect against the excesses of big business and political machines. For the middle class, the base of support and the source of leadership for the movement, there was a reaction also to the more radical political and labor activities of the 1890s.

The industrial collapse of 1893 produced hardships for 4 million factory workers made jobless and for small businessmen, farmers, and investors. Many demanded a change in power relationships and the development of a more equitable system of distribution of wealth and income. The march of "General" Jacob Coxey's army of the unemployed on Washington, D.C., in 1894, the increased prevalence of strikes and industrial violence, the growth of union membership (particularly in the Western Federation of Miners and the United Mine Workers), and the strength of the Populist Movement were part of an agrarian/working-class coalition for reform.

In the early years of the twentieth century the reform movement shifted toward the center. The AFL, representing more highly paid craft workers than the older, industrial unions, became the dominant force in the labor movement. Writers and educators undertook an exposé of the "robber barons"; new political leadership took on the task of city and state reforms; social workers worked on behalf of the poor segregated into urban slums. Social protest became the property of intellectuals and professionals.

The economic changes of the early twentieth century involved a shift from an agrarian and commercial economy to an urban and industrial one. Along with that came a change in the style of living and in values—from the individualism of the nineteenth century to a recognition of collective interdependence. The era of small business firms engaged in competition had supported a model of individual achievement, but the emergence of large corporations or trusts engaged in monopolistic market control increasingly made this model appear unlikely. In a competitive, individualistic society the dominant social theorists had argued for social reform based on individual reformation; the corporate universe of the twentieth century seemed to require a reform of institutions. By 1900 laissez faire looked like an inappropriate social doctrine and a new social truth was proclaimed: social justice through legal regulation and protection. Research would provide knowledge of social and political problems; extension of democratic institutions in government would lead to enactment of the appropriate legislation. In retrospect it was a romantic and an optimistic belief in rational, peaceful, and democratic processes.

Characteristic of the reform activity of the Progressive Era was its emphasis upon opportunity for the underdog. Change in social conditions through the provision, improvement, or regulation of government programs and services was meant to facilitate the individual's chance for assimilation into the mainstream of society, as well as to enhance the potential for successful living. For immigrants this constituted an especially important opportunity to become like "us"—that is, like the dominant Anglo-Saxon members of the society. For immigrants and for blacks opportunity was to be the road to independence through the American self-help image. The focus on independence and the image of self-help constituted another, somewhat contradictory facet of this multidimensional reform movement—that is, the desire to return to a pre–big business era in which true competition flowed and success resulted from individual merit.

The reform activities of the Progressive Era were spearheaded by many groups, some working independently, some working cooperatively as particular issues warranted cooperation, some working for individual aggrandizement, and some working altruistically for the larger society. One group was composed of small businessmen who were anxious to control and stop the domination of trusts and banking establishments. They were joined by writers and social workers, as well as by lawyers and clergymen, two professional groups for whom the rise of big business had especially meant a loss of status. Lawyers had lost status by a shift from being independent professionals to employed representatives of *nouveau riche* industrialists; the clergy had lost status by the secular, impersonal thrust of the process of industrialization and the wholesale abandonment of the church by the working class. Farmers, in search of easy credit, also became a part of the struggle against the domination of "organized money."

The Socialist party joined the coalition too. Starting with a membership of less than 5,000 in 1900, it enrolled 118,000 members by 1912, including many of the nation's leading intellectuals—John Dewey, Stuart Chase, Paul Douglas, Jack London, Walter Lippmann, and Alexander Meikeljohn. Eugene Debs, running for president as the Socialist candidate, polled 6 percent of the popular vote in 1912. More important perhaps was the Socialists' success that same year in electing over 1,000 members to various public offices. Socialist doctrines were widely reviewed, discussed, and quoted. Socialists were sometimes allied in specific causes with other reform groups. The growth of the Socialist party and its increased visibility served as a threat and catalyst for more moderate reform groups seeking regulation of industry.[24]

In 1902 President Roosevelt instructed the attorney general to bring suit under the Sherman Antitrust Act against the Northern Securities Company, a consolidation of railways including the Northern Pacific, the Great Northern, and the Chicago, Burlington, and Quincy systems. The Supreme Court sustained the government's appeal and effectively frustrated the plan of E.H. Harriman to bring all the important railways in the country under his control. Regulation of big business was begun in 1906 with the passage of the Hepburn Act, which permitted the Interstate Commerce Commission (ICC) to fix the rates of railroads, of storage, refrigeration, and terminal facilities, and of sleeping car, express, and pipeline companies. In 1910 authority was extended to the ICC to regulate telephone and telegraph companies.

Economic and regulatory reforms took various shapes. As a result of Upton Sinclair's *The Jungle* and of other exposés of the food and pharmaceutical industries, editors of popular journals and the American Medical Association, among others, formed a coalition to secure passage of the Food and Drug Act in 1906. In 1909 the Sixteenth Amendment, which established a federal income tax, was introduced in Congress by Cordell Hull. By 1913 it had been ratified by the required number of states, and the income tax with its potential for redistribution of income was instituted. During this same year, Congress created the Federal Reserve System, bringing about major reforms in banking.

Labor's cause and the frequency with which the lower courts had found against that cause were increasingly arousing sympathy. 1914 saw the enactment of the Clayton Antitrust Act, representing a culmination of the struggle between labor and small business, on the one hand, and big business on the other. Passage of this act, then, was an indication of labor sympathy and strength and of the success of the reform coalition. The Supreme Court had already begun to reverse the antilabor decisions of lower courts. Now, by an act of Congress, a base was laid for further restricting corporate monopolies, while simultaneously exempting labor unions from much of the antitrust legislation. The Clayton Act was supplemented by the Federal Trade Commission Act, establishing a commission whose purpose was to bring to bear the knowledge and advice of a group of economic experts on "unfair" methods of competition and alleged infractions of antitrust laws.

The "democratic" thrust of the Progressive Era made political reform a partner to economic reform. Just as muckraking publications had reported lurid instances of fraud and graft and of monopolistic control in industry, in railroading, and in public utilities,[25] they detailed corruption in state and local governments, in the courts, and in the United States Senate.[26] A veritable avalanche of widely read, eagerly awaited exposés of the "shame of the cities," of "treason in the Senate" led the way to political change. The effort was twofold: to provide for greater citizen participation in political affairs and to increase governmental responsiveness and honesty. The first strengthened the movement for women's suffrage, the secret ballot, direct primaries, direct election of senators, the initiative, referendum, and recall, and municipal home rule. The second led to demands for civil service reform, the short ballot, regulation of campaign expenditures, accountability and leadership on the part of elected officials, and for the commission and city manager plans for municipal government. A few highlights suggest the thrust of the changes.

On the federal level, Congress in 1907 banned political contributions by corporations. In 1913 the Seventeenth Amendment to the Constitution provided for direct election of senators. In 1919 the Nineteenth Amendment, providing for women's suffrage, was passed. It was ratified by the required 36 states just one year later, bringing victory to this cause after almost 75 years of campaigning.

On a state and local level, 20 states introduced the initiative (making it possible for the citizenry to propose legislation) and the referendum (making it possible for voters to pass on measures introduced in legislative bodies). By 1915 direct primary and presidential preference laws were on the books of two-thirds of the states, thus giving a blow to the power of political bosses. The drive for efficiency, economy, and honesty in the administration of local governments began in Galveston, Texas, in 1900, when the entire political machinery of mayor, council, and bureaus was abolished and replaced by a board of commissioners. Thereafter, the commission form of government spread rapidly, especially in smaller cities, where its structure—generally five commissioners elected at large and each responsible for a particular department—was most appropriate. Starting with Dayton, Ohio, in 1914, the city manager type of government—a government run by an appointed expert in city administration—also found widespread acceptance.

In public welfare administration, change resulted in an initial shift of responsibility from local overseers of the poor to local or county departments of welfare. Kansas City, Missouri, established a city department of welfare in 1910, with authority to provide for the relief of the poor and the care of delinquents, the unemployed, and other needy groups. St. Joseph, Missouri, established a county-city department of public welfare and Chicago set up the Cook County Bureau of Public Welfare, both in 1913.

Nor did the country's entry into World War I completely stop local governmental restructuring. Westchester County, New York, established a department of welfare in 1916. In 1917 an important reorganization of the Illinois state government occurred with the passage of the Civil Administrative Code, which provided for the grouping of all state functions and activities into nine departments, each with its own director. Among the nine, was a Department of Welfare with its director of public welfare responsible for administering the state's assistance, services, and institutional programs. The Illinois code was emulated by other states and was the start of a new era in public administration. In many states, for example, public welfare services were consolidated into statewide systems administered by appointed heads of state departments of welfare. Both in the statewide scope of the organizations and in the removal of department

executives "from current political responsibility, except through [the ultimate political responsibility of] the governor,"[27] the trend foreshadowed the
requirements of the Social Security Act of 1935.

No reform activities were more representative of the Progressive Era
than those that occurred in the arena of social welfare. The aura of justice, of
social consciousness, of morality and ethics, most logically reposed here. The
reform movement responded to and fostered the new profession of social
work. Individual social workers through research, persistence, and expertise
moved to the forefront of advocacy for social legislation. Theodore Roosevelt
himself, acting on the commonly held conviction that all were personally
responsible for the current state of affairs depicted so graphically in
muckraking literature, called upon each citizen to contribute to "reform
through social work."[28] Social work, acting on society's will for social change,
carried that projection in two sometimes converging but basically different
operations—the Charity Organization and Settlement House movements.

Those who labored for social reform were primarily concerned, as a
matter of social justice, "to bring the power of the state and national
governments into the economic struggle on the side of women, children, and
other unprotected groups."[29] Whether prompted by the Charity Organization hope to sustain and strengthen individuals in their own efforts to cope,
or by the Settlement House conviction that any intervention short of
intrinsic societal restructuring must be considered only "a down payment
toward justice,"[30] social workers could find common ground for the work
that needed doing.

At the height of the reform movement, between 1905 and the beginning
of World War I, leaders of the Charity Organization and Settlement House
movements came together in behalf of social reform activity. The participation of Charity Organizations in reform was impelled by their changing view
of the family. In 1900 Charles Faulkner's presidential address at the National
Conference of Charities and Corrections had labeled the family "the unit of
social order" and laid out a program of education in the home and in the
school for the moral improvement of individuals. His Darwinian bent took
him from a concern for the maintenance of "the blessings and protection of
society through its family life" to call for avoiding "unrestrained conmingling
of . . . defectives with the people. . . ."[31] By 1908, however, Mary
Richmond was arguing for the protection of family life against the onslaughts
of a hostile environment.[32]

Miss Richmond referred to the family as "the great social unit, the
fundamental social fact." She demanded changes in agency practices, action
in regard to child labor laws, industrial safety regulations, and protection of
working women, as well as administrative changes in industrial operations to
strengthen family life. She challenged the members of her social work
audience to ask themselves: "Have we at least set plans in motion that will
make the children better heads of families than their parents have been?"
Miss Richmond's challenge was based on a new recognition of "the over-

whelming force of heredity *plus* the environment that we inherit." Social workers and their allies strove for legislation to regulate tenement and factory construction; to prevent and compensate for industrial accidents and diseases; to prohibit child labor and provide for compulsory education; to improve sanitary and health conditions; to provide social insurance as security against unemployment, retirement, or death of the breadwinner; and to protect workers—especially women—in regard to minimum wages and working hours.

Improvement in housing conditions had been a concern of social workers at least since 1882, when the Boston Associated Charities appointed a Committee on Dwellings of the Poor. In the same year, the New York and Buffalo Charity Organization Societies combined to get a tenement housing bill through the state legislature. During the next decade, they allied themselves with settlement residents and others to investigate and publicize the housing conditions of the poor. The New York City Tenement House Law was passed in 1901. Aimed at preventing the construction of lightless, airless tenements, the law become a model to follow. Similar legislation was passed for Chicago in 1902; and by 1910 most large cities had inaugurated some housing reform.

Social Reform: Working Conditions

Child labor and women's working hours were matters of gravest concern. In 1900 nearly 2 million children aged 10 to 15 and almost 5 million women over 15 were in a labor force totaling about 29 million.[33] Twenty-eight states had already adopted some legal protections for children. By 1914, as a result of the continued assault by the National Child Labor Committee, the National Consumer's League, the General Federation of Women's Clubs, and others, almost all the states had laws covering hours and conditions of child labor in factories, mills, and workshops and setting minimum ages for leaving school.[34]

But the laws were weak and inadequate. Owen R. Lovejoy, secretary of the National Child Labor Committee and chairman of the Committee on Standards of Living and Labor of the National Conference of Charities and Corrections, reported the following:

> No state has made any adequate plan to protect its children to sixteen years from bare-handed contact with the red hot tools of our industrial competition. Nearly half the states have no effective way of protecting children even to the fourteenth birthday. Several permit their employment at twelve or even younger.[35]

Much of the problem occurred in industries engaged in interstate commerce and, therefore, federal intervention seemed necessary. The first formal attempts to bring child labor under federal control were made in 1906, when bills were introduced in Congress to prohibit the interstate shipment of articles produced in factories or mines employing children. The bills were not passed. A few years later, President Roosevelt directed the secretary of labor to investigate the situation. In 1912, the Children's Bureau was created to report, among other things, on "dangerous occupations, accidents and diseases of children, employment legislation affecting children."[36] The Bureau's investigations bolstered the report of the secretary of labor as to the need for child protections, and further efforts to obtain federal regulation of child welfare followed. The Keating-Owen bill was passed by Congress in 1916, but it was found unconstitutional two years later on the ground that it transcended "the authority delegated to Congress over commerce."[37] Subsequent improvements in child labor legislation remained with the states; and by 1930 all the states and the District of Columbia had taken legal measures to safeguard the employment and working conditions of children. In many instances old provisions had been strengthened.[38]

In the country as a whole, child labor had shown a steady decline, so that by 1930 less than 5 percent of the children between 10 and 15 years of age were employed, compared to 18 percent in 1900. Even in the South, which had lagged in regulatory legislation, the ratio of children employed in its newly developing textile industry was no higher than in its Northern counterpart. These advances were chronicled in the census of 1930. Despite within-industry equivalency, however, there were wide interindustry distinctions, reflecting geographic and racial differences. For example, only 3 percent of children between 10 and 15 were at work in industrial Rhode Island, whereas 24 percent were at work in Mississippi, where child welfare laws were loosely enforced and the cheap farm labor of black children was deemed necessary. Nor did the census takers secure information concerning the paid employment of children under 10.[39] One can only surmise what that meant for black children, especially in those Southern states where legislation provided minimal protection.

Efforts to effect child labor legislation were paralleled by efforts to regulate conditions and hours of female workers, who constituted 20 percent of the labor force. The coalition of groups working to obtain legislation for each was largely the same.

The Consumer's League, under the leadership of its executive, Florence Kelley, was particularly active in regard to legal protections for working women. Under the aegis of the League, Mrs. Kelley and Josephine Goldmark, a social worker, completed research that was successfully used by Louis Brandeis in arguing the constitutionality of Oregon's law limiting working hours for women to ten hours per day. When, in 1908, the Supreme Court upheld the constitutionality of the law, the right of states to protect women from excessive hours of labor was established, and virtually all the states moved to enact laws in this field. By 1912, the year in which the Committee on Standards of Living and Labor of the National Conference of Charities and Corrections made its report, the battle was for such specific protections as the eight-hour day and the six-day workweek. The Committee

"Breaker Boys," Working in Ewen Breaker, Pittstown, Pennsylvania.
Courtesy of The National Archives

predicted: "the day will come—come tripping on the heels of social regulation—when our manufacturers and merchants will be able to distribute . . . [their products] without compelling the sacrifice of the health of our mothers or burning out the eyes of our little children who now bend over their work . . . at all hours of the night."

Success in obtaining protections for women from excessive work hours was achieved in the course of the larger struggle to attain a shorter workday. This particular fight began during the Jacksonian reform era as a ten-hour movement designed to provide leisure time during which workers could "give themselves to moral and mental improvement." In 1840 President Van Buren ordered a ten-hour day for all federal workers. Following this, the movement showed some success in state legislation, but legal loopholes made for very slow progress in attaining the goal on an industrywide basis.

The average work day at the close of the Civil War was still 11 hours,[41] and organized labor began to campaign for an eight-hour day. The eight-hour movement, such as it was, collapsed in 1886, when the violence and aftermath of Chicago's Haymarket Square riot proved disastrous to the Knights of Labor. In 1900, according to an estimate based on information of the Bureau of Labor Statistics, the average standard work week was still over 57 hours, having declined very little during the previous decade.[42] For industry as a whole, there was wide variation, so that unorganized workers, such as those in the blast furnaces of steel mills, normally worked a 12-hour

140

day, 84-hour week, whereas organized workers in the building trades had achieved a 48-hour week, working eight hours a day, six days a week.[43]

After 1900 reduction in working hours might not have occurred without organization on the part of workers, who were panicked by the threat of unemployment posed by technological advance. The eight-hour day was seen, in effect, as "job making," a method of spreading available employment among the greatest number of workers. At the same time, the demand for fewer working hours coincided with higher labor-hour productivity and with increased sales from lowered prices. Differentials in work hours between unionized and nonunionized industries indicate the significance of unionization for reduced work hours. Average weekly hours in 1900 for unionized manufacturing industries were 53, compared to 62 for nonunion manufacturing. By 1920, unionized manufacturing hours had declined to 46 per week and nonunion manufacturing to 54. Unionized manufacturing had achieved the eight-hour day and nonunion manufacturing had made significant gains. The gap between organized and unorganized labor narrowed.[44]

Social Reform: Women, Work, and Suffrage

In 1900 the National American Woman's Suffrage Association, representing the joining of the two earlier rivals in the women's suffrage movement, was still unclear as to directions for achieving votes for women. The Association's flirtation with "educated suffrage," offering to counter the votes of lower-class blacks and immigrants with those of middle-class women, contributed to a separation of white women from black women, middle-class women from lower-class women, nonworking women from working women, and native-born women from immigrant women. There were seemingly irreparable divisions.

In the Progressive Era, racism and nativism, as integral parts of the suffrage movement, began to subside. Josephine Shaw Lowell's statement of 1888, pointing up the discrepancy between middle-class rhetoric and lower-class reality in the matter of working mothers signified a beginning shift in her own stance towards people in need.[45] The National American Woman's Suffrage Association moved away from a position which not only failed of success but which was generally untenable in the climate of the times. In addition, the limiting nature of a single-issue organization became apparent as other women's groups moved to the fore. These new organizations—for example, The National Consumers' League, The National Women's Trade Union League, and the Young Women's Christian Association—were at once concerned with matters affecting women as women and with the potential of the vote for righting wrongs. The National American Woman's Suffrage Association broadened its view. Its publication, *The Woman's Journal*, supported the garment workers' strike of 1909 and 1910 and reported the tragic Triangle Shirt-Waist Company fire of 1911 as demonstrating the need for women's votes to assured "more effective factory legislation and a larger number of [factory] inspectors."[46] This broadening of

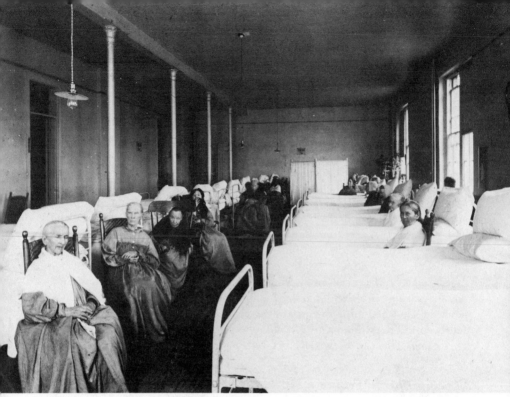

Charity, Kings County Alms House, 1900.
Photograph by Byron, The Byron Collection, Museum of the City of New York

view resulted in increased membership. By 1910, the official numbers in NAWSA had risen to 100,000; in 1917, the membership stood at 2 million.

Part of the reality of the Progressive Era was the increasing participation of women in the labor force. In 1900, there were more than 5 million gainfully employed female workers. Most worked as unskilled factory hands or as domestics; most were foreign born or black; some were married. The number of female workers increased rapidly to meet the demands of this generally prosperous era, later the added demands of a Europe at war, and finally, in 1917, the demands of the United States itself as its own male workers, drafted to wartime service, had to be replaced. By 1910, the number of gainfully employed women had risen to 8 million. With the war over, labor force adjustments resulted from the return of soldiers to the work force and of many women to working solely in the home. Nevertheless, by 1920, the number of gainfully employed women had risen to more than 8½ million.[47] The formation of the National Women's Trade Union League and its activities in supporting existing unions of women wage earners and of assisting in the formation of new women's unions attest to the increase in the numbers of women workers, their beginning entrance in skilled positions, and their increasing political consciousness.

Progress toward the unionization of women was nevertheless slow and fraught with difficulty. Much of the history was characterized by spontaneous work stoppage and strikes against low wages and torturous working conditions. These strikes resulted in efforts to organize; but even when success in gaining demands followed, unionization tended to fall apart. In skilled industry the responsibility for this can be traced to the overall antagonism of male workers, who accused women of scabbing during strike actions on the part of male-dominated unions, of taking men's jobs, and of lowering wage rates. These antagonisms carried over in the half-hearted attempts by the American Federation of Labor, an organization of craft unions made up of skilled workers, to organize women's unions or to admit women into existing organizations. The Federation, like its constituents, was suspicious of women's commitment to work, of their staying power during strikes, and of their effect upon wages. The Federation's lack of interest was encouraged by the fact that by far the largest number of women continued to work in unskilled jobs—in textiles, in garments, shirt, and waist making, in laundries, in domestic service. Among these unskilled workers, foreign-born and black women predominated. Black women particularly suffered exclusion from unionizing efforts, even from the efforts of other unskilled workers.

The task of bringing together the work-related and suffrage-related concerns of women was not easy. Concern for their physical, moral, and emotional well-being welled out of the conviction that "the prime function of woman must ever be the perpetuating of the race . . . . The woman is worth more to society . . . as the mother of healthy children than as the swiftest labeler of cans."[48] The result was a great deal of effort to estimate "a living wage" for women and to clarify the special needs of women in regard to working hours and working conditions. Although similar concerns were being explored in connection with all workers, very special legislative protection was sought for the unique circumstances of women.[49] The culmination of these concerns for women, reflecting the additional burdens they had assumed during World War I, came with the establishment by Congress in 1920 of the Women's Bureau within the Department of Labor.

By the time of the armistice in 1918, women's groups had become accustomed to cooperation. This unity of action comprised a powerful political force. Under the direction of Carrie Chapman Catt, who had been reelected its president in 1915, the National American Woman's Suffrage Association was revitalized and led the final march toward victory. Mrs. Catt was able to gain President Wilson's support. Not the least of that support derived from the contribution of women and of women's organizations to the war efforts. The Nineteenth Amendment to the Constitution was approved by Congress on June 4, 1919. The amendment was ratified by the required number of states on August 26, 1920. The National American Woman's Suffrage Association went out of existence but was revived as the League of Women voters.

The end of World War I also brought success to another women led movement, the drive for prohibition. In fact, the strength of the National Woman's Christian Temperance Union combined with the government's wartime conservation efforts—i.e., the need to limit the use of grain for the production of liquors—to win Congressional approval for prohibition sooner than woman's suffrage. The Eighteenth Amendment to the Constitution prohibiting the manufacture, sale, and import or export of liquor was ratified in 1919. The disastrous results of attempts to enforce its provisions led to its being rescinded in 1933 by the Twenty-First Amendment.

With the passage of the Eighteenth and Nineteenth Amendments to the Constitution the women's movement went into an eclipse, a part of the decline in all reform activity suffered in the aftermath of World War I. The women's movement was not to revive until the 1960s.

Social Reform: Income Security

Social welfare legislation was additionally sought to protect against loss of income from the major hazards of the industrial society—accident, illness, death of the breadwinner, old age and retirement, and unemployment. Industrialization and urbanization required enormous change on the part of the family. Economic survival required mobility, freedom to move from farms to industrial sites where jobs existed. The mobile family was almost by definition a small family. Having moved to the cities the families were then trapped by low wages and a lack of resources, and by a lack of industrial skills. Most family members had to stand ready to work in order to meet the costs of urban living. The family became increasingly dependent for income on factory owners, who themselves felt no responsibility for their workers' welfare, and on non-family members for services previously performed internally—child care for working mothers, for example. The family of the Progressive Era was a unit caught in the stress of a period of social change, a unit socially and economically insecure in its day-to-day living and vulnerable to anxieties about an unknown future.

The changes forced upon the family by industrial society, coupled with the dependence upon others for the means of production and for money payments, led to a sharp decline in the economic independence of the family unit. Thus there was a need for safeguards to alleviate economic insecurity.

Workmen's compensation for injuries resulting from industrial accidents was first discussed at the American Sociological Conference of 1902. During this same year, when the National Conference of Charities and Corrections appointed a committee to investigate the topic, Maryland's Workmen's Compensation Act was declared illegal. The fact that no one could be found to appeal this decision of the lower court did not impede growing national enthusiasm for such a measure. Action was spurred by the realization that "the industries of our country every year claim an army of 15,000 men killed, and some half a million injured."[50] President Roosevelt's enthusiastic support of Senate action eventuated in the Federal Employee's Act of 1906.

In 1904 a Massachusetts commission and in 1907 an Illinois commission each recommended industrial insurance to their respective states. The recommendations went unheeded; nevertheless, agitation continued. Discussion of workmen's compensation occurred again at the annual meetings of the National Conference of Charities and Corrections in 1905 and 1906; and a National Conference on Workmen's Compensation was held in 1909. By 1910, the year of the second National Conference on Workmen's Compensation, a groundswell of support had developed. The American Association for Labor Legislation, the National Civic Federation, the American Federation of Labor, the American Economic Association, and, though reluctantly, the National Association of Manufacturers were all encouraging the enactment of industrial insurance. During 1911, the year regarded "as the beginning of an intelligent grappling with the problem," ten states enacted workmen's compensation laws.[51]

The issue of old age security was raised for discussion in the United States in the decade before World War I. The number of older people in the population had risen, and, at the same time, industrialization increased the likelihood of dependency in old age. The more advanced European industrial nations, France, Germany, and England, had already instituted old age support systems. Both the National Conference of Charities and Corrections and the Progressive party endorsed the principles of social insurance as a response to economic need from unemployment, illness, and old age, in 1912. Case studies documented the inability of individuals to save for their own old age, the inadequacy of private charity, and the inability or unwillingness of industry to provide private pensions. Nonetheless, attempts to provide income in old age either through public or private pensions failed. At the outbreak of World War I only Arizona and Alaska had even limited pension plans and less than 1 percent of American workers were covered by private insurance. The economic status of the elderly declined and their dependence on public welfare rose steadily.

In the years immediately following World War I, reform groups, especially the National Consumers' League, the American Association for Labor Legislation, and the Women's Trade Union League, gave health insurance their first priority, and the impetus toward old age pensions came to a standstill.

The old age pension movement began to gather support once more in the 1920s. But this time the research and leadership of social reformers, economists, and social scientists had a new political base of support. The Fraternal Order of Eagles, a broad-based popular group, began to organize community pension clubs and lobby for state pension bills. Three states— Montana, Nevada, and Pennsylvania—passed voluntary, limited pension bills in 1923. Most other states followed suit in the next few years. The first mandatory system was legislated in California in 1929. In every case the payments were too low and the coverage inadequate, but a major precedent of state responsibility for old age security had been set.[52]

Social Reform: Family Welfare

Legislation to regulate the working conditions of women and children and to insure against loss of income due to industrially caused illness and accident was the first part of a package that might loosely be identified with family welfare. Additional elements of the package were those that dealt with the development of juvenile courts and widows' pensions. The juvenile court movement was an expression of a growing consensus as to the importance of differentiating the needs of children. The first juvenile court law, An Act to Regulate the Treatment and Control of Dependent, Neglected, and Delinquent Children, had been enacted in 1899 by Illinois, where the Illinois State Conference of Charities had taken responsibility for having the act drafted. The law applied to children under 16 years of age and provided for a special juvenile courtroom and record-keeping system and for probation officers "to take charge of any child before and after trial as may be directed by the court."[53] Within ten years similar laws had been passed in 22 states. By 1919 all the states except Connecticut, Maine, and Wyoming had enacted juvenile court laws emphasizing the "principle of separate treatment of juvenile delinquents and. . . cure rather than punishment . . . ."[54] Once again Illinois set the character of juvenile probation services, when several agencies assigned social workers to the court in the hope of making the state's new juvenile court law operate effectively by providing casework services.

As professional services developed, social research became a tool for advancing social legislation. Social work's contribution to social reform during the Progressive Era was in large measure derived from its introduction of systematic social surveys to the study of social problems. This was best illustrated by the Pittsburgh Survey of 1907–1908, directed by Paul Kellogg, a social worker and assistant editor of *Charities and the Commons*, the national journal published under the auspices of the New York Charity Organization Society. An article in the March 1906 issue of *Charities and the Commons*, "Neglected Neighborhoods in the Alleys, Shacks and Tenements of the National Capitol," led to the suggestion by the chief probation officer of the Allegheny County (Pennsylvania) Juvenile Court that a similar investigation be made in the Pittsburgh area. The suggestion was favorably received by the Publications Committee of the Charity Organization Society and an Advisory Committee was formed. Among the members of the committee, in addition to Kellogg, were William H. Matthews, head worker at Kingsley House in Pittsburgh; Robert A. Woods, another leading settlement house worker and former Pittsburgh resident; Florence Kelley, director of the National Consumers League; and John R. Commons, a well-known economist. Funding was secured from a number of sources but primarily from the Russell Sage Foundation, which used the survey as its initial large investment in social research.

The Pittsburgh Survey was "the first major attempt to survey in depth the entire life of a single community,"[55] and for this purpose Kellogg pulled together a study team of workers and students of social welfare and the social sciences. The findings, published serially in *Charities and the Commons* and later in book form, covered "wages, hours, conditions of labor, housing,

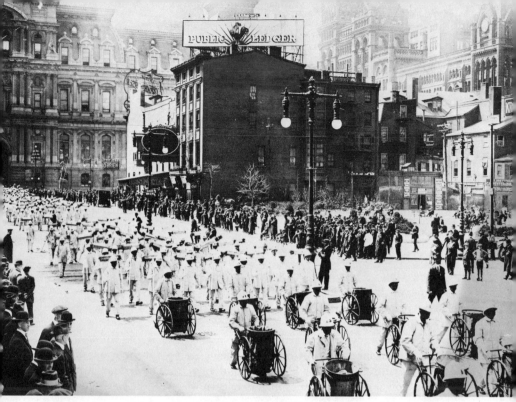

Social reform measures of the Progressive Era places emphasis upon sanitation as an area of environmental change designed to enhance the social well-being of the entire citizenry. Sanitation Parade, Philadelphia, 1911.

Courtesy City of Philadelphia

schooling, health, taxation, fire and police protection, recreation [and] land values."[56] They became widely known not only through their publication in professional literature but also through their being brought to the public's attention in such popular periodicals as *Collier's Weekly*. The result was a factual base for use in social action.

Similarly, social research was a major weapon of the National Child Labor Committee, whose primary interest was child labor legislation. The officers of the National Child Labor Committee included persons who were active on the many fronts of the social reform movement. Edgar Gardner Murphy had seen to the formation of the Committee. Also on the Committee were Jane Addams, founder of Hull House; Florence Kelley; Felix Adler, of Columbia University and longtime crusader for tenement housing reform; Lilliam Wald, founder of the Henry Street Settlement House; and Edward T. Devine and Robert W. DeForest, executive and president, respectively, of the New York Charity Organization Society. An awareness of the value of coalitions for achieving social welfare goals was demonstrated when the Committee set up headquarters in Chicago's United Charities Building, which also sheltered the Association for the Improvement of the Conditions of the Poor, the Charity Organization Society, the Children's Aid Society, and the National Consumer's League.

As early as 1906 the National Child Labor Committee was able to have introduced in Congress a bill for the establishment of a children's bureau. As part of a campaign to have the bill passed, the Committee was successful in influencing President Roosevelt to call the 1909 White House Conference on Child Dependency. The President established the theme of the Conference by extolling the virtues of home life and by urging that children "not be deprived of it except for urgent and compelling reasons."[57] The Conference went on record as favoring home care for children—own home care, as well as foster home care—and recommended the creation of a publicly financed bureau to collect and disseminate information affecting the welfare of children and a national voluntary organization to establish and publicize standards of child care. The first, the Children's Bureau, was created in 1912; the Child Welfare League of America followed in 1921. Equally important was the establishment of the principle of federal interest in child welfare, a principle that has resulted in the reconvening of the Conference at ten-year intervals.

The federal government's interest in the well-being of children was demonstrated again in 1921 with the passage of the Act for the Promotion of the Welfare and Hygiene of Maternity and Infancy, better known as the Sheppard-Towner Act. The Act's major concern was with the health of rural children.

Annual appropriations for five years were made to states designating a state child hygiene or child welfare division to carry responsibility for the local administration of the Act's provisions. The general purpose of the Act was educational, and instruction in maternal and infant care was conducted by nurses and physicians either through itinerant conferences held in homes or at established health centers. Instruction in maternal and infant care was also offered to professionals involved in teaching or caring for mothers and young children. The life of the Sheppard-Towner Act was extended for two years in 1927, with the understanding that the Act would lapse after June 30, 1929. At the time of its expiration, 45 states and Hawaii were cooperating. The decision to continue the work begun was left with the states.

The recommendation of the White House Conference that children not be deprived of home care except for "urgent and compelling reasons" stimulated controversy. On one side were those social workers who supported the Conference's position that private—not public—funds be used to prevent the removal of children from their own homes. On the other were such prominent juvenile court judges as Ben Lindsey and Merritt Pinckney, whose daily practice required the institutionalization of children of poor (though competent) mothers. There was an underlying conflict, too, posed by the question of whether mothers should work at all. Before the enactment of the first mother's pension in 1911, while the possibility of such pensions was still being verbally explored, the question of balance between pension and earnings was major. A speaker at the National Conference of Charities and Corrections in 1910 stated the problem:

The first question to consider, after regular relief on a pension basis has been decided upon, is whether it should be a full pension or whether the widow should be encouraged to earn. At a recent meeting of the Secretaries of the Boston Associated Charities . . . most . . . felt that a day or two of work a week outside was really better for the mother than to keep her always at home, for life can be too dull some times. . . .[58]

The first mother's pension law was passed by Missouri in April 1911. The law had been enacted at the behest of a single county and its provisions were permissive in that it left the decision to provide assistance to the individual counties. The first statewide mandatory law, the Funds to Parents Act, was passed by the General Assembly of the State of Illinois in June 1911. With the sudden adoption of laws providing public funds for the aid of dependent children in their own homes, the development of Mother's Aid as a public movement was a *fait accompli*. Leaving aside such Settlement House leaders as Lillian Wald, social workers were shocked. Mary Richmond's outcry that the Funds to Parents Act had been "drafted and passed without consulting a single social worker"[59] expressed the general view.

After the passage of the act, social workers did rally to help establish the program and to survey its operation. But Mary Richmond, for all her concern with the burdens that society placed on family life, maintained that families pensioned under the system were without the competent supervision of social workers to assure that "the children of the widow are in school, that they are morally protected, that their health is safeguarded, that they have a good chance to grow up right."[60] Frederic Almy, secretary of the Buffalo Charity Organization Society, was more willing to permit experiments in public relief giving. Nevertheless, he viewed private charity as safer. He warned that "to the imagination of the poor the public treasury is inexhaustible and their right, and that they drop upon it without thrift, as they dare not do on private charity."[61] Almy stresssed the importance of professional casework help in investigating the need for relief and for redeeming recipient families. And since such help was not characteristic of public relief giving, he favored having public relief funds administered by voluntary agencies. He objected to relief's being dispensed without professional help, for "like undoctored drugs, untrained relief is poisonous to the poor. . . . Poor charity is worse than none."[62]

The number of states with Mother's Assistance programs increased rapidly. Within two years of the passage of the Illinois Funds to Parents Act, 20 states had provided cash relief programs for widows with children, and within ten years, 40 states had done the same.[63] The Children's Bureau's study of Mother's Assistance, conducted in ten representative localities during the period October 1923 to April 1924, reported that "the principle of home care for dependent children as a public function is generally accepted in this country."[64] The Bureau also reported generally good relationships between voluntary agencies and the public agencies studied and, of most importance, that families were functioning with the help of Mother's Assistance "on a par with . . . self-supporting families."[65] Thus, in the Mother's Assistance or Widow's Pension Movement, a movement basically concerned with help for children, the changing nature of social welfare was demonstrated. A beginning change of relationships between voluntary and public welfare agencies and a beginning recognition of governmental responsibility for family welfare were shown.

The policy intent that mothers were not to be expected to work was clear, but the reality was that the policy was being undermined by inadequate funding of budgets. Emma O. Lundberg, director of the Children's Bureau, and C. C. Carstens, executive of the Child Welfare League of America, made this clear when they addressed the national conference in 1921. Carstens said this:

> The granting of this aid [Mother's Pensions] was intended to meet the needs of the budget. . . . In theory this was a clearly established policy . . . but in practice . . . in many of the states the mother is expected to earn a very large share of the budget and much more than it is best that she should earn in view of her own needs and those of her children.[66]

A Children's Bureau report of a study of the administration of mother's pensions suggests the latent intent of inadequate budgets.

> It was the testimony of the workers in the field and of the executives that the aid did not tend to develop a spirit of dependency but on the contrary developed self-confidence, initiative, and generally a desire for economic independence as at early a date as possible.[67]

The example of someone in the family working was important. To be expected then was the failure of another intent of the various state mother's and widow's pensions—that is, the education of women, particularly immigrant women, for American motherhood:

> The degree to which mothers receiving aid were encouraged to join clubs and classes of an educational character varied greatly. . . . In some communities the grants were too small to permit the mothers to give their time to anything more than housekeeping and gainful employment.[68]

The inability of the Mother's Pension Movement to fulfill its intent because of inherent conflicting values need not detract from its contribution to publicizing the plight of women in the American economic structure. Despite reform efforts, however, it was not until the Great Depression that there were any federal programs to maintain female-headed families. After World War I federal programs were restricted to insuring federal employees against a loss of income due to retirement or disability and to insuring the families of veterans against the loss of the breadwinner's life. Insurance programs operated or required by the states were few, scattered, and inadequate. In the private sector—notably in the railroad industry—pension systems were started and then collapsed.[69] For the most part, then, the responsibility for resolving family economic problems continued to fall on local public welfare departments or on private agencies. The sparcity of the public effort is shown in the data on public welfare expenditures at federal, state, and local levels. In 1913 they totaled only $57 million—1 percent of total government expenditures and only 0.1 percent of the gross national product.[70]

Social Work and the Black Population

Neither the public nor the private sector was responsive to the needs of black families. The overall indifference of white social welfare workers to black problems was demonstrated by the thrust of interests of the Charity Organization and Settlement House Movements, those movements that had taken the lead in social welfare. In 1905, the year in which W. E. B. Du Bois and his followers met at Niagara Falls to consider legal solutions to Negro problems, an entire issue of *Charities and the Commons* was devoted to "The Negroes in the Cities of the North."[71] In 1909 and in 1910 *The Survey* gave the news of the first and second national Negro conferences, at which the National Association for the Advancement of Colored People was organized.[72] In 1913 *The Survey* carried a special collection of articles on the status of negroes.[73]

The primary interest of Charity Organizations, however, was not in blacks, not in their deprivation or segregation as factors requiring broad social reform. Nonetheless, their emphasis on character reform might have helped fuel public discussions of the black's ability to function in a civilized society. In the 1905 examination of blacks in the cities of the North, for example, the famous anthropologist Franz Boas said:

> There is every reason to believe that the Negro when given facility and opportunity will be perfectly able to fill the duties of citizenship as well as his white neighbor. It may be that he will not produce as many great men as the white race and that his average achievement will not quite reach the level of the average achievement of the white race, but there will be endless numbers who will be able to outrun their white competitors, and who will do better than the defectives whom we permit to drag down and to retard the healthy children of our public schools.[74]

Such interest in the plight of blacks as might have developed from direct contact was stifled by the relatively few blacks in the caseloads of Charity Organization Societies. Again, the small number of blacks in the North was partially responsible. In Chicago in 1900, for example, blacks numbered 108,000 in a total population of 1,698,000. They ranked tenth among the city's ethnic groups.[75] The black population did, of course, have major social welfare problems, and in 1910 the National Urban League was established to help with those problems, as well as to promote interracial cooperation.

Settlement house workers were more geared to social change. But they, too, tended to lump the problems of blacks with those of immigrant groups and then to expend their energies on the latter. Among the leaders and allies of the Settlement House Movement, however, were those who recognized the problem as a prohibition of common rights to a particular group of Americans. Louise de Koven Bowen, Sophenisba Breckenridge, and others spoke out in opposition to discrimination and prejudice that held minorities responsible for the economic and social inferiority to which they had been condemned. Florence Kelley and Lillian H. Wald were among those who gathered for the first meeting of the National Committee on the Negro held in New York on May 31, 1909. Jane Addams was among a group of distinguished white reformers who joined Du Bois and the Niagara group in founding the National Association for the Advancement of Colored People. When antiblack discrimination surfaced at the Progressive party's presidential convention of 1912, Miss Addams debated leaving. Her decision to remain suggests again the tenor of the times. The party's nominee, Theodore Roosevelt, eventually lost the election, partly perhaps because his having entertained Booker T. Washington at the White House dashed all hope of gaining votes in the solid South.

The sparcity of governmental programs for blacks and for whites and the overall absence of a sense of responsibility for helping families meet the risks of industrial living demonstrate how little acceptance there was of societal causation of family problems. Indeed, in official circles the nineteenth-century belief still held. Family problems were indicative of the deviant family, the family that was unable and unwilling to make use of its own potential for taking advantage of opportunities offered so abundantly by society. Unquestionably, a great deal had been accomplished as America's attention shifted to the war in Europe. Nevertheless, the amount of reform activity should not obscure the fact that basic inequities remained intact and basic needs unmet.

The End of Reform

The end of World War I did not see a return to reform activity. The years between the close of the war and the depression of the 1930s were a time of peace during which many Americans achieved individual prosperity. They found it through credit and installment buying and through participation in the glittering promises of speculation. They did not concern themselves with the problems of those brushed aside by society's advances or with the obvious abuse of power and influence by those who led the way in speculative activity. Despite the recession of 1921, urban standards of living moved up. Booming profits, high levels of employment, and rising real wages meant that Americans felt able to purchase and enjoy a flood of new products—cars, radios, home electricity, motion pictures, silk stockings. There was new life in the doctrine of laissez faire and a renewed belief that what was good for business was good for the nation. The solution to poverty did not lie in corporate regulation, minimum wages, social insurance, or public welfare, but rather in providing an atmosphere that was encouraging to business.

Americans were determined to believe assurances offered by President Hoover in his inaugural address:

> We in America today are nearer to the final triumph over poverty than ever before in the history of any land. The poorhouse is vanishing among us. We have not yet reached the goal, but given a chance . . . we shall soon with the help of God be in sight of the day when poverty will be banished from this nation.[76]

At the close of the war, it became clear that the era of the reform coalition had come to an end and that a new era of professionalization of social work had begun. The change seems attributable to a number of factors. The war itself had wrought havoc among social work leaders who, prior to the events leading to the country's involvement, had in the main counted themselves pacifists. Jane Addams was a leader in pacifist causes. Her membership on the Platform Committee of the Progressive party in 1912 was an effort to further specific social goals despite her disagreement with the party's stand in regard to war and defense.[77] World War I of necessity split those who could not abandon a lifetime's philosophical stance from those who supported the war and saw this support as serving their country in a time of crisis. The Russian Revolution effected a further split in the reform spirit of social workers; some moved closer to revolutionary positions, some moved further away from an interest in social action. All were subject to the threatening atmosphere created by the investigations and raids of U.S. Attorney General Mitchell Palmer. The wartime and postwar fear of subversive activity, sparking a demand for law and order, led to severe political repression, to expulsion of radical aliens, and, in turn, to hostility toward expressions of need for political change or political redress. Emphasis shifted to personality reform, as psychoanalysis—the work of Sigmund Freud—offered a new professional direction for social workers and social work education.

The push for social reform was further dissipated by the stemming of the flow of immigrants. The increase in immigration during the early years of the twentieth century, with masses of immigrants coming from Eastern Europe at a time of anarchy and revolution there and of labor unrest and wartime preparation here, had stimulated efforts for social reform and socialization. Severe legal restrictions caused the numbers to drop dramatically and almost disappear during the late 1920s. This cessation of immigration and of the needs associated with immigrants now lessened the priority of efforts for social reform.

The prosperity of the 1920s—with its surge of economic growth and affluence accompanied by the hope for the imminent disappearance of poverty—came on top of the seeming achievement of many of the goals of the reform movement and decreased the pressure for further social legislation. In actuality, the reform spirit of the agencies regulating business was often reversed by administrative practices; new political bosses arose to negotiate the ballot reforms, and much of the social legislation passed by the states was thrown out by the courts. The moral fervor, the Social Gospelism, that pervaded the Progressive Movement shifted to the drive against alcoholic beverages. The success of Prohibition became a crowning moral victory.

With social reform abandoned, character reform was revived as an orientation toward people in need. Emil Frankel's *Poor Relief in Pennsylvania*, a statewide survey published in 1925, demonstrated renewed suspicion of public relief and of relief recipients. In a report that generally attacked historic fears of public welfare, Frankel supported the significance of professional social work service, if only to allay the fear that public aid would be considered a right. Frankel wrote:

> Outdoor relief without constructive service can lead only to increasing dependency because while a certain portion of the families receiving relief may pull themselves out of a rut with the aid of the grants, a good many will not. . . .
>
> A good many have the feeling that inasmuch as the poor fund is raised through public taxation they have a right to demand relief and are entitled to it as a matter of course. And a good many families feel that although they may not be in need of relief they can see no reason why they should not get it when other families do.[78]

Public and voluntary orientations toward relief giving—especially toward public relief—seemed to have changed little since the inception of the Charity Organization in 1877. The views and foreboding of Frankel, a public official, were not unlike those of Josephine Shaw Lowell, who had argued in 1890 that public relief should be given only in cases of extreme distress, "when starvation is imminent." The refuge from pauperism, according to Mrs. Lowell, was self-support or help provided by private sources.[79] The similarity in their views is probably not surprising when one considers the 1918 appeal of Francis McLean, director of the American Association for Organizing Charities, that member agencies aid "in the socialization [i.e., professionalization] of both staff and methods of work of . . . public family social work agencies."[80] Not until 1921 was membership in the Association extended to public agencies, and their joining was indicative of a common voluntary/public social welfare viewpoint.

The Social Welfare of Veterans

As in past periods, veterans escaped the overall diminution of social welfare entitlements and benefits. Armed forces participants in World War II numbered 4,744,000.[81] Prior to the outbreak of war in 1914, the chief benefits being received by veterans and their families were pensions, which were being paid at an annual rate of $174 million. The war brought about an enormous expansion of benefits and services, first to attract enlistees, later to compensate veterans and their families for services rendered.

On September 2, 1914, only one month after the declaration of war in Europe, Congress passed the War Risk Insurance Act, insuring enlistees in the merchant marines against the hazards of submarine warfare. In 1917 President Wilson appointed a Council of National Defense to review and make recommendations in regard to veterans' benefits. The Council's report, incorporated shortly after into law, introduced a new concept: the offer of readjustment and rehabilitation services, along with monetary benefits. The new package of benefits and services included:

1. Compulsory allotments and allowances to families of soldiers, paid for by the soldiers themselves and by the government.
2. A system of voluntary insurance against death and total disability.
3. Medical and surgical hospital treatment, as well as prosthetic appliances for those injured in the line of duty.
4. Vocational rehabilitation services for injured veterans who could not resume prewar occupations.

The close of the war, on November 11, 1918, compelled further consideration of veterans' benefits. Not only had an enormous number of Americans served in the armed forces, but a large number—116,000—had died and an even greater number—204,000—had been wounded. By mid-1920 the Public Health Service had increased its total available beds to 11,639 in 52 hospitals. A year later the use of available beds in army and navy hospitals and in National Homes for Disabled Volunteer Soldiers was also authorized. The necessarily rapid expansion of in-hospital services to meet the needs of wounded veterans helped clarify the returning veterans' need for outpatient and nonmedical services. The urgency of the need also pointed up the extent to which veterans' benefits were fragmented by the historical delegation of responsibility for benefits among the Bureau of War Risk Insurance, the Rehabilitation Division of the Federal Board for Vocational Education, the Public Health Service, and the armed services themselves.

Early in 1921 President Harding appointed the Dawes Commission to devise a program for the immediate and future needs of ex-servicemen "to the end that the intention of Congress to give the full measure of justice to ex-servicemen may be adequately, promptly, and generously met." The Commission's report concluded that "no emergency of war itself is greater than is the emergency which confronts the Nation in its duty to care for those disabled in its service and now neglected."

The new Congress, which convened on April 11, 1921, took up consideration of the Commission's report and incorporated most of its recommendations in Public Law No. 47, passed on August 9, 1921. The Commission's most important recommendation, the creation of a single entity to administer veterans' affairs, resulted in the establishment of the Veterans' Bureau. The Bureau brought together most veterans' benefits,* including medical care, insurance payments, and vocational rehabilitation services.

A still further expansion of benefits for veterans occurred in 1924, when Congress made hospital services available for honorably discharged veterans with non-service-connected disabilities. The recommendation for this particular benefit had been submitted jointly by the director of the Veterans' Bureau, the American Legion, the Disabled American Veterans, and the Veterans of Foreign Wars to the House Committee on World War Veterans' Legislation. The enactment of this law highlighted the continuing, enlarging interest that Congress and the American people had in providing special consideration for the needs of veterans. Additionally, the 1924 enactment demonstrated the strength of the constituencies organized to advance and to protect the social welfare rights of this particularly "worthy" group of Americans.

The Professionalization of Social Work

No such constituencies as supported veterans' rights—neither the Charity Organization nor the Settlement House Movement—stood ready to support public relief giving as a major requirement for the maintenance of family welfare. In voluntary social welfare as well as in corporate management the 1920s were years of bureaucratization and professionalization. For Charity Organization Societies and for Settlements, "scientific philanthropy" had led to internal organizational changes paralleling the managerial changes of corporate enterprise. The developing of supervision, of supervisors accountable for the successful operation of professional workers, was a further example of internal adherence to structural authority. Beyond that, Charity Organization Societies were largely responsible for the formation of Councils of Social Agencies accountable for social welfare planning and of Federated Funds that undertook "effective economy" in funding the social welfare establishment.[82]

The definition of "scientific philanthropy" was broadened to encompass developments in helping methodology. The failure of friendly visiting, the hiring of paid agents, and, finally, the emergence of social workers were sequential steps in the search for techniques to deal with the variety of situations uncovered by individualized investigations of families. The body of techniques that were codified in Mary Richmond's *Social Diagnosis*, published in 1917, further explicated in *What Is Social Casework?*, published in 1922, and enriched by the newly discovered psychological theories of Freud, established casework as a major methodology of social work. Casework represented a therapeutic model of professional service. In addition, the development of casework from friendly visiting, at a time when these

*Not including pensions of the pre–World War I veterans.

Charity Organization societies were relinquishing responsibility for social reform, not only reawakened an old image of the rich helping the poor but also strengthened the view of individual and family responsibility for social and economic problems.

The overriding interest of Charity Organizations in relief, their longtime charity organizing purposes, and their slowness in moving toward an explicit family welfare stance are demonstrated in the successive names given the Societies' national association:

  1911: National Association of Societies for Organizing Charity
  1912: American Association of Societies for Organizing Charity
  1917: American Association for Organizing Charity
  1919: American Association for Organizing Family Social Work
  1930: Family Welfare Association of America
  1946: Family Service Association of America

Not until 1919, when the era of professionalization had begun to take hold, did the Association's name include the word "family": American Association for Organizing Family Social Work. Not until 1930, with the adoption of Family Welfare Association of America as its name, did the title suggest an aggressive force for the welfare of families. This slow evolution of purpose from charity organization to social work organization to family welfare can be traced through a relatively cursory perusal of the *Proceedings of the National Conference of Charities and Corrections* (1880¬1929) for the contributions of Charity Organization leaders. Particularly striking in the *Proceedings* is the extreme fragmentation of topics discussed. There is limited concern with the family as a unit or with the interaction between family life and social institutions.

The Settlement Movement shifted to its own brand of professionalism. Social reform activity diminished as an area of functional responsibility and "social group work," a methodological approach to helping through recreational and educational activities, became the core of Settlement House programming. The extent of the shift was indicated by George Bellamy of Cleveland's Hiram House in 1914, when he addressed the National Conference on the use of recreational programs by neighborhood centers to help neighborhood residents maintain community control and strengthen family life. "It is far better," he said, "for the city to throw the responsibility of self-support and self-improvement upon the people themselves than to hire at great expense . . . others to entertain the community. We need a recreation by the people, not, for the people."[83] In 1926 Mary K. Simkhovitch addressed the National Federation of Settlements on Settlement goals for the "next third of a century." She argued that Settlements had "turned the social welfare corner" and were "launched on the larger task of social education" in an effort to democratize and civilize industrial society by popularizing art and developing the creative instinct.[84] A far cry from social reform!

The Evolution of Family Agencies. The picture is of an exhibit of posters showing the evolution of a Charity Organization Society into a Family Service Agency. In 1878, the Society's main functions were "sporadic relief and friendly visiting." In 1902, the emphasis shifted to "activities initiated to meet social needs." By 1934 the focus was on "changing behavior by changing attitudes."
Courtesy of Family Service of Philadelphia

The definitive statement on the professionalization of social work was made by Porter R. Lee in his presidential address at the National Conference in 1929. Lee traced the development of social work as "a movement directed toward the elimination of an entrenched evil" and its culmination as a profession with a professional responsibility for operating "a methodical, organized effort . . . to make enduring the achievement of the cause."

> In the last analysis I am not sure that the greatest service of social work as a cause is contributed through those whose genius it is to light and hand on the torch. I am inclined to think that in the capacity of the social worker, whatever his rank, to administer a routine functional responsibility in the spirit of the servant in a cause is the explanation of the great service of social work.[85]

Amazingly rapid development occurred in social work during the period 1900–1929. The organization and professionalization of social work was carried out by the Charity Organization and Settlement House Movements. Both movements claimed a concern with the family as the core unit of society, and each, to its own lights, developed its program so as to try to bring stability and fulfillment to family living. While the economy appeared to prosper, social work turned to family dynamics and individual personality development. Therapy had become the door to social well-being.

DOCUMENTS
Progress and Reform

The three documents that follow, Florence Kelley's statement on *The Family and the Woman's Wage* (1909), the text of the first *Funds to Parents Act* (1911), and the National Conference of Charities and Corrections discussions of *Public Pensions to Widows* (1912), highlight major conflicts in social welfare during the Progressive Era.

Florence Kelley, both as an individual and in her position as secretary of the National Consumer's League, was in the forefront of social welfare reform activity during the Progressive Era. Her close personal connections with leaders in the Settlement House Movement and the coalitions they formed with other groups on behalf of an array of social welfare measures make her utterances a reflection of the Settlement view. She pictured the family and family members as needing economic and legal protections against industrial and political hindrances that prevented their full democratic participation in society. Mrs. Kelley's special interest was in wages and working hours and their meaning for family welfare. In "The Family and the Woman's Wage" she challenges the depth of the value placed on the home as "the fundamental thing in our national life." Her point is that truly valuing the home and the family would require legislation to regulate the conditions and places of employment of children—in this instance, girls—and the working hours and wages of women. She is convinced of the importance of home life for children and, therefore, of the necessity for making it financially possible for mothers and children to remain in the home. Her outcry against the economic exploitation of women and children is, therefore, not only a demand for higher wages but also a condemnation of conditions that make it necessary for them to work at all. The necessity to work, she believed, distracted the mother from the care of children; and "if one really thought about the family and the home . . . one should have none of that work today."

One result of the kind of agitation for reform encouraged by Mrs. Kelley was the Funds to Parents Act, passed by the state of Illinois in June 1911. The act provided public funds for the care of dependent and neglected children, making it unnecessary to remove them from their own homes when parents were otherwise adequate. The significance of the act resides in its being the first demonstration of public responsibility for supporting the care of children at home. The act is, therefore, the predecessor of the Aid to Dependent Children program included in the Social Security Act in 1935.

159

The discussions of Frederick Almy, Mary Richmond, Homer Folks, and Merritt Pinckney of "public pensions to widows" indicate the controversy resulting from the passage of the Funds to Parents Act. Supporting widows and dependent children in their own homes was still a controversial issue for workers in charities and corrections, despite the recommendation of the first White House Conference on Children. By 1912, however, the discussants of public pensions no longer addressed themselves to this particular question. Their arguments centered on the use of public, rather than private, funds and on the necessity for social work professionals to oversee the use of funds.

Frederick Almy, secretary of the Buffalo Charity Organization, wavers in his opinion. He is not entirely afraid of public funds—"neglect is the great pauperizer, not relief"—but he is afraid of relief that is not professionally dispensed: "untrained relief is poisonous to the poor." Mary Richmond, a most eminent figure in social work, is also fearful of the possible lack of supervision over the use of funds by recipients. For Mary Richmond, the question is twofold. First, there is the issue of money versus service as a key to helping. Second, there is the fear that increases in public funding will dry up sources of private funding—that bad money will drive out good money—and that private agencies might themselves become pauperized through dependence on government grants. Homer Folks, Secretary of New York's State Charities Aid Association, also argues for private funds and private agency control. He concludes, however, ". . . if we do not secure from private sources sufficient funds, then, without hesitation we ought to have a system of public relief for widows." As might be expected, Judge Pinckney, who spearheaded the drive to make public funds available for the care of dependent children, disagrees with opponents of public funding; and speaking from experience now, he insists that his court is "doing something toward administering this law efficiently, intelligently, and honestly, too, and through public channels."

PROCEEDINGS OF THE
NATIONAL CONFERENCE OF CHARITIES
AND CORRECTIONS

1909

THE FAMILY AND THE WOMAN'S WAGE

BY MRS. FLORENCE KELLEY, SECRETARY OF THE NATIONAL
CONSUMER'S LEAGUE

There is no subject concerning which we more persistently live in a fool's paradise than this of woman's wage. We say on all occasions that we consider the home the fundamental thing in our national life. If we really valued the home, such things could not happen as I saw last Thursday in the night court in the city of New York. A girl, seventeen years of age, was taken away by a policeman from her two-year-old, fatherless boy to spend three years in a prison which, with the bitterest irony, we call a house of mercy. No charge has been proved against her. As a little cash girl, at fourteen years, in the enlightened city of New York, she went out from her home and worked under the temptations of a great department store. Before her fifteenth birthday her little fatherless boy was born, because of the conditions under which our laws allowed her to work. Her mother thought that the home needed the little girl's wages more than the little girl needed protection. When she was seventeen years old she had been working nearly a year, every night, in a telephone exchange, and she could bear it no longer. She was so weary that she could not even endure being with her little boy during the day. Finally she left her work, which meant taking six dollars a week out of her mother's family budget. She took her child and went away to look for other work, for her mother refused to keep the child unless the six dollars a week were paid. After a week she confessed herself beaten and sent the little boy back through a neighbor to his grandmother, with word that she believed she would have work in a few days and could take care of him. This mother sent her daughter to prison for three years under no other charge than that, for less than a week, the girl had not been able to maintain herself and her little boy and was therefore "a wayward girl."

That girl, after she comes out of prison, will never make a home for her little boy. Her heart is effectively broken; three years hence it will be effectively hardened. There are thousands of little cash girls working in our stores, and thousands of young girls never before did in the history of the world, because there never were telephone exchanges to be served in the dead of night.

If we valued home life as we hypocritically say that we do, there would not be one of these young girls away from the family home in the dead of night serving the public, not because they serve it better than men would do, but because they are cheaper and because the interest of the stockholders and the bondholders of the corporation is of greater importance than the sacrifice of these young girls. Now every man and woman of us who passively consent, as we do, to be served by telephone exchanges which employ these young victims in the night, everyone of us who is not striving to get legislation, and protesting as only subscribers can protest, is *particeps criminis* with these employers and stockholders. If there be a telephone exchange in this country which is served at night exclusively by men over twenty-one years of age, I beg that its patrons stand up now. I have never been able to hear of one in any city.

Lest anyone should believe that the young girls in New York City are less cherished in this service than those of other cities, I know of a city not far from Buffalo, where, within a month, a factory inspector took out of a leading hotel a girl under sixteen years of age who worked regularly until three o'clock in the morning serving a telephone exchange in that lobby, subject to the insults of passing travelers. But on her sixteenth birthday there will be no legal offense if her cruel father sends her back insisting, like the mother of the telephone girl, upon having six dollars a week.

The telephone exchange commands girls chiefly because there they are paid fifty-two weeks in the year, while the rest of our industries are so ill-organized that very few of them offer steady work throughout the year.

It may be said that I have spoken unjustly of the store where the first little girl was working. It is true that many young girls go as cash girls into stores and advance until they become clerks, and come out unhurt, so far as one can see, from that experience. It is also true that some of our boys came home sound in wind and limb from the Cuban war. Some children do not take scarlet fever, although exposed to it. Some unvaccinated people never take smallpox. But the risk is not greater which the families took who sent their sons to the Cuban war, than the risk these parents take who send their little girls into department stores. The protest cannot be made too strong, to those who believe that they value the home, against sending future mothers and makers of homes out of the schools knowing nothing of that which they should know when they shall have homes of their own, into institutions, commercial and otherwise, which, as Mr. Lee has said, "diseducate" the children and unfit them for life in the home.

It is not only the earnings which the future mothers bring into the homes that are earned at a frightful social price. The widows of working men, cleaning the filthy floors of railway stations, and hotels, and stores, and offices on their knees, after inhaling first the dust from the dry broom—is there any greater exposure to tuberculosis conceivable than that of the weary mother of little children doing such work at night? A friend of mine has conceived the monstrous idea of having a night nursery to which women so employed might send their children. And this idea was seriously described in so modern a publication as Charities and the Commons "before it changed its name" without a word of editorial denunciation. The mothers of young children cannot be sent away from their homes to do such work without the gravest social injury, any more than daughters can be sent away so young and untrained as they are sent in this country today. The proper place for a workingman's widow who has young children is in her home taking care of those children, unless she is a bad woman or a drunkard, or so ill that her proximity is a menace to the health of her children. But assuming that the mother is bad or ill, there is nothing gained by sending the children away for a few hours a day to a nursery. If she is infectious she would infect the children in their close sleeping quarters.

There is no subject concerning which we are more foolish than this of the wages of women in their homes, this idea of establishing institutions to take little children away from good mothers during their working hours, insisting that widowed mothers shall perform the tasks of fathers while some hired person pretends to be mother to their little ones.

There are conditions under which the day nursery is acceptable. For instance, where the mother is temporarily in the hospital for treatment from which her convalescence may be reasonably prompt; or, if there is illness in a home and the mother ought to be relieved temporarily of the care of the children. But when Americans boast of a national, or state, or city society of day nurseries (instead of humbly apologizing that we need more than one in Greater New York) we show how little we value the presence of the mother in her home. The day nursery which encourages the mother to go out to work, leaving the larger children to spend their day on the street and to buy penny lunches, is an argument for school luncheons for the larger children. No money earned in the United States costs so dear, dollar for dollar, as the money earned by the mothers of young children.

When we permit mothers to work in the homes industrially, on a large scale, as is the case in New York, we have the degradation of the home by industry, and the mother distracted from the care of the children through the invasion of the home. If we really thought about the family and the home as we say we do, we should have none of that work today.

• • •

LAWS
of the
STATE OF ILLINOIS
Enacted by the
FORTY-SEVENTH GENERAL ASSEMBLY
at the
REGULAR BIENNIAL SESSION

BEGUN AND HELD AT THE CAPITOL, IN THE CITY OF
SPRINGFIELD, ON THE FOURTH DAY OF JANUARY
A.D. 1911, AND ADJOURNED SINE DIE ON THE
FIRST DAY OF JUNE, A.D. 1911.

Printed by authority of the General Assembly
of the State of Illinois.

Juvenile Courts—Funds to Parents

1. Amends section 7, Act of 1907. 7. As amended, provides for funds to parent or parents.

(Senate Bill No. 403. Approved June 5, 1911.)

AN Act to amend an Act entitled, "An Act relating to children who are now or may hereafter become dependent, neglected or delinquent, to define these terms, and to provide for the treatment, control, maintenance, adoption and guardianship of the person of such children," approved June 4, 1907.

Section 1. Be it enacted by the People of the State of Illinois, represented in the General Assembly: That section 7 of the Act entitled "An Act relating to children who are now or may hereafter become dependent, neglected or delinquent, to define these terms and to provide for the treatment, control, maintenance, adoption and guardianship of the person of such children," approved June 4, 1907, be and the same is hereby amended so as to read as follows:

7. If the court shall find any male child under the age of seventeen years or any female child under the age of eighteen years to be dependent or neglected within the meaning of this Act, the court may allow such child to remain at its own home subject to the friendly visitation of a probation officer, and if the parent, parents, guardian or custodian consent thereto, or if the court shall further find that the parent, parents, guardian or custodian of such child are unfit or improper guardians or are unable or unwilling to care for, protect, train, educate or discipline such child, and that it is for the interest of

such child and the people of this State that such child be taken from the custody of its parents, custodian or guardian, the court may make an order appointing as guardian of the person of such child, some reputable citizen of good moral character and order such guardian to place such child in some suitable family home or other suitable place, which such guardian may provide for such child or the court may enter an order committing such child to some suitable State institution, organized for the care of dependent or neglected children, or to some training school or industrial school or to some association embracing in its objects the purpose of caring for or obtaining homes for neglected or dependent children, which association shall have been accredited as hereinafter provided.

If the parent or parents of such dependent or neglected child are poor and unable to properly care for the said child, but are otherwise proper guardians and it is for the welfare of such child to remain at home, the court may enter an order finding such facts and fixing the amount of money necessary to enable the parent or parents to properly care for such child, and thereupon it shall be the duty of the county board, through its county agent or otherwise, to pay to such parent or parents, at such times as said order may designate the amount so specified for the care of such dependent or neglected child until the further order of the court.

APPROVED June 5, 1911.

• • •

PROCEEDINGS OF THE
NATIONAL CONFERENCE OF CHARITIES
AND CORRECTIONS

1912

PUBLIC PENSIONS TO WIDOWS.
EXPERIENCES AND OBSERVATIONS WHICH LEAD ME TO
OPPOSE SUCH A LAW.

By Frederic Almy, Secretary Buffalo Charity Organization Society.

This paper will not discuss the recent laws giving pensions to widows in Illinois, Missouri, California, Michigan and Oklahoma, or the bills now pending in New York and Ohio, or the State Commission studying this subject in Massachusetts, or the efforts in Colorado, but will discuss general principles. I find I am scheduled to oppose such laws, though for over a year in the SURVEY and elsewhere I am on record as well disposed towards them, though of the opinion that private charity is, for the present, safer.

Widowhood is a most innocent cause of poverty, especially pitiful because of its pain and waste, and very costly to society because the poverty is apt to increase in geometrical progression, two-fold, four-fold, or even more in each generation, as the neglected children mature. Sickness is also usually an innocent cause of poverty, though there are sexual diseases of appetite. The poverty of a family is still greater when the husband is not dead but is a living cost and danger. In such cases, the children have a father's counsel but less food than if they had none.

Neglected childhood is, in all the world, the very most innocent, appealing and frequent cause of poverty and crime. Poverty is often chosen, but the pauper child never chooses his poverty and his curses punish the society which has so foolishly neglected him. The cry of the children has been heard; street children are gone, factory children are going and the institution child must go. Home made children give the best results and even the foster home must go, unless the parents of the child are unfit.

A stupid fear of spending on the part of the Philistines of charity, who do not comprehend it, and a fear of pauperizing on the part of the Pharisees of charity, who have made a creed of it has made us penny wise and pound foolish. Neglect is the great pauperizer, not relief. The devil of pauperizing has been made a bogy of. That devil has his claws cut long ago by organized charity; but organized charity hates to give, and in some cities gives only in secret. When organized charity learns to be generous, without blushing, it will come into its own, and the widowhood of poverty will then get as liberal indemnity as the widowhood of industrial disaster. Such widowhood is just as innocent; and it is just as dangerous to society if not relieved.

I should like to see in every city a survey of all the children who are in institutions and in foster homes, and then a statement of the cost of maintenance of those children among them whose own homes are more fit except for poverty. I have always favored private out-door relief, but it is inadequate, and to-day all over the country, except in a few cities, families of widows are being ruthlessly scattered for lack of charity. Will public out-door relief be more adequate or better? Students of public out-door relief know well how it increases pauperism, but does not neglected childhood increase pauperism even more?

For nearly twenty years I have been a charity organization secretary and a special student and opponent of public outdoor relief. In Charities for 1899, I had elaborate articles on the public and private out-door relief of forty cities. I know the dangers of relief, but last year at Boston I said, with Devine, "Our resources for relief are woefully inadequate. Our use of relief has most sparing and timid. I am inclined to believe that we have caused more pauperism by our failure to provide for the necessities of life, for the education and training of children, and for the care and convalescence of the sick, than we have by excessive relief, even if we include indiscriminate alms." Can we harness public relief as we have harnessed steam and electricity through skillful engineers, so that we can have its power without its danger?

Why am I opposed to this plan of public pensions for widows? My opposition is not academic. I do not care whether the relief is a public or a private function, or whether it is given by the poor master, or by the Juvenile Court as in Chicago, or by children's guardians, or by a board of home assistance as proposed in New York. I think much, very much, of Thomas Mackay's classic argument that to the imagination of the poor the public treasury is inexhaustible and their right, and that they drop upon it without thrift, as they dare not do on private charity, and this argument is one that cannot be met by any excellence of administration; but I remember too that pauperizing by alms is no worse than pauperizing by neglect. Moreover, Mackay's argument applies mainly to indolence and improvidence, which are voluntary. The poverty of widowhood is not usually due to lack of thrift, and what widow ever became a widow because aid was public rather than private?

The crux of my opposition to public pensions to-day is that the public does not stand for fit salaries for relief. I am an advocate of more adequate relief, but I am an advocate first of more adequate brains and work for the poor. Relief without brains is as bad as medicine without doctors. I would much rather see doctors without medicine, or salaries without relief, as is the practice of some of the best of our charity organization societies. Like undoctored drugs, untrained relief is poisonous to the poor. Good charity is expensive, and poor charity is worse than none, yet what city would support adequate case work for its public aid?

In Buffalo where we have had organized charity for thirty-five years and for five years much talk and less practice of adequate relief, public opinion supports adequate salaries for a large staff in the charity organization society. Nevertheless, the city poor office has but five investigators, while we have fourteen, of better ability. Moreover, the city investigators merely investigate, while we make plans, find friends and find money from natural sources. Last month the money found by our paid visitors from relatives, employers and friends nearly equalled the total of their salaries, and if we add the wages for work found by them it would have exceeded their salaries. Of course these visitors gave the poor also a service which is worth ten times more than the money they get for them; but I find that the monthly statement of this money got by them for their poor, does much to justify the salaries in the eyes of the public.

Will the voters stand in any city for the salaries without which charity is a pest and curse? Even in Chicago where a bad law in a good cause is redeemed by a good judge, I do not find any indication of adequate case work. Judge Pinckney has voluntarily associated with himself a salaries case committee, paid for by private charities and not from the public treasury; but the record stories, which I have glanced at in the few days since I undertook this paper, would not pass muster for case work in some cities. They show good diagnosis and study of temperament, but I have not noticed in them search for relatives who can give, or attempts to find work or to find better paid work, or official records of the school attendance of children as a condition of aid, or constructive plans for removing poverty. A pension committee needs all of these things for its action. Even under Judge Pinckney, the Chicago relief looks like mere relief, which keeps the family from deteriorating after the bread-winner has gone. Indemnity relief may have no higher function than to prevent deterioration, but charity relief aims to redeem the family. It is not too much to ask that the tax payers' money should be educational and constructive.

How does the adequacy of Judge Pinckney's relief compare with private charity relief? I have only Buffalo to compare with. Judge Pinckney has pretty nearly carte blanche; his work has been splendidly guarded and intelligent and is the high-water mark of what can be expected to-day of public charity. In eleven months (to June 1, 1912) 316 families had an average of $262.00 each per year. In Buffalo, which is above the average in private relief, 707 widows applied last year, of whom 230 had money aid, averaging $35.00 a year each. This means nothing, however, for the figures include old widows without children, widows who had one month's casual aid, etc., twenty-four widows, who had our aid for twelve consecutive months, averaged $152.00 per annum from us or with city aid included, $180.00 per annum, which is 70 per cent of the Chicago aid. The Buffalo families have earnings, however, and aid from relatives, as the Chicago families must have had also. The only fair comparison would be the budgets rather than the pensions, and these I have not on tap for Buffalo, though I have been given the Chicago figures. The maximum C. O. S. pensions in Buffalo were $301.00 and $307.00 per year. An adequate family budget for the poor is not less than $700.00 a year.

A fact of the very first importance in this connection was stated last year in my Boston paper at this Conference that out of 2,240 families treated in that year by the Buffalo Society only seven were found to be absolutely dependent for as much as even six months with no income at all from earnings, relatives, lodgers, or any source except charity. This shows clearly both the danger of exaggeration and the need of investigation.

Salaries are usually far more adequate with private charity than with public. Money relief is inadequate with either, but bad, very bad, as the relief given by private charity has been in many cities it has not been so bad or so niggardly with individual families as public outdoor relief. We still find doles with either public or private charity, though $2.00 a week orders to widows every one, two, or three weeks (with $2.00 weekly or $104.00 a year as a maximum for the family) is still typical with public charity, but the rare exception with private. The private charity which has not the energy to find adequate relief will not be likely to have the wisdom to use it wisely when found. The valuable pension system of private charity is not half developed as a money raiser. It is my belief that modern organized charity is the most liberal as well as the most tender, personal and effective charity that the world has ever known. Politics exist with either public or private charity, but more with public charity. Fit men are more often found by private charity than by public where the tail of a long ticket is often designated by party managers with little public attention. The valuable co-operation of volunteers through case committees is a splendid part of the Chicago plan and exists with Boston out-door relief but is as exceptional with public charity as it is universal with private charity.

Will public relief check the giving of private relief as suggested in Chalmers "seven fountains" so that nothing will be gained because private givers will leave it all to the public treasury? May elaborate study in Charities, in 1899 seemed to show that just this happened, and that private giving was trifling in cities where public aid was given. Dr. Devine thinks this and said at the last New York State Conference of Charities at Watertown that public out-door relief would require at least a million dollars a year in New York City and that he firmly believed from ample experience in Berlin, Paris, and this country, that with it there would be more neglected poverty and distress than without it. Dr. Devine thinks private relief most inadequate, however, and so do Alexander Johnson, Folks, Hebberd, Tucker, Kingsley and many others who differ as to public pensions.

The question is active in New York State where the report of the congestion commission February 28, 1911, which was reviewed at length in the Survey for March 11, 18, and 25, 1911, was followed by the report to the New York City Conference of Charities and Correction rendered last May after a year's consideration. This report advocated public pensions to widows. Both this report and the New York bill recognize the danger of public administration as inadequate and provide that the public money shall go through private charities. If this is a return to public subsidies to private charities it seems to me indescribably bad, for such subsidies lead to sectarian appeals, to lobbying and to a scrambing at the public trough for patronage.

I have the detail of many of the state bills and laws, but they cannot be described in a paper so short as this must be if there is to be time for discussion.

It is no light thing to reverse a policy of many years in regard to public outdoor relief. It was abolished in New York and Brooklyn thirty years ago, and in many of our chief cities and it was thought to be a dead issue in this Conference. Times change, however, and I am not willing to believe that in this day public outdoor relief cannot be successful. It weighs with me that the equally delicate work of child placing is successfully done by public charity, though the arguments against it would be similar. Over and over private charity has blazed the way for what became public safely after standards had been developed and established, and this process I believe in. The curse of the old name of city out-door relief is something and the new and better associations will make it easier to keep up the new and better standards.

I am myself still opposed to public pensions, though with their aims I am so much in sympathy that I shall welcome experiments, in states not my own which may demonstrate whether they will succeed. Even if in the beginning such public relief does not reach the best standards of private relief I shall be willing to wait before judging if it improves steadily. Universal suffrage does not give immediate good government.

This paper has been prepared under extreme pressure as a basis for discussion. It is not a straddle, but voices the doubts which I have been expressing publicly for some time. I am here to learn.

DISCUSSION

MR. HOMER FOLKS—It seemed to me I could best make my thoughts on this matter clear by asking a few questions in serial order and then answering them as best I could. So far as I deal with facts I have in mind entirely the facts in New York City.

The first question is this: Is it desirable that children of widows of good character and efficiency be kept with their mothers? Is poverty alone a sufficient cause for breaking up families?

I think that all of us here probably without exception would answer this first question in the affirmative. There are those who would answer it in the negative, but they don't come to conferences, and we have to deal with them when we get home. I think we can assume that substantially all those present would agree with the conclusion of the White House Conference in that regard. I, at least, stand without qualification on the answer as stated in those conclusions.

Again, if such families should be kept together, should the relief come preferably from private sources?

I take it that there is difference of opinion. A very considerable, and perhaps an increasing number, probably, would say that they would have no special preference, or even prefer public relief. Personally, I take the other side. Under present circumstances I decidedly prefer the relief of such families from private sources for these three reasons:

First, it is desirable to develop and maintain private relief giving, and that this offers a clear and easy division of the field—the public authorities to maintain the public institutions and the private societies to give the family relief.

Second, the administration of public family relief is perhaps admitted by all to be decidedly difficult. I do not agree with Mr. Almy that the difficulty lies in getting adequate salaries for relief officers. I think it is the rule that public work pays better salaries than private work. Charity may be the one exception, but if it is, I believe we can change that particular exception, and that adequate money for adequate salaries for an adequate number of officers, could be had.

But the more difficult point is the clumsiness of the machinery by which public employes are selected. It is still difficult, to be sure, by any process that we now know of to get competent people at a given time for a given job in the public service.

But the most serious objection of the three is, that I think there is a subtle psychological, but very important difference between the feeling of reliance upon private relief and the feeling of reliance upon public charity claimed as a matter of right. I am not so sure, in the case of widows, that it is not a matter of right. A feeling of reliance upon a steady and regular income wisely adapted to the family needs and the family budget, ought to be a good thing. I am not so sure that it is not a desirable thing in the home of the widow or where the totally disabled wage earner is concerned, but certainly it is a very dangerous thing in other households where there is a wage earner, able-bodied, but disposed to shirk his responsibility.

If it is preferable that relief come from private sources, is sufficient relief now given from private sources to such families? Speaking as to New York: I doubt if any person would have the hardihood to say that such is the case at the present time and for one, I have to state most emphatically, that it is not sufficient, and that families of that character are not kept together and that considerable numbers of children of widows who should be kept at home are committed, and that the process which Judge Pinckney described of the tearing apart of children from their mothers for poverty alone, occurs from time to time in every borough of the City of New York.

Third. If it is desirable that such families should be kept together and if the relief should come preferably from private sources, and if sufficient relief does not come now, is it, after all, a very serious thing to break up such families and send the children to institutions? I doubt whether any person present would answer that question thus put, in the negative, and yet some of our best friends do by their actions, answer it in the negative, because, while this breaking up of families goes on admittedly and openly, they do not actually do anything in a large way to stop it.

It is suggested sometimes that the proper course is to relieve in the best and finest and most constructive and up-to-date method such families as can be aided by existing resources. As to what is to happen to the other families not so aided, no particular reply is made.

What should we think of a city which had a thousand destitute aged persons and which was about to construct a new almshouse, and which proposed plans for an entirely modern building to accommodate two hundred persons, and pointed with pride to its sanitary arrangements, its bath rooms and cottage plan, and spoke of this as a model provision for the aged poor, but refused to answer the question as to what is to happen to the other eight hundred? What would the people of the city think of that sort of a municipal policy? But in my judgment that would be far more defensive, far less serious than to provide adequately for a few families leaving others to the tender resources of nothing.

Now, if it is desirable that these families be kept together, and if the relief should come preferably from private sources, and if it is really a very serious matter, is it possible to find from private sources sufficient relief? Some say yes and some say no, and I say that I do not think any of us know, for the reason that in New York it has never been intelligently tried.

We have possibly between six and seven thousand children of widows in institutions in New York City. Not all of them should be at home. Is it possible to secure from private sources sufficient additional funds to provide for them? I am not sure, and I hope the relief societies will make one more combined serious, final effort to secure such funds. But I think they should distinctly realize that this is the last call for dinner, and if they don't get together and secure such funds they will be provided from some other source in some other way.

Now, just one question more: If it develops that sufficient private resources are not to be had, is the evil of breaking up families as we are now doing, a lesser evil than public relief to widows? A good many say yes. My opinion is distinctly not; and that if we do not secure from private sources sufficient funds, then, without hesitation we ought to have a system of public relief for widows.

HON. MERRITT W. PINCKNEY—I am not convinced, notwithstanding what I have heard, against the "Funds to Parents" law—no, I am not convinced. I have listened with great interest to a very able and intelligent paper read by Mr. Almy. Anybody who knows him, knows of his ability to grasp this subject, must treat what he says with the highest consideration, and I do. If I had known him as well and liked him as well as I do now, before I came to Cleveland, I don't know whether I would have taken the opposite side of any question that he was to discuss. He certainly looks to me as though he was by experience authorized to speak, and I want to thank him personally, too, for the way he treated the subject. He didn't shut the door in our faces and say, "Stay outside." He didn't say to us, "The honest and judicious administration of the law of the Funds to Parents Act is impossible, go away and don't bother me." He left the door open, as I always believe he has left his mind open, for honest, intelligent thought, regardless of what his years of experience have been, and regardless of what his thought was on any particular subject, and I want to thank him for that consideration.

It comes to me now that someone of the speakers said it will cost a million dollars to try this out in the City of New York. I have read with interest the report of the State Board of Charities for the State of New York for the year 1911, and I recognize Mr. Hebberd as the Secretary of that Board. I assume that those gentlemen in their experience and grasp of this subject, and in their study of it, in their service to the State of New York, have made investigation and inquiry and have consulted with the various organizations, private and otherwise, through the State of New York, and therefore, when I read in their report that it is confessedly admitted by the private charities in the City of New York that they have not the adequate means to meet the needs of the dependents in that city, that it stands for something; and when I see in that report that thirty-four thousand five hundred and thirty children were in dependent institutions at the close of the fiscal year ending September 30, 1910, that it must take three hundred and fifty thousand dollars of New York's money to take care of those children for one month and that it must take for the year something over four million of dollars. I say, when these gentlemen, after their investigation, tell us these things and report that many of the children could have been taken care of at home in the normal condition of family life, that it means something, and I say it would pay the City of New York, as an experiment, to keep some of those children at home with their mothers instead of sending them away to institutions, even if it did cost one million dollars.

I want to say to Judge Baker from Boston, when you say that the administration of this relief ought not to be left to the Juvenile Court of Chicago, or to any Juvenile Court, I say, Amen! but I do say it is possible to so frame a law that public officials will be able to administer this relief.

Now, Mr. Persons, I want to say to you that it is probably due to the short time allowed me that I did not explain about these eight hundred and fifty families who were refused relief. I have the figures here on those families and I think there must be three hundred and fifty of them who were, through undisclosed property interests, money or funds of some kind, amply able to take care of themselves. That shows, if it shows anything, that we have a committee that is doing its work of investigation and inquiry well.

So, out of eight hundred and fifty families, three hundred and fifty were able to take care of themselves, and naturally, under the law, we couldn't give them relief. And of the other five hundred there are various reasons set down for refusing them relief. They were turned over to other agencies to be taken care of. Under the law, we say that these families, for reasons set down by the conference group after consultation with the Court, are not entitled to relief, but they are taken care of wherever it is necessary to take care of them.

Now, with reference to supervision, I wish to say to Miss Richmond that she is mistaken when she says that there is no supervision in Chicago. I will admit, ladies and gentlemen, after eleven months, under a law that is too brief, and into which we have had to read certain essentials before we undertook to administer it—I will admit that the law is not complete. I will admit that we are in the beginning of the dawn, but I say we are doing something toward administerinng this law efficiently, intelligently and honestly, too, and through public channels.

Don't let us be satisfied with what is partial, but let us ask for all. Why, we have been working for years now, for what? For compulsory insurance against accident, sickness, old age and invalidity.

Let us nail our colors to the mast and insist on what we have been asking for these many years, the full program; insurance against industrial accident, insurance against sickness, insurance against old age, insurance against invalidity, and compulsory insurance against all these four items in every State of the Union.

MISS M. E. RICHMOND—Mr. Senior has struck the keynote, I think. We must not attempt to meet our present difficulties, serious though they be, in such a bungling way as to put up permanent barriers against their solution. So far from being a forward step, "funds to parents" is a backward one—public funds not to widows only, mark you, but to private families, funds to the families of those who have deserted and are going to desert!

The breaking up of homes through poverty alone is, as I have said, a serious evil, but its prevention demands elements that this Chicago experiment, so carefully watched and safeguarded by some of the best known social workers in the country, conspicuously lacks. Even here, with their hearty good will and earnest co-operation, and with a judge willing to aid them, there has been practically no competent supervision of the pensioned families; there has been, in some cases, less adequate relief than private charity was giving, and far less supervision. If this has been the case in Chicago, what may we expect, at this stage of social service development, from experiments less co-operative and under administrations less able to withstand undue influence?

Another point in my too brief four minutes: This Illinois bill was drafted and passed without consulting a single social worker, and then they had to ask the social workers to come to their rescue in order that the worst might not happen. Watch your Legislatures carefully, when you go back to your several states, and see that the social workers are consulted in time.

Miss Lathrop has said that the private charities have been "pauperized" in Chicago by the new law, and are turning their cases over to the court. There is another aspect of that. No private fund for relief can successfully compete very long with a public fund, whether the latter is adequate or not. Inevitably the sources of private charitable relief dry up. A greater danger threatens in the state of New York, where it is actually proposed publicly to pay private charities for the relief of widows one hundred cents for every fifty that they spend in relief from their own funds—a two for a cent plan that will be an admirable way of hammering down our standards of adequate treatment in such cases. If we spend any of the fifty cents in seeing that the children of the widow are in school, that they are morally protected, that their health is safeguarded, that they have a good chance to grow up right, we are to get less than a dollar for the family; but if we, or our colleagues, spend all of the fifty cents on material relief, we get a dollar. The methods of public pensioning so far proposed are full of such incongruities as I have pointed out.

When a widow is granted relief under the law, the last thing that is said to her in court by myself, is to explain to her the necessity of accounting to a regular probation officer as to how she spends her money. And she is cautioned to keep her receipts, and that probation officer's duty is to visit that family regularly, and report on that family, giving it such supervision as it is possible for him or her to give. I don't say that this is enough, but I say that somewhere along the line, when we have had the experience and we get right down to what is possible to do under public administration, that we can rightly supervise and investigate and control this situation.

Now, I noticed in Mr. Almy's paper, the argument which he read, that to the imagination of the poor the public treasury is inexhaustible, and they drop on it without thrift—that is a forceful statement, that is true, but which is the worse, the pauperizing by alms or by neglect? For my part, I would rather have a pauper with a well-filled stomach than a pauper who is starving to death.

Chapter 6
The Depression
and the New Deal:
1930–1940

The depression of the 1930s was preceded by nearly a decade of economic prosperity accompanied by extravagance and flamboyance. Speculation and fraud in stock investments were widespread and, in the existing Midas-touch atmosphere, even admired. The new emphasis on consumer goods and the ready availability of purchase credit lent a sense of mastery over one's world in the push and pull toward an ever-higher standard of living. The rudeness of the stock market crash of October 24, 1929, the near collapse of the whole credit structure of the American economy, and the spiral of falling sales, rising unemployment, declining income, further production cuts, and more unemployment touched all and shattered the confidence that had recently heralded the approaching "triumph over poverty."

The crisis that descended upon the country had not come without forewarning. In addition to the large-scale bull market speculation and the credit-buying rampage, several other factors indicated the precariousness of the "permanent" prosperity that preceded the crash. A study by the Brookings Institution analyzed the income and savings of families in our richest year, 1929, and found that almost 6 million families, 21 percent of the population, had annual incomes of less than $1,000. These families of necessity spent more than they earned—$2.1 billion more. The next income group, the 5.8 million families with incomes between $1,000 and $1,500, had very slight savings—less than $200 million. Thus 40 percent of the population had no reserves to fall back on when the depression set in. The fact was that 30 percent of American families had incomes under $3,100 and had saved only 2 percent of all that families had saved during 1929. And could it have been any different? The Brookings study had declared that $2,000 in 1929 prices was sufficient to supply a family with only basic necessities. An annual income of $2,500 was a very moderate one. Nevertheless, 60 percent of all families had incomes below $2,000, and 71 percent of all families had incomes below $2,500.[1] Under such circumstances the necessity for and temptation of credit buying seems clear.

Equally clear is the reason for the cessation of purchasing once the unsoundness of the economic situation became evident and the fear of its consequences took hold. The country beat a hasty retreat, with consequent increased unemployment, from "overproduction of capital; overambitious expansion of business concerns; overproduction of commodities . . . the maintenance of an artificial price level for many commodities. . . . "[2] The gross national product dropped yearly from an all-time high of $103.1 billion in 1929 to reach $55.6 billion in 1933. GNP started upward in 1934, reached $90.4 billion in 1937 but fell back to $84.7 billion the following year. Not until 1941 did national income reach precrisis levels.[3]

Other economic indicators followed the same pattern. Unemployment, which had stabilized at about 4 percent of the civilian labor force in the 1920s, averaged 4 million, or about 9 percent during 1930. In 1933, the year that marked the depth of the depression, an average of 13 million persons, 25 percent of the civilian labor force, were unemployed, and many more could find only part-time employment. Despite recovery programs, 14 percent of the American work force was still jobless in 1937; and by 1938 that figure was up again to 19 percent.[4] The crash of 1929 was the start of a 12-year period of deprivation.

In a situation in which earnings for so large a sector of the population were generally near a poverty level and thus made saving impossible, security was necessarily measured in terms of steady employment. Unemployment of a breadwinner was obviously disastrous for a family. The finding of the Relief Census conducted by the Federal Emergency Relief Administration during October 1933 that 3 million families, consisting of more than 12.5 million persons (about 10 percent of the population),were dependent upon unemployment relief suggests the disaster that had befallen the country. Clearly a new view of poverty and of the poor was in order.

Despite earlier economic crises, Americans had remained convinced that the United States was the land of opportunity and that anyone who really wanted to work could find a job. That some people could not manage—that some apparently ablebodied individuals could be classed as permanently poor—had been observed, of course. The Yates report of 1824 was a notable example of an effort to deal with this class of "inferior" people. The concept of the poor as a class of inferiors who needed to be driven or enticed from their unwholesome, lethargic state of being held sway as late as 1924. In that year, a ten-year study (1914—1924) reported by the New York

Association for Improving the Condition of the Poor argued that assistance levels were too low and that raising them might enable recipients to break the "vicious circle of poverty."[5] The depression brought forceably to consciousness the point that one could be poor and unemployed as a result of the malfunctioning of society. The temporary relief programs developed to meet the exigencies of the depression acknowledged the existence of this kind of poverty and of a "new poor." The later permanent programs of the Social Security Act recognized the possibility of inherent societal malfunctioning. Thus for the time being, the "old poor" were caught up in a larger whole and were included in programs originating in the economic crisis.

There was, of course, dissent from the dominant view of poverty as a self-induced condition. Illustrative and factual support for such dissent began to appear in the publications of the Family Welfare Association of America (FWA) and of the National Federation of Settlements. The FWA journal, *The Family*, reported a study of breakdown in family income during 1928. One thousand cases, including 3,996 individuals known to three Boston family relief agencies, were analyzed for factors associated with dependency. Of the total of 1,000 cases, 41 percent showed that "some form of physical incapacity made charitable aid necessary."[6] Although the report, as part of letting the facts speak for themselves, made no comment about 30 percent of the cases in which dependency was associated with unemployment or underemployment, the intention that such dependency be generally disassociated from personal failure was implied by the establishment of a separate statistical category, "Bad Character." Only 7 percent fell into this category. The researcher pointed out that of the total of 164 cases in which dependency was associated with bad character, only 38—1 percent of the total study population—were the result of intemperance. This was in sharp contrast with the results of Amos Warner's classical study, *American Charities*, of 1892, which found intemperance to be the cause of dependency in one-fifth of the cases studied. The principal researcher of the 1928 study hoped that the analysis would contribute to an understanding of "the inevitable economic maladjustments in a society which distributes its wealth to individuals capable of earning it . . . and assumes that the family system of consumption surviving from an earlier economic organization will have its needs supplied."[7]

In 1931 the Unemployment Committee of the National Federation of Settlements published *Case Studies of Unemployment*, an account of 150 cases offering "cross-sections of human experience where unemployment is due to industrial rather than individual causes."[8] The volume was distributed widely and the impact of its illustrations from life contributed not only to the eventual acceptance of federal participation in emergency relief measures but also to the recognition of the need for permanent insurance against the risks of the industrial society. Looking beyond the immediate crisis, the National Federation declared:

Experience has taught us to recognize broken work not merely as a symptom of financial crises, but as a recurring fault of modern production. We are confronted by unemployment, not as a single episode in the history of a household, but as something that may come again and again, impeding and stopping the normal development of the family.[9]

The Hoover Response to Crisis

The years that elapsed between the early recognition by social workers of rising unemployment and the beginning of federal participation in the financing and administration of direct relief highlight the inability and unwillingness of the federal government to recognize the depth of the crisis. During much of 1930 President Hoover engaged in a major campaign of optimistic rhetoric and a minor campaign of public works that failed to stop the precipitous economic descent. This refusal to depart from traditional political and ideological thinking imposed serious restraints on responses considered appropriate to deal with the event. Trapped by the hope of his own prediction of an early return to economic normalcy and by his belief in balanced budgets, laissez faire, and states' rights, Hoover was reluctant to have the federal government assume new responsibilities and powers. This was especially true in matters of social welfare, long considered a province for state and local activity as well as the special domain of private voluntary activity. Not until 1932 did Congress charter the Reconstruction Finance Corporation (RFC) "to provide emergency financing facilities for financial institutions to aid in financing agriculture, commerce and industry, and for other purposes."[10]

During the Hoover administration the Corporation's ability to stimulate economic recovery was stymied by its being restricted largely to making loans to help maintain the stability of financial, industrial, and agricultural institutions. In effect, the RFC became federally mandated aid for businessmen, whereas individuals and families were left to the mercy of inadequate state and local treasuries. Later in 1932 the powers of RFC were extended to permit federal loans to states "for relief and work relief to needy and distressed people and in relieving the hardship resulting from unemployment."[11] But even then the need for direct relief, as indicated by the findings of the National Federation of Settlements' case studies of unemployed families, generally went unheeded:

> Neither savings in cash, nor in homes, furniture, or personal keepsakes, neither charity nor getting into debt to butcher and baker, neither moving to cheaper quarters nor scrimping on food, nor the enforced labor of mothers and children gave adequate assurance of livelihood. . . . All combined, these makeshifts did not offer a reasonable solution of their predicament nor one which we should tolerate as part of our going life.[12]

The platform statements of the Republican and Democratic parties demonstrated the essential conservatism of both parties as they entered the presidential campaign of 1932. Of the two statements, that of the former party unexpectedly gave more explicit recognition to the human suffering occasioned by the widespread economic depression and to the need "to bring encouragement and relief to the thousands of American families that are sorely afflicted."[13] The Democratic platform did not use the word "depression" at all; and although it did mention the "unprecedented economic and social distress of the times,"[14] it did not refer to the human, familial consequences of this distress. Nevertheless, the Democratic platform, with its advocacy of public works and unemployment and old age insurance, did focus directly on changing the situation for people. The Republican platform "true to American traditions and principles of government . . . [confirmed] the relief problem as one of State and local responsibility"[15]—and, furthermore, as primarily a voluntary, rather than public responsibility.

FDR and the New Deal

In his acceptance speech and during the 1932 campaign itself, the Democratic nominee for the presidency, Franklin D. Roosevelt, moved somewhat unevenly toward a more open position as he pledged a New Deal for the American people. On the one hand, he advocated increased spending for the unemployed and more public works; on the other hand, he advocated a 25 percent cut in federal expenditures.[16] Programs became bolder and federal leadership more vigorous throughout Roosevelt's first term. There was widespread fear of permanent economic stagnation and the end of growth and progress, but most people wanted to maintain the established system against the threat of fascist inroads from the political right and communist inroads from the left. Initially, certainly, the New Deal changes and a belief in their effectiveness were welcomed by a people aware that dramatic means might be necessary to save a desperate situation.

The effects of the crisis were visible for all to see. In addition to the inability of the stock market to sustain a rally, banks were closing, industries were failing, and farms were going into bankruptcy. Corporate profits, farm income, and wage earnings all fell, and the need for money brought the meaning of economic standstill literally and painfully into almost every home. Everywhere there was agreement based on experience as to the necessity for more governmental action. By the time that Roosevelt came into office, governmental intervention in social and economic affairs was expected and accepted—particularly on the federal level. As one contemporary commentator noted:

> There is a country-wide dumping of responsibility on the Federal Government. If Mr. Roosevelt goes on collecting mandates, one after another, until their sum is startling, it is because all the other powers—industry, commerce, finance, labor, farmer and householder, state and city—virtually abdicate in his favor. America today literally asks for orders. . . . .

Among all the phenomena on the landscape, viewed from any angle, none is more striking than the reversal of the traditional relation between the country and the capital; for once Washington is the center of activity and the states beyond are passive, waiting for direction. Here is the stage, scene of a performance partly rehearsed, partly prompted by events; the nation is like a vast audience, hanging on to their seats to see what happens.[17]

New Deal policy contained a combination of three different, sometimes contradictory, courses in economic policy. First, there was a basic belief in the efficacy of the market system as a tool of economic "control," if only prices could be started upward. Second, there was the traditional view of the importance of a balanced budget, and, whenever possible, the Roosevelt administration moved to cut expenditures and reduce deficits. Finally, and often in conflict with what was seen as "sound" fiscal policy, there was the Keynesian theory of "effective demand," which saw the key to recovery in increased spending—government programs to increase purchasing power and direct spending for public works to increase employment. The regulated economy and the free market economy, compensatory finance and debt reduction, all played their parts in the New Deal package.

The early responses of the New Deal were, despite the rhetoric of change, very much in the Hoover tradition. Roosevelt's initial emphasis was to try generally to instill confidence and specifically to induce inflation in the expectation that a price rise would increase profits and thus stimulate output. A variety of measures were instituted to this end.

The banking crisis required immediate attention. There were 4,400 bank failures between 1930 and the end of 1932, and by January 1933 panic was widespread. Runs and heavy withdrawals led one state after another to declare "bank holidays." When Roosevelt took office on March 4, 1933, banks were either closed or severely curtailed in 47 states. Within two days, on March 6, FDR had declared a bank holiday, forbidden all gold payments and exports, and instituted new penalties for hoarding gold. Three days later Congress met in special session, the start of the "Congress of the Hundred Days" and passed an emergency Banking Bill. The emergency legislation that supervised the reopening of the banks and the more permanent banking reforms instituted within the next few years demonstrated the determination of the Roosevelt administration to maintain and preserve the American enterprise system. Banking was not nationalized. Instead, the federal government, through the Federal Reserve Banks, the Reconstruction Finance Corporation, and the Treasury Department, was to aid and regulate the banking industry so as to permit the emergence of a strengthened system of private financial institutions. In order to extend the system of control and to offer increased security to investors as well as depositors, there was legislation regulating stock exchanges and the financial operations of holding companies.

In housing, too, the New Deal moved to preserve the concept of private property. Homeowners threatened with foreclosure were helped to refinance their mortgages through the Home Owners Loan Corporation, established in June 1933.* The home construction industry, almost at a standstill in 1933, was revived through the Federal Housing Administration, which insured loans for home repairs and mortgages for new houses.

A major thrust was the attempt to induce inflation through experimental monetary policy measures. There was a retreat from the gold standard, forced devaluation of the dollar, and a program of gold and silver purchases. The hope was that currency manipulation, support and regulation of credit institutions, along with rising prices, would make an increase in business investment possible and profitable, at the same time that the creation of government-financed work and new programs in agriculture and industry stimulated the demand for goods.

Despite the talk and promise of inflation, prices did not rise. In part this was due to the reluctance of the Federal Reserve to expand the money supply and in part to the deflationary impact of fiscal policy. The Economy Act of March 11, 1933 called for a major retrenchment of government spending in an effort to balance the budget. Although Congress restored the cuts and put aside the goal of debt reduction, never during the entire period from 1933 to 1941 was there an understanding and use of fiscal policy as a compensatory device to maintain consumer purchasing power. Budget deficits were kept small, seen as a problem more than an aid; and, in fact, when production started to show real signs of recovery in 1937, government spending was cut and taxes increased. As a result, production, which in 1937 finally reached 1929 levels for the first time since the stock market crash, dropped precipitously in 1938 and unemployment rose again.[18]

The conflicting thrusts of New Deal policies were particularly dramatic in the development of agricultural legislation. For farmers, the horrors of the depression of the 1930s seemed an extension and deepening of a crisis that had descended with the close of World War I and the collapse of domestic and European demand for farm commodities. At first the problem seemed part of the general economic recession that plagued the country during 1920 and 1921; but subsequent improvements, during the twenties, in the overall situation did not bring full recovery to farmers. Thus, whereas the share of agriculture in the national product had been 13 percent in 1919, its share was only 10 percent in 1929.[19] The situation became desperate during the thirties. The ratio of prices for commodities sold by farmers to prices paid for purchases—using 1909–1914 as the base period—fell from 92 percent in 1929 to 58 percent in 1932.[20] Total farm income dropped to $2.5 billion in 1932, less than one-half of total farm income in 1919.[21] Individual farm income dropped from $945 per farm in 1929 to $379 per farm in 1933.[22] Ironically, farm production fell by less than 5 percent, dashing hopes for an increase in prices of farm commodities. Farm debt soared as the value of

*Two hundred fifty thousand families had lost their homes in 1932, and more than a thousand homes were being foreclosed each month early in 1933.

farm property declined precipitously. Farmers organized, demonstrated, and threatened a nationwide strike.

Despite agricultural difficulties, the depression brought about a brief reversal of the long-term trend in which the percentage of the country's population on farms had been dropping. In 1929, 30.6 million persons—25 percent of the total population—lived on farms; by 1933 the farm population had risen to 32.4 million—26 percent of the total population. After 1933 the number of persons living on farms resumed its downward trend.[23] Disenchantment with the realities of farm living had set in, industrial production had started a slow recovery, and, perhaps most important, relief, when needed, was more readily available in the cities. As with farm population, the number of farms rose during the early depression years and then began to fall.

The Roosevelt administration's New Deal package responded to the farmers' plight and unrest with legislation and administrative regulations designed to ease credit and to raise commodity prices through restricting output. In particular, the Agricultural Adjustment Act, approved by Congress on May 10, 1933, authorized the imposition of production controls. Its purpose was to achieve a balance between production and consumption of farm commodities at the index parity level of farm income enjoyed during the 1909–1914 period.

The restriction of output contributed to a decline in the number of farms during the depression years. By 1940 the number of farms stood at 6,097,000, representing a ten-year loss of almost 200,000 farms.[24] Since the number of farms owned or operated by whites remained essentially unchanged, the loss was almost entirely in black farms—down from 15 percent of the total number of farms in 1930 to 12 percent in 1940.[25] This suggests the kind of dislocation to which blacks were subjected, especially in the early years of the depression, as circumstances forced farm owners into bankruptcy and to foreclosure.

As the depression progressed, the percentage of fully owned farms increased despite the decrease in the number of farms extant. This was true for black-owned as well as white-owned farms. The percentage of fully owned farms rose from 46 in 1930 to 51 in 1940; the percentage of black farms that were fully owned rose from 17 to 23 in the same period.[26] Farm ownership was accompanied by a steady increase in farm size—from an average of 150.7 acres in 1930 to an average of 167.1 acres in 1940.[27] Growth in farm ownership and in the average size of farms was stimulated directly and indirectly by New Deal policies.

Following his inauguration, President Roosevelt consolidated all federal agricultural credit agencies into the Farm Credit Administration. Congress authorized loans to save farmers from the immediate danger of foreclosures, to underwrite production costs, and to regain lost property on easy credit terms. The result of this package of New Deal farm legislation, including the Agricultural Adjustment Act (AAA), was to raise net farm income from $2.5

Sharecropper Families Evicted from the Dibble Plantation near Parkin, Arkansas, January 1936. These evictions followed charges that the sharecroppers, by membership in the Southern Tenant Farmers' Union, were engaging in a conspiracy to retain their homes. This contention was granted by the court. The evictions, though at the point of a gun, were considered legal. The picture was taken just after the eviction near Parkin, Cross County, Arkansas, before the sharecroppers were moved into a tent colony.

Photograph by J. Vachon, reproduced from the collection of the Library of Congress.

billion in 1932 to more than $5.9 billion in 1935.[28] Additionally, the $9.6 billion farm mortgage debt load of 1930 was reduced to $7.6 billion in 1935 and to $6.6 billion in 1940.[29]

The success of early New Deal legislation, designed to help farmers through easy credit, supported not only farm ownership but also the introduction of farm machinery, which, in turn, encouraged the development of larger farms. The Farm Security Administration had authority to lend money to make it possible, among other things, for farmers to become landowners and to refinance and rehabilitate their lands. The withdrawal of submarginal land was encouraged.

In its early years, New Deal legislation spelled disaster for the most marginal group of farmers—tenants. In general, government support was for large farmers, with little assistance going to the small farmer. Not until 1935 was a tenant clause added to the AAA requiring farmers to keep the same number of tenants they had when they joined the program. Thus, between 1930 and 1940, while the number of full-farm owners increased by 172,000, the number of tenants decreased by 303,000. All of the decrease was accounted for by changes occurring in the South where the number of white

183

tenant farmers dropped by 149,289 and the number of black tenants by 192,291. Blacks accounted for 56 percent of the total decrease in the number of tenant farmers. In terms of total numbers of tenant farmers, the loss represented a 28 percent decrease in the total number of black tenant farmers and a 14 percent decrease in the total number of white tenant farmers.[30] As the most marginal part of the farm population, tenant farmers and sharecroppers bore the heaviest burden of the agricultural depression. Homeless, they joined the other jobless and dispossessed who wandered the country.

In industry, as in agriculture, recovery was to be achieved through regulation of prices and output, and large firms tended to dominate policy. The major legislation aimed at bringing about a manufacturing revival was the National Industrial Recovery Act (NIRA) presented to Congress on May 15, 1933. The NIRA was designed to meet a combination of labor's demand for limited hours of work in order to spread employment, of business's demand for the relaxation of antitrust laws in order to stabilize output and raise prices, and of the generally accepted need for a public works program to provide immediate employment.

Title I of the NIRA provided for the establishment of a set of industry codes that would end "cutthroat" competition, raise prices, limit output, and provide for workers a reasonable work week at a reasonable wage. Each industry was, in theory, to be regulated by a tripartite committee representing management, labor, and the public. FDR signed the bill on June 16, 1933. Its appeal was immediate. An interim, blanket code was established with the Blue Eagle, as posted by business, as its symbol of acceptance. Within a few weeks, almost 2.5 million employers, with 16 million workers, had signed codes. By September, within three months of the inception of the codes, the ten largest industries were brought under the National Recovery Administration (NRA). All the codes contained minimum wage and maximum hour scales; all contained provisions for collective bargaining. In practice, however, the industry codes reflected the price and output policies of the dominant firms in each industry, and competition restraint operated to the serious disadvantage of small businessmen. When the NRA was declared unconstitutional by the Supreme Court in May 1935, it was already under severe attack.

How successful was this organization of industry for recovery? During its two years of operation, employment rose by 2 million, industrial production rose from 62 percent to 79 percent of the 1929 level of output, and gross national product increased from $55.6 billion to $72.2 billion.[31] But 20 percent of the labor force was still unemployed, industrial output was 21 percentage points less than before the crash, and GNP was still far below the level of prosperity. Paralleling the irony of the AAA's curtailment of food production and destruction of livestock when people were starving, the NRA limited competition and output when what was needed for prosperity was an expansion of industry.

Title II of the NIRA provided for a Public Works Administration (PWA) and allocated $3.3 billion for this program. Had this money been used speedily to increase employment and purchasing power, it might have been an extremely helpful stimulant. PWA was intended, however, for capital investment and pump priming. Under the cautious direction of Harold Ickes, its immediate expansionary potential was never exercised.

Labor and Social Welfare

Perhaps the most significant and long-lasting result of the experiment in industrial control was its impact on organized labor and the precedent for social legislation it established. As the United States entered the decade of the 1930s and economic depression, labor was largely unorganized. Union gains made during World War I under the protections of a government anxious to avoid labor unrest during wartime were lost in a postwar situation of generally steady employment, increasing real wages, and political repression. Furthermore, the AFL, representing skilled labor, tended to cooperate with management in a "welfare capitalism" effort. Ignored by that effort was the great mass of workers, generally unskilled, in the basic industries. Trade union membership declined from 5 million in 1920 to 3.4 million in 1930; membership in the AFL declined from 4.1 million in 1920 to 3 million in 1930.[32] The violent and largely unsuccessful strikes led by the United Mine Workers in 1921 and 1922 and by the United Textile Workers in 1929 contributed further to weakness and helplessness on the part of organized labor as the depression settled in.

The fortunes of labor began to turn in 1932 with the passage of the Norris-LaGuardia Act, which restricted the right of the federal courts to issue injunctions against unions engaged in peaceful strikes and to enforce "yellow dog" contracts. In 1933 the newly formulated codes of the NRA reaffirmed the right of collective bargaining in covered industries, established the 44-hour week, outlawed child labor, and set minimum wages ranging from 30 to 40 cents an hour. The underlying motive was to maintain wages at the same time that the elimination of child labor and the reduction in working hours spread jobs among a larger number of adult workers. Concurrently, there was a stimulus for workers to organize and for unions to recruit membership. By 1935 union membership had grown to 3.7 million.[33]

Labor's success was not easily attained. Its efforts to organize and to force concessions were matched by management's determination to prevent unionization and to preserve the open shop. In August 1933 President Roosevelt established the National Labor Board to mediate labor disputes. When it failed for lack of authority to enforce decisions, it was replaced by the National Labor Relations Board. The new Board, authorized to hold elections to determine the right of unions to conduct collective bargaining, but lacking authority to prevent unfair management practices, was equally unsuccessful in preventing and settling labor disputes. By May 1935, when the NRA was declared unconstitutional, business had generally revolted against the labor provisions of the codes; labor believed itself betrayed.

The National Labor Relations Act—the famous Wagner Act—was signed into law on July 5, 1935. The new law contained all that had been foreshadowed in the Norris-LaGuardia and National Industrial Recovery acts. In addition, it outlawed company-dominated unions and gave the new National Labor Relations Board authority to supervise elections and determine the appropriate bargaining unit, to hear complaints of unfair labor practices, and, when necessary, to petition the courts for enforcement of its orders. The legal authorization of collective bargaining led to the unionization of large numbers of unskilled workers in basic industries. By 1937 the new industrial unions, organized into the Congress of Industrial Organizations (CIO), had achieved major victories in the automobile and steel industries, initially, and most significantly, with United States Steel and General Motors.

A report of the La Follette Civil Liberties Committee, the first part of which was made public in December 1937, strengthened the hand of the National Labor Relations Board and ultimately assured the passage of the Fair Labor Standards Act of June 1938. The report publicized in detail industry's disregard for labor's legal rights. Not the least of its revelations was the fact that a selected list of companies had spent a total of $9.4 million for labor spies, strikebreakers, and munitions between 1933 and 1936.[34] The disclosures were important in moving management toward collective bargaining. As the decade of the thirties ended, organized labor could boast a total membership of 10.6 million. Of the total, 5 million workers belonged to the CIO and 4.6 million belonged to the AFL.[35]

The Fair Labor Standards Act legislatively retrieved those provisions of the NRA that had dealt with work hours, minimum wages, and child labor. The act established a minimum wage of 25 cents an hour (rising to 40 cents an hour in seven years), a 44-hour week to be reduced to 40 hours in three years, and 16 years as the age below which a child could not work in industries whose products entered interstate commerce.[36] The Act's provisions were, for the most part, already a reality for much of organized labor, so that largely affected were nonunionized, unprotected workers—women, minors, and minority group members, the rank and file of the unskilled. As a result, the hourly pay of 300,000 workers was immediately raised and the work week was shortened for 2,382,000 people.[37]

The triumph of the CIO in its beginning efforts to organize the mass industries was enormously significant for unskilled workers. Such workers were frequently members of minority groups, women, and children; and their status was easily exploited in times of labor strife or economic recession. In the strikes of 1921 and 1922, unorganized blacks had been extensively used as strikebreakers. Blacks were often the first to feel the crush of the incipient depression of the 1930s as social discrimination played its role in decisions to release workers. An Urban League survey of 106 cities disclosed that 20 to 30 percent of the black population was unemployed in 1931.[38] As the economic situation worsened, many industries replaced men with women at cheaper rates; and many replaced men and women with children. In other situations, "desperate heads of families took women's jobs at women's wages, Negro jobs at Negro wages, leaving the minority groups without means of support."[39]

The size of the labor force increased between 1930 and 1940. This was true for both male and female workers.[40] As with blacks, the severity of the unemployment situation aggravated long-established patterns of prejudice and discrimination against women. The notion of women's "proper place" was enhanced by the urgency of "Get the Men Back to Work." The country as a whole was convinced that employment for men was the priority, and this was the view of many social workers and social scientists as well as the official position of unions and government. Congresswoman Florence Kahn said: "Woman's place is not out in the business world competing with men who have families to support."[41] In 1932, Congress established a "married persons' clause" for all federal and service employees, whereby the first employees to be considered redundant when reductions in personnel were necessary were those whose spouses were also federal employees.[42] For the most part, this meant that women were dismissed.

Actually, the Get-the-Men-Back-to-Work slogan was aimed at all women; and single, as compared to married, women seem to have suffered even greater discrimination. Whether out of family necessity or the leniency of employers, the percentage of married female workers rose. In 1920, married women comprised 23 percent of female workers; by 1930, one of the earlier years of the depression, the percentage had risen to 28.9; and in 1940, married women represented 36.7 percent of women in the labor force.[43] Married or single, the fact was that employers found in women a pool of workers suitable for employment at low levels of wages.

Veterans and the Bonus

The depression years were years of distress for veterans as for others, but the difference was that their visibility as veterans and as a strongly organized constituency meant a continuing ability to elicit special consideration. Almost immediately after World War I, veterans began pushing for a bonus that would provide an economic redress to balance the wartime earnings of workers in industry. A bill making such provisions in the form of "adjustment compensation certificates" was passed over President Coolidge's veto in 1924. Payments were to come due in 1945. By 1930, with unemployment mounting, demands for immediate payment began to be made. The demand culminated in June 1932 in the "bonus march" on Washington, D.C., of some 15,000 to 20,000 veterans, many accompanied by their families. The march ended a month later when, on the order of President Hoover, army

Bonus Army, 1932. Shacks, put up by the Bonus Army on the Anacostia flats, burning after the battle with the military. The Capitol is in the background.

troops were dispatched to clear the veterans out of their Washington campsites. Despite Hoover's objections, however, and over his veto, Congress passed a bill allowing veterans to obtain, in cash, half the value of the certificates.

Smaller bonus marches were attempted in 1933 and 1934, but with little immediate success. Payment of the bonus was made in 1937, the year that saw a disastrous reversal of the long climb out of the depression. The bonus succeeded in putting almost $3.5 billion into the hands of veterans and, eventually, into the nation's economy.

The bonus marches of 1933 and 1934 were triggered by the Economy Act of March 1933, the same act that had cut congressional salaries and reduced federal expenditures. The act also cut veterans' benefits—the slate of benefits, the amount of benefits, and the number of eligible recipients. Especially hard hit were thousands of veterans who needed care for non-service-connected conditions and who were caught in a double-jeopardy situation because of the depression. The resulting outcry was such that in 1934 Congress passed new legislation, in effect rescinding the Economy Act. The liberality of newly enacted monetary, medical, and hospital benefits brought about a presidential veto, which also was overridden. In connection with the provisions for money payments, the new legislation stressed the word "compensation" to define the uniqueness of such payments to veterans.

Veterans were given special attention in the matter of job opportunities, too. From the bonus armies of 1933 and 1934, more than 10,000 veterans—transients stranded in Washington—were enrolled in the Civilian Conservation Corps (CCC) and assigned to work camps. Additional camps were established by the Federal Emergency Relief Administration (FERA) for veterans whose physical condition made them ineligible for CCC camps. Still other veterans were assigned to Works Progress Administration (WPA) projects. In all, some 17,000 veterans were certified by the Veterans Administration for CCC, FERA, or WPA employment between 1933 and 1935.[44] The bonus payment of 1937 was, of course, of much greater significance because of the number of individuals reached and the dollar amount of benefits received. The bonus concept, joined to the benefit structure of the veterans' legislation of 1934, set a pattern that would influence veterans' legislation during and after World War II.

Public Money for Relief

One of the most urgent and immediate problems of Roosevelt's first year in office was certainly the problem of relief; and in response he proposed three types of remedial legislation: (1) grants to states for direct relief, (2) public works programs to stimulate investment, and (3) immediate public employment programs.

A most commonly held belief had been that anyone who really wanted to work could find a job. This particular myth had been shattered by every household's firsthand experience, by newly developed systems of statistical fact-finding in regard to unemployment, and by social agency revelations of the causes and effects of dependency. More difficult to dispel were the myths that the chief burden of relief was being carried by privately supported agencies and that, in any case, relief was a local responsibility. The development of a powerful, voluntary family welfare movement and the existence of local public welfare departments that were "stereotyped, inarticulate, politics-ridden, and generally of lower standards"[45] had obscured the shift to public relief that had already occurred in 1929.

The larger part of relief was being paid with public funds, although it was generally administered by voluntary family agencies directly or by family agency workers on loan to public agencies. This realization stimulated a reconsideration of alignments between voluntary family and public welfare agencies. In effect, the depression had created a functional crisis for family agencies. These agencies had historically opposed the giving of public relief and the development of public welfare agencies, arguing that they themselves were best equipped to handle relief problems. Now, with the coming of the depression, they could not meet the financial demands no matter how much they wanted to help. Furthermore, mushrooming caseloads of "new poor" families whose only need was money distracted attention from families requiring professional casework services. Necessity was forcing the separation of professional service from the provision of financial help.

Noting that the four large family agencies of Manhattan had had, during

Soup Kitchen, 1931. Unemployed men queued outside a depression soup kitchen opened in Chicago by Al Capone, who is standing at the left. The storefront sign reads "Free Soup, Coffee & Doughnuts for the Unemployed."
Photograph by U.S. Information Agency, in the National Archives

November 1930, 5,739 applications for "material need" and only 669 other types of applications, so prominent a social worker as Gordon Hamilton admitted that voluntary agencies had "attempted to carry. . . many types of problems which should be carried under public auspices."[46] She suggested the appropriateness of a public family agency geared primarily to offering financial help but also offering casework help when requested by the family. In such a realignment of public-private welfare relationships, "the contribution of private social work to welfare administration is chiefly through urging a professional rather than political considerations in the selection of personnel, the idea of budgeted rather than fixed relief, and the attempt to offer trained casework service to those who desired it. "[47]

Hamilton's presentation of the situation in New York was borne out by information derived from 51 agencies reporting to the Russell Sage Foundation for the period between March 1929 and March 1931. As might be expected, all the agencies had been confronted with the necessity of dealing with enormously increased numbers of families. They had met the emergency by classifying the unemployment cases as a separate and distinct group, by using volunteers and "junior" workers for routine duties, and by protecting the intensive treatment of "regular run" cases from being swamped.[48] Overall, the 51 reporting agencies had emphasized "the urgent need for giving individualized treatments so far as possible, and . . . stood out against such mass methods of treatment as bread lines and soup kitchens, with the result that these primitive, inadequate, and demoralizing devices for giving large scale relief . . . [had] been used but very little"[49] with families.

A compilation of the Department of Statistics of the Russell Sage Foundation of relief expenditures of 81 American cities showed that 74 percent of such expenditures ($31 million) had come from public funds during 1929. Expenditures in 1930 for relief were about double those of 1929. Seventy-five percent of relief expenditures ($51 million) had come from public funds. An emergency appeal for private funds reduced the share of public relief expenditures to 66 percent during 1931, but public relief expenditures had, nevertheless, increased to $54 million.[50] Obviously, voluntary giving could not meet the demand.

By 1931 it was clear too that local units of government could not keep pace with the need for public funding. Municipal welfare payments, where they existed, were painfully small. As the depression deepened, the need for relief increased, and it became less and less possible for cities to meet that need.

New York—with its Temporary Relief Administration set up in 1931— was the first state to appropriate funds to be disbursed to cities and counties for home relief and work relief programs. Other states followed suit, so that by the close of 1931, New Jersey, Rhode Island, Illinois, Wisconsin, Ohio, and Pennsylvania had joined New York in making relief funds available to localities. Efforts to obtain federal participation in relief funding also occurred during 1931 but were defeated by presidential veto. Be that as it may, New York, in setting up its Temporary Relief Administration to administer that state's relief appropriations, provided the prototype for the federal program to come.

Federal Emergency Relief Administration

On May 12, 1933, acting on the overwhelming need of states for money for relief, Congress established the Federal Emergency Relief Administration to channel a half billion dollars in relief money through state and local welfare agencies. That same month the Public Works Administration was established as a stimulant to business investment. In November 1933, recognizing the urgent need for jobs, and interpreting flexibly the provisions of the National Industrial Recovery Act, President Roosevelt established the Civil Works Administration (CWA) and made $400 million of PWA money available to

View of Squatter Shacks Under the D Street Bridge, Marysville, Yuba County, California, February 1940.

Photograph by Dorothea Lange Taylor, in the National Archives

finance programs of "civil works." Both the Federal Emergency Relief Administration and the Civil Works Administration came under the direction of Harry Hopkins. When CWA proved too expensive a means of job creation, the Emergency Work Relief Program was established within FERA. Subsequent "temporary" measures to deal directly with unemployment and the needs of the unemployed led to the creation of the Federal Surplus Commodities Corporation, the Civilian Conservation Corps, and finally, when direct federal relief was phased out, to the Works Progress Administration. From the beginning of the New Deal a threefold approach to income maintenance was envisioned: cash relief, short-term work relief, and the expansion of employment through the pump-priming effects of public works.

The major direct relief effort of the federal government was the FERA. It was established "To provide for cooperation by the Federal government with the several States and Territories and the District of Columbia in relieving the hardship and suffering caused by unemployment and for other purposes." Half of the appropriation was to be made available to the states on a matching basis—$1 of federal money for every $3 of state and local expenditures; the other $250 million was to be distributed to the states on the basis of need without matching funds.[51] In authorizing direct grants to states for relief, the legislation set a major precedent for a new fiscal relationship between the federal government and the states and for a new interpretation of the responsibility of the federal government for social welfare.

Of more immediate importance, however, was the speedy flow of cash to the needy. Grants for seven states were approved one day after Harry Hopkins took office in May 1933; and by the end of the next month, $51 million had been paid out to 45 states, the District of Columbia, and the Territory of Hawaii. During the last half of 1933, about 3.5 million people were supported; and by the end of December 1933, $324.5 million had been distributed—with all states and territories participating. In the three years of its existence, FERA spent over $3 billion. Despite some tendency of state and local governments to substitute federal money for local effort, the states too increased their relief expenditures during this period. In all, something over $4 billion was distributed in cash and work relief by federal and state governments.[52]

There were problems, of course. The money was not always distributed fairly. A disproportionate amount seems to have gone to rural areas. Racial discrimination in the administration of funds was a major problem, particularly in Southern rural areas where the black population found it difficult to get on relief rolls. Blacks were more apt to receive relief in Northern cities. Overall they suffered much higher rates of unemployment and poverty and this was reflected in the relief rolls. In 1933 nearly 18 percent of all black family heads were certified for relief and about 15 percent in 1935—about twice the rate for white breadwinners.[53] For all, black and white, grants were pitifully low throughout the period.

In part, the shortfalls of the relief effort reflect the speed with which the federal government tried to establish a federal-state public welfare program. The need was widespread and immediate, and the administrators of FERA tried to provide cash to meet that need as quickly as possible. The difficulties arose, too, from a conflict between ideology and necessity. The philosophy of the New Deal was relief for the unemployed through the provision of jobs. Direct relief was to be a temporary, necessary expedient until those who were employable could be employed. For the moment, in the emergency, "employables" and "unemployables" were brought together in one program; but direct relief for the ablebodied was only a stopgap measure.

Harry Hopkins, the president's mentor on welfare matters, had indicated as much in his clarification of the purpose of the Federal Emergency Relief Act. Addressing the National Conference of Social Workers, Hopkins had said:

> The intent of this act is that relief should be given to the heads of families who are out of work and whose dependency arises from the fact that they are out of work, and to transient families, as well as the transient men and women roaming about the country. . . .
>
> Our job is to see that the unemployed get relief, not to develop a great social work organization throughout the United States.[54]

FDR's distaste for relief can be measured by his statement two years after assuming office:

> The Federal Government must and shall quit this business of relief.
>
> I am not willing that the vitality of our people be further sapped . . . . We must preserve not only the bodies of the unemployed from destitution but also their self-respect, their self-reliance and courage and determination.[55]

This fear of relief, the "subtle destroyer of the human spirit,"[56] and the threat to old values posed by a citizenry awakened to the hazards of unrestricted private enterprise had already led to the appointment by Executive Order of a Committee on Economic Security to develop a plan of income security for individuals and families. The Committee's recommendations were to echo the president's concern that the productivity of American workers be secured at the same time that their loyalty to the American "free" market system be assured.

In his congressional message of January 4, President Roosevelt had separated the productive from the nonproductive poor, accepting primary responsibility for the former, the group that was "the victim of a nation-wide depression caused by conditions which were not local but national."[57] Approximately 5 million families and single people were then on the relief rolls. FERA estimated that 3.5 million of these recipients were employable, and FDR was determined to give them employment "pending their absorption in a rising tide of private employment."[58] Although not abandoning the additional 1.5 million people remaining on the relief rolls, he nevertheless stated his intention that those who in the past had been "dependent upon local efforts" be maintained again "by State, by counties, by towns, by cities, by churches, and by private welfare agencies."[59]

The fact that excessive unemployment continued year after year and gave rise to the specter of a huge demoralized and unproductive class dependent upon a public dole required not only insurance against future industrial hazards but also an immediate new approach to unemployment relief. With a program of work-related social insurance already in the making by the Committee on Economic Security, the president's interim solution was the establishment of the Works Progress Administration to "supersede the Federal Emergency Relief Administration with a coordinated authority . . . charged with the orderly liquidation of our present relief activities and the substitution of a national chart for the giving of work."[60] As for those who could not work, said the president, "I stand ready through my personal efforts, and through the public influence of the office that I hold, to help these local agencies to get the means necessary to assume this burden."[61]

The WPA, funded in 1935 at $4.9 billion, actually spent more than twice that amount in its lifetime. Eventually it provided jobs for 8 million Americans in a wide range of activities, from heavy construction to the painting of murals in local libraries and orchestral performances in the schools. For those for whom jobs were provided, life was much improved. Wages were higher than relief payments, and there was no deterrent income eligibility test. But work projects got under way slowly and many "employables" never found work at all.

The federal government did not immediately substitute the proposed program of work relief for all direct relief. Congress did not pass the Emergency Appropriation Act until April 1935 and included requested funds to cover a period of transition from home relief to work relief. The Works Progress Administration was constituted by Executive Order in May, and Harry Hopkins was appointed its administrator. Actual liquidation of the FERA was not begun until the closing months of the year, and the final emergency relief grants went out to the states in December 1935.

By the end of 1935, with the phasing out of federal participation in direct relief under way, with the inability or unwillingness of many states to replace the lost funds, and with the transfer of employables to WPA projects slower than had been contemplated, the transition period became a "bitter one for families on relief in many parts of the country."[62] The problem was exacerbated by the slowness with which the public assistance programs of the Social Security Act—programs designed to help some categories of unemployables—were being put into operation among the states.

Social workers were wary of the phasing out of federal funding for direct relief. Some had been catalysts for the organization of client groups of which they were themselves members. Many had a personal and professional intimacy with problems resulting from unemployment and a new understanding of poverty and the poor.[63]

Private agencies were not able to pick up the slack as they had prior to 1933 because the events of the depression had begun to define a new role for them. Harry Hopkin's administration of FERA had revolutionized public relief giving and formalized the changed relationship between public and voluntary family agencies. This revolution was proclaimed in the *Rules and Regulations* promulgated by FERA. The most famous and far-reaching of these was Regulation No. 1, which required that public relief funds be administered by public agencies. Recognition was given to the thousands of private family agency workers who had helped with the administration of public funds, but Regulation No. 1 required that they be designated as public officials working under the control of public authority.[64] The process by which private family agencies had already begun to delineate the uniqueness of their service was now accelerated and suddenly required consideration not only of alignments with public agencies but also with private child welfare agencies.

The fact that the historical relationships between private family and child welfare agencies would be changing had been foreshadowed by the 1932 report of the Committee on Family and Child Welfare, entitled "External and Internal Forces in Family and Child Welfare Work." The Committee had made two assumptions:

First, that goals of the family and children's agencies . . . are the same, namely to aid families and individuals in distress toward normal living; and second, that there are not essential differences in their casework methods and processes except perhaps those of approach and emphasis. The difference which appears to exist between the two fields because of the family agency's use of relief is not a real one. Material relief is simply one tool in the casework process and is used in both family and children's agencies. Whether it is given as food for a family or board for a child in a foster home, it is still relief.[65]

Having begun with the above assumptions, the Committee did not proceed to explore their meaning for the future relationship of private family and child welfare but, rather, explored the effects of the depression on each. Nevertheless, the future would require acceptance of the basic similarity of their functions and would eventuate in administrative mergers. Of more immediate significance for the development of public agencies was the Committee's statement of principles, which might be "used as controls in preserving the human values which the present wholesale methods [of giving relief] tend to destroy."[66] These principles supported a sympathetic individual service approach that required the use of trained personnel in administering relief.

FERA's Regulation No. 3 clarified further the separation of public and private agencies in regard to administering public relief funds. At the same time, the regulation revealed the extent to which public officials were influenced by private agency experience. Regulation No. 3 required the investigation and the demonstration of need on the part of the individual family. Means testing and budgeting to assure that "no relief is given to persons unless they are actually in need and that such relief . . . is adjusted to . . . actual needs"[67] was the outcome. The use of trained and experienced investigators, at least in supervisory positions, regular home visiting, and attention to state relative responsibility laws were required.

FERA's *Rules and Regulations* represented an advance in standard setting when compared with predepression approaches to public giving. They also established certain operating principles that were to have negative consequences in later years: administrative discretion, rather than legal definitions, for establishing eligibility for aid; a professional casework service orientation toward relief giving; and a subtly pervading, if unnoted, reservation that relief was somehow a necessary evil. For the moment, however, people were helped and their need was of primary importance. Harry Hopkins stated:

> We are now dealing with people of all classes. It is no longer a matter of unemployables and chronic dependents, but of your friends and mine who are involved in this. Everyone of us knows some family of our friends which is or should be getting relief.[68]

Hopkins's statement, his administration of FERA, and his realization that "however well this thing is administered, this enormous relief business can never be anything more than a makeshift"[69] set the stage for a major shift in the federal approach to income maintenance. The change had several facets.

For the short run, there had been a switch in the allocation of federal funds to employment—work relief—programs and a return to the states of responsibility for the direct relief of "unemployables." For the long run, there were to be permanent social security programs.

The shift in approach to income maintenance must be considered in a context of the essential conservatism of President Roosevelt and of most Americans, a conservatism hard pressed by the realities of the depression and by the appeal of radical solutions. In his 1932 speech accepting the presidential nomination, Roosevelt had stated:

> The great social phenomenon of this depression, unlike others before it, is that it has produced but a few of the disorderly manifestations that too often attend upon such times.
>
> Wild radicalism has made few converts, and the greatest tribute that I can pay to my countrymen is that in these days of crushing want there persists an orderly and hopeful spirit on the part of the millions of our people who have suffered so much.[70]

The inspirational wording of the speech, the eloquence of its delivery, and the breaking of tradition that brought the presidential nominee to the convention could not mask the traditionalism of the proposed program for recovery: economy in government, shorter working hours, public works financed and self-sustained by the issuance of government bonds, protective tariffs for industry and agriculture, increased prices for industrial and farm products. The pledge of assistance with "distress relief" seemed almost an afterthought.

The Social Security Act

The Social Security Act, approved by President Roosevelt on August 15, 1935, was the major piece of social welfare legislation resulting from the depression and the New Deal. It was a landmark in American political and social history, reflecting a shift from public, governmental concern for property rights to a concern for the rights of people and, consequently, extending federal responsibility for social welfare. The act, from the point of view of program provisions, administrative structuring, and federal/state fiscal arrangements, represented a watershed for the mingling of old and new orientations toward people as social and economic beings.

The Social Security Act evolved from the work of the Committee on Economic Security, which submitted its report to the president on January 15, 1935. The report was accompanied by drafts of bills representing an expedient "piecemeal approach" whose primary aim was "the assurance of an adequate income to each human being in childhood, youth, middle age, or old age—in sickness or in health."[71] Within an overall recommendation that the federal government assume responsibility for employment assurance, the Committee made specific recommendations in regard to security against the risks of unemployment, retirement in old age, and ill health. Additional recommendations provided for the current security of old people and children through the provision of federally aided, state-administered "pensions." Finally, the Committee recommended an array of employment, health, educational, and rehabilitative services. Many of these were to be administered by the states, with standard setting to be stimulated by the federal government through the offer of financial and other types of assistance.

Having made sweeping recommendations in regard to federal involvement in a program of assurances against the hazards of life, the Committee recognized the need for residual relief for "genuine unemployables—or near unemployables." The Committee commended the care and guidance of this group to the states—and to social workers:

> With the Federal Government carrying so much burden for pure unemployment, the State and local governments . . . should resume responsibility for relief. The families that have always been partially or wholly dependent on others for support can best be assisted through the tried procedures of social casework, with its individualized treatment.[72]

The Committee could not foresee that the recipients of old age and mothers' "pensions" would also be subjected to such treatment.

President Roosevelt recommended the Committee's report to Congress in January 1935 as the basis for legislation. His message emphasized the soundness of the Committee's proposals and the caution with which they should be considered.

> The detailed report of the Committee sets forth a series of proposals that will appeal to the sound sense of the American people. It has not attempted the impossible nor has it failed to exercise sound caution and consideration of all the factors concerned: the national credit, the rights and responsibilities of States, the capacity of industry to assume financial responsibilities and the fundamental necessity of proceeding in a manner that will merit enthusiastic support of citizens of all sorts.[73]

The president's sense of fiscal and political realities led him to specifying legislative principles that necessarily ordained a modest beginning program of social assurances: no health insurance, no federal administration of relief programs and only fiscal administration of unemployment insurance, and no use of the general revenues for old age insurance. Not unexpectedly, then, the Social Security laws, when enacted, were rather more conservative than the recommendations of the Committee on Economic Security.

The policy of the United States in regard to permanent programs of income maintenance was stated in the preamble to Public Law No. 271:

> An Act to provide for the general welfare by establishing a system of Federal old-age benefits, and by enabling the several States to make more adequate provision for aged persons, blind persons, dependent and crippled children,

maternal and child welfare, public health, and the administration of their unemployment compensation laws. . . .[74]

Ensuing program provisions covered loss of income due to temporary loss of job (Unemployment Compensation), inability to participate in the labor force due to age or disability (Federal Old Age Insurance, Old Age Assistance, Aid to the Blind, Aid to Dependent Children), the promotion of the welfare of mothers and children (Maternal and Child Health Services, Services for Crippled Children, Child Welfare Services), and the encouragement of adequate state and local public health services. Provisions for the extension and improvement of maternal and child health services offered by local health authorities restored programs that had languished or collapsed when the Sheppard-Towner Act had been permitted to expire in 1929. Nonetheless, the decision against legislating health insurance at that time effectively stopped the movement toward the development of a health insurance mechanism. Not until 30 years later did the movement again become viable. The decision was especially constraining since the overall thrust of the Social Security Act toward cash payments as opposed to in-kind services simultaneously limited federal contributions toward the development of a comprehensive health care delivery system.

The enactment of Federal Old Age Insurance and of Grants to States for Unemployment Compensation recognized flaws in the country's private enterprise market system and the need for institutional change to mitigate unavoidable economic and social distress. Insurance against the hazards of unemployment and of retirement in old age bolstered the security of beneficiaries and of the private enterprise system itself because these institutional reforms, aimed at meeting universal needs, guaranteed permanent economic stabilizers for both. Thus, social insurance benefits, based on a joint employee-employer contributory scheme, assured an income for individuals who had worked but could not necessarily be expected to maintain the burden of self-support in retirement or unemployment. The social insurance approach assumed the essential viability of the market system while acknowledging the need to support the public's purchasing power. This assumption by the federal government of responsibility for the worker's income security suggested that the flaws in society were, after all, correctable. But the social insurance programs did not cover loss of income due to disability, absence of the breadwinner, or, in many cases, old age. In addition, for those groups it did cover, the programs needed time to build up funds from which benefits might be dispensed. These factors meant that programs of temporary assistance were required; and categorical programs that made federal grants-in-aid available to the states were designed to assist the destitute aged, the blind, and dependent children.

The Social Security Act established a dual system for federally supported income maintenance. The result for the country was a tripartite approach to public relief. The act provided for federally administered insurance programs and federally aided, state-administered assistance programs for selected groups. The grant-in-aid, state-administered financial assistance programs served to separate again the old poor from the new. The new poor, the unemployed, were covered by social insurance; the old "worthy" poor, by categorical public assistance. Left to the states was the third group, the "unworthy poor," for whom states and localities were to develop programs without federal aid.

The creation of federally aided categories of assistance evolved from long-time state efforts to help certain classes of the poor whose circumstances could not readily be attributed to personal inadequacy and who, therefore, were not to be stigmatized as recipients of the dole. State provisions of aid for the aged, the blind, and the widowed were generally viewed as pensions without stigma. By 1935 aid to the blind was available in 24 states; aid to the aged, in 34 states; and aid to mothers, in all states and jurisdictions except Alabama, Georgia, and South Carolina. The decision of the Congress to lend federal support for the beneficiaries of these programs acknowledged the legitimacy of their claim. Besides, it was believed that the necessity for such programs would recede as federal measures for social insurance, maternal and child welfare, and public health work took hold.

The provision of public assistance on the basis of requirements in addition to need and the decision for state, rather than federal, administration indicated continuing ambivalence about all non-work-related relief. Continuing reliance on local surveillance of recipients followed. Categorization separated out those who could not work and for whom public benefits were acceptable and relatively noncontroversial. At the same time, the system tried to meet the service needs of these exceptional groups and to assure the proper use of income benefits. Be that as it may, the federal categories, as designed in 1935, were no return to traditional, almshouse-oriented relief programs. The popularity of the old age pension movement, the past success with wholly state-financed categorical programs, and the new understanding of the causes of poverty would not permit this. The federal public assistance categories were community oriented in that they required that recipients be living in their own homes. Furthermore, the Social Security Act defined assistance as "money payments," requiring that grants be made in cash. Finally, the act mandated the opportunity for a fair hearing for any individual whose "claim" for assistance was denied. These particular provisions, plus the fact that they legislatively joined insurance and assistance programs, gave some support to the concept of the "right to assistance" for eligible recipients. The concept of entitlement was strengthened by the absence of any requirement that the claimant's own capital assets be taken into account when determining benefits.

Additional factors contributed to the standard-setting character of the Social Security Act. The act required that participating states submit plans making assistance programs mandatory in all political subdivisions, appointing a single state agency responsible for administering or supervising the state's assistance program, assuring the efficiency of state program administration, and guaranteeing compliance with the Social Security Board's regulations and reporting requirements. Of equal standard-setting significance was the act's rejection of unusual and deterring residence requirements. For all the differences still possible under its essentially permissive requirements, the act did succeed in bringing the federally funded public assistance programs to all the states and in giving the various programs an identifiable common base.

The Social Security Act had profound significance for family welfare generally and for the welfare of poor families in particular. For the larger society, Old Age insurance and Old Age Assistance meant that a major portion of the financial burden of caring for aged parents was lifted from adult children. The money thus freed could be shifted to the care of minor children. The ability of Aid to Dependent Children (ADC) to provide adequately for children who remained financially dependent was questionable from the start, however.

The Committee on Economic Security had described mothers' pensions as "defensive measures for children."

> They are designed to release from the wage-earning role the person whose natural function is to give her children the physical and affectionate guardianship necessary not alone to keep them from falling into social misfortune, but more affirmatively to rear them into citizens capable of contributing to society.[75]

Despite the Committee's encouragement and the seeming popularity of Mother's Aid among the states, limited professional social work attention was given to Aid to Dependent Children during congressional hearings. Leaving aside the testimony of Katherine Lenroot, chief of the Children's Bureau,[76] and Jacob Kepecs, president of the Child Welfare League of America,[77] little interest was demonstrated. Edwin Witte, paid executive for the Committee, stated after the passage of the Social Security Act that the poor outcome of provisions for dependent children, as compared to provisions for other needy groups, was mainly due to this lack of interest.[78]

The inattention to provisions for dependent children resulted, first, in the administration of ADC along with the adult categories of assistance. The original intent that the program be under the jurisdiction of the Children's Bureau was thus ignored. Second, the phrase "aid to dependent children" was defined to mean money payments with respect to a dependent child or children and not to include caretakers. Third, the grant-in-aid formula limited federal payments to one-third of a total of $18 per month per family provided for one dependent and to one-third of $12 per month provided for additional dependent children. The formula contrasted sharply with that used for Old Age Assistance. In the latter instance, the federal government offered payment monthly of one-half of $30 for each eligible person. Aid to Dependent Children obviously provided less than the "defense measures" envisioned by the Committee on Economic Security. In fact, there was such contrast between the provisions for dependent children and for the aged and the blind that one might wonder whether aiding such children was still subject to suspicion despite the widespread adoption of mothers' pensions by the states.

Family Life and Social Workers

A summary of staff reports prepared for the Committee on Economic Security declared that "the chief aim of social security is protection of the family life of wage earners, and the prime factor in family life is the protection and development of children."[79] As the depression deepened, social workers became increasingly insistent that the economic base of the family be strengthened and that the federal government share in the cost.

Changes in the family were particularly evident in the reduced economic importance of women in the home and, consequently, in their move to outside occupations. The number of wage-earning women, 16 years and over, increased from 1,701,000 in 1870, when the Bureau of the Census first collected such data, to 10,546,000 in 1930.[80] During the 1920s the increase in female employment was 29 percent, while the increase of the female population was 22 percent.[81] The number of employed married women had reached 3,071,000 in 1930, a 300 percent increase over the 769,000 employed at the beginning of the century.[82] Were it not "for the retardation of business activity which was well under way at the time of the 1930 census, probably even more women would have reported themselves as occupied."[83] As it was, 33 percent of those who worked were in domestic and personal services, 18 percent were in manufacturing and mechanical industries, 19 percent were in clerical occupations, and 12 percent were in trade and transportation. The vast majority were in semiskilled or unskilled positions.[84]

The unemployment crisis of the 1930s of necessity affected family life. The formation of new families—getting married and having children—was delayed. The marriage rate per 1,000 unmarried women declined from 92 percent in 1920 to 68 percent in 1930.[85] In 1933 the birthrate was 18.4 per 1,000 of population, down from 27.7 per 1,000 of population in 1920 and from 21.3 in 1930.[86] The psychological climate, as well as economic reality, was one of depression for families already formed. Unemployment struck women as well as men, with discrimination falling heavily upon the former as jobs became scarcer and men displaced women. At the same time, the well-paid industrial and construction work performed by most men was more liable to layoff than the lower-paid, unskilled work performed by most women. One result was role reversal, wherein wives worked and supported families while husbands were confined to the home. Although the divorce rate showed no appreciable change between 1920 and 1940—actually the rate for 1930 (7.5 per 1,000) married women was slightly lower than the 1920 rate (8.0 per 1,000)[87] family instability was evidenced by an increase in suicide and desertions by the fear of becoming "superfluous people."[88] And the plight of older people forced permanently out of the labor force by the depression was frightening to contemplate.

Thus the attitude of the social work and social welfare community toward the Social Security Act as a family welfare measure is worth exploring. The act itself had been approved on August 15, 1935, but federal funds did not become available until February 1936. Beyond that, the process of having states submit plans for the administration of public assistance and of having those plans approved by the newly created Public Assistance Board proved slow. By mid-November 1936, 42 states had finally received grants for Old Age Assistance. Only 26 states had received grants for Aid to Dependent Children, bearing out the lack of concern for this group of recipients. The states, in their reluctance to move into this category of assistance, reflected the attitude of the federal government in its differential treatment of children.

All in all, social workers were alarmed by the course of events, and the Delegate Conference of the American Association of Social Workers, held in Washington, D.C., February 14–16, 1936, considered carefully "this business of relief." The delegates gave public hearing to a number of convictions and concerns:[89]

1. That the factors that made relief necessary were demoralizing, not the act of receiving relief itself.
2. That the work provided by WPA should be productive in itself and not just a technique for avoiding idleness.
3. That need should be the criterion for federal assistance and that separating employables from unemployables left the matter to the uncertain mercies of states and localities.
4. That there was a residual relief problem caused by the fact that WPA work relief payments were inadequate to cover the needs of large families and by the fact that some groups were not covered by the federally aided public assistance categories at all.
5. That permissive requirements for state participation in federally aided public assistance programs threatened irresponsibility.

The dissatisfaction expressed at the Delegate Conference did not alter the course of events. This does not mean that social workers were without political influence, for it must be remembered that both Harry Hopkins, the administrator of FERA and of WPA, and Frances Perkins, the secretary of labor, had themselves come from professional social work backgrounds. Secretary Perkins (as chairman) and Harry Hopkins had been two of the five members of the Committee on Economic Security; and social workers were prominent members of the Committee's Advisory Council and of the Committee's technical and consultative groups. Moreover, Aubrey Williams, deputy administrator for WPA, appeared at the Delegate Conference to plead the political wisdom of supporting the federal government's programs.[90] The collapse of social work's pressure for a return to a federal program geared primarily to direct relief seems first of all due to the political unreality of such a return but also to a conflict among social workers as to their professional view of the poor and of the needs of the poor.

Aubrey Williams expressed his bewilderment and concern at the "growing disposition on the part of social workers to advocate the return of the federal government to direct relief." He implied that this pressure resulted from the tendency on their part to see caseworkers as necessary to the poor and casework as a necessary adjunct to poor relief. "To put caseworkers into the old poor relief system," Williams arqued, "is to put new wine into old bottles that will crack." He warned that the demolition of WPA would give social workers "3.5 million people on direct relief and nothing else" and, in a final thrust, said that "the sooner social work as a profession can turn its back on direct relief as a valid form of social treatment, the better off will be the nation and the higher the standing of social work." Like Harry Hopkins back in 1933, Williams seemed to be saying that federal programs should not be used "to develop a great social work organization throughout the United States." Those who led the attack against WPA could not easily dismiss the accusation.

Having been admonished by Williams to think of new approaches to unemployment and income security, the delegates were also treated to Ewan Clague's description of the potentialities of the provisions of the Social Security Act.[91] Perhaps because it did join, no matter how uneasily, new social insurance and old public relief measures, the act offered some satisfaction to those social workers who had urged social reform through social insurance and to those who urged reform through the professionalization of relief giving.

The early years of the depression were ones during which social workers clarified their own views about relief and about people who needed financial help. The professional literature between 1930 and 1935 abounds with discussion and controversy. One issue, federal versus state and local responsibility for relief, was settled quite easily. State and local coffers were empty. The issue of public versus private responsibility for relief was similarly resolved. A third issue was that of cash versus kind. In 1933 Dorothy Kahn, director of the Philadelphia County Relief Board and soon to become chairman of the American Association of Social Workers, made "an ardent appeal for one form [of relief giving], namely, cash."[92] As demonstrated by the categorical programs of the Social Security Act, the proponents of cash payments won the day. The literature would suggest that social workers believed the issue of right versus privilege as a basis for financial aid to have been settled in favor of the right to assistance. Certainly this was true for the social insurances whose benefits were related to worker contributions. As for the categorical programs, the Social Security Act's use of the word "claim" in connection with the receipt of benefits distributed in cash and the right to a fair hearing both indicated an entitlement to public assistance, no matter how conditioned that entitlement might be. Harry Hopkins thought the federal administering agency, along with state and local boards, would pass benefits on "as a pension without stigma."[93]

Perhaps most important to an understanding of the fate of Aid to

Dependent Children was the social insurance versus public assistance issue. Although both types of programs were included in the Social Security Act, the reality was that the social insurance mechanism was favored as an approach to income security. The strengthening of the work ethic by relating premiums and benefits to earnings and the attempted simulation of actuarial, private insurance soundness (with almost no contribution from the general revenue) assured the political attractiveness of social insurance.

Of course, the current unemployment crisis required public relief programs; but whatever fears remained about supporting public, non-work-related programs could be allayed with the belief that such programs would wither away. The need for Old Age Assistance would disappear as Old Age Insurance matured and covered an increasing number of workers. Of importance, too, was the fact that survivors of workers, although not sufficiently provided for, had not been entirely forgotten. The Committee on Economic Security had recommended that a death benefit be paid to a worker's surviving dependents should the worker die before the age of 65 or before the amount of his own contributions had been paid to him as an annuity.[94] The Committee had also given consideration to the future when "families and widows would be given primary consideration in broad plans for survivors' insurance or insurance for widows and orphans."[95] The Social Security Act did in fact provide for a lump sum benefit to survivors as recommended by the Committee on Economic Security. There was reason to believe that insurance coverage would eventually be extended to widows and orphans* and that Aid to Dependent Children, like Old Age Assistance, would fade in significance. Perhaps that is why the Senate and House committees heard only perfunctory social work support for Aid to Dependent Children and only perfunctory social work criticism of its deficiencies as a program.

New Alignments in Social Welfare

An exploration of social work's attitude toward Aid to Dependent Children must take into account that the depression required social workers to clarify not only their views about relief and relief recipients but also alignments between public and private social welfare. Inevitably this meant a reconsideration of the functions of professional social work. Regulation No. 1 had begun the reversal of a tradition whereby voluntary agencies shaped the contribution of public agencies to social welfare. The enactment of the Social Security Act furthered the process and established the dominance of public welfare. The impact on voluntary agencies—on voluntary family agencies, in particular—was enormous. Voluntary family agencies and family agency personnel had impeded the development of public welfare prior to the depression. And despite their beginning development of casework as a

---

*The act was amended to provide survivors' insurance and benefits for dependents in 1939.

professional methodology and of family counseling as a professional function, they had remained absorbed with problems of relief giving. With the onset of the depression they became involved in cooperative efforts to help families needing relief because of the unemployment crisis, and their day-to-day practice consisted chiefly of relief-related activities. The Family Welfare Association of America described the extent of its member agencies' involvement:

> Every good public program owes something to the pioneer work of private agencies. . . . Private agencies have readily loaned or released trained persons for service in public agencies, often at a great cost to their own programs. Supervisory and advisory aid have been accorded continuously by many private agencies to public agencies. In addition . . . private agencies have also engaged actively in obtaining general support of public welfare programs.[96]

Now, with the passage of the Social Security Act, family agencies seemed devoid of a viable social welfare function. Family agency workers, who in large measure carried the professional status for social work, seemed similarly affected. Both agencies and workers needed to find a raison d'être; and it was perhaps the knowledge of this, as much as anything else, that underlay the heated discussions of public welfare at the February 1936 Delegate Conference of the American Association of Social Workers. The apparent collapse of organized social work support for unemployment relief suggests a perception that professional social work practice and relief giving were separate entities, however overlapping their concerns.

This recognition was confirmed in March 1936, when the Family Welfare Association of America published a report of responses by member agencies to questions related to "the crisis in community programs."[97] Of the total of 93 agencies responding, 89 agreed that "it would be folly for private agencies . . . to attempt to meet any appreciable part of the unemployment relief burden . . . being abandoned by the Federal Government." They agreed that it was essential "to hold firmly to the principle that intensive casework treatment is the primary function of a family service organization." Nevertheless, when asked to list developments of new or more clearly defined channels of services to the community, the agencies gave "a great variety of answers which constitute[d] a confusing picture." Many listed their emphasis on "intensive casework" as a new development.

The extent to which voluntary agencies were threatened by the Social Security Act's establishment of a permanent public welfare structure and by the vacuum created by the loss of a primary relief-giving responsibility can also be discerned from FWAA's report of responses to its questionnaire. When asked what they were doing to rally community support for public welfare, one-third of the respondents expressed interest in helping but were inactive; another one-third were indifferent.[98] Perhaps they felt all the more upset by the fact that the problem was again largely of their own making. If earlier they had impeded the development of an adequate public sector of social welfare, now they must share responsibility for the existence of a permanent, powerful establishment they could not control. Furthermore, the existence of such an establishment required change at the core of the voluntary agency.

Despite the frequent reference in the social work literature to a "right to assistance," this view was inconsistent with the philosophy that had impelled the development of voluntary social welfare. The latter had begun with an assumption of a character flaw for which—as with man's original fall—man was himself responsible. This view of human nature as essentially evil and of society as the blameless victim of human frailty led to religious, eventually voluntary, social welfare efforts to change the human being. The Protestant ethic was particularly concerned with work, thrift, and financial independence. When voluntary social welfare secularized this ethic, the family agency tied social work practice and relief giving into a single package. In a situation where societal, public responsibility was not admitted, there was no need for public welfare.

The depression of the 1930s revolutionized conventional thinking about social need. The discovery that people could be unemployed and in need through no fault of their own led, first, to an admission of fault in the economic and social system and, second, to a conception of the individual-at-risk in the system. Society therefore had an obligation to help. In such a circumstance, financial need was truly secularized—one might say, publicized—and the need for public welfare was inherent. Furthermore, the acceptance of societal responsibility for financial need led quite naturally to the depersonalization of relief giving. Relief recipients needed money, not service. They did not require the skill of professional service and could best be helped by government aid administered objectively. Federal and state aid represented the elimination of the control of individuals by local communities and was all to the good.

The message for voluntary social agencies was stark, and they renewed efforts to define a unique professional service function. At that moment, when they were themselves psychologically desperate for a new orientation, they discovered the psychological vulnerability of people. Moreover, the widespread dissemination of Freudian theory demonstrating the significance of parent-child relationships brought home the psychological underpinnings of family survival. Having helped achieve economic security for families, voluntary family agencies moved to the further development of highly skilled "casework treatment to assist individuals in removing their own handicaps."[99] The Freudian symbiotic tie of parent to child, however, required family, rather than individual treatment; and again attention was focused on the relationship between voluntary family and children's agencies and on the possibility of their merging.

In November 1937 the Family Welfare Association of America distributed an outline of points discussed in meetings of its Committee on Relationship between Family and Children's Work in a meeting of that

Committee with a similar committee of the Child Welfare League of America.

> In considering the relationship between family and children's case work . . . it is evident that they have the same roots in social case work, as far as the basic knowledge and equipment of the case worker are concerned. . . .
>
> Any family case work agency is also a children's case work agency, in the sense that it has the same obligation for skilled treatment of the problems of children in families as it does for meeting the needs of adults. Any children's case work agency, dealing with children in their own homes or in foster homes, is or should be a family case work agency, in so far as it attempts to treat children's needs in relation to the family setting, or to deal with those difficulties in family relationships that affect the child.[100]

Relationships between voluntary family and children's agencies were to be the subject of controversy throughout the 1940s and 1950s; but already in 1937, mergers between family and children's agencies were being considered. The reasons were: (1) the similarity of casework base, (2) the development of cooperative structures between agencies offering family and children's services, and (3) the development of children's services within family agencies and vice versa. In the *Social Work Year Book, 1951*, Frank J. Hertel reported the following:

> Figures available to FSAA [Family Service Association of America] over the past eight years show that the number of its member agencies engaging in this multiple service [family and child welfare services] increased from 46 in 1942 to 82 (33 percent of the member agencies) by the close of 1949. Of these, 42 had expanded their services to include child placement, whereas 40 represented the merging of two or more agencies . . . to provide the services formerly considered special to each.[101]

By 1960 the number of merged family and children's agencies holding common membership in FSAA and CWL had risen to 60. In 1974 FSAA and CWL were themselves considering a merger, which they finally rejected.

Conclusion

The depression of the 1930s left an indelible mark on the United States and on a generation of Americans. Despite the effort expended in the attempt to wrest the country out of the crisis, neither Franklin Roosevelt nor the New Deal programs achieved success until World War II boosted the economy to full employment. Nevertheless, the president had been able to invest the people with psychological endurance and, in the face of severe challenges from the political right and the left, to preserve the basic economic system of private property.

The essential conservatism of the New Deal, however, does not negate the fact that the federal government had emerged prime promoter of social welfare. Voluntary welfare as well as state and local governments had been tried and found wanting. The extent to which a new realism had taken hold was exhibited in the Supreme Court opinion delivered by Justice Cardozo upholding the constitutionality of the Social Security Act:

> The concept of the general welfare is not static. Needs that were narrow or parochial a century ago may be interwoven in our day with the welfare of the nation. What is critical or urgent changes with the times.[102]

The United States emerged from the depression aware of the hazards of the industrial society and having accomplished a major structural change in its income transfer system. The provision of social insurance—and, for the moment, public assistance too—represented aggressive federal responsibility for guaranteeing minimum financial security as a matter of right.

Unquestionably, the Social Security Act was the major legislative accomplishment of the New Deal. The act declared the birth of the welfare state and established a direction for its growth and development. As a start, the necessity for opening up jobs for young adults (which required that the elderly be retired from the labor market) and the political clout of older people meant that the welfare measures of the act were geared primarily to persons over age 65. The risks suffered by children and young adults were given short shrift, a situation not really retrieved by the minimum wage and hour or child labor provisions of the Fair Labor Standards Act of 1938. For the most part, the Fair Labor Standards Act did little more than give federal sanction to provisions that already existed in many of the states. Nevertheless, precedent for societal protection for all had been established and would serve as a base for substantial expansion of old programs and the creation of new ones.

For social work, the return to prosperity meant a return to a period of further introspection and professionalization. In 1934 the general sessions and section meetings of the National Conference of Social Work strongly emphasized unemployment, health, and justice as social welfare policy concerns and social legislation as the route to social change. By 1936 the meetings emphasized social work methodology, social agency administration, and social work education.[103]

DOCUMENTS
The Depression and the New Deal

The documents used to demonstrate social welfare issues during the depression of the 1930s are excerpts from the *Monthly Reports of the Federal Emergency Relief Administration* (1933) and from the Social Security Act (1935) as originally passed by Congress. The two documents illustrate continuity and change in social policy.

The Monthly Reports of the FERA set forth the famous *Rules and Regulations,* which not only governed the administration of developing public welfare programs but also revolutionized the relationship between the public and private sectors of social welfare. The most famous of these regulations, Regulation No. 1, ordered that relief funds be administered by public agencies. This new principle— "public funds in public hands"—removed voluntary agencies from the business of relief. Taking into account the enormous significance of relief giving for social welfare during the depression, the dominance of the public sector was immediately established.

Nevertheless, the influence of voluntary agency experience and tradition can be detected. Regulation No. 3 requires that need be determined on the basis of individual budgeting and that a variety of individual and family resources be taken into account in establishing the final amount of the relief grant. The requirements for individualized budgeting and resource determination lead directly to the investigations of applications and the use of trained investigators at least in supervisory positions.

The Social Security Act was the most important piece of social welfare legislation of the depression era. It substituted a group of permanent programs for the temporary programs of the FERA and, in so doing, acknowledged long-term federal responsibility for social welfare. This new thrust did not, however, make a total break with the past. In fact, a major characteristic of the act is its dual nature, its putting together of old and new orientations.

On the one hand, the Social Security Act establishes a number of social insurance programs to meet the hazards of old age and unemployment. The insurance programs are meant to cover those with former or current work force connections. They are financed through payroll-tax deductions. Simultaneously, the act provides for a group of categorical non-work-related programs of assistance for the elderly, the blind, and for dependent children. These programs are funded through a grant-in-aid formula providing a joint federal-state funding device. They are to be administered by states.

The social insurance and public assistance programs differ markedly in their orientation to people in need. The former, perhaps because of the direct taxation involved, makes carefully spelled-out benefits available to claimants as a matter of right. The public assistance categories, because they are based on a "demonstrated need" approach, continue the practice of investigation and individualized budgeting.

The delineation of categories of public assistance recipients indicates the extent to which need per se as a determinant for helping was compromised. Nevertheless, the new public assistance programs were also a break with the past. The Social Security Act requires that each participating state develop a state plan for public assistance and that the plan meet certain requirements. In this regard, the act is standard setting. In addition, the act requires that grants be made in cash and to people living in their own homes, marking the end of institutional almshouse care for the poor. Finally, the act provides for a "fair hearing" for those applicants who believe they have been unfairly treated. The changes are such that social welfare workers began to talk of a "right to assistance."

MONTHLY REPORT
OF
THE FEDERAL EMERGENCY RELIEF

LETTER OF TRANSMITTAL

JULY 1, 1933

SIR: Pursuant to subsection (d) of section 3 of the Federal Emergency Relief Act of 1933, the Federal Emergency Relief Administration has the honor to submit this report of its activities from May 22, 1933, to June 30, 1933, inclusive. . . .

RULES AND REGULATIONS

Rules and Regulations Nos. 1, 2, and 3 were promulgated by the Federal Emergency Relief Administrator, and were printed and distributed to the governors and State Emergency Relief Administrators. They read as follows:

No. 1

(a) Grants of Federal emergency relief funds are to be administered by public agencies after August 1, 1933.

Just as all State commissions responsible for the distribution of Federal and State funds to local communities are public bodies, so in turn should those local units be public agencies responsible for the expenditure of public funds in the same manner as any other municipal or county department.

This policy obviously must be interpreted on a realistic basis in various parts of the United States. Hundreds of private agencies scattered throughout the land have freely and generously offered their services in the administration of public funds. It would be a serious handicap to relief work if the abilities and interests of these individuals were lost. But these individuals should be made public officials, working under the control of public authority. Thousands of these workers are serving and will continue to serve without pay, but if paid, they should be compensated in the same manner as any other public servant.

It is not the intention of this regulation to instruct the several States to make hasty changes in agreements which the State administration may have made with the private agencies. Adjustment, however, to this policy is to be made no later than August 1, 1933.

This ruling prohibits the turning over of Federal emergency-relief funds to a private agency. The unemployed must apply to a public agency for relief, and this relief must be furnished direct to the applicant by a public agent.

(b) Grants made to the States from Federal funds under the Federal Emergency Relief Act of 1933 may be used for the payment of medical attendance and medical supplies for those families that are receiving relief.

(c) These funds may also be used to pay the cost of shelter for the needy unemployed.

(d) These funds may not be used for the payment of hospital bills or for the boarding out of children, either in institutions or in private homes, or for providing general institutional care. These necessary services to the destitute should be made available through State or local funds.

(e) The personnel employed on work relief projects by the States or their subdivisions are not Federal employees and must not be considered as such; therefore, premiums for accident insurance in connection with work relief programs may not be paid from Federal funds, but should be paid out of State or local moneys.

No. 2

Grants of Federal relief funds cannot be made on the basis of expenditures for rental of buildings used for relief operation; salaries of regularly employed public employees other than those employed full time in connection with emergency unemployment relief and under the supervision of the unemployment relief authority; salaries of relief workers not working directly under the supervision of the unemployment relief authority; and the purchase of automobiles and other equipment used in connection with relief administration.

No. 3

SUPPLEMENT TO RULES AND REGULATIONS NO. 1

Rule No. 1 stated: "Grants of Federal emergency relief funds are to be administered by public agencies after August 1, 1933." The rule further stated, "This ruling prohibits the turning over of Federal Emergency Relief funds to a private agency. The unemployed must apply to a public agency for relief and this relief must be furnished directly to the applicant by a public agent."

Three points need to be clarified:

(*a*) Public agency.

(*b*) Public agent or public official.

(*c*) Use of private agency personnel.

(*a*) *Public agency.*—A public welfare department, supported by tax funds and controlled by local government, if approved by the State emergency relief administration to administer unemployment relief, is a "public agency." Where a public welfare department does not exist and a local unemployment relief administration is responsible for unemployment relief this local unemployment relief administration, in order to be recognized as a "public agency" in the meaning of that term as used in Rules and Regulations No. 1, must have the following factors:

(1) It must have the full sanction and recognition of the State emergency relief administration.

(2) It must be vested with full authority and control in the expenditure of State and Federal public funds appropriated for local relief purposes.

(3) It must conform to the rulings of the State emergency relief administration.

(4) It must keep such records and forms as are required by the State emergency relief administration.

NOTE.—This interpretation recognizes as a "public agency," an agency created and sustained by Executive action in the absence of creative local legislation.

(*b*) *Public official or public agent.*—"Public official" or "public agent" in the meaning of the term as used in Rules and Regulations No. 1, includes every person who is engaged in carrying out the purposes of the public agency, and so must be:

(1) A member of the official staff of the public agency responsible to the chief executive employed by the public agency to administer the entire organization of unemployment relief. This relationship must be made official by definite appointment and acceptance of such appointment.

(2) The compensation of the "public official" or "public agent" may or may not be paid from public funds. Such official may be loaned by a private agency, but when so loaned must become a member of the official staff of the public agency.

(*c*) *Use of personnel loaned by private agency.*—The public agency may make use of personnel of private agencies provided—

(1) Where such personnel is used for the giving of unemployment relief it becomes for the time being an integral part of the public agency. The public agency must assume full responsibility over personnel loaned by the private agency.

(2) That visible evidence of the integration into the public agency is provided as follows:

a. The name of the public agency clearly set out on the office door so that clients may know that they are applying to a public agency for relief.

b. All order forms must be those of the public agency; receipts must be made out to the public agency; identification cards of relief workers must be as staff members of the public agency and relief workers at all times in handling unemployment relief clients must report themselves as public agents or officials.

c. All bills for direct relief, wages for work relief, service or administration costs must be paid directly by the public agency; e.g., when grocery orders are issued by the relief worker the bills must be paid by the public agency directly to the grocer and not through a private agency.

d. It is expected that on other matters than the determination of relief there will be cooperative relationships established between public agencies and private agencies, but the public agency shall not pay for supplemental services so rendered by private agencies.

ADEQUACY OF RELIEF

(Either work relief or direct relief)

Relief shall be given as provided in this act to all needy unemployed persons and/or their dependents. Those whose employment or available resources are inadequate to provide the necessities of life for themselves and/or their dependents are included.

This imposes an obligation on the State emergency relief administration and on all the political subdivisions of the States administering relief, insofar as lies in their power, to see to it that all such needy unemployed persons and/or their dependents shall receive sufficient relief to prevent physical suffering and to maintain minimum living standards.

It also imposes an obligation on the part of the State emergency relief administration and the local relief administration to see that no relief is given to persons unless they are actually in need, and that such relief as is allowed is adjusted to the actual needs of each individual or family.

At the same time the obligation exists to develop maximum efficiency and economy in the furnishing of relief, with a minimum of delay in providing relief to those in distress.

The amount of relief to be given must be based on the following:

(1) An estimate of the weekly needs of the individual or family including an allowance for food sufficient to maintain physical well-being, for shelter, the provision of fuel for cooking and for warmth when necessary, medical care and other necessities. Taxes may be allowed in lieu of allowances for shelter, and not to exceed the normal rent allowance—providing such tax allowance is necessary in order to maintain the shelter or home of the relief recipient.

(2) An estimate of the weekly income of the family, including wages or other cash income, produce of farm or garden, and all other resources.

(3) The relief granted should be sufficient to provide the estimated weekly needs to the extent that the family is unable to do so from its own resources.

Any or all of the following types of relief may be allowed under direct relief or under work relief:

(1) Food, and/or food orders or allowance, determined by the number, ages, and needs of the individual members of the family in general accordance with standard food schedules.

(2) Orders or allowances for the provision of shelter, or its equivalent, where necessary.

(3) Orders or allowances for light, gas, fuel, and water for current needs.

(4) Orders or allowances for necessary household supplies.

(5) Clothing or orders or allowances for clothing sufficient for emergency needs.

(6) Orders or allowances for medicine, medical supplies, and/or medical attendance to be furnished in the home.

See further interpretation under *"Direct relief."*

INVESTIGATION AND SERVICE

(Work relief and direct relief)

To carry out the purposes of the Federal Emergency Relief Act of 1933 the investigation of all applications for direct and/or work relief is required. The following rules are hereby established:

(1) Each local relief administration should have at least one trained and experienced investigator on its staff; if additional investigators are to be employed to meet this emergency, the first one employed should have had training and experience. In the larger public welfare districts, where there are a number of investigators, there should be not less than 1 supervisor, trained and experienced in the essential elements of family case work and relief administration, to supervise the work of not more than 20 investigating staff workers.

(2) Registration records of all local applications for relief should be kept at a central office. Where no such central registration index now exists, one should be established by the local relief administration. This is absolutely necessary if duplication is to be avoided where there is more than one agency, either public or private, administering relief.

(3) The minimum investigation shall include a prompt visit to the home; inquiry as to real property, bank accounts, and other financial resources of the family; an interview with at least one recent employer; and determination of the ability and agreement of family, relatives, friends, and churches and other organizations to assist; also the liability under public welfare laws of the several States, of members of a family, or relatives, to assume such support in order to prevent such member becoming a public charge.

(4) Investigation shall be made, not only of persons applying directly to the office but also of those reported to it. In this emergency, it is the duty of those responsible for the administration of unemployment relief to seek out persons in need, and to secure the cooperation of clergymen, school teachers, nurses, and organizations that might assist.

(5) There must be contact with each family through visits at least once a month, or oftener if necessary. The local field worker should be in sufficiently close touch with the family situation to avoid the necessity of applicants reapplying to the office for each individual order.

(6) Investigators should not be overloaded with cases. While no exact standard is being set as to the number of cases per worker, State emergency relief administrators should see to it that a sufficient number of workers are utilized in each local relief district to insure reasonable investigation procedure.

(7) Relief should be given only to persons in need of relief, and on the basis of budgetary deficiency established after careful investigation.

(8) Duplication of relief must be avoided, and every precaution should be taken to prevent overlapping of relief agencies, both public and private.

(9) Frequent and careful reinvestigation should be undertaken at regular intervals in order to establish the continued need of those who are receiving relief in order to determine whether or not some member of the family may have obtained part or full-time work, which would indicate the necessity for cutting down or cutting off on relief. Where adequate staff for investigation is provided, under able direction and supervision, these reinvestigations may be carried out automatically and the relief rolls kept clear of those who do not qualify.

DIRECT RELIEF

Such relief shall be in the form of food, shelter, clothing, light, fuel, necessary household supplies, medicine, medical supplies, and medical attendance, or the cash equivalent of these to the person in his own home.

Direct relief does not include relief—where provision is already made under existing laws—for widows or their dependents, and/or aged persons. There is further disallowed the payment of hospital bills or institutional care, and the costs of the boarding out of children.

Any or all of the following types of relief may be granted:

(1) Food, in the form of food orders, determined by the number, ages, and needs of the individual members of the family in general accordance with standard food schedules.

(2) Orders for the payment of current rent, or its equivalent, where necessary.

(3) Orders for light, gas, fuel, and water for current needs.

(4) Necessary household supplies.

(5) Clothing or orders for clothing sufficient for emergency needs.

(6) Orders for medicine, medical supplies, and/or medical attendance to be furnished in the home.

A broad interpretation of direct relief may be followed by the State relief administration where such is called for in meeting the immediate needs of individuals or families, or in aiding such needy persons in providing the necessitites of life for themselves and/or their dependents.

Feed for livestock cannot be allowed as a relief expenditure except feed for domestic livestock may be allowed as a relief expenditure where such allowance makes it possible for the distressed family to produce additional food for the immediate family need.

Seed for gardens under the same reasoning may likewise be allowed as a relief measure.

Tax or mortgage interest payments on real property (home and land) may be allowed in lieu of rent as a relief measure where such allowance is no greater than the normal minimum relief rent allowance and when such payment of tax or mortgage interest is vitally necessary in preventing the loss of the home and the eviction of the owner.

A liberal interpretation of direct relief as above indicated must be controlled by the rule of reason and public policy. Under no circumstances shall an allowance be made which makes provision for other than the emergency needs of the immediate family. State relief administrations are not authorized to make allowances for feed or seed to such an extent that provision is made possible for more than the individual family requirements.

Likewise, tax or mortgage interest payments in lieu of rent shall be allowed only on properties occupied and held title to by relief recipients. In no event shall a relief grant be made which directly or indirectly makes possible an increased capital investment in private properties.

WORK RELIEF

(Work relief wages and projects)

Work relief wages in cash or in kind are to be interpreted as follows:

(1) All work relief wages shall be based upon the relief need of the individual and/or his dependents.[1]

(2) The rate of wages should be a fair rate of pay for the work performed. Total compensation should meet the budgetary requirement of the relief recipient.

(3) Payment shall be by check, in cash, or in kind.

(4) Allowance should be on the basis of days' wages, or the equivalent, for the hours worked.

(5) Work relief should be allowed only to those who are employable.

(6) There shall be no discrimination because of race, religion, color, noncitizenship, political affiliation, or because of membership in any special or selected group.

(7) Where skilled personnel is required, skilled wages for skilled work must be paid. Such personnel taken from the work relief lists should be staggered. Where such skilled personnel is required full time, it should be provided otherwise than on a work relief basis.

(8) Work relief projects must be projects undertaken on Federal, State, or local public properties. Work projects for private institutions or agencies, nonprofit or otherwise, are therefore prohibited except as such projects, undertaken by governmental units, may benefit the public health or welfare as, for example, the prosecution of a drainage project which may benefit private interests but is withal of definite benefit to the public health of the community.

It therefore follows that work relief may not be used in the improvement of hospitals, libraries, churches, parks, cemeteries, etc., which are privately owned or incorporated, except that if State or local public moneys are regularly contributed to the support of such institutions, and such public support creates a quasi-public institution which may receive the benefit of work relief.

(9) Work relief projects under this act must be for work undertaken by a State or local relief administration independent of work under a contract or for which an annual appropriation has been made. It must be, in general, apart from normal governmental enterprises and not such as would have been carried out in due course regardless of an emergency.

The construction, as a work relief project, of public buildings, such as schools, firehouses, garages, etc., would in general not be acceptable as a

---

[1]See further interpretaion under "Direct relief" and "Adequacy." Allowances on work relief may be made to cover food, shelter, clothing, light, fuel, necessary household supplies, medicine, medical supplies, and medical attendance.

proper work relief project, such construction falling within the usual contract work which would provide labor for those unemployed at large.

(10) Persons employed on work-relief projects are not Federal employees and the premiums for their compensation or accident insurance may not be paid from Federal funds. If such insurance is provided, it therefore must be carried by State or local moneys.

Persons employed on work-relief projects by the States and their subdivisions ought to be covered by compensation or accident insurance.

(11) All local work-relief projects must be submitted for approval to the State emergency relief administration.

$$\bullet\ \bullet\ \bullet$$

THE SOCIAL SECURITY ACT

Approved, August 14, 1935

[Public—No. 271—74th Congress]
[II. R. 7260]

AN ACT

To provide for the general welfare by establishing a system of Federal old-age benefits, and by enabling the several States to make more adequate provision for aged persons, blind persons, dependent and crippled children, maternal and child welfare, public health, and the administration of their unemployment compensation laws; to establish a Social Security Board; to raise revenue; and for other purposes.

Be it enacted by the Senate and House of Representatives of the United States of America in Congress assembled,

TITLE I—GRANTS TO STATES FOR OLD-AGE ASSISTANCE

APPROPRIATION

SECTION 1. For the purpose of enabling each State to furnish financial assistance, as far as practicable under the conditions in such State, to aged needy individuals, there is hereby authorized to be appropriated for the fiscal year ending June 30, 1936, the sum of $49,750,000, and there is hereby authorized to be appropriated for each fiscal year thereafter a sum sufficient to carry out the purposes of this title. The sums made available under this section shall be used for making payments to States which have submitted, and had approved by the Social Security Board established by Title VII (hereinafter referred to as the "Board"), State plans for old-age assistance.

STATE OLD-AGE ASSISTANCE PLANS

SEC. 2 (a) A State plan for old-age assistance must (1) provide that it shall be in effect in all political subdivisions of the State, and, if administered by them, be mandatory upon them; (2) provide for financial participation by the State; (3) either provide for the establishment or designation of a single State agency to administer the plan, or provide for the establishment or designation of a single State agency to supervise the administration of the plan; (4) provide for granting to any individual, whose claim for old-age assistance is denied, an opportunity for a fair hearing before such State agency; (5) provide such methods of administration (other than those relating to selection, tenure of office, and compensation of personnel) as are found by the Board to be necessary for the efficient operation of the plan; (6) provide that the State agency will make such reports, in such form and containing such information, as the Board may from time to time find necessary to assure the correctness and verification of such reports; and (7) provide that, if the State or any of its political subdivisions collects from the estate of any recipient of old-age assistance any amount with respect to old-age assistance furnished him under the plan, one-half of the net amount so collected shall be promptly paid to the United States. Any payment so made shall be deposited in the Treasury to the credit of the appropriation for the purposes of this title.

(b) The Board shall approve any plan which fulfills the conditions specified in subsection (a), except that it shall not approve any plan which imposes, as a condition of eligibility for old-age assistance under the plan—

(1) An age requirement of more than sixty-five years, except that the plan may impose, effective until January 1, 1940, an age requirement of as much as seventy years; or

(2) Any residence requirement which excludes any resident of the State who has resided therein five years during the nine years immediately preceding the application for old-age assistance and has resided therein continuously for one year immediately preceding the application; or

(3) Any citizenship requirement which excludes any citizen of the United States.

PAYMENT TO STATES

Sec. 3. (a) From the sums appropriated therefore, the Secretary of the Treasury shall pay to each State which has an approved plan for old-age assistance, for each quarter, beginning with the quarter commencing July 1, 1935, (1) an amount, which shall be used exclusively as old-age assistance, equal to one-half of the total of the sums expended during such quarter as old-age assistance under the State plan with respect to each individual who at the time of such expenditure is sixty-five years of age or older and is not an inmate of a public institution, not counting so much of such expenditure with respect to any individual for any month as exceeds $30 and (2) 5 per centum of such amount, which shall be used for paying the costs of administering the State plan or for old-age assistance, or both, and for no other purpose: *Provided,* That the State plan, in order to be approved by the Board, need not provide for financial participation before July 1, 1937 by the State, in the case of any State which the Board, upon application by the State and after reasonable notice and opportunity for hearing to the State, finds is prevented by its constitution from providing such financial participation. . . .

DEFINITION

Sec. 6. When used in this title the term "old-age assistance" means money payments to aged individuals.

TITLE II—FEDERAL OLD-AGE BENEFITS

OLD-AGE RESERVE ACCOUNT

Section 201. (a) There is hereby created an account in the Treasury of the United States to be known as the "Old-Age Reserve Account" hereinafter in this title called the "Account". There is hereby authorized to be appropriated to the Account for each fiscal year, beginning with the fiscal year ending June 30, 1937, an amount sufficient as an annual premium to provide for the payments required under this title, such amount to be determined on a reserve basis in accordance with accepted actuarial principles, and based upon such tables of mortality as the Secretary of the Treasury shall from time to time adopt, and upon an interest rate of 3 per centum per annum compounded annually. The Secretary of the Treasury shall submit annually to the Bureau of the Budget an estimate of the appropriations to be made to the Account. . . .

OLD-AGE BENEFIT PAYMENTS

Sec. 202. (a) Every qualified individual (as defined in section 210) shall be entitled to receive, with respect to the period beginning on the date he attains the age of sixty-five, or on January 1, 1942, whichever is the later, and ending on the date of his death, an old-age benefit (payable as nearly as practicable in equal monthly installments) as follows:

(1) If the total wages (as defined in section 210) determined by the Board to have been paid to him, with respect to employment (as defined in section 210) after December 31, 1936, and before he attained the age of sixty-five, were not more than $3,000, the old-age benefit shall be at a monthly rate of one-half of 1 per centum of such total wages;

(2) If such total wages were more than $3,000, the old-age benefit shall be at a monthly rate equal to the sum of the following:

(A) One-half of 1 per centum of $3,000; plus

(B) One-twelfth of 1 per centum of the amount by which such total wages exceeded $3,000 and did not exceed $45,000; plus

(C) One-twenty-fourth of 1 per centum of the amount by which such total wages exceeded $45,000.

(b) In no case shall the monthly rate computed under subsection (a) exceed $85.

(c) If the Board finds at any time that more or less than the correct amount has theretofore been paid to any individual under this section, then, under regulations made by the Board, proper adjustments shall be made in connection with subsequent payments under this section to the same individual.

(d) Whenever the Board finds that any qualified individual has received wages with respect to regular employment after he attained the age of sixty-five, the old-age benefit payable to such individual shall be reduced, for each calendar month in any part of which such regular employment occurred, by an amount equal to one month's benefit. Such reduction shall be made, under regulations prescribed by the Board, by deductions from one or more payments of old-age benefit to such individual.

PAYMENTS UPON DEATH

SEC. 203. (a) If any individual dies before attaining the age of sixty-five, there shall be paid to his estate an amount equal to 3½ per centum of the total wages determined by the Board to have been paid to him, with respect to employment after December 31, 1936.

(b) If the Board finds that the correct amount of the old-age benefit payable to a qualified individual during his life under section 202 was less than 3½ per centum of the total wages by which such old-age benefit was measurable, then there shall be paid to his estate a sum equal to the amount, if any, by which such 3½ per centum exceeds the amount (whether more or less than the correct amount) paid to him during his life as old-age benefit.

(c) If the Board finds that the total amount paid to a qualified individual under an old-age benefit during his life was less than the correct amount to which he was entitled under section 202, and that the correct amount of such old-age benefit was 3½ per centum or more of the total wages by which such old-age benefit was measurable, then there shall be paid to his estate a sum equal to the amount, if any, by which the correct amount of the old-age benefit exceeds the amount which was so paid to him during his life.

PAYMENTS TO AGED INDIVIDUALS NOT QUALIFIED FOR BENEFITS

SEC. 204. (a) There shall be paid in a lump sum to any individual who, upon attaining the age of sixty-five, is not a qualified individual, an amount equal to 3½ per centum of the total wages determined by the Board to have been paid to him, with respect to employment after December 31, 1936, and before he attained the age of sixty-five.

(b) After any individual becomes entitled to any payment under subsection (a), no other payment shall be made under this title in any manner measured by wages paid to him, except that any part of any payment under subsection (a) which is not paid to him before his death shall be paid to his estate. . . .

OVERPAYMENTS DURING LIFE

SEC. 206. If the Board finds that the total amount paid to a qualified individual under an old-age benefit during his life was more than the correct amount to which he was entitled under section 202, and was 3½ per centum or more of the total wages by which such old-age benefit was measurable, then upon his death there shall be repaid to the United States by his estate the amount, if any, by which such total amount paid to him during his life exceeds whichever of the following is the greater: (1) Such 3½ per centum, or (2) the correct amount to which he was entitled under section 202. . . .

DEFINITIONS

Sec. 210. When used in this title—

(a) The term "wages" means all remuneration for employment, including the cash value of all remuneration paid in any medium other than cash; except that such term shall not include that part of the remuneration which, after remuneration equal to $3,000 has been paid to an individual by an employer with respect to employment during any calendar year, is paid to such individual by such employer with respect to employment during such calendar year.

(b) The term "employment" means any service, of whatever nature, performed within the United States by an employee for his employer, except—

(1) Agricultural labor;

(2) Domestic service in a private home;

(3) Casual labor not in the course of the employer's trade or business;

(4) Service performed as an officer or member of the crew of a vessel documented under the laws of the United States or of any foreign country;

(5) Service performed in the employ of the United States Government or of an instrumentality of the United States;

(6) Service performed in the employ of a State, a political subdivision thereof, or an instrumentality of one or more States or political subdivisions;

(7) Services performed in the employ of a corporation, community chest, fund, or foundation, organized and operated exclusively for religious, charitable, scientific, literary, or educational purposes, or for the prevention of cruelty to children or animals, no part of the net earnings of which inures to the benefit of any private shareholder or individual.

(c) The term "qualified individual" means any individual with respect to whom it appears to the satisfaction of the Board that—

(1) He is at least sixty-five years of age; and

(2) The total amount of wages paid to him, with respect to employment after December 31, 1936, and before he attained the age of sixty-five, was not less than $2,000; and

3 Wages were paid to him, with respect to employment on some five days after December 31, 1936, and before he attained the age of sixty-five, each day being in a different calendar year.

TITLE III—GRANTS TO STATES FOR UNEMPLOYMENT COMPENSATION ADMINISTRATION

APPROPRIATION

Section 301. For the purpose of assisting the States in the administration of their unemployment compensation laws, there is hereby authorized to be appropriated, for the fiscal year ending June 30, 1936, the sum of

$4,000,000, and for each fiscal year thereafter the sum of $49,000,000, to be used as hereinafter provided.

PAYMENTS TO STATES

SEC. 302. (a) The Board shall from time to time certify to the Secretary of the Treasury for payment to each State which has an unemployment compensation law approved by the Board under Title IX, such amounts as the Board determines to be necessary for the proper administration of such law during the fiscal year in which such payment is to be made. The board's determination shall be based on (1) the population of the State; (2) an estimate of the number of persons covered by the State law and of the cost of proper administration of such law; and (3) such other factors as the Board finds relevant. The Board shall not certify for payment under this section in any fiscal year a total amount in excess of the amount appropriated therefor for such fiscal year.

(b) Out of the sums appropriated therefor, the Secretary of the Treasury shall, upon receiving a certification under subsection (a), pay, through the Division of Disbursement of the Treasury Department and prior to audit or settlement by the General Accounting Office, to the State agency charged with the administration of such law the amount so certified.

PROVISIONS OF STATE LAWS

SEC. 303. (a) The Board shall make no certification for payment to any State unless it finds that the law of such State, approved by the Board under Title IX, includes provisions for—

(1) Such methods of administration (other than those relating to selection, tenure of office, and compensation of personnel) as are found by the Board to be reasonably calculated to insure full payment of unemployment compensation when due; and

(2) Payment of unemployment compensation solely through public employment offices in the State or such other agencies as the Board may approve; and

(3) Opportunity for a fair hearing, before an impartial tribunal, for all individuals whose claims for unemployment compensation are denied; and

(4) The payment of all money received in the unemployment fund of such State, immediately upon such receipt, to the Secretary of the Treasury to the credit of the Unemployment Trust Fund established by section 904; and

(5) Expenditure of all money requisitioned by the State agency from the Unemployment Trust Fund, in the payment of unemployment compensation, exclusive of expenses of administration; and

(6) The making of such reports, in such form and containing such information, as the Board may from time to time require, and compliance with such provisions as the Board may from time to time find necessary to assure the correctness and verification of such reports; and

(7) Making available upon request to any agency of the United States charged with the administration of public works or assistance through

public employment, the name, address, ordinary occupation and employment status of each recipient of unemployment compensation, and a statement of such recipient's rights to further compensation under such law.

(b) Whenever the Board, after reasonable notice and opportunity for hearing to the State agency charged with the administration of the State law, finds that in the administration of the law there is—

(1) a denial, in a substantial number of cases, of unemployment compensation to individuals entitled thereto under such law; or

(2) a failure to comply substantially with any provision specified in subsection (a);

the Board shall notify such State agency that further payments will not be made to the State until the Board is satisfied that there is no longer any such denial or failure to comply. Until it is so satisfied, it shall make no further certification to the Secretary of the Treasury with respect to such State.

TITLE IV—GRANTS TO STATES FOR AID TO DEPENDENT CHILDREN

APPROPRIATION

SECTION 401. For the purpose of enabling each State to furnish financial assistance, as far as practicable under the conditions in such State, to needy dependent children, there is hereby authorized to be appropriated for the fiscal year ending June 30, 1936, the sum of $24,750,000, and there is hereby authorized to be appropriated for each fiscal year thereafter a sum sufficient to carry out the purposes of this title. The sums made available under this section shall be used for making payments to States which have submitted, and had approved by the Board, State plans for aid to dependent children.

STATE PLANS FOR AID TO DEPENDENT CHILDREN

SEC. 402. (a) A State plan for aid to dependent children must (1) provide that it shall be in effect in all political subdivisions of the State, and, if administered by them, be mandatory upon them; (2) provide for financial participation by the State; (3) either provide for the establishment or designation of a single State agency to administer the plan, or provide for the establishment or designation of a single State agency to supervise the administration of the plan; (4) provide for granting to any individual, whose claim with respect to aid to a dependent child is denied, an opportunity for a fair hearing before such State agency; (5) provide such methods of administration (other than those relating to selection, tenure of office, and compensation of personnel) as are found by the Board to be necessary for the efficient operation of the plan; and (6) provide that the State agency will make such reports, in such form and containing such information, as the Board may from time to time require, and comply with such provisions as the Board may from time to time find necessary to assure the correctness and verification of such reports.

(b) The Board shall approve any plan which fulfills the conditions specified in subsection (a), except that it shall not approve any plan which imposes as a condition of eligibility for aid to dependent children, a residence requirement which denies aid with respect to any child residing in the State (1) who has resided in the State for one year immediately preceding the application for such aid, or (2) who was born within the State within one year immediately preceding the application, if its mother has resided in the State for one year immediately preceding the birth.

PAYMENT TO STATES

SEC. 403. (a) From the sums appropriated therefor, the Secretary of the Treasury shall pay to each State which has an approved plan for aid to dependent children, for each quarter, beginning with the quarter commencing July 1, 1935, an amount, which shall be used exclusively for carrying out the State plan, equal to one-third of the total of the sums expended during such quarter under such plan, not counting so much of such expenditure with respect to any dependent child for any month as exceeds $18, or if there is more than one dependent child in the same home, as exceeds $18 for any month with respect to one such dependent child and $12 for such month with respect to each of the other dependent children. . . .

DEFINITIONS

SEC. 406. When used in this title—

(a) The term "dependent child" means a child under the age of sixteen who has been deprived of parental support or care by reason of the death, continued absence from the home, or physical or mental incapacity of a parent, and who is living with his father, mother, grandfather, grandmother, brother, sister, stepfather, stepmother, stepbrother, stepsister, uncle, or aunt, in a place of residence maintained by one or more of such relatives as his or their own home;

(b) The term "aid to dependent children" means money payments with respect to a dependent child or dependent children.

TITLE V—GRANTS TO STATES FOR MATERNAL AND CHILD WELFARE

PART 1—MATERNAL AND CHILD HEALTH SERVICES

APPROPRIATION

SECTION 501. For the purpose of enabling each State to extend and improve, as far as practicable under the conditions in such State, services for promoting the health of mothers and children, especially in rural areas and in areas suffering from severe economic distress, there is herby authorized to be appropriated for each fiscal year, beginning with the fiscal year ending June 30, 1936, the sum of $3,800,000. The sums made available under this section shall be used for making payments to States which have submitted, and had approved by the Chief of the Children's Bureau, State plans for such services.

ALLOTMENTS TO STATES

SEC. 502. (a) Out of the sums appropriated pursuant to section 501 for each fiscal year the Secretary of Labor shall allot to each State $20,000, and such part of $1,800,000 as he finds that the number of live births in such State bore to the total number of live births in the United States, in the latest calendar year for which the Bureau of the Census has available statistics.

(b) Out of the sums appropriated pursuant to section 501 for each fiscal year the Secretary of Labor shall allot to the States $980,000 (in addition to the allotments made under subsection (a), according to the financial need of each State for assistance in carrying out its State plan, as determined by him after taking into consideration the number of live births in such State.

(c) The amount of any allotment to a State under subsection (a) for any fiscal year remaining unpaid to such State at the end of such fiscal year shall be available for payment to such State under section 504 until the end of the second succeeding fiscal year. No payment to a State under section 504 shall be made out of its allotment for any fiscal year until its allotment for the preceding fiscal year has been exhausted or has ceased to be available.

APPROVAL OF STATE PLANS

SEC. 503. (a) A State plan for maternal and child-health services must (1) provide for financial participation by the State; (2) provide for the administration of the plan by the State health agency or the supervision of the administration of the plan by the State health agency; (3) provide such methods of administration (other than those relating to selection, tenure of office, and compensation of personnel) as are necessary for the efficient operation of the plan; (4) provide that the State health agency will make such reports, in such form and containing such information, as the Secretary of Labor may from time to time find necessary to assure the correctness and verification of such reports; (5) provide for the extension and improvement of local maternal and child-health services administered by local child-health units; (6) provide for cooperation with medical, nursing, and welfare groups and organization; and (7) provide for the development of demonstration services in needy areas and among groups in special need.

(b) The Chief of the Children's Bureau shall approve any plan which fulfills the conditions specified in subsection (a) and shall thereupon notify the Secretary of Labor and the State health agency of his approval . . . .

PART 2—SERVICES FOR CRIPPLED CHILDREN

APPROPRIATION

SEC. 511. For the purpose of enabling each State to extend and improve (especially in rural areas and in areas suffering from severe economic distress), as far as practicable under the conditions in such State, services for locating crippled children, and for providing medical, surgical, corrective, and other services and care, and facilities for diagnosis, hospitalization, and aftercare, for children who are crippled or who are suffering from conditions which lead to crippling, there is hereby authorized to be appropriated for each fiscal year, beginning with the fiscal year ending June 30, 1936, the sum of $2,850,000. The sums made available under this section shall be used for making payments to States which have submitted, and had approved by the Chief of the Children's Bureau, State plans for such services.

ALLOTMENTS TO STATES

SEC. 512. (a) Out of the sums appropriated pursuant to section 511 for each fiscal year the Secretary of Labor shall allot to each State $20,000, and the remainder to the States according to the need of each State as determined by him after taking into consideration the number of crippled children in such State in need of the services referred to in section 511 and the cost of furnishing such services to them.

(b) The amount of any allotment to a State under subsection (a) for any fiscal year remaining unpaid to such State at the end of such fiscal year shall be available for payment to such State under section 514 until the end of the second succeeding fiscal year. No payment to a State under section 514 shall be made out of its allotment for any fiscal year until its allotment for the preceding fiscal year has been exhausted or has ceased to be available.

APPROVAL OF STATE PLANS

SEC. 513. (a) A State plan for sevices for crippled children must (1) provide for financial participation by the State; (2) provide for the administration of the plan by a State agency or the supervision of the administration of the plan by a State agency; (3) provide such methods of administration (other than those relating to selection, tenure of office, and compensation of personnel) as are necessary for the efficient operation of the plan; (4) provide that the State agency will make such reports, in such form and containing such information, as the Secretary of Labor may from time to time require, and comply with such provisions as he may from time to time find necessary to assure the correctness and verification of such reports; (5) provide for carrying out the purposes specified in section 511; and (6) provide for cooperation with medical, health, nursing, and welfare groups and organizations and with any agency in such State charged with administering State laws providing for vocational rehabilitation of physically handicapped children.

(b) The Chief of the Children's Bureau shall approve any plan which fulfills the conditions specified in subsection (a) and shall thereupon notify the Secretary of Labor and the State health agency of his approval. . . .

PART 3—CHILD-WELFARE SERVICES

SEC. 521. (a) For the purpose of enabling the United States, through the Children's Bureau, to cooperate with State public-welfare agencies in establishing, extending, and strengthening, especially in predominantly rural areas, public-welfare services (hereinafter in this section referred to as "child-welfare services") for the protection and care of homeless, dependent,

and neglected children, and children in danger of becoming delinquent, there is hereby authorized to be appropriated for each fiscal year, beginning with the fiscal year ending June 30, 1936, the sum of $1,500,000. Such amount shall be allotted by the Secretary of Labor for use by cooperating State public-welfare agencies on the basis of plans developed jointly by the State agency and the Children's Bureau, to each State, $10,000, and the remainder to each State on the basis of such plans, not to exceed such part of the remainder as the rural population of such State bears to the total rural population of the United States. The amount so allotted shall be expended for payment of part of the cost of district, county or other local child-welfare services in areas predominantly rural, and for developing State services for the encouragement and assistance of adequate methods of community child-welfare organization in areas predominantly rural and other areas of special need. The amount of any allotment to a State under this section for any fiscal year remaining unpaid to such State at the end of such fiscal year shall be available for payment to such State under this section until the end of the second succeeding fiscal year. No payment to a State under this section shall be made out of its allotment for any fiscal year until its allotment for the preceding fiscal year has been exhausted or has ceased to be available
. . . .

PART 4—VOCATIONAL REHABILITATION

SEC. 531. (a) In order to enable the United States to cooperate with the States and Hawaii in extending and strengthening their programs of vocational rehabilitation of the physically disabled, and to continue to carry out the provisions and purposes of the Act entitled "An Act to provide for the promotion of vocational rehabilitation of persons disabled in industry or otherwise and their return to civil employment," approved June 2, 1920, as amended (U.S.C., title 29, ch. 4; U.S.C., Supp. VII, title 29, secs. 31, 32, 34, 35, 37, 39, and 40), there is hereby authorized to be appropriated for the fiscal years ending June 30, 1936, and June 30, 1937, the sum of $841,000 for each fiscal year in addition to the amount of the existing authorization, and for each fiscal year thereafter the sum of $1,938,000. Of the sums appropriated pursuant to such authorization for each fiscal year, $5,000 shall be apportioned to the Territory of Hawaii and the remainder shall be apportioned among the several States in the manner provided in such Act of June 2, 1920, unamended. . . .

PART 5—ADMINISTRATION

SEC. 541. (a) There is hereby authorized to be appropriated for the fiscal year ending June 30, 1936, the sum of $425,000, for all necessary expenses of the Children's Bureau in administering the provisions of this title, except section 531.

(b) The Children's Bureau shall make such studies and investigations as will promote the efficient administration of this title, except section 531.

(c) The Secretary of Labor shall include in his annual report to Congress a full account of the administration of this title, except section 531. . . .

TITLE X—GRANTS TO STATES FOR AID TO THE BLIND

APPROPRIATION

SECTION 1001. For the purpose of enabling each State to furnish financial assistance, as far as practicable under the conditions in such State, to needy individuals who are blind, there is hereby authorized to be appropriated for the fiscal year ending June 30, 1936, the sum of $3,000,000, and there is hereby authorized to be appropriated for each fiscal year thereafter a sum sufficient to carry out the purposes of this title. The sums made available under this section shall be used for making payments to States which have submitted, and had approved by the Social Security Board, State plans for aid to the blind.

STATE PLANS FOR AID TO THE BLIND

SEC. 1002. (a) A State plan for aid to the blind must (1) provide that it shall be in effect in all political subdivisions of the State, and if administered by them, be mandatory upon them; (2) provide for financial participation by the State; (3) either provide for the establishment or designation of a single State agency to adminster the plan, or provide for the establishment or designation of a single State agency to supervise the administration of the plan; (4) provide for granting to any individual, whose claim for aid is denied, an opportunity for a fair hearing before such State agency; (5) provide such methods of administration (other than those relating to selection, tenure of office, and compensation of personnel) as are found by the Board to be necessary for the efficient operation of the plan; (6) provide that the State agency will make such reports, in such form and containing such information, as the Board may from time to time require, and comply with such provisions as the Board may from time to time find necessary to assure the correctness and verification of such reports; and (7) provide that no aid will be furnished any individual under the plan with respect to which he is receiving old-age assistance under the State plan approved under section 2 of this Act.

(b) The Board shall approve any plan which fulfills the conditions specified in subsection (a), except that it shall not approve any plan which imposes, as a condition of eligibility for aid to the blind under the plan—

(1) Any residence requirement which excludes any resident of the State who has resided therein five years during the nine years immediately preceding the application for aid and has resided therein continuously for one year immediately preceding the application; or

(2) Any citizenship requirement which excludes any citizen of the United States.

PAYMENT TO STATES

SEC. 1003. (a) From the sums appropriated therefor, the Secretary of the Treasury shall pay to each State which has an approved plan for aid to the blind, for each quarter, beginning with the quarter commencing July 1, 1935, (1) an amount, which shall be used exclusively as aid to the blind, equal to one-half of the total of the sums expended during such quarter as aid to the blind under the State plan with respect to each individual who is blind and is not an inmate of a public institution, not counting so much of such expenditure with respect to any individual for any month as exceeds $30, and (2) 5 per centum of such amount, which shall be used for paying the costs of administering the State plan or for aid to the blind, or both, and for no other purpose. . . .

SHORT TITLE

Sec. 1105. This Act may be cited as the "Social Security Act."
Approved, August 14, 1935.

Chapter 7
War and Prosperity:
1940–1970

The period from 1940 to 1970 was one of contradiction—of growth and of conflict, of affluence and of the rediscovery of poverty. First in Europe and the Pacific, later in Indochina, the United States was involved in warfare. The military mobilization and wartime production of World War II led initially to economic recovery and subsequently to a "revolution of rising expectations" at home. The 1950s and 1960s were decades of internal as well as external conflict, of battles at home against discrimination on the basis of race and sex and against poverty, while abroad we waged war in Korea and Vietnam.

Supported by military and civilian demand, the years from 1940 to 1970 were prosperous ones that marked a transition from the consumer demand deficiency of the depression to a "supply deficiency" of the 1970s, from the problem of mass unemployment to the problem of spiraling inflation. The gross national product had managed to climb to almost $100 billion by 1940 as a result of efforts to rearm and to supply future allies. By 1970 the gross national product had soared almost tenfold to $976 billion. True, much of the increase was due to inflation; but even in constant prices, GNP had tripled.[1] Real disposable personal income—that is, purchasing power available to consumers—had more than doubled by 1970; and per capita consumer expenditures and savings had risen dramatically.[2] As might be expected, family income, and therefore family welfare measured in money terms, showed significant improvement.

All income groups of the population shared in the prosperity, as did most racial and ethnic groups. Median family income grew for whites and nonwhites. Nonwhite families had a median income of $1,614 in 1947, 51 percent of white family median income. In 1950 nonwhite family income was 54 percent of white; in 1960, 55 percent; and in 1970, 61 percent. This was an improvement in one sense, but the actual dollar gap between white and nonwhite families widened as all incomes grew: the gap went from $1,543 in 1947, to $1,576 in 1950, to $2,602 in 1960, and to $3,957 in 1970.[3]

The same mixed picture of prosperity is demonstrated through the use of the poverty index developed by the Social Security Administration (SSA) to measure the minimum income needed for purchasing a subsistence level of goods and services. In 1960 a nonfarm family of four required $3,022 in order to escape poverty as defined by SSA. In that year, almost 40 million individuals were counted poor, 22.4 percent of the population. Ten years later, in 1970, the poverty index for a nonfarm family of four had risen to $3,968. The number of individuals counted poor had dropped to 25.4 million, 12.6 percent of the population. But again, there was a differential between the progress of whites and nonwhites. The 17.5 million whites counted poor in 1970 represented 10 percent of all whites in the population; the 8 million nonwhites counted poor represented 32 percent of all nonwhites. The poverty rate for blacks was more than three times that for whites.[4]

The increase in income was in part a result of the expansion of the labor force. The civilian labor force grew from 55.6 million in 1940 to 82.7 million in 1970. The expansion was due partially to population growth and partially to a long-time secular increase in labor force participation rates from 56 percent in 1940 to 61 percent of the population in 1970.[5] The trend was accelerated by World War II when there was a major infusion of women into the labor force. In 1940, 24 percent of all women of working age were in the labor force; by 1970 the figure had risen to over 43 percent. In 1970, as in 1940, economic necessity made for a higher labor force participation rate among black women—49 percent as against 42 percent for white women— but the gap had closed appreciably.[6]

The state of the economy was demonstrated by its ability to resist major recessions at the same time that it absorbed an ever-expanding labor force. In 1940 the unemployment rate stood at 14.6 percent. In 1943, with war production in full swing, the unemployment rate dipped as low as 1.2 percent. Unemployment averaged 4.5 percent during the 1950s; 5.7 percent between 1960 and 1965; and 3.8 percent between 1965 and 1970. The apparent strength of the economy at first obscured, but then increasingly made visible, the extent to which unemployment struck disproportionately at certain groups. In 1960, when white unemployment averaged 4.9 percent, the rate for nonwhites was 10.2 percent. For teenagers it stood at 14.7 percent. Structural imbalance persisted throughout the era. The rates averaged 4.5 percent and 8.2 percent for whites and nonwhites, respectively, in 1970.[7]

Satisfaction with the state of the economy, and with the social and economic choices it made possible, tended to suppress recognition of the connection between the rapid exit out of poverty of male-headed families and the entrance of wives in such families into the labor force. There was even slower recognition of the discriminatory differential between male and female earnings. By the close of the 1960s, women's wages averaged only 59 percent of wages and salaries received by male workers.[8] And beyond reluctance to recognize the contribution to familial economic well-being attributable to increased labor participation by women was the slowness in coming to grips with the significance of their working. Their growing financial independence had implications for the development of new family forms, for changes in the roles of family members, and for new child care arrangements.

Population Shifts

The military and social eruptions of the 1940–1970 period were accompanied by huge changes in population size and distribution. Total U.S. population grew from 132.1 million in 1940 to 204.8 million in 1970. Since congressional action during the 1920s had slowed immigration to a trickle, most of the growth was due to natural population increase reflecting changes in the birth and death rates. By the middle of the 1930s, decisions to delay marriage and childbearing had lowered the birthrate to about 17 per 1,000 persons in the population. As the depression ended at the beginning of World War II and as young people faced the initial prospect of separation, the birthrate briefly increased—and then fell again. Immediately after the war, however, the birthrate soared, reaching a high of 26.6 per 1,000 persons in 1947 and remaining high until the mid-1960s.[9]

The increased birthrate was accompanied by an increase in years of life expectancy and by a decline in the death rate. In 1940 the estimated average length of life in the United States was 62.9 years. Life expectancy had risen to 68.2, 69.7, and 70.8 years by 1950, 1960, and 1970 respectively. During this same period, the estimated average life expectancy among nonwhites rose from 82.7 percent to 90 percent of estimated average life expectancy among whites. Simultaneously, death rates declined for the total population from 10.8 per 1,000 individuals in the population in 1940 to 9.4 in 1970. Most significantly, the death rate among nonwhites declined from 13.8 in 1940 to approximate the national average at 9.5 in 1970.[10] These remarkable changes in life expectancy reflected better nutrition as incomes rose as well as widespread availability of sulfa and penicillin and of new medical and surgical procedures. The visibility of actual and potential results from improved medical and health care sustained an increased vigorous concern for further progress. The demand, too, was for assured availability of care to the general public.

Changing birth and death rates produced changing demographic patterns. Over the years, the country's population grew both younger and older. The percentage of those under 19 grew from 34.2 percent of the total population in 1940 to 37.9 percent of the population in 1970. The percentage of the population over 65 grew from 6.8 percent to 10.2 percent in the same time. Clearly, a declining percentage of "productive" individuals was being called upon to support a growing percentage of the "nonproductive." Added to this was the nonproductivity of groups who wanted jobs but could not find them. In this regard, the effect of racial discrimination upon employment opportunities for blacks intensified as the percentage of blacks in the total population grew.[11]

Population growth was accompanied by population shifts and dislocations. World War II accelerated the historical process of industrialization and mechanization. The wartime necessity for spreading industry, shipping, and the training of service personnel across the country in order to engage in a war being fought on two fronts reinforced the continuous westward movement of the center of population. Rapid development of the Pacific states ensued. Equally important was the movement of the population from rural to urban areas. The pull of jobs in urban centers and the push of technical advances making small marginal farms obsolete and therefore unprofitable impelled the move of 20 million people from rural to urban areas between 1940 and 1970. Of the total, about 16 million were white and about 4 million were black.[12] By 1950, 64 percent of the country's total population lived in urban areas—64 percent of the white population and 62 percent of the nonwhite population—and the rest lived in rural areas. By 1970, 72 percent of the white population and 81 percent of the nonwhite population lived in urban areas.[13]

In the search for factory employment, large numbers of blacks had left the South. The percentage of the black population residing in the South dropped from 77 percent in 1940 to 52 percent in 1970. Despite a continuous migration to Northeastern and North Central states, however, a heavy concentration of blacks continued to live in the South.

Perhaps of more importance than place of residence was the fact of black urbanization itself, a response to changes in agriculture. For the country as a whole, the relative share of employment in agriculture fell from 15 percent of the civilian labor force in 1940 to 4 percent in 1970.[14] At the same time, mechanization increased the real value of farm output by $6.4 billion between those same years.[15] Technological developments—increased mechanization that had led to increased productivity—had necessitated the development of larger farms to ensure adequate monetary returns. Average farm size increased from 167 acres in 1940 to 373 acres in 1970. The size of farms owned by whites more than doubled; but the size of farms owned by blacks grew only 20 percent.[16] Since average black-owned and -operated farm holdings had historically been small and only marginally profitable, black families and farm workers suffered disproportionate dislocation. Black migration was inherent in the changed economic situation.

The black migration of the early 1940s was caught up and hidden in the general necessity for wartime mobility. More than 16 million men were transported for military reasons; women, wives, and families followed. Another 16 million men and women moved for job-related reasons. The general wartime atmosphere was characterized by migration and mobility. Family life and the family unit were severely challenged. Between 1940 and the close of the war in 1946 the number of divorces increased from 264,000 to 610,000 annually.[17] The divorce rate had shot from 2.0 to 4.3 per 1,000 of population. Between 1940 and 1950 the number of illegitimate births per 1,000 unmarried women, 15 to 44 years of age, increased from 3.6 to 6.1 for white women and from 35.6 to 71.2 for nonwhite women.[18] Many high school students left school to take jobs, so that as early as September 1942, the National Child Labor Committee reported that of the 4 million juveniles who had been employed in industry and agriculture during the preceding summer months, 3 million were still employed as the new school term began. About 75,000 were under age 16.[19] During the midst of the war, J. Edgar Hoover, head of the Federal Bureau of Investigation, reported "an alarming" increase in juvenile delinquency.[20]

The postwar years aggravated, even institutionalized, the trend toward mobility and its concomitant social risks. The creation of a "mobile attitude," with its seeming homogenization of values, was sustained by the increased ease of transportation and communication. Moving was no longer unusual or frightening in a world made familiar by commercial civilian flying and by television. And as automobile ownership mushroomed and discontent with city dwelling surfaced, suburbanization followed upon urbanization. As families moved from their home base, they moved too from the support and help of relatives and long-time friends.

Technology, Productivity, and Economic Insecurity

The key to postwar affluence, consumerism, and leisure was increased output per man-hour. A continuous development of new materials, new products, and new industries called forth an evolution of new processes involving greater efficiency in harnessing the uses of energy. The building of specialized, labor-saving machinery, the increasing attention to standardization and use of interchangeable machinery parts, and the extension of mass production techniques further increased productivity. These new processes were enhanced by the development of computer technology, advanced information systems, and systems engineering. World War II had given a major boost to the chemical and airplane industries, to the development and exploitation of synthetics such as nylon and metals such as aluminum, and to the expansion of the importance of electricity. The postwar period saw the continuation of the preeminence of the automobile industry but saw, too, the emergence of major new industries—television, space technology, commercial aviation, and others. Industrial and technological advances were reflected in worker productivity and work hours. Between 1950 and 1970 the real gross national product per capita rose 50 percent while average annual working hours per worker dropped 8.5 percent.[21]

The impact of industrial and technological change on worker output was reflected not only in a reduction in average work hours but also in the occupational distribution of employees. By 1970, the significance of manufacturing as a source of employment had peaked and declined to 25 percent of the total employment picture. At the same time, growing wealth and increasing societal complexity led to rapid expansion in service industries— health, recreation, and so on—and in government. By 1970 employment in services had risen to 17 percent and in government to 18 percent of the total employment picture.[22]

The postwar era saw too a public acceptance of the expansion of governmental activities in specified areas. The Employment Act of 1946 had set "maximum employment, production and purchasing power" as goals of governmental policy. The act's creation of the Council of Economic Advisors led to the conscious use of fiscal and monetary policy and of the federal budget as tools to control employment, production, and price levels—that is, to plan economic stability. In a related area, there was continued and growing acceptance of the responsibility of government for the income security of those with lifetime attachments to the labor force. The government's program of Old Age and Survivors Insurance was expanded first to disability and then to health insurance for the aged; with little opposition, payroll taxes were increased from 2 percent of the first $3,000 of income in 1940 to 9.6 percent of $7,800 in 1970. The popularity of "Social Security" showed little sign of abating.

Public attitudes did not change appreciably toward the acceptance of an expanded governmental role in regard to direct relief for the nonworking poor. Categorical public assistance programs had been included in the Social Security Act and were accepted as temporary programs. To the extent that minor program expansions did not challenge the belief that the need for relief would "wither away," little opposition appeared. When, however, it became clear that the public assistance programs—particularly Aid to Dependent Children—were expanding, not withering away, resistance developed. The discovery that poverty in America included a substantial group of working poor at the same time that ADC was becoming identified as a "black program" almost guaranteed hostility and opposition. Beyond that, however, was the vigor of renewed confidence in the work ethic and in economic growth as a way out of poverty.

The depression had shaken the confidence of Americans in the ability of society to control economic fluctuations. It introduced fears of a permanent "mature" economy that would stagnate. The events of World War II and the postwar period seemed to most Americans to demonstrate the ability of government to develop control mechanisms to moderate the ups and downs of business cycles and the continued vigor of the economy. A renewed faith in the productive process took hold. The final reality was that organized labor, that segment of society that might have been expected to become allied with the poor, had itself become part of the establishment. Beginning with the New Deal, government had legalized almost all of labor's demands: the right to organize and bargain collectively, workmen's compensation, minimum wages, old age insurance and unemployment insurance, limitations on hours, and the prohibition of injunctions. Through the process of collective bargaining, labor had not only been able to raise and even control its wage position relative to prices, but it had also been able to have a whole series of fringe benefits instituted comprising a private health and welfare security system. Membership in unions rose to 20 million by 1970.[23] Organized labor increasingly identified itself with the status quo and separated itself from the poor.

World War II

The most dramatic changes of the 30-year period from 1940 to 1970 occurred during World War II. The upheaval of war brought full employment and rising incomes. For oppressed groups, particularly blacks and women, the period offered increased opportunity for economic, educational, and social equality and laid the groundwork for the civil rights and feminist movements of the 1950s and 1960s.

Indicators of change between 1940 and 1945 abound. The gross national product, for example, rose from $99.7 billion in 1940 to $211.9 billion in 1945; and although this was a period of rapidly advancing prices, GNP rose 56 percent in "real" terms—that is, in constant dollars.[24] Furthermore, full employment and progressive taxation brought about basic changes in income distribution—changes that the New Deal had hoped, but failed, to achieve.

In 1940 the total noninstitutional population of the United States was 100.4 million. Of this total 56 million were in the labor force, including 540,000 in the armed services. Civilian employment stood at 47.5 million. By 1945 the population had risen to 105.5 million. The total labor force had increased to 65.3 million, including the 11 million men and women in the armed forces. The huge increase in the number of armed forces personnel took these people out of the civilian work force. Nevertheless, total civilian employment rose by 5 million, or 11.1 percent. The increase was made possible by the sharp decline in unemployment and the expansion of the labor force as women, retirees, and children went to work. By 1945 civilian employment had reached 52.8 million. Between 1940 and 1945 unemployment declined from 8 million to 1 million.

Whereas income redistribution during the 1930s had benefited middle income groups, redistribution during the World War II period favored the lowest income groups. Real income rose for families in all income ranges between 1941 and 1947; but it rose proportionately more for poor families than for rich ones. The average increase in real income of families in the lowest quintile of family income rankings was 41.6 percent; the average increase for families in the highest fifth was 18.3 percent.[25]

Still, poverty had not disappeared. In 1947, 31 percent of all family units still had annual incomes, after taxation, under $2,000, and 51 percent of all family units had annual incomes under $3,000. But this compared with 62 percent of all family units having had annual incomes, after taxation, under $2,000, and, with 84 percent of all family units having had annual incomes under $3,000 in 1941. At the same time, the share of income of individuals ranked in the top 5 percent had declined from 23 percent to 17 percent in 1947.[26] Within these limits, therefore, democratization of income had occurred. A combination of factors—decrease in unemployment, an increase in the number of multiearner families, the opening up of job opportunities for minority groups—was responsible. Of major consequence for income redistribution was the influx of women into the labor force and the shift of blacks from farm to higher-paying factory jobs.

Rising incomes combined with restrictions on the availability of civilian goods increased personal savings. During the worst of the depression in 1933, savings were negative; almost $1 billion of dissaving occurred. In 1940 personal savings totaled $3.8 billion. They climbed throughout the war, reaching a peak of $37.3 billion in 1944.[27] Thus during the war years a huge backlog of savings developed—about 24 percent of annual disposable income, as compared to 3.4 percent of disposable income in prewar years and 6 to 7 percent in postwar years.

The wartime redistribution of jobs and income was not achieved easily. Tremendous resistance to the employment of blacks in defense industries was encountered, and race riots occurred in 1940 and 1941. A march on Washington, D.C., by 50,000 to 100,000 blacks to highlight the demand for jobs was threatened by A. Philip Randolph, president of the Brotherhood of Sleeping Car Porters. The march, planned for July 1941, was canceled when the March on Washington Movement, under Randolph's leadership, was able to negotiate the establishment of the Fair Employment Practices Committee (FEPC).

FEPC was established by Executive Order 8802 on June 25, 1941, and promised "no discrimination in the employment of workers in defense industries or Government because of race, creed, color, or national origin . . . [and] the full and equitable participation of all workers in defense industries, without discrimination. . . ."[28] Widespread defiance of the Committee's recommendations, the lack of power to punish offenders, and reluctance to have war contracts and the manufacturing of war equipment canceled rendered FEPC ineffectual.

The response of the black community to the failure of FEPC was strong and immediate, as several factors came together. First, of course, was the fact that blacks had been migrating to urban industrial centers, where their congregating under conditions of segregation lent strength for joint action. Second, a significant number of blacks had been educationally prepared and were ready for greater participation in the work opportunities opened up by the war. Experience on WPA projects, vocational training received by way of the National Youth Administration's vocational work program, defense training financed through programs sponsored by the U.S. Office of Education, all pointed up a source of untapped and underutilized labor. The training was in itself a promise of opportunity that remained unfulfilled, joining other promises to a string of disappointments. The National Defense Advisory Committee's statement against discriminatory hiring practices in defense plants and President Roosevelt's inclusion of a similar statement in a message to Congress, both in 1940, failed to change the situation. The efforts of the Office of Production Management's Negro Employment and Training Branch to facilitate the hiring of blacks in defense industries were unsuccessful. Finally, the ineffectiveness of FEPC was demonstrated when its scheduled public hearings into discrimination on railroads were canceled by the War Manpower Commission despite widespread support by the negro press and civil rights leaders. This particular affront loosened the cap that Executive Order 8802 had placed on a well of discontent.

Underpinning all that set the stage for resistance to racial discrimination was the fact that the black community was organized in ways that had not previously been true. Union membership, especially in black unions such as Randolph's Brotherhood of Sleeping Car Porters, was one indication of organization. The emergence of spokesmen for the black community, Randolph himself, for example, and, among others, the corps of men in the government who became identified as the "Black Brain Trust" was another indication. In addition, there was the evolution of an influential Negro press—Baltimore's *Afro-American,* Harlem's *Amsterdam Star News,* the *Chicago Defender,* the *Houston Informer,* and so on—which pressed editorially for black rights and simultaneously encouraged blacks to make their own demands.

Discrimination and resistance to discrimination in defense employment and in the armed forces eventuated in a series of racial clashes in Newark, New Jersey; Philadelphia, Pennsylvania; Centreville, Mississippi; and Mobile, Alabama. A particularly severe outbreak in Detroit left 35 dead, 700 wounded, and 1,300 under arrest. Riots occurred in Texas, Massachusetts, New York, and California. In the latter instance the rioters were largely Mexican-Americans.

The growing militancy of minority groups resulted in the creation of a second FEPC in May 1943, and greater headway against discriminatory employment practices was achieved. By 1943 black workers held 1 million factory jobs, though largely as unskilled laborers. Black union membership had increased to 500,000. The number of blacks in government rose from 50,000 in 1939 to 200,000 in 1944. Resistance to the induction of blacks under the provisions of the Selective Service Act of 1940 yielded, so that by the end of the war, about 1 million black men and women had served in the armed forces—a remarkable achievement considering that only about 2,000 were drafted during the first year of the act's operation. The war had brought about gains for blacks as a response to economic pressures and to the successful mobilization of protest. That white Americans' attitude toward other races had not changed is seen in the treatment of the 112,000 Japanese-Americans who were removed from their homes on the West Coast to internment camps in the Western deserts and the swamplands of Arkansas.[29]

Wartime Economic and Social Advances

The general improvement in levels of living, as measured by increased income, during the war years was paralleled by major improvement in the nation's health. Concern about physical and mental health developed as armed services induction procedures revealed serious deficiencies; the inability of large numbers of young people to meet induction standards caused a startling rejection rate. A shift toward improved health conditions occurred for the civilian and noncivilian populations. Routine health care, including dental care, was provided for servicemen and their families. In 1943 Congress appropriated special funds for the Emergency Maternity and Infant Care Program. This program, which was administered by the Children's Bureau through state health departments, provided regular health care for the wives and children of servicemen in the lower pay grades of the armed services. More than 1.2 million women and 230,000 infants were given care during the war years.[30] For servicemen themselves, the armed services offered both corrective and preventive care through regular physical and dental examinations and emergency clinic care for minor illnesses. Beyond that, "military medicine" fostered improvements in standards of physical fitness through balanced diets, better clothing, and "more and better hospitals completely staffed."[31]

Rising incomes made for better, healthier living conditions for the civilian population. In addition, rising incomes made it possible for the civilian population to take advantage of the discovery and development of new drugs and new medical and surgical procedures. Attention to health needs and health care as matters of daily living was demonstrated in new practices such as the stepping up of various inoculation programs. Increased labor participation by women led to improved safety conditions in factories. The wartime attention to health and mental health continued during the postwar period and resulted in the passage of the National Mental Health Act of 1946. The act provided a funding mechanism for research and training programs and for state assistance in establishing community mental health services. In 1948 President Truman proposed a national health insurance scheme. The National Mental Health Act was not funded until 1948; the proposal for national health insurance was defeated after a gigantic attack by the American Medical Association. Delays aside, however, events of the future had begun to take shape.

The passage of the Emergency Maternal and Infant Care Act serves to point up the extent to which wartime improvements in economic and social well-being flowed from exigencies of the war rather than from social welfare concerns per se. At the beginning of the war, even as large-scale unemployment continued, pressure began to mount for phasing out the many New Deal social welfare programs; and during the war very little explicit social legislation was passed. The Civilian Conservation Corps was abolished in 1941, and WPA was abolished in 1943. Expenditures for work relief declined year after year.[32] The figures are as follows:

1940	$1,861,421,985
1941	1,451,910,183
1942	937,272,410
1943	317,385,759
1944	23,009,726
1945	4,640,335

The National Youth Administration survived as a mechanism for administering vocational training for recruits to war industries.

The social legislation of the time was primarily related to the needs of communities disrupted by army camps and war plants and to the needs of families dislocated by the absence of husbands and fathers as they left for the armed forces or for war industries and by the absence of mothers as women took jobs. Housing, day care, education, health, recreation, and transportation needs as they affected "home front" preparations became the focus of concern.

In November 1940 President Roosevelt named the administrator of the Federal Security Agency as coordinator of the Office of Health, Welfare and Related Defense Activities with special responsibility for providing service in defense communities and communities near training camps. In May 1941 the Office of Civilian Defense was created in the Office of War Management for the purpose of integrating the provision of health, welfare, and recreation services with other defense activities. The two departments underwent considerable reorganization as experience demonstrated conflicting areas of jurisdiction and the need for clarifying their relationships with a variety of national and local public and voluntary social welfare organizations. By 1943 the government had organized the Office of Community War Services under the Federal Security Agency to take responsibility for coordinating state and local efforts to provide health, welfare, recreation, family, and community services for members of the armed forces and for the civilian population. The Community Facilities Act of 1941 (the Lanham Act) provided federal funds to defense-impacted communities for the construction of houses, schools, day care centers, hospitals, water and sanitation plants, and recreational facilities.

Lanham Act funds helped many communities, but many others suffered upheaval without federal funds to ease the problems of population movement. Local community chests and councils of social agencies took on some of the planning and financing of social services early in the war. Six major voluntary agencies* combined efforts through the United Service Organization for National Defense (USO) to provide services for military personnel, war workers, and transients. Over 1,000 USO centers were established.

Fund-raising efforts in the voluntary sector were united by the National War Fund, which combined and regulated the money-raising campaigns of community chest funds with those of the war relief agencies so that traditional social services of local agencies could be financed. Overall control of the whole effort was exercised by the federal government through the War Relief Control Board, which licensed agencies and held authority over all secular wartime charities, except for the Red Cross.[33]

Wartime measures for education, like those for health, had implications for future developments. Army examinations had revealed an illiteracy rate of one in five among recruits. At the start of the war, the army asked the WPA to set up programs of adult and worker education and the NYA, a student vocational work program. Their activities were phased out or reduced as the army itself took on some of their tasks and especially after the U.S. Office of Education was expanded. Perhaps most important in the long run is the fact that federal aid was made available for elementary and secondary education in "impacted areas" and for agricultural extension services in rural areas. Education on the college level was also fostered as the federal government let out enormous contracts for research in engineering, science, and civil aeronautics, for education in defense industry management, and for ROTC.

Veterans and the G.I. Bill

The major social legislation of the war and immediate postwar years centered on the welfare needs of soldiers and veterans. There were 16,535,000 United States participants in the war. Deaths sustained in battle numbered 292,000; deaths from other causes were 114,000; the wounded numbered 671,000.

The income security needs of the dependents of members of the armed forces were met through a program of family allotments financed jointly by the individual soldier, through a pay deduction, and by the federal government. The allowances were provided for by the Servicemen's Dependents Allowance Act of 1942[34] and were administered by the Office of Dependency Benefits of the War Department. During its first year of operation, ending June 30, 1943, a total of $797 million was disbursed, of which the government had contributed 50 percent. By 1945 allotment payments totaled $3 billion, with the government's contribution rising to $2 billion.[35]

Family allotments were seen as wage supplements and were available to

*YMCA, YWCA, National Catholic Community Service, Jewish Welfare Board, Salvation Army, National Travelers Aid Society.

dependents of the six lowest pay grades of enlisted personnel. Entitlement to benefits for wives and children was based upon relationship. Need, given salary levels, was assumed. Dependents of servicemen were additionally protected by the National Life Insurance Act of 1940,[36] which (with later amendments) insured against death or total disability from service and non-service-connected causes.

Benefits for veterans of World War II included those benefits available to soldiers and veterans of previous wars. In the past, concern had been primarily with income security for dependents of the dead and disabled and with the vocational rehabilitation of the latter. There had long been dissatisfaction with the fact that "veterans without service-connected disabilities were left to their own devices in the matter of their readjustment to civilian life."[37] A first approach to help with readjustment problems was contained in the Selective Training and Service Act of 1940, which provided that inductees "be reemployed at the termination of their period of service in positions of like seniority, status and pay."[38] On November 13, 1942, President Roosevelt appointed the Armed Forces Committee on Postwar Education Opportunities for Service Personnel to study the educational problems that servicemen and servicewomen might encounter after the war. The president's appointment followed upon the urging of the resolution, adopted earlier in 1942, by the American Legion at its annual convention. The Servicemen's Readjustment Act of 1944[39]—the famous G.I. Bill of Rights—was largely the product of the American Legion.

The G.I Bill was described by the Senate Finance Committee as "a fundamental bill of rights to facilitate the return of service men and women to civilian life."

> It is a comprehensive statement of the measures presently necessary and . . . represents the very least that should be done at this time in justice to veterans and in enlightened self-interest for the remainder of the country.[40]

The G.I. Bill represented the triumph of the "rehabilitation idea," that is, of "the idea that the country owes an obligation to the veteran to restore him to the civilian status and opportunities he would have enjoyed had there not been a war."[41] Restoration to civilian status was to be facilitated through provisions for education and training; loans for the purchase of a home, business, or farm; unemployment insurance payments; and veterans' employment services.

A number of factors converged to aid the passage of the G.I. Bill. There was, of course, very real concern for the welfare of veterans, especially as they returned to an uncertain economy in the midst of reconversion to peacetime operation. Involved, too, was a recognition of the educational and financial deficit suffered by men and women who had to delay customary educational and job pursuits for wartime service. Added to this, there was a concern over the stability of political and economic institutions, should large numbers of veterans be unable to find jobs. Pervading all was the fear of a postwar depression and the memory of the unemployment of the prewar period. The discharge of millions of veterans into the labor force at a time when war production had ended and thousands of workers were already looking for jobs was seen as a major problem. Thus the G.I. Bill was designed to delay and ease entrance to the labor market. Actual federal government expenditures for veterans' services and benefits rose to about $3.4 billion for fiscal year 1946. They reached a peak of $9.3 billion, 23 percent of total federal expenditures, in 1950.[42]

Postwar Optimism

For a number of reasons, a postwar recession did not occur. The liberal monetary and educational provisions of the G.I. Bill and the beginning contribution of the provisions of the Social Security Act to economic stability were two cushioning factors. Even more important was the enormous backlog of demand for major consumer goods that had been unavailable during the war—new housing and automobiles, for example. The postwar spurt in marriages and births added to market demand for goods. The combination of needs and wartime savings stimulated the expansion of older industries and the development of such new products as television. The depression-born fear of a "mature," "stagnating" economy was replaced with a new faith in the vigor of the economic system.

With concern about a return to economic recession and unemployment allayed, the United States entered a period of social complacency. The country seemed pleased with continuing economic growth and intrigued with the promise of automation, of a cybernetic revolution that would provide affluence for all.

However, despite this postwar air of social optimism, economic laissez faire, and political conservatism, some new welfare programs were legislated: the National School Lunch Program in 1946; the Housing Act of 1949; the special Milk Program in 1954; and finally, in 1960, the Kerr-Mills Act, which provided aid to the medically indigent. On a judicial level, at the height of the McCarthy period, a major decision on civil rights was handed down. In 1954, in *Brown v. Board of Education*,[43] the Supreme Court decided unanimously that in public school education, separate facilities for racial groups were "inherently unequal."

Public welfare had expanded early in the decade through incremental legislative changes that increased the number of potential program recipients and through benefit formula changes that liberalized payments. In 1956 disability insurance was added to the social security programs; a new category of public assistance—Aid to the Physically and Totally Disabled—was instituted; federal aid for medical expenses incurred by families receiving welfare was begun; and, in the Aid to Dependent Children program, a caretaker provision was introduced whereby there was, for the first time, federal money to support the parent of a dependent child. Later in the decade, new groups were offered social insurance coverage and public assistance payments were raised as the federal government increased its contribution and attempted to equalize the payment efforts of poor and wealthy states. In 1956 federal funding for social services was added to ADC; and 1958 saw extension of child welfare services from rural to urban areas.

If the 1950s were years of overall self-satisfaction, they were also years of frustration—internationally and domestically. By the close of the decade, John F. Kennedy was campaigning for the presidency on a promise to get the country "moving again" toward "new frontiers." Abroad, the Korean War had ended in a stalemate. At home, Senator Joseph McCarthy of Wisconsin had accused the Democratic party of having subjected the country to "20 years of treason" during the Roosevelt and Truman terms. Senator McCarthy spearheaded a witch hunt against those who had been "soft on communism," and the political repression that ensued paralleled closely the Palmer raids of the post-World War I era. The Senate committee charged with investigating McCarthy's accusations found them "a fraud and a hoax perpetrated in the Senate of the United States, and on the American people," but not until the Senate's censure of McCarthy tactics in 1954 did the country's hysteria over possible communist influence on the nation's political and social institutions begin to subside. Almost as a fallout, however, the late 1950s saw an increasingly virulent series of attacks on public welfare and health insurance, both viewed as overtures to an un-American welfare state.

The Attack on Public Welfare

An attack on public welfare began to take shape. From 1950 to 1960 the number of recipients of public assistance grew only slightly—by less than 800,000, despite a rise in unemployment of more than 2 million. Why then the outcry? Two factors seem to have played a major role. One was the rising costs; although the number of beneficiaries grew only 13 percent from 1950 to 1960, expenditures were up much more sharply. Total public assistance payments stood at $2.5 billion in 1950; by 1960 they had risen almost 60 percent to reach $4.0 billion. The second factor was the changing nature of the relief rolls. The number of old age recipients was decreasing; the number of mothers with children was increasing. In 1950 the aged constituted half the public assistance population; in 1960 they were only 37 percent. For the Aid to Dependent Children program, the percentages were almost the reverse. The program was expanded to include over 3 million beneficiaries by 1960. Expenditures for ADC increased between 1950 and 1960 by 92 percent to total more than $1 billion. During 1961, the first year of John F. Kennedy's presidency, the number of ADC recipients increased another 502,000; expenditures for the year rose to $1.2 billion.[44]

The efforts to contain the growth of ADC were generally restrictions on entitlement to benefits. State discretion was signaled by the Eisenhower administration's shift away from federal government centralization of authority and the reemergence of states' rights and local control. In state after state, punitive administrative policies were used to remove recipients from the welfare rolls and to deter new applications. State residency requirements were strictly enforced, so that black migrants who moved from the South to Northern cities, for example, were successfully prevented from receiving assistance. Drives to publicize the names of welfare recipients were widespread. As a way of weeding out suspected "frauds," entire caseloads were closed and all recipients required to undergo new application investigations. Beyond the overt intention of weeding out ineligible recipients was the covert hope that attrition would result from the unwillingness of large numbers of individuals to experience new eligibility investigations set up to deter them.

In a number of states, "suitable home" and "man-in-the-house" policies became bases for determining that the presence of an unrelated man made a home unsuitable for children. The presence of a man, even though unrelated, also was considered evidence that financial need did not exist. In the summer of 1960 the state of Louisiana was found to have used the "suitable home" pretext for closing 6,281 cases, involving 23,549 children. The practice was halted in 1961, when Secretary of Health, Education, and Welfare Arthur Fleming ruled that cases could no longer be closed as a result of unsuitable home findings, unless other suitable living arrangements had been made for the children.[45] Midnight raids to uncover men living with ADC mothers continued well into the 1960s, when they were effectively halted by the March 27, 1967, decision of the Supreme Court of California, which declared that public assistance workers could not be fired for refusing to participate in an unconstitutional invasion of privacy.[46*]

The most notorious example of attempts to reduce the welfare rolls— the effort that became symbolic of all—was the one that occurred at Newburgh, New York, during 1961. In that year the Newburgh city manager promulgated a 13-point code of welfare regulations that included in one package many of the devices being used across the country to control the size of the welfare rolls and to reduce welfare expenditures: for example, applicants new to Newburgh were to give evidence of having come to the city with a concrete offer of employment; assistance was to be denied to applicants who had left a job voluntarily; all new cases were to be reviewed in the city manager's office prior to certification; active cases were to be reviewed monthly by the city's corporation counsel; work was to be mandated for all ablebodied males receiving money payments; voucher payments were to be substituted for cash. Leaving aside the question of ethics, the danger of Newburgh—to itself and to the entire state of New

---

*Man-in-the-house rules and durational residence requirements were finally eliminated by *King* v. *King*, 392 U.S. 309 (1968) and by *Shapiro* v. *Thompson*, 364 U.S. 618 (1969), respectively.

York—was that its practices could be found to be out of compliance with federal grant-in-aid regulations. Federal funds for New York's welfare programs could be withheld. Thus the New York State Social Welfare Board ordered Newburgh's welfare officials to refrain from implementing the city manager's directive.

The various attacks on public assistance programs highlighted a slowly changing perception of the adult recipient of public assistance. The image of that recipient was changing from the worthy, responsible aged or widowed beneficiary to the unworthy, unpopular, young, ablebodied, unemployed female or male. Most significantly, attention was focused on urban ADC mothers who were increasingly perceived as women who had illegitimate children as a way of avoiding work and as blacks, despite the fact that residency requirements had effectively prevented black migrants from swelling the expanding rolls. During the fifties, at least, increased expenditures for public welfare resulted from normal population growth, from expanded programs, and from liberalized benefits. Be that as it may, the new image of the welfare recipient meant that the base of public support for public welfare had eroded.

Poverty and the Reform of Welfare

By the 1960s some of the optimism of the postwar era began to fade. A series of recessions started in 1948: 1948–1949, 1953–1954, 1957–1958, and 1961–1963. A renewed and growing concern with unemployment developed when unemployment rates approached 7 percent in 1958 and again in 1961. After each recession, the economy bounced back, but with less than full vigor. Indeed, each period of recovery was less energetic than that which preceded it; and definitions of full employment moved from the 2 percent of the 1940s to where some considered 4 percent as unrealistically low.

Despite this, the general view of the 1950s as the era of the affluent society held. What had changed was the view of poverty and of the poor. Kenneth Galbraith, writing in 1958, implied that poverty was spotty and scattered, not systemic. He identified two types of poverty: "insular" and "case." "Insular" poverty covered problems that arose from structural unemployment and differential unemployment rates—the special problems of the Appalachian region, for example. "Case" poverty denoted poverty arising from a personal deficiency, such as ill health, lack of education, or even racial or sexual discrimination.[47] Whether "insular" or "case" in nature, the problem was considered one of employability rather than of poverty per se. In fact, the United States rediscovered poverty as a serious social problem only in the early 1960s, when a series of studies and publications made reality unavoidable. The Social Security Administration, using 1959 data, established a poverty index and, for the first time, provided an official statistical measure of individuals and groups in poverty. Increased attention came with the publication of Michael Harrington's *The Other*

America: Poverty in the United States in 1962 and Dwight MacDonald's "Our Invisible Poor" in 1963.[48] The 1964 *Annual Report* of the Council of Economic Advisors dealt with the situation at length and was transmitted to the Congress along with the *Economic Report of the President*.[49]

Slowly the response to poverty emerged, shaped by three factors: (1) the identification of depressed geographical areas, (2) the civil rights revolutions, and (3) the shift in the composition of public assistance rolls that began early in the 1960s. Overall, there was a programmatic emphasis on employment; the opening up of employment opportunities and the upgrading of labor market skills of the poor.

The first thrust of legislation was directed at the specialized problems of depressed areas. The Area Redevelopment Act of 1961 focused on problems of regional unemployment. If the poverty in an area was due to a depletion of natural resources and a decline in the demand for the traditional products of the area, then new industry was to be induced to move into the area. If the people of Appalachia suffered from the decrease of jobs in coal mining, then the expansion of factory employment seemed appropriate. In subsequent years the 1961 legislation was expanded, and a broader program, the Economic Development Act, was passed in 1965. Federal grants and loans provided aid to build industry in six depressed regions of the United States: Appalachia, New England, the Coastal Plains, the Ozarks, the Upper Great Lakes, and a poverty-stricken sector of the Southwest.

The statistical count of the poor made the special plight of the minority population dramatically clear. The risk of poverty for blacks was three times as great as that for whites. Discriminatory employment practices were scored as one major factor. The developing civil rights movement of the 1960s was increasingly forceful in pointing up areas of social, political, and economic discrimination and the consequences of this discrimination for unemployment and relief rolls. The Civil Rights Act of 1964 included a section prohibiting racial, sexual, or ethnic discrimination in employment[50] and established an enforcement mechanism, the Equal Employment Opportunity Commission.

The change in the public assistance rolls in the 1960s was the third major force behind the social legislation of the decade. During the previous decade, the number of unemployed had risen faster than the number of relief recipients, but the increases could be related to each other—they went up and down together. But in 1963 this shifted, and from 1963 to 1970 unemployment rose by less than 300,000 while the number of public assistance recipients increased by over 6 million![51] The sharp rise in public assistance recipients was really a jump in ADC recipients, despite the fact that by 1960 the Survivor's Insurance program, in its tenth year of existence, was covering 1.5 million children and 396,000 widows. A picture of ADC as harboring, and even creating, families broken by illegitimacy and desertion developed. This new picture was brought into even sharper focus by the program's continuing emphasis on the unemployable female parent in the

Faces of a Breadline, Biddeford, Maine, 1958. The young and the old, even a baby in arms, made up the breadline twice a day in this hard-hit textile and machinery city. Food came from government surplus, neighboring cities, and from Boston where Girl Scouts aided in its collection. The Overseer of the Poor, at whose office the line formed, said 2,749 people were on the relief lists out of a population of just over 20,000.

Courtesy of Wide World Photos, Inc.

home—the worthy-widow halo—at a time when the larger society was insistently labeling that parent "unworthy" and employable.

Solutions to case poverty, whatever the cause, were sought in employment training, work incentives, and, above all, counseling services. The addition of federal funding for services to ADC recipients in 1956 was an expression of alarm at the new composition of the ADC rolls and of hope that services might lead to employment and financial independence. In 1962 the Manpower Development and Training Act was intended to provide training or retraining for workers displaced by economic or technological change. This reemphasis on labor market participation—on enhancing occupational potential—was, in part, an extension of the intent of the G.I. Bill. As regards welfare recipients, however, it represented a shift from the cash programs of the New Deal to a service approach, which came to full development in the Public Welfare Amendments of 1962.

President Kennedy's assumption of office in January 1961 and the appointment of Abraham Ribicoff as secretary of health, education, and welfare provided the opportunity to get public assistance moving away from "the outlook of 1935" toward two new objectives: "Eliminating whatever abuses have crept into these programs and developing more constructive approaches to get people off assistance and back to useful roles in society."[52] In May 1961 the secretary appointed an Ad Hoc Committee on Public Welfare to study "the problems and prospects for public assistance in the next decade."[53] At about the same time, George K. Wyman, an administrator with experience in local, state, and federal welfare and in voluntary social welfare posts, was asked to make a report offering "recommendations and suggestions for administrative and program actions relating to procedures and operations in the Children's Bureau and the Bureau of Public Assistance."[54] The Ad Hoc Committee was composed of 25 public and voluntary social welfare leaders, mostly social workers. Despite the fact that three members of the Committee were deans of schools of social work, a fourth was appointed to be the Committee's consultant. Wyman drew on essentially the same group in preparing his report. The essential similarity of recommendations is not surprising.

The recommendations of the Ad Hoc Committee were released in September and were "designed to reinforce and support family life through rehabilitation, prevention and protection." Basic to the Committee's proposals were adequacy of financial assistance to needy persons and families, efficient administration and organization of public welfare programs, research into the causes of dependency and family breakdown, and, foremost, the provision of rehabilitative services by professionally trained personnel. In a statement reminiscent of Frederick Almy's 1912 warning against the provision of "untrained relief," the Committee wrote: "Financial assistance to meet people's basic needs for food, shelter, and clothing is essential, but alone is not enough. Expenditures for assistance not accompanied by rehabilitation services may actually increase dependency and eventual costs to the community."[55]

The Committee's statement was repeated by its consultant in hearings before the Committee on Ways and Means: "We feel that the very essence of a vital program should be full use of our rehabilitative service, including but not confined to, financial assistance."[56] The conviction was that public welfare, through rehabilitation services, could become a "positive wealth-producing force in society" by contributing to an "attack on such problems as dependency, juvenile delinquency, family breakdown, illegitimacy, ill health, and disability."[57]

Of the Committee's ten recommended immediate steps for change in public welfare, four were aimed directly at ADC. It was recommended:

1. That "Aid to Dependent Children Families" be strengthened by the initiation of an accelerated, intensive program of rehabilitation services offered by trained personnel
2. That the temporary (1961) provisions of federal support for unemployed parents and for foster home care for ADC children be

extended and a provision to include support for disabled and unemployed fathers living at home be added
3. That measures for studying and dealing with the problems of illegitimacy be undertaken
4. That earnings of youths be exempted as a deduction from the amount of assistance granted a family

Other recommendations for immediate action included appropriations for day care, the removal of residence requirements that conflict with "the freedom of movement . . . essential to economic progress," the limited use of voucher payments for persons with severe problems of money management, and the support of research and demonstration projects concerned with dependency and family breakdown. Although these recommendations were applicable to all public assistance programs, they, too, held special meaning for change in ADC.

The Ad Hoc Committee concluded with four recommendations for "further action." Considering the services thrust of the Committee's report, the most far-reaching of these final proposals was Recommendation 12: "To make possible the rehabilitative services so strongly advocated, the goal should be established . . . that one-third of all persons engaged in social work capacities in public welfare should hold masters' degrees in social work."[58] But the significance of professionally trained social workers went beyond the direct provision of service. The Ad Hoc Committee had interpreted the occurrence of fraud in public welfare as a reflection of a "basic weakness in the standards of moral responsibility in modern society." Committee members thought that well-qualified social workers could offer knowledgeable, well-directed help to build self-respect and reinforce "capacities of persons to meet their problems and to behave responsibly."[59] No wonder then that the Public Welfare Amendments of 1962, which were largely based on the Committee's recommendations, were familiarly known as the Social Services Amendments.

George K. Wyman's report had been submitted to Secretary Ribicoff one month prior to that of the Ad Hoc Committee. Although Wyman's task was concentrated on administrative and procedural matters of concern to the Children's Bureau and the Bureau of Public Assistance, his recommendations were basically in line with those of the Ad Hoc Committee.

On December 6, 1961, Secretary Ribicoff addressed a memorandum to the commissioner of social security setting forth a series of changes that would be made in public welfare programs. Along with encouraging the locating of deserting fathers and the detection of fraud, the changes were designed "to promote rehabilitation services and develop a family-centered approach." Specific changes looked to the improvement of state staff training and development programs and the development of services to families. Each state was to be required to have "a statewide staff development plan which would include inservice training and opportunities for professional and technical education." And in order to emphasize that "our efforts must involve a variety of helpful services, of which giving a money payment is only one, and . . . that the object of our efforts must be the entire family," the name of the Bureau of Public Assistance was to be changed to the Bureau of Family Services.[60] A conference of state welfare department administrators was called one month later to promote support for the proposed reforms.

The reports of the Ad Hoc Committee and of George K. Wyman, the memoranda of Abraham Ribicoff to the commissioner of Social Security and to the administrators of state welfare departments, and the combined report of the state welfare administrators were all preludes to President Kennedy's message to Congress on February 1, 1962—the first presidential message entirely on the subject of public welfare. The president expressed concern about poverty that persisted in the midst of abundance and stated that the "reasons are often more social than economic."

> Merely responding with a relief check to complicated social or personal problems . . . is not likely to provide a lasting solution. Such a check must be supplemented, or in some cases made unnecessary, by positive services and solutions, offering the total resources of the community to meet the total needs of the family to help our less fortunate citizens help themselves.[61]

The legislative actions recommended by the president were those previously designated by Secretary Ribicoff as necessary to reduce the welfare rolls. He suggested, in addition, the appointment of an Advisory Council on Public Welfare to evaluate public welfare programs in the light of "the changing nature of the economic and social problems of the country."

President Kennedy's recommendations had considerable influence upon the substance of the amendments to the Social Security Act, the Public Welfare Amendments of 1962. Their promise of a new approach to the problems of dependency was based upon extensive advice from social welfare experts who implied future savings in public welfare expenditures. The promised new approach was, of course, an old approach, a return to seeking the cause of poverty within the individual—a return to helping individuals change themselves in order to operate successfully in an apparently well-functioning economy. This time, however, the personal counseling was to be buttressed by employment services—job training and job placement.

A significant outcome of this reversion to tradition was the president's recommendation that federal money be available for services not only for persons who are already dependent, but also for persons who *might become* dependent. The extent to which the prevention of dependency was focused on mothers with children was shown by the suggestion that Congress offer the states the option of combining into a single category of assistance their programs for the aged, blind, and disabled. The need to simplify and coordinate the administration of public assistance programs in order to "improve the adequacy and consistency of assistance and related services" did not extend to that category of assistance for families whose members were potentially employable.

Public Law 87-543, the Public Welfare Amendments of 1962, were signed by President Kennedy on July 25, 1962.[62] The new law, incorporating the recommendations of the president's message, encouraged the states to provide social services leading to self-care and self-support. Encouragement took the form of a change in the grant-in-aid formula, making the federal share of costs 75 percent of expenditures for services to reduce dependency and for training staff to achieve the intent of the law. In line with this intent, the law offered federal money for services not only to current recipients of public assistance but also to former recipients and to persons who were likely to become recipients. The intent was further strengthened by the provision of funding for demonstration projects aimed at experimenting with new methods for offering money payments and social services.

Although the amendments brought about change for all categories of public assistance and for the Child Welfare provisions of Title V of the Social Security Act, the most striking were those dealing directly or indirectly with Title IV, Aid to Dependent Children. The name of the program was changed to Aid and Services to Needy Families with Children and the program would henceforth be known as AFDC, Aid to Families with Dependent Children. The intent of public policy in providing assistance for needy families was expanded:

> For the purpose of encouraging the care of dependent children . . . by enabling each State to furnish financial assistance and rehabilitation and other services . . . to needy dependent children and the parents or relatives with whom they are living to help maintain and strengthen family life and to help such parents or relatives to attain or retain capability for the maximum self-support and personal independence consistent with the maintenance of continuing parental care and protection.[63]

The temporary legislation enacted in 1961 authorizing federal financial participation in aid to children deprived of parental care and support because of the unemployment of a parent was extended,* but assistance was to be denied to an unemployed parent who refused to accept retraining without good cause.[64] In providing for community work and training programs, the amendments attempted to heed President Kennedy's suggestion that work projects "be an opportunity for the individual on welfare, not a penalty." The projects were to be "of a constructive nature, [geared to] the conservation of work skills and the development of new skills." The secretary was to assure appropriate health, safety, and pay standards for those referred to projects and appropriate arrangements for the care and protection of the child during the parent's absence. An additional work incentive provided that expenses

---

*This program was familiarly known as AFDC-UP, Aid to Families with Dependent Children—Unemployed Parent.

reasonably attributable to work participation be considered in determining the amount of the family's assistance grant.[65]

The 1962 amendments required that a service plan be developed and applied for each child recipient in the light of his or her particular home conditions. Such a plan would include the use of protective payments, if the assistance grant were being mismanaged. Funds for day care for children of working parents were authorized, as were funds for the extension of public child welfare services to all political subdivisions of the separate states, in effect paralleling the coverage of AFDC. The services were to be provided, to the extent feasible, by trained personnel. Their purpose was spelled out in a definition of "child-welfare services":

> "Child-welfare services" means public social services which supplement, or substitute for, parental care and supervision for the purpose of (1) preventing or remedying, or assisting in the solution of problems which may result in, the neglect, abuse, exploitation, or delinquency of children, (2) protecting and caring for homeless, dependent, or neglected children, (3) protecting or promoting the welfare of children of working mothers, and (4) otherwise protecting and promoting the welfare of children, including the strengthening of their own homes where possible or, where needed, the provision of adequate care . . . in foster family homes or day-care or other childcare facilities.[66]

The amendments were hailed by social workers. They were extolled as approaches to strengthening family welfare. Mostly ignored was the important connotation that the legislation measured "strengthened family life" in terms of success in achieving financial independence.[67] Also ignored by some social workers was the extent to which Congress had taken seriously the implication that expenditures for public assistance would decline as social workers freed recipients for work and independence. When the rolls did not decline, but instead began to expand at a faster rate than unemployment, "embarrassing questions" began to be asked. The American Public Welfare Association, a national organization of people concerned with public welfare issues, had predicted such difficulties.[68] Social workers and social work services became increasingly suspect.

For the moment, however, the huge expansion in public services gave renewed attention to relationships between public and private agencies and between family and child welfare agencies. The creation of the Bureau of Family Services and its assumption of a family services approach threatened a further encroachment into social welfare areas generally considered the domain of voluntary social welfare agencies. Efforts were made to define the essential uniqueness of both public and voluntary welfare in preparation for "a new era of partnership."[69] It became clear not only that developments in social welfare were being shaped by public welfare, but also that the burden of responsibility for defining a relationship between public and voluntary agencies was, at that moment at least, the responsibility of the latter. The development of a professional generic methodology of social work helping and the growing need for administrative economy had earlier sparked a series of mergers between voluntary family and children's casework agencies. The enactment of the 1962 amendments to the Social Security Act (moving the public agency into the family and children's counseling services areas) and the voluntary agencies' continuing problem of funding raised questions about the necessity for voluntary agency services at all.

The possibility for a new era of partnership had to await the discovery of a new technique of funding. The purchase-of-service mechanism was embedded in the service amendments. The Social Security Act made federal funds available for contracting for services

> prescribed by the Secretary which in the judgment of the State agency cannot be as economically or as effectively provided by the staff of such State or local agency and are not otherwise reasonably available to individuals in need of them, and which are provided . . . (whether . . . by contract with public . . . or nonprofit private agencies).[70]

In 1962, whatever the problem with relationships between voluntary and public agencies, the future of social work as a profession seemed assured. The social service amendments had reversed Harry Hopkins's 1933 decision that public welfare not be a haven for professional social work practice. The extent of the reversal was indicated by the announcement of prescribed social services to be offered by "State public assistance agencies . . . in order to claim increased Federal funds." The commissioner of Social Security also announced the means by which services were to be made effective: "Caseloads of no more than 60 per worker, 1 supervisor for each 5 workers, and home visiting as frequently as necessary. . . ."[71]

The War on Poverty

By 1964 a number of forces had come together to make an even more vigorous attack on poverty seem necessary. One factor certainly was the continuing, seemingly uncontrollable, increase in AFDC recipients. In December 1964 a total of 1 million families received assistance; the total number of recipients had reached more than 4 million, including more than 3 million children.

Perhaps more important than the rise in AFDC rolls to the development of indignation against the persistence of poverty in the land of plenty was the growing awareness of the extent of need. The annual reports of the U.S. Department of Commerce were especially effective in identifying poverty groups, those individuals and families particularly vulnerable to the risks of an industrial society. Year after year, the poverty groups were identified as children, the aged, large families, and families headed by women. A double risk was suffered by rural families and minority group members. Surprisingly, work—even full-time work—was no guarantee against poverty; and the "working poor" became identified as a poverty group.

Support for an attack on hunger and poverty was furthered by the growing strength of the civil rights movement. A demonstration climaxed by an historic speech by Reverend Martin Luther King, Jr., brought an unprecedented 200,000 people to Washington, D.C., in a march for "jobs and freedom" and an interracial display of solidarity. President Lyndon B. Johnson's decision to include the elimination of poverty among his plans for a "Great Society" came at a fortuitous time. A tax cut in 1964 had succeeded in reversing a downward economic cycle and a renewed faith in an affluent society made a successful war on poverty seem feasible.

In his message urging Congress to "declare war on a domestic enemy which threatens the strength of our Nation and the welfare of our people," President Johnson wrote: "Today, for the first time in our history, we have the power to strike away the barriers to full participation in our society. Having the power, we have the duty."[72]

The Economic Opportunity Act was passed on August 20, 1964. Its declaration of purpose established public policy in relation to the elimination of poverty:

> The United States can achieve its full economic and social potential as a nation only if every individual has the opportunity to contribute to the full extent of his capabilities and to participate in the workings of our society. It is therefore the policy of the United States to eliminate the paradox of poverty in the midst of plenty in this Nation by opening to everyone the opportunity for education and training, the opportunity to work, and the opportunity to live in decency and dignity."[73]

The various Titles of the act represented a continuation and intensification of the Kennedy thrust, that is, a further continuation of work training, work incentives, services, and special programs for particular regions.

The Economic Opportunity Act provided, first of all, for a series of youth programs designed to give young people of low income and minority group families the education, skills, and experiences deemed necessary for success. The youth programs included: federally established Job Corps training centers for out-of-school and unemployed youths requiring general and vocational education and help with social and physical difficulties; a work-training program supporting state and local governmental and private nonprofit activities aimed at preventing school dropouts; and a work-study program enabling young people to continue their education in secondary schools, colleges, and universities.

Titles III and IV provided for special programs to combat poverty in rural areas and for programs of employment and investment incentives in poverty areas beyond the reach of the provisions of the Area Redevelopment Act. Grants and loans to farmers and small businesses were the core of these Titles. The aim of Title V, described as "Family Unity Through Jobs" by presidential assistant Sargent Shriver, was the development of short-term training and retraining courses leading to the transfer of trainees from relief rolls to jobs. Its central concern was for unemployed parents—fathers and mothers—receiving assistance through the AFDC-UP program. Title V was meant to "demonstrate that public assistance with work and training can be used as a positive instrument to keep families together, to increase employability, and to brighten our communities."[74] An important section created an adult volunteer corps—"Volunteers in Service to America" (VISTA)—to help with the rehabilitation and improvement of slums and other impoverished areas.

The most controversial, perhaps most important, provisions of the Economic Opportunity Act were those included in Title II, "Urban and Rural Community Action Programs." Community Action Programs (CAP) were defined as those that promised progress toward the elimination of poverty, that provided for "the maximum feasible participation" of residents of the geographic areas of group members covered, and that were conducted by public or private, nonprofit community action organizations. The initial popularity of the Office of Economic Opportunity (OEO) stemmed from its ability, through the CAP concept, to fund projects administered by public and voluntary agencies freed from the administrative control of city halls and united funds. Among the more popular programs funded were Head Start (a preparatory education program for preschool, low-income children), Upward Bound (an educational program meant to prevent school dropout and to encourage dropouts to return to school), day care centers, neighborhood recreation centers, and neighborhood health centers.

The Economic Opportunity Act reemphasized the 1962 view that work and jobs were the keys to strengthened family life. The act accelerated the spate of programs designed to remove parents and children from the home and from each other. Job training, job placement, and counseling for a variety of psychological and social ills represented a crash effort to reduce the welfare rolls. Day care, Head Start, Upward Bound, and so on served several purposes at once. For children, they were to be compensation for the failures of parental upbringing and enhancement of potential for adult economic independence. For parents, they represented an immediate freeing for job hunting. The act clearly indicated that employment as an American value was at least equal to the value placed on family life and family unity.

The OEO soon came under attack. Mayors of cities around the country were politically threatened by the federal funding of projects over which they had no control. Members of Congress were upset by legal suits brought by government-funded community legal services against federal programs. Communities were shaken by the aggressiveness and hostility of the poor who had found voice in the "maximum feasible participation" concept. Stories of mismanagement, radicalism, and fraud abounded. In time, President Johnson, increasingly enmeshed in the Vietnam War, became disenchanted with a War on Poverty that was not only costly, but was creating political and social dissensions while seeming to make little direct contribution to its stated goal. The race riots of the summer of 1967 brought renewed attention to the problems of the ghetto poor. Nonetheless, the administration's overall support began to fade.

The Economic Opportunity Act and the war on poverty did make important contributions to change. The "maximum feasible participation" concept opened new sources of psychological, financial, and political power as the poor found themselves having a say in, and in some instances even controlling, the programs and institutions that affect their lives. The concept became integral to other legislated social welfare programs, as in the Model Cities legislation of 1966, for example. The poor and other consumers of services became increasingly involved in education and health, as well as welfare, programs. As skills developed, their participation ranged from service to managerial to policymaking positions. Community action programs opened opportunities for large numbers of minority group members who were educationally prepared for executive and professional jobs but to whom such opportunities had been closed by discrimination. They helped make the poor and the members of minority groups not only visible but increasingly audible.

An equally significant legacy of community action programs was the development of community legal services. These services were not specifically mentioned in the Economic Opportunity Act as originally enacted. Once developed as community action programs, the importance of legal services for testing and securing the legal rights of the poor through a wide variety of class action suits became obvious, and amendments to the act made specific provision for inclusion. Community legal services, applying pressure for administrative action to implement judicial victories, appeared to be a most important governmental contribution to the welfare of the poor.

An unexpected result of the development of community action programs was a shift in social workers' views of social welfare, of social agencies, and of their profession. Originally ignored by officials of the Office of Economic Opportunity, social workers were soon brought into community action programs because of their competencies in community organizing, administration, and direct work with clients and client groups. The thrust of the war on poverty and particularly of community action programs moved many social workers, and the profession itself, from a therapeutic to a reform approach, from a psychoanalytic to a social science base. The move led some to a seemingly antiprofessional stance as they pushed for community and consumer participation in policymaking and decision making; for the input of nonprofessionals into service design and delivery; and for social action to "change the system." Social workers helped public assistance clients organize, and the Welfare Rights Organization became a substantial force for change.

Cross currents of opinion in regard to social welfare became sharper during the second half of the 1960s. In 1965, 1966, and 1968, Congress extended the federal government's role in social welfare. Health insurance was provided for the elderly, a high risk group in terms of vulnerability to illness and to poverty, and to the medically indigent by Title XVIII (Medicare) and Title XIX (Medicaid), respectively, amendments to the Social Security Act in 1965. Also in 1965 the Elementary and Secondary Education Act marked the first extension of federal aid for general purposes to local schools. In 1966 the Demonstration (Model) Cities Act proposed to demonstrate, through a concentration and coordination of housing, health, education, employment, and social services, the ability to transform decaying urban areas into settings for the good life. The Housing and Urban Development Act of 1968 gave impetus to President Johnson's intent to provide 6 million new dwellings for low- and moderate-income groups within the next ten years. Overall, the civil rights movement and the publicity it gave to the needs of the poor and of minority groups continued to push movement toward improved social well-being. Counterpressures were evident, however, in the monitoring of public assistance and public assistance recipients.

Reform of Welfare: 1967

Neither the Public Welfare Amendments of 1962 nor the Economic Opportunity Act of 1964 succeeded in reducing the AFDC rolls. The number of recipients and total expenditures continued a steep climb. More of the poor were being helped, but not in the way Congress had intended. Despite this, the 1966 report of the Advisory Council on Public Welfare urged a continuation of the services approach to change.

The Advisory Council on Public Welfare had been appointed by the secretary of health, education, and welfare pursuant to the 1962 public welfare statutes. The title of the Council's report, *Having the Power, We Have the Duty,* was derived from President Johnson's messages to Congress urging the War on Poverty. Selection of the title for a report published in June 1966 suggested a misreading of current congressional opinion of public welfare and of current efforts to change its direction. The overall tenor of the report was that Congress should make public assistance more effective by seeing to the provision of more aid and more services "as a matter of right." Greater effectiveness, it was suggested, could come from a new pattern of federal-state cooperation by which the federal government would set nationwide standards for relief grants and asssume their full cost above individually stipulated state shares. Discrepancies among state standards would thus be eliminated, and the states, freed of pressures to find new sources of revenues, would be able to concentrate on meeting human needs. Since the fulfillment of objectives would depend on a sharp increase in the available number of professional social workers, social work aides, and related auxiliary personnel, special legislation appropriating funds to encourage expansion and training was deemed necessary.[75]

The recommendations of the Advisory Council have been cited as "the last hurrah of the social welfare professionals who had long dominated public assistance policy development."[76] And, indeed, those who influenced the shape of the report, despite its fresh declaration of a right to assistance and service, were in some ways out of touch with fellow professionals who were moving in a different direction.* For at the very moment that the Council's report, supporting a continuing administrative tie between money payments and social services, was being released, a number of influential professionals were beginning to pressure for their separation. In fact, the proposal for separation had already been made in an unpublicized report by a special task force headed by James Dumpson, the New York City commissioner of welfare and a social worker.[77] Neither group, however, foresaw the congressional approach to be adopted in 1967.

The Social Security Amendments of 1967 legislated a stick-and-carrot attack on the rising AFDC caseload. Using January 1967 as a base for purposes of federal withholding, a freeze was imposed on the number of children under 21 who would be allowed to receive AFDC because of absence of a parent from the home. Secondly, a Work Incentive Program (eventually known as WIN, after having initially and disastrously been referred to as WIP) was instituted. The welfare freeze deliberately exempted AFDC cases attributable to a father's death or a parent's unemployment. Its aim, therefore, was to pressure state efforts against dependency due to desertion and illegitimacy. The Work Incentive Program disqualified adults and out-of-school older children—female as well as male—for AFDC payments, if they refused to accept employment or to participate in training programs without good cause. Work incentives included a mandated reduction of the 100 percent tax on earnings; that is, working recipients would be permitted to retain the first $30 and subsequent one-third of earnings before suffering a reduction in their grants. Another proposed work incentive was additional funding for day care. Thus the inducements of the 1962 amendments were "strengthened"!

The punitive aspects of the 1967 welfare amendments caused dismay and then outrage. The welfare freeze, especially, caused consternation among client groups interpreting the freeze as punishment of helpless children, among state administrations facing the prospect of increased and intolerable burdens on state budgets, and among social welfare professionals foreseeing state reductions in relief grants. President Johnson and his successor, President Nixon, both delayed implementation of the freeze, which was repealed by congressional action in 1969.

The full effects of the WIN program were temporarily delayed by the adminstrative discretion permitted state and local departments of welfare in requiring recipient participation. Nevertheless, the intent of Congress and of the secretary of health, education, and welfare was proclaimed on August

---

*Although the Council's report was open to criticism, it should be pointed out that among its recommendations were: (1) the introduction of a new public assistance program based on need alone, and (2) the use of a simple client declaration form in establishing eligibility. Both were to become important elements in later proposals for welfare reform.

15, 1967, in an announcement of a major administrative restructuring of the department. The Welfare Administration and Bureau of Family Services, established in 1962, were abolished, and a new agency, the Social and Rehabilitation Service (SRS), was created to administer public assistance, rehabilitation, and social services. The secretary's announcement indicated a planned deemphasis on family and community services and the substitution of "services aimed at rehabilitation in the broadest sense of the word."[78] The work orientation of SRS was further indicated by the appointment of the former commissioner of the Vocational Rehabilitation Administration as administrator of the new unit.

Gradually, through a series of administrative shifts, a new policy became clear: a national intent to separate money payments from services. It was the end of the service approach to public assistance. By 1969 the separation idea was the order of the day, and eventually federal regulations ordered that separation of money payments from services be achieved at state and local levels by January 1, 1974.

"Separation" was attractive on a number of counts. For those who were determined to infuse AFDC with a work orientation, separation quite literally meant separation of recipients from the requirement of services offered by professional social workers. In line with this, the institution of simple client declaration systems for establishing eligibility for cash benefits eliminated the need for professional skills in all aspects of the money payment process. For clients, separation meant the right to choose service voluntarily, when needed, without fear of losing a grant. For most professionals, separation meant a further delineation of the rights of clients and of the poor and of minority group members.

The National Association of Social Workers stated its reason for supporting separation in a policy statement. Among others, they were:

1. Service, when offered within the context of eligibility investigation, tends to become a condition for obtaining financial assistance. This undermines the concept of assistance as a right and . . . interferes with . . . self-determination in seeking and accepting service.

2. There is no reason to assume that financial need, in itself, necessarily calls for the provision of social services. . . . Separation of assistance from social services will make it possible to organize services so that they reach those who have specific need for them.[79]

The concept of separation had helped social workers clarify their relation to public welfare as well as the meaning of professional social work service. They were now free to join other social scientists and social welfare theorists in a search for new forms of income transfers and for new ways of achieving a more equal distribution of income.

Civil Rights and Juvenile Justice

Social workers saw separation of money payments and services as a part of a new concern for the rights of the poor. This was well in line with a strand of social welfare that unraveled throughout the 1960s. Spurred by the civil rights revolution, questions about the rights of various groups in our society to social well-being were asked and answers were demanded. Judicial and administrative decisions strengthened the rights of the aged, the rights of the mentally ill, the rights of the retarded, the rights of tenants, the rights of prisoners, the rights of minority groups, the rights of women.

Some legal rights of children were established by the Supreme Court's decision, *in re: Gault,* of 1967. As originally conceived in 1899, the juvenile court sought to protect children from the impersonal legal processes of adult courts. Instead of an adversary approach, the child was to be offered the friendly help of a fatherly judge who would see to individualized treatment and, if necessary, rehabilitation. Seventy years of experience with juvenile courts had demonstrated the reality that services for rehabilitative purposes were a myth. In practice, the pretext of service was a substitute for justice. Children were incarcerated for indefinite periods. The rhetoric claimed training for a productive adult life; the actuality most often proved quite the contrary.

In 1967 the Supreme Court decided that children in trouble with the law had legal rights: to counsel, to confidentiality, to silence. Justice Abe Fortas, writing the majority decision, stated:

> While due process requirements will . . . introduce a degree of order and regularity to juvenile court proceedings to determine delinquency, and in contested cases will introduce some elements of the adversary system, nothing will require that the conception of the kindly juvenile judge be replaced by its opposite . . . .[80]

The child could have both, justice and service.

The juvenile's sudden right to "due process" galvanized the entire judicial and probation systems to a reconsideration of legal practices in regard to children. In addition, the fact that there are legal aspects to all child welfare programs and that workers in these programs have frequent contacts with courts and lawyers fostered a reawakening of interest in the law on the part of all social agencies and social welfare personnel engaged in services to children.

The *Gault* decision pointed up the need for a resolution of continuing value conflicts in all areas of social welfare.

War and Prosperity

The documents used to support post-World War II occurrences in social welfare are President Kennedy's *Message on the Public Welfare Program* (1962), excerpts from the *Economic Opportunity Act* (1964), and the Supreme Court decision *in the matter of Gault* (1967). The documents are all products of the 1960s and represent the climax of post-World War II effort to bring economic affluence to bear on the promises of American democracy. The documents represent executive, legislative, and judicial responses to the social welfare issues of the period.

President Kennedy's message to Congress on public welfare programs was historic in its having been the first presidential message entirely devoted to the subject. The message, in effect, reiterates the thrust of Secretary of Health, Education, and Welfare Abraham Ribicoff's memorandum to the commissioner of Social Security. That memorandum bridged the efforts of the late 1950s to contain the growth of the public assistance rolls and the new approach to public welfare legislated by the 1962 Public Welfare Amendments. The secretary's concern was to eliminate fraud, but more than that to infuse public welfare—in reality, AFDC—with a philosophy geared to family stability and family independence. The approach implied a pathological base for poverty and dependence; therefore, the secretary pointed up the need for each state to assess its personnel and training needs to carry out the objectives of "a service-oriented program."

President Kennedy's message announces the new orientation to family welfare. It demonstrates administrative discretion at the federal level in shaping and regulating the public assistance programs. It shows, too, the need for congressional action for authorizing and funding new programs. In his leadership capacity, the president recommends congressional support of a new approach to public assistance by providing for the relief of unemployed parents, for community work and training projects, for the expansion and upgrading of social work personnel, and for a consultative Advisory Council on Public Welfare. The president's recommendation of the "rehabilitative road" to change in public welfare is couched in terms that plead for a demonstration of "the compassion of free-men . . . in the light of . . . constructive self-interest."

The Economic Opportunity Act of 1964 and its heralded war on poverty were President Johnson's extension of his predecessor's compassion for the poor. The act was also a response to a rediscovery of poverty, this time in the midst of economic plenty. The demand of the poor and particularly of the black minority for participation in the country's economic life, for a share of its wealth, seemed eminently reasonable. In 1964 the country was not yet so embroiled in the Southeast Asia conflicts that decisions about guns or butter had to be made. It seemed possible to have both, and the president, believing that we had the power to eliminate poverty, convinced the Congress that we had the duty to do so.

Ultimately the Economic Opportunity Act was an abortive attempt to eliminate poverty. Nevertheless, it was historically important as an effort to do so. Additionally, the act made significant, perhaps permanent, contributions to social welfare in the United States through the introduction of the "maximum feasible participation" concept, which, at the least, led to some psychological and political gains in the power of minorities. This new power was demonstrated and furthered by the community action programs, among them Head Start and community legal services, funded by the act. It must be pointed out, however, that the overall thrust of the Economic Opportunity Act was one of "blaming the victim." The act was meant to change the poor and, in this way, open opportunities for them. Only incidentally did organizations for structural change in "the system" arise.

The War on Poverty was waged in the context of a civil rights revolution. Led by the black community, the United States was swept by demands for increased political, social, and economic equality. Other racial and ethnic groups, Puerto Ricans and Indians, for example, added their protests. Many other groups banded together in a fight for social justice. The Supreme Court decision, *In re: Gault*, represents a judicial response to demand on behalf of the rights of one group of children.

The juvenile court had been formed to provide individualized treatment for children. The erosion and subversion of the intent of the juvenile court is delineated in the opinion written for the Supreme Court by Justice Abe Fortas. In effect, the Court's opinion requires attention to due process, to legal rights, as the path to individualized justice for children. The opinion denies that legal justice necessarily eliminates sympathy and compassion or attention to therapeutic and rehabilitative needs of children. In fact, suggests the opinion, "The essentials of due process . . . may be a more impressive and more therapeutic attitude so far as the juvenile is concerned."

The Fortas opinion had sweeping significance for children, for juvenile courts, and for professionals operating in juvenile courts. By extension, the opinion had significance for all of social welfare.

MESSAGE FROM PRESIDENT JOHN F. KENNEDY

PUBLIC WELFARE

February 1, 1962

H. Doc. No. 325

TO THE CONGRESS OF THE UNITED STATES:

Few nations do more than the United States to assist their least fortunate citizens—to make certain that no child, no elderly or handicapped citizen, no family in any circumstances in any State, is left without the essential needs for a decent and healthy existence. In too few nations, I might add, are the people aware of the progressive strides this country has taken in demonstrating the humanitarian side of freedom. Our record is a proud one—and it sharply refutes those who accuse us of thinking only in the materialistic terms of cash registers and calculating machines.

Our basic public welfare programs were enacted more than a quarter century ago. Their contribution to our national strength and well-being in the intervening years has been remarkable.

But the times, the conditions, the problems have changed—and the nature and objectives of our public assistance and child welfare programs must be changed, also, if they are to meet our current needs.

The impact of these changes should not be underestimated.

People move more often—from the farm to the city, from urban centers to the suburbs, from the East to the West, from the South to the North and Mid-west.

Living costs, and especially medical costs, have spiraled.

The pattern of our population has changed. There are more older people, more children, more young marriages, divorces, desertions, and separations.

Our system of social insurance and related programs has grown greatly: In 1940, less than 1 percent of the aged were receiving monthly old-age insurance benefits; today over two-thirds of our aged are receiving these benefits. In 1940, only 21,000 children, in families where the breadwinner had died, were getting survivor insurance benefits; today such monthly benefits are being paid to about 2 million children.

All of these changes affect the problems public welfare was intended to relieve as well as its ability to relieve it. Moreover, even the nature and causes of poverty have changed. At the time the Social Security Act established our present basic framework for public aid, the major cause of poverty was unemployment and economic depression. Today, in a year of relative prosperity and high employment, we are more concerned about the poverty that persists in the midst of abundance.

The reasons are often more social than economic, more often subtle than simple. Some are in need because they are untrained for work—some because they cannot work, because they are too young or too old, blind or crippled. Some are in need because they are discriminated against for reasons they cannot help. Responding to their ills with scorn or suspicion is inconsistent with our moral precepts and inconsistent with their nearly universal preference to be independent. But merely responding with a relief check to complicated social or personal problems—such as ill health, faulty education, domestic discord, racial discrimination, or inadequate skills—is not likely to provide a lasting solution. Such a check must be supplemented, or in some cases made unnecessary, by positive services and solutions, offering the total resources of the community to meet the total needs of the family to help our less fortunate citizens help themselves.

Public welfare, in short, must be more than a salvage operation, picking up the debris from the wreckage of human lives. Its emphasis must be directed increasingly toward prevention and rehabilitation—on reducing not only the long-range cost in budgetary terms but the long-range cost in human terms as well. Poverty weakens individuals and nations. Sounder public welfare policies will benefit the Nation, its economy, its morale, and, most importantly, it people.

Under the various titles of the Social Security Act, funds are available to help the States provide assistance and other social services to the needy, aged and blind, to the needy disabled, and to dependent children. In addition, grants are available to assist the States to expand and strengthen their programs of child welfare services. These programs are essentially State programs. But the Federal Government, by its substantial financial contribution, its leadership, and the standards it sets, bears a major responsibility. To better fulfill this responsibility, the Secretary of Health, Education, and Welfare recently introduced a number of administrative changes designed to get people off assistance and back into useful, productive roles in society.

These changes provided for:

The more effective location of deserting parents;

An effort to reduce that proportion of persons receiving assistance through willful misrepresentation, although that proportion is only a small part of the 1.5 percent of persons on the rolls found to be ineligible;

Allowing dependent children to save money for educational, employment or medical needs without having that amount deducted from their public assistance grants;

Providing special services and safeguards to children in families of unmarried parents, in families where the father has deserted, or in homes in danger of becoming morally or physically unsuitable; and

An improvement in the training of personnel, the development of services and the coordination of agency efforts.

In keeping with this new emphasis, the name of the Bureau of Public Assistance has been changed to the Bureau of Family Services.

But only so much can be done by administrative changes. New legislation is required if our State-operated programs are to be fully able to meet modern needs.

I. PREVENTION AND REHABILITATION

As already mentioned, we must place more stress on services instead of relief.

I recommend that the States be encouraged by the offer of additional Federal funds to strengthen and broaden the rehabilitative and preventive services they offer to persons who are dependent or who would otherwise become dependent. Additional Federal funds would induce and assist the States to establish or augment their rehabilitation services, strengthen their child welfare services, and add to their number of competent public welfare personnel. At the present time, the cost of these essential services is lumped with all administrative costs—routine clerical and office functions—and the Federal Government pays one-half of the total of all such costs incurred by the States. By separating out and identifying the cost of these essential rehabilitation, social work and other service costs, and paying the States three-fourths of such services—a step I earnestly recommend for your consideration—the Federal Government will enable and encourage the

States to provide more comprehensive and effective services to rehabilitate those on welfare. The existing law should also be amended to permit the use of Federal funds for utilization by the State welfare agency of specialists from other State agencies who can help mount a concerted attack on the problems of dependency.

There are other steps we can take which will have an important effect on this effort. One of these is to expand and improve the Federal-State program of vocational rehabilitation for disabled people. Among the 92,500 disabled men and women successfully rehabilitated into employment through this program last year were about 15,000 who had formerly been receiving public assistance. Let me repeat this figure: 15,000 people, formerly supported by the taxpayers through welfare, are now back at work as self-supporting taxpayers. Much more of this must be done—until we are restoring to employment every disabled person who can benefit from these rehabilitation services.

The prevention of future adult poverty and dependency must begin with the care of dependent children—those who must receive public welfare by virtue of a parent's death, disability, desertion, or unemployment. Our society not only refuses to leave such children hungry, cold, and devoid of opportunity—we are insistent that such children not be community liabilities throughout their lives. Yet children who grow up in deprivation, without adequate protection, may be poorly equipped to meet adult reponsibilities.

The Congress last year approved, on a temporary basis, aid for the dependent children of the unemployed as a part of the permanent aid-to-dependent-children program. This legislation also included temporary provisions for foster care where the child had been removed from his home, and an increase in Federal financial assistance to the aged, blind, and disabled. The need for these temporary improvements has not abated, and their merit is clear. I recommend that these temporary provisons be made permanent.

But children need more than aid when they are destitute. We need to improve our preventive and protective services for children as well as adults. I recommend that the present ceiling of $25 million authorized for annual appropriations for grants to the States for child welfare services be gradually raised, beginning with $30 million for 1963, up to $50 million for the fiscal year ending June 30, 1969, and succeeding years.

Finally, many women now on assistance rolls could obtain jobs and become self-supporting if local day-care programs for their young children were available. The need for such programs for the children, the children of working mothers has been increasing rapidly. Of the 22 million women now working, about 3 million have children under 6, and another 4½ million have school-age children between 6 and 17. Adequate care for these children during their most formative years is essential to their proper growth and training. Therefore, I recommend that the child welfare provisions of the Social Security Act be changed to authorize earmarking up to $5 million of grants to the States in 1963 and $10 million a year thereafter for aid in establishing local programs for the day care of young children of working mothers.

II. PROMOTING NEW SKILLS AND INDEPENDENCE

We must find ways of returning far more of our dependent people to independence. We must find ways of returning them to a participating and productive role in the community.

One sure way is by providing the opportunity every American cherishes to do sound and useful work. For this reason, I am recommending a change in the law to permit States to maintain with Federal financial help community work and training projects for unemployed people receiving welfare payments. Under such a program, unemployed people on welfare would be helped to retain their work skills or learn new ones; and the local community would obtain additional manpower on public projects.

But earning one's welfare payments through required participation in a community work or training project must be an opportunity for the individual on welfare, not a penalty. Federal financial participation will be conditioned upon proof that the work will serve a useful community or public purpose, will not displace regular employees, will not impair prevailing wages and working conditions, and will be accompanied by certain basic health and safety protections. Provisions must also be made to assure appropriate arrangements for the care and protection of children during the absence from home of any parent performing work or undergoing training.

Moreover, systematic encouragement would be given all welfare recipients to obtain vocational counseling, testing, and placement services from the U.S. Employment Service and to secure useful training wherever new job skills would be helpful. Close cooperative arrangements would be established with existing training and vocational education programs, and with the vocational and on-the-job training opportunities to be created under the manpower development and training and youth employment opportunities programs previously proposed.

III. MORE SKILLED PERSONNEL

It is essential that State and local welfare agencies be staffed with enough qualified personnel to insure constructive and adequate attention to the problems of needy individuals—to take the time to help them find and hold a job—to prevent public dependency, and to strive, where that is not possible, for rehabilitation—and to ascertain promptly whether any individual is receiving aid for which he does not qualify, so that aid can be promptly withdrawn.

Unfortunately, there is an acute shortage of trained personnel in all our welfare programs. The lack of experienced social workers for programs dealing with children and their families is especially critical.

At the present time, when States expend funds for the training of personnel for the administration of these programs, they receive Federal grants on a dollar-for-dollar basis. This arrangement has failed to produce a sufficient number of trained staff, especially social workers. I recommend, therefore, that Federal assistance to the States for training additional welfare personnel be increased; and that in addition, the Secretary of Health, Education, and Welfare be authorized to make special arrangements for the training of family welfare personnel to work with those children whose parents have deserted, whose parents are unmarried, or who have other serious problems.

IV. FITTING GENERAL CONDITIONS OR SAFEGUARDS TO INDIVIDUAL NEEDS

In order to make certain that welfare funds go only to needy people, the Social Security Act requires the States to take all income and resources of the applicant into consideration in determining need. Although Federal law permits, it does not require States to take into full account the full expenses individuals have in earning income. This is not consistent with equity, common sense, or other Federal laws such as our tax code. It only discourages the will to earn. In order to encourage assistance recipients to find and retain employment, I, therefore, recommend that the act be amended to require the States to take into account the expenses of earning income.

Among relatives caring for dependent children are a few who do not properly handle their assistance payments—some to the extent that the well-being of the child is adversely affected. Where the State determines that a relative's ability to manage money is contrary to the welfare of the child, Federal law presently requires payments to be made to a legal guardian or representative, if Federal funds are to be used. But this general requirement may sometimes block progress in particular situations. In order to recognize the necessity for each State to make exceptions to this rule in a very limited number of cases, I recommend that the law be amended to permit Federal sharing to continue even though protective payments in behalf of children—not to exceed one-half of 1 percent of ADC recipients in each State—are made to other persons concerned with the welfare of the family. The States would be required to reexamine these exceptions at intervals to determine whether a more permanent arrangement such as guardianship is required.

When first enacted, the aid to dependent children program provided for Federal sharing in assistance payments only to the child. Since 1950, there has been Federal sharing in any assistance given to one adult in the household as well as to the child or children. Inasmuch as, under current law there may be two parents in homes covered by this program, one incapacitated or unemployed, I recommend in the interest of equity the extension of Federal sharing in assistance payments both to the needy relative and to his or her spouse when both are living in the home with the child.

V. MORE EFFICIENT ADMINISTRATION

Under present public assistance provisions, States may impose residence requirements up to 5 of the last 9 years for the aged, blind, and disabled. Increased mobility, as previously mentioned, is a hallmark of our times. It should not operate unfairly on either an individual State or an individual family. I recommend that the Social Security Act be amended so as to provide that States receiving Federal funds not exclude any otherwise eligible persons who have been residents of the State for 1 year immediately preceding their application for assistance. I also recommend that the law be amended to provide a small increase in assistance funds to those States which simplify their laws by removing all residence requirements in any of their federally aided programs.

In view of the changing nature of the economic and social problems of the country, the desirability of a periodic review of our public welfare programs is obvious. For that purpose I propose that the Secretary of Health, Education, and Welfare be authorized to appoint an Advisory Council on Public Welfare representing broad community interests and concerns, and such other advisory committees as he deems necessary to advise and consult with him in the administration of the Social Security Act.

No study of the public welfare program can fail to note the difficulty of the problems faced or the need to be imaginative in dealing with them. Accordingly, I recommend that amendments be made to encourage experimental, pilot or demonstration projects that would promote the objectives of the assistance titles and help make our welfare programs more flexible and adaptable to local needs.

The simplification and coordination of administration and operation would greatly improve the adequacy and consistency of assistance and related services. As a step in that direction, I recommend that a new title to the Social Security Act be enacted which would give to States the option of submitting a single, unified State plan combining their assistance programs for aged, blind and disabled, and their medical assistance programs for the aged, granting to such States additional Federal matching for medical payments on behalf of the blind and disabled.

These proposed far-reaching changes—aimed at far-reaching problems—are in the public interest and in keeping with our finest traditions. The goals of our public welfare programs must be positive and constructive—to create economic and social opportunities for the less fortunate—to help them find productive, happy, and independent lives. It must stress the integrity and preservation of the family unit. It must contribute to the attack on dependency, juvenile delinquency, family breakdown, illegitimacy, ill health, and disability. It must reduce the incidence of these problems, prevent their occurrence and recurrence, and strengthen and protect the vulnerable in a highly competitive world.

Unless such problems are dealt with effectively, they fester, and grow, sapping the strength of society as a whole and extending their consequences in troubled families from one generation to the next.

The steps I recommend to you today to alleviate these problems will not come cheaply. They will cost more money when first enacted. But they will restore human dignity; and in the long run, they will save money. I have recommended in the budget submitted for fiscal year 1963 sufficient funds to cover the extension of existing programs and the new legislation here proposed.

Communities which have—for whatever motives—attempted to save money through ruthless and arbitrary cutbacks in their welfare rolls have found their efforts to little avail. The root problems remained.

But communities which have tried the rehabilitative road—the road I have recommended today—have demonstrated what can be done with creative, thoughtfully conceived and properly managed programs of prevention and social rehabilitation. In those communities families have been restored to self-reliance, and relief rolls have been reduced.

To strengthen our human resources—to demonstrate the compassion of free men—and in the light of our own constructive self-interest—we must bring our welfare programs up to date. I urge that the Congress do so without delay.

• • •

THE WAR ON POVERTY
THE ECONOMIC OPPORTUNITY ACT OF 1964

88th Congress   Document
2d Session   No. 86

PUBLIC LAW 88-452—Aug. 20, 1964 [78 Stat.]

Public Law 88-452

AN ACT

August 20, 1964
(s. 2642)

To mobilize the human and financial resources of the
Nation to combat poverty
in the United States
Be it enacted by the Senate and the House of Representatives of the United States of America in Congress assembled.

Economic Opportunity Act of 1964.

That this Act may be cited as the "Economic Opportunity Act of 1964."

FINDINGS AND DECLARATION OF PURPOSE

SEC. 2. Although the economic well-being and prosperity of the United States have progressed to a level surpassing any achieved in world history, and although these benefits are widely shared throughout the Nation, poverty continues to be the lot of a substantial number of our people. The United States can achieve its full economic and social potential as a nation only if every individual has the opportunity to contribute to the full extent of his capabilities and to participate in the workings of our society. It is, therefore, the policy of the United States to eliminate the paradox of poverty in the midst of plenty in this Nation by opening to everyone the opportunity for education and training, the opportunity to work, and the opportunity to live in decency and dignity. It is the purpose of this Act to strengthen, supplement, and coordinate efforts in furtherance of that policy.

TITLE I—YOUTH PROGRAMS

PART A—JOB CORPS

STATEMENT OF PURPOSE

SEC. 101. The purpose of this part is to prepare for the responsibilities of citizenship and to increase the employability of young men and young women aged sixteen through twenty-one by providing them in rural and urban residential centers with education, vocational training, useful work experience, including work directed toward the conservation of natural resources, and other appropriate activities.
. . .

PART B—WORK-TRAINING PROGRAMS

STATEMENT OF PURPOSE

Unemployed youth, work experience opportunities

SEC. 111. The purpose of this part is to provide useful work experience opportunities for unemployed young men and young women, through participation in State and community work-training programs, so that their employability may be increased or their education resumed or continued and so that public agencies and private nonprofit organizations (other than political parties) will be enabled to carry out programs which will permit or contribute to an undertaking or service in the public interest that would not otherwise be provided, or will contribute to the conservation and development of natural resources and recreational areas. . . .

PART C—WORK-STUDY PROGRAMS

STATEMENT OF PURPOSE

Students, part-time employment.

SEC. 121. The purpose of this part is to stimulate and promote the part-time employment of students in institutions of higher education who are from low-income families and are in need of the earnings from such employment to pursue courses of study at such institutions. . . .

TITLE II—URBAN AND RURAL COMMUNITY ACTION PROGRAMS

PART A—GENERAL COMMUNITY ACTION PROGRAMS

STATEMENT OF PURPOSE

Definition.

SEC. 201. The purpose of this part is to provide stimulation and incentive for urban and rural communities to mobilize their resources to combat poverty through community action programs.

COMMUNITY ACTION PROGRAMS

SEC. 202. (a) The term "community action program" means a program—

(1) which mobilizes and utilizes resources, public or private, of any urban or rural, or combined urban and rural, geographical area (referred to in this part as a "community"), including but not limited to a State, metropolitan area, county, city, town, multicity unit, or multicounty unit in an attack on poverty;

(2) which provides services, assistance, and other activities of sufficient scope and size to give promise of progress toward elimination of poverty or a cause or causes of poverty through developing employment opportunities, improving human performance, motivation, and productivity, or bettering the conditions under which people live, learn, and work;

(3) which is developed, conducted, and administered with the maximum feasible participation of residents of the areas and members of the groups served; and

(4) which is conducted, administered, or coordinated by a public or private nonprofit agency (other than a political party), or a combination thereof. . . .

PART C—VOLUNTARY ASSISTANCE PROGRAM FOR NEEDY CHILDREN

STATEMENT OF PURPOSE

SEC. 219. The purpose of this part is to allow individual Americans to participate in a personal way in the war on poverty, by voluntarily assisting in the support of one or more needy children, in a program coordinated with city or county social welfare agencies.

AUTHORITY TO ESTABLISH INFORMATION CENTER

SEC. 220. (a) In order to carry out the purposes of this part, the Director is authorized to establish a section within the Office of Economic Opportunity to act as an information and coordination center to encourage voluntary assistance for deserving and needy children. Such section shall collect the names of persons who voluntarily desire to assist financially such children and shall secure from city or county social welfare agencies such information concerning deserving and needy children as the Director shall deem appropriate.

(b) It is the intent of the Congress that the section established pursuant to this part shall act solely as an information and coordination center and that nothing in this part shall be construed as interfering with the jurisdiction of State and local welfare agencies with respect to programs for needy children. . . .

TITLE III—SPECIAL PROGRAMS TO COMBAT POVERTY IN RURAL AREAS

STATEMENT OF PURPOSE

SEC. 301. It is the purpose of this title to meet some of the special problems of rural poverty and thereby to raise and maintain the income and living standards of low-income rural families and migrant agricultural employees and their families.

PART A—AUTHORITY TO MAKE GRANTS AND LOANS

SEC. 302. (a) The Director is authorized to make—

(1) loans having a maximum maturity of 15 years and in amounts not exceeding $2,500 in the aggregate to any low income rural family where, in the judgment of the Director, such loans have a reasonable possibility of affecting a permanent increase in the income of such families by assisting or permitting them to—

(A) acquire or improve real estate or reduce encumbrances or erect improvements thereon,

(B) operate or improve the operation of farms not larger than family sized, including but not limited to the purchase of feed, seed, fertilizer, livestock, poultry, and equipment, or

(C) participate in cooperative associations; and/or to finance nonagricultural enterprises which will enable such families to supplement their income.

(b) Loans under this section shall be made only if the family is not qualified to obtain such funds by loan under other Federal programs. . . .

TITLE IV—EMPLOYMENT AND INVESTMENT INCENTIVES

STATEMENT OF PURPOSE

Small business concerns, assistance.

SEC. 401. It is the purpose of this title to assist in the establishment, preservation, and strengthening of small business concerns and improve the managerial skills employed in such enterprises; and to mobilize for these objectives private as well as public managerial skills and resources. . . .

TITLE V—WORK EXPERIENCE PROGRAMS

STATEMENT OF PURPOSE

SEC. 501. It is the purpose of this title to expand the opportunities for constructive work experience and other needed training available to persons who are unable to support or care for themselves or their families. In carrying out this purpose, the Director shall make maximum use of the pro-grams available under the Manpower Development and Train-ing Act of 1962, as amended, and Vocational Education Act of 1963. . . .

76 Stat.23, 42 USC2571 note.77 Stat. 403, 20 USC 35 note.

VOLUNTEERS IN SERVICE TO AMERICA

Recruitment and assignment

SEC. 603. (a) The Director is authorized to recruit, select, train, and—

(1) upon request of State or local agencies or private nonprofit organizations, refer volunteers to perform duties in furtherance of programs combating poverty at a State or local level; and

(2) in cooperation with other Federal, State, or local agencies involved, assign volunteers to work (A) in meeting the health, education, welfare, or related needs of Indians living on reservations, of migratory workers and their families, or of residents of the District of Columbia, the Commonwealth of Puerto Rico, Guam, American Samoa, the Virgin Islands, or the Trust Territory of the Pacific Islands; (B) in the care and rehabilitation of the mentally ill or mentally retarded under treatment at non-profit mental health or mental retardation facilities assisted in their construction or operation by Federal funds; and (C) in furtherance of programs or activities authorized or sup-ported under title I or II of this Act.

• • •

U.S. SUPREME COURT'S DECISION
In Re Gault et al. No. 116
Argued December 6, 1966; Decided May 15, 1967

I

On Monday, June 8, 1964, at about 10 A.M., Gerald Francis Gault and a friend, Roland Lewis, were taken into custody by the Sheriff of Gila County. Gerald was then still subject to a six months' probation order which had been entered on Feb. 25, 1964, as a result of his having been in the company of another boy who had stolen a wallet from a lady's purse. The police action on June 8 was taken as a result of a verbal complaint by a neighbor of the boys, Mrs. Cook, about a telephone call made to her in which the caller or callers made lewd or indecent remarks. It will suffice for purposes of this opinion to say that the remarks or questions put to her were of the irritatingly offensive, adolescent, sex variety. . . .

The judge committed Gerald as a juvenile delinquent to the State Industrial School "for the period of his minority [that is, until 21], unless sooner discharged by due process of law." [Gerald was 15.] . . .

II

It is claimed that juveniles obtain benefits from the special procedures applicable to them which more than offset the substance of normal due process. As we shall discuss, the observance of due process standards, intelligently and not ruthlessly administered, will not compel the States to abandon or displace any of the substantive benefits of the juvenile process. But it is important, we think, that the claimed benefits of the juvenile process should be candidly appraised. Neither sentiment nor folklore should cause us to shut our eyes, for example, to such startling findings as that reported in an exceptionally reliable study of repeaters or recidivism conducted by the Stanford Research Institute for the President's Commission on Crime in the District of Columbia. This commission's report states:

"In fiscal 1966 approximately 66 per cent of the 16- and 17-year-old juveniles referred to the court by the Youth Aid Division had been before the court previously. In 1965, 56 per cent of those in the receiving home were repeaters. The S.R.I. study revealed that 61 per cent of the sample juvenile court referrals in 1965 had been previously referred at least once and that 42 per cent had been referred at least twice before."

Certainly, these figures and the high crime rates among juveniles could not lead us to conclude that the absence of constitutional protections reduces crime, or that the juvenile system, functioning free of constitutional inhibitions as it has largely done, is effective to reduce crime or rehabilitate offenders. We do not mean by this to denigrate the juvenile court process. . . .

But the features of the juvenile system which its proponents have asserted are of unique benefit will not be impaired by constitutional domestication. For example, the commendable principles relating to the processing and treatment of juveniles separately from adults are in no way involved or affected by the procedural issues under discussion.

Further, we are told that one of the important benefits of the special juvenile court procedures is that they avoid classifying the juvenile as a "criminal." The juvenile offender is now classed as a "delinquent. . . ." It is disconcerting, however, that this term has come to involve only slightly less stigma than the term "criminal" applied to adults. It is also emphasized that in practically all jurisdictions, statutes provide that an adjudication of the child as a delinquent shall not operate as a civil disability or disqualify him for civil service appointment. There is no reason why the application of due process requirements should interfere with such provisions.

Beyond this, it is frequently said that juveniles are protected by the process from disclosure of their deviational behavior. As the Supreme Court of Arizona phrased it in the present case, the summary procedures of Juvenile Courts are sometimes defended by a statement that it is the law's policy "to hide youthful errors from the full gaze of the public and bury them in the graveyard of the forgotten past."

This claim of secrecy, however, is more rhetoric than reality. Disclosure of court records is discretionary with the judge in most jurisdictions. Statutory restrictions almost invariably apply only to the court records, and even as to those the evidence is that many courts routinely furnish information to the F.B.I. and the military, and on request to government agencies and even to private employers. Of more importance are police records. In most states the police keep a complete file of juvenile "police contacts" and have complete discretion as to disclosure of juvenile records. Police departments receive requests for information from the F.B.I. and other law-enforcement agencies, the Armed Forces, and social service agencies, and most of them generally comply. . . .

In any event, there is no reason why consistently with due process, a State cannot continue, if it deems it appropriate, to provide and to improve provision for the confidentiality of records of police contacts and court action relating to juveniles. It is interesting to note, however, that the Arizona Supreme Court used the confidentiality argument as a justification for the type of notice which is here attacked as inadequate for due process purposes. The parents were given merely general notice that their child was charged with "delinquency." No facts were specified. The Arizona court held, however, that in addition to this general "notice," the child and his parents must be advised "of the facts involved in the case" no later than the initial hearing by the judge. Obviously, this does not "bury" the word about the child's transgressions. It merely defers the time of disclosure to a point when it is of limited use to the child or his parents in preparing his defense or explanation. . . .

The early conception of the juvenile court proceeding was one in which a fatherly judge touched the heart and conscience of the erring youth by talking over his problems, by paternal advice and admonition, and in which, in extreme situations, benevolent and wise institutions of the state provided guidance and help "to save him from a downward career."

Then, as now, goodwill and compassion were admirably prevalent. But recent studies have, with surprising unanimity, entered sharp dissent as to the validity of this gentle conception. They suggest that the appearance as well as the actuality of fairness, impartiality and orderliness—in short, the essentials of due process—may be a more impressive and more therapeutic attitude so far as the juvenile is concerned. . . .

It is not suggested that juvenile court judges should fail appropriately to take account, in their demeanor and conduct, of the emotional and psychological attitude of the juveniles with whom they are confronted. While due process requirements will, in some instances, introduce a degree of order and regularity to Juvenile Court proceedings to determine delinquency, and in contested cases will introduce some elements of the adversary system, nothing will require that the conception of the kindly juvenile judge be replaced by its opposite, nor do we here rule upon the question whether ordinary due process requirements must be observed with respect to hearings to determine the disposition of the delinquent child.

Ultimately, however, we confront the reality of that portion of the Juvenile Court process with which we deal in this case. A boy is charged with misconduct. The boy is committed to an institution where he may be restrained of liberty for years. It is of no constitutional consequence- –and of limited practical meaning—that the institution to which he is committed is called an Industrial School. The fact of the matter is that, however euphemistic the title, a "receiving home" or an "industrial school" for juveniles is an institution of confinement. His world becomes "a building with white-washed walls, regimented routine and institutional hours. . . ."

Instead of mother and father and sisters and brothers and friends and classmates, his world is peopled by guards, custodians, state employees, and "delinquents" confined with him for anything from waywardness to rape and homicide.

In view of this, it would be extraordinary if our Constitution did not require the procedural regularity and the exercise of care implied in the phrase "due process." Under our Constitution, the condition of being a boy does not justify a kangaroo court. . . .

If Gerald had been over 18, he would not have been subject to Juvenile Court proceedings. For the particular offense immediately involved, the maximum punishment would have been a fine of $5 to $50, or imprisonment in jail for not more than two months.

Instead, he was committed to custody for a maximum of six years. If he had been over 18 and had committed an offense to which such a sentence might apply, he would have been entitled to substantial rights under the Constitution of the United States as well as under Arizona's laws and constitution. The United States Constitution would guarantee him rights and protections with respect to arrest, search and seizure, and pretrial interrogations. It would assure him of specific notice of the charges and adequate time to decide his course of action and to prepare his defense. He would be entitled to clear advice that he could be represented by counsel, and, at least if a felony were involved, the state would be required to provide counsel if his parents were unable to afford it.

If the court acted on the basis of his confession, careful procedures would be required to assure its voluntariness. If the case went to trial, confrontation and opportunity for cross-examination would be guaranteed. So wide a gulf between the State's treatment of the adult and of the child requires a bridge sturdier than mere verbiage, and reasons more persuasive than cliche can provide. . . .

III

Notice of Charges

Appellants allege that the Arizona juvenile code is unconstitutional or alternatively that the proceedings before the juvenile court were constitutionally defective because of failure to provide adequate notice of the hearings.

No notice was given to Gerald's parents when he was taken into custody, on Monday, June 8. On that night, when Mrs. Gault went to the Detention Home, she was orally informed that there would be a hearing the next afternoon and was told the reason why Gerald was in custody. The only written notice Gerald's parents received at any time was a note on plain paper from Officer Flagg delivered on Thursday or Friday, June 11 or 12, to the effect that the judge had set Monday, June 15, "for further hearings on Gerald's delinquency."

A "petition" was filed with the court on June 9 by Officer Flagg, reciting only that he was informed and believed that "said minor is a delinquent minor and that it is necessary that some order be made by the honorable court for said minor's welfare."

The applicable Arizona statute provides for a petition to be filed in juvenile court, alleging in general terms that the child is "neglected, dependent, or delinquent." The statute explicitly states that such a general allegation is sufficient, "without alleging the facts." . . .

We cannot agree with the court's conclusion that adequate notice was given to this case. Notice, to comply with due process requirements, must be given sufficiently in advance of scheduled court proceedings so that reasonable opportunity to prepare will be afforded, and it must "set forth the alleged misconduct with particularity." . . .

IV

Right to Counsel

Appellants charge that the Juvenile Court proceedings were fatally defective because the court did not advise Gerald or his parents of their right to counsel, and proceeded with the hearing, the adjudication of delinquency and the order of commitment in the absence of counsel for the child and his parents or an express waiver of the right thereto.

The Supreme Court of Arizona pointed out that "[t]here is disagreement [among the various jurisdictions] as to whether the court must advise the infant that he has a right to counsel." . . . It referred to a provision of the juvenile code which it characterized as requiring "that the probation officer shall look after the interests of neglected, delinquent and dependent children," including representing their interests in court. The court argued that "the parents and the probation officer may be relied upon to protect the infant's interests."

Accordingly it rejected the proposition that "due process requires that an infant have a right to counsel." It said that juvenile courts have the discretion, but not the duty, to allow such representation; it referred specifically to the situation in which the juvenile court discerns conflict between the child and his parents as an instance in which this discretion might be exercised.

We do not agree. Probation officers in the Arizona scheme are also arresting officers. They initiate proceedings and file petitions which they verify, as here, alleging the delinquency of the child; and they testify, as here, against the child.

The probation officer cannot act as counsel for the child. His role in the adjudicatory hearing is as arresting officer and witness against the child. Nor can the judge represent the child. There is no material difference in this respect between adult and juvenile proceedings of the sort here involved. In adult proceedings, this contention has been foreclosed by decisions of this court. A proceeding where the issue is whether the child will be found to be "delinquent" and subjected to the loss of his liberty for years is comparable in seriousness to a felony prosecution.

The juvenile needs the assistance of counsel to cope with problems of law, to make skilled inquiry into the facts, to insist upon regularity of the proceedings, and to ascertain whether he has a defense and to prepare and submit it. . . .

We conclude that the Due Process Clause of the Fourteenth Amendment requires that in respect of proceedings to determine delinquency which may result in commitment to an institution in which the juvenile's freedom is curtailed, the child and his parent must be notified of the child's right to be represented by counsel retained by them, or if they are unable to afford counsel, that counsel will be appointed to represent the child.

At the habeas corpus proceeding, Mrs. Gault testified that she knew that she could have appeared with counsel at the juvenile hearing. This knowledge is not a waiver of the right to counsel which she and her juvenile son had, as we have defined it. They had a right expressly to be advised that they might retain counsel. . . .

V

Confrontation, Self-Incrimination, Cross-Examination

Appellants urge that the writ of habeas corpus should have been granted because of the denial of the rights of confrontation and cross-examination in the Juvenile Court hearings, and because the privilege against self-incrimination was not observed. . . .

It would indeed be surprising if the privilege against self-incrimination were available to hardened criminals but not to children. The language of the Fifth Amendment, applicable to the states by operation of the 14th Amendment, is unequivocal and without exception. . . .

With respect to juveniles, both common observation and expert opinion emphasize that the "distrust of confessions made in certain situations" is imperative in the case of children from early age through adolescence.

In New York, for example, the recently enacted Family Court Act provides that the juvenile and his parents must be advised at the start of the hearing of his right to remain silent. The New York statute also provides that the police must attempt to communicate with the juvenile's parents before questioning him, and that a confession may not be obtained from a child prior to notifying his parents or relatives and releasing the child either to them or the Family Court. . . .

It is also urged, as the Supreme Court of Arizona here asserted, that the juvenile and presumably his parents should not be advised of the juvenile's right to silence because confession is good for the child as the commencement of the assumed therapy of the juvenile court process, and he should be encouraged to assume an attitude of trust and confidence toward the officials of the juvenile process.

United States Reports, Vol. 387, Cases Adjudged in the Supreme Court (Washington, D.C.: U.S. Government Printing Office, 1967), pp. 1–81.

Chapter 8
Social Change and Economic Stagnation: The 1970s and 1980s

At the start of the 1980s the economy of the United States appears to be in trouble. Unemployment is rising sharply. In May 1980 the overall unemployment rate stood at 7.8 percent; for the black population it was almost twice that; for teenagers, three times. As unemployment rose and production fell, many government officials predicted that the economic turn would develop into a major depression—the first since the 1930s.

The depression of the early eighties followed a decade of stagflation, inflation with little economic growth. Unemployment during the 1970s averaged 5.4 percent in the first half of the decade then jumped to 8.5 percent in the recession of 1975, recovering, but still at 5.8 percent, in 1979. Gross national product and median family income grew during the period, but at a disappointing pace. In dollar terms GNP grew from $982 billion in 1970 to $2,369 billion in 1979, but inflation took most of that. Despite large nominal growth, real median family income grew only 5 percent during the ten-year period.

Despite the numerous recommendations to be expected in an election year, solutions were not close at hand. During the 1970s OPEC made dramatically clear the extent to which the American economy is subject to world pressures, with shortages here reflecting shortages and demands in other parts of the world. Domestic inflation had disturbing implications for those who live on fixed incomes especially, as well as for those who work and find their ability to purchase goods and services declining. Rising prices combined with rising unemployment have hit most heavily those least able to withstand wage and job loss. Campaigning in 1976, President Carter promised inflation control and an expansion of jobs, with a "misery rate" (the sum of the inflation rate and the unemployment rate) of 8 by the end of his first term. But now, in mid-1980, we have a misery index of 18.7 for the population as a whole—7.8 percent unemployment added to 10.9 percent inflation. For blacks, despite the gains of the period, the misery rate stands at 25.6—a full two points higher than during the recession of 1974–1975.[1]

The search for economic security grew more intricate during the 1970s. The previous two decades had welcomed economic growth, consumerism, and affluence as panaceas for almost all economic and social problems. The problems of the 1970s were not amenable to these cure-alls. Even more, they became suspect as questions were raised about continuing urban decay, the costs of environmental control, and an overall decline in productivity. Union demands for wage increases to offset the erosions of inflation, industry's demand for tax relief as a stimulant to investment in new equipment and new ventures, taxpayer "revolts" against rising taxes and government expenditures, and the resulting demand for restrained governmental budgets all contributed to the complexity of the economic situation.

Government intervention was increasingly suspect as a method for matching rising expectations with economic and social realities. After 40 years, the American love affair with the federal government came to an end. Its failure to resolve environmental issues, to eliminate poverty and discrimination, and to "fine tune" the economy, combined with a hangover of Watergate sentiment to lead Americans back to their historical distrust of planning and of planners. *Common Cause*, a privately financed consumer's group addressed its national constituency with this "plain and simple" truth:

> The reason the United States cannot solve the urgent problems that are plaguing our country, is because the government *is the problem.*[2]

From the start of the 1980 presidential campaign, the Republican candidate, Ronald Reagan, argued that the Democratic Party had been unable to meet new and serious economic and social conditions. Candidate Reagan recognized that the optimism of earlier decades had been tempered and not without a reservoir of anger.

As we enter the 1980s, family life is under question too. Birthrates in the United States are down, approaching zero population growth, but illegitimacy rates continue high. The continuing popularity of marriage is countered by rising divorce rates, and worries about that are not allayed by high remarriage rates. Our concern with family instability led to the calling of the White House Conference on Families. But debate about the acceptability of alternative family forms and mores made for major difficulties in devising an acceptable Conference agenda and a near shambles of its implementation. Although the viability of the nuclear family in this "postindustrial" society is being reevaluated and some believe that the family in any organized form is threatened, there is as yet no consensus about the need for governmental family policy.[3]

"Jobs and Security" *The Morning Sun,* Baltimore, reports that 26,205 applications had been distributed by the Woodlawn, Maryland, office of the Social Security Administration to persons responding to an advertisement publicizing 75 unskilled, entry level openings. September 20, 1980.

Courtesy *The Sunpapers,* Baltimore, MD.

Two other shifts that will shape social welfare in the 1980s need to be noted. One has to do with the graying of the population, the other with work habits. These changes alter the size of the groups at risk and the perception of those in need by those called upon to support them.

In 1900, persons 65 years of age and over represented 6 percent of the total population; by 1970, the percentage had risen to 9.7; by 1980, more than 11 percent of the total population. The proportion of the working population—persons between 18 and 64 years of age—has declined.[4] Falling birthrates, combined with increased life expectancy, would seem to lead to further weakening of the dependency ratio in the future. The expectation that the working segment of the population can and will continue to finance the welfare of those not expected to work at the same level is increasingly questioned.[5] With increased numbers the aging have become more politically effective: they are needing and demanding new programs and expanded benefits, as the working population feels less able to meet these needs. The decrease of children needing education and support will ease the situation somewhat—but only in the short run.

Nor will the increase in women in the labor force solve the financial straits in which retirement programs find themselves. The proportion of women working has risen sharply in this century. In 1900, 20 percent of adult women worked. By 1960, on the eve of the civil rights and feminist revolutions, that proportion had increased to 30 percent; in 1970 it stood at 43 percent. Today more than 50 percent of women of working age are in the labor force.[6] The reality of women in the work force, and, consequently, the increased expectation that women hold jobs outside the home has an impact not only on family social and economic status, but also on many social welfare programs. The potential for competition for available jobs during periods of high unemployment will, for example, impact upon public employment policies and programs. The social insurance system is under scrutiny for its treatment of working women. Issues of child care move to the fore of public attention; while programs for poor women "not expected to work" will almost certainly become more suspect than in the past.

The 1970s were years of dilemma and debate about social welfare in the United States. Significant changes occurred, but they neither solved all dilemmas nor stilled all debates. Moreover, the social changes and economic stagnation of the period in combination seem to suggest that further expansion of social welfare will be slow, with budget constraints dominating welfare decisions.

The decade brought a current of economic, social, and political malaise to American life. The circumstances surrounding the Watergate scandal and President Richard Nixon's resignation led to a reexamination of the political process. Basic political reform—honesty in government—was promised by the presidential candidates during the 1976 campaign. Implicit were social and economic reforms to follow. As in other eras leading to periods of reform, old values and old beliefs were scrutinized. But the frustrations and disappointments of the 1970s widened discrepancies among reality, possibility, and hope. Indeed, as distrust of government and of political leaders deepened and the economic situation worsened, the general citizenry seemed to lose hope that positive change would occur for the country as a whole; and individuals and self-interest groups began to look even more to their own. As faith in collective action faded, the traditional American confidence in the efficacy of individual effort prevailed. Ronald Reagan, won the presidential election of 1980 on the promise of a return to conservative traditions which would restore the country's greatness.

Poverty and Income Distribution

Data from the Social Security Administration have traced a decline in the numbers of those counted poor from 39.5 million in 1959—the first year of the poverty count—to 29.3 million in 1980, a reduction in the poverty rate from 22.4 percent of the population to 13.0 percent.[7] The poverty count is based on the receipt of money income alone, however. The rapid growth of in-kind programs—food stamps, housing subsidies, medical care payments—has, of course, increased the real income of the lowest income groups and further reduced the number of poor. Indeed, some observers have argued that, with the expansion of noncash transfers, and the suspected underreporting of income that occurs,

> One can conclude that the goal of eliminating income poverty as stated by President Johnson in 1964 had been virtually achieved before the onset of the 1974–75 recession.[8]

Nonetheless, there are still major poverty concerns in the United States. For one thing, the reduction in the official poverty count all occurred during the 1960s. Indeed, more people were counted as poor in 1980 than in 1969.

Secondly, the distribution of poverty is far from random. On the contrary, it is structured by race, ethnicity, sex, family situation, and employment status. For whites, the official poverty rate was about 10.2 percent in 1980; for Hispanics, 25.7 percent; for blacks, 32.5 percent. Adult men had a poverty risk of 8.3 percent; women, 11.3 percent. The rate for families where the head works full-time was down to 2 percent; the rate for nonworking families, 21 percent.

Poverty among two-parent families decreased sharply. Only 6.2 percent of husband-wife families were counted poor in 1980. During much of the 1970s, increased job opportunities and wage hikes helped. But much of the financial success was dependent upon the higher labor force participation of women, of working wives and mothers. The poverty rate for single-parent families was higher—11.0 percent for male-headed families; 32.7 percent for female-headed families. Obviously, two-parent (and possibly two-earner) families were in better financial shape, but the implications of having both parents working and out of the home remained unexplored. Major questions about marriage, family life, and child care remained unanswered.

The biggest decline in numbers counted poor has been among the aging. Between 1959 and 1970 the incidence of poverty among the elderly was reduced by about one-third, from 35.2 percent to 24.5 percent. It fell by more than one-third more by 1980, falling to 16 percent, despite the increase in the number of persons 65 years and over in the population. The exit from poverty experienced by the elderly was largely due to the effectiveness of income transfer programs, particularly of old age insurance. In 1972, an increase of 20 percent in old age insurance benefits was legislated; and in 1974, an 11 percent increase. Starting in 1975, increases in retirement income were tied to increases in prices and average wages. Additionally, the passage of the Supplemental Security Act, which began operation in January 1974, provided a means-tested income transfer program guaranteeing a minimum income for the elderly and disabled. Furthermore, SSI benefits, like social insurance, were indexed to keep pace with inflation. Automatic increases in transfer payments should continue to help this group if food, heat, and housing costs do not outstrip gains. Nevertheless, the aging continue to be vulnerable to poverty, with an incidence rate several points above the average.

The situation of female-headed families was far less satisfactory. The incidence of poverty for all in this group remained extraordinarily high at 33 percent. For black and Hispanic female-headed families, living in double jeopardy, the poverty rate was over 50 percent. "Quality control" measures succeeded in slowing and even reversing the growth of the AFDC rolls, the major income transfer program available to single-parent families despite the increase in numbers of potential recipients. Single parenthood appears to be a "time of transition," with many women marrying or remarrying and moving out of poverty after a few years. This means, however, that in the course of growing up, more than one-third of our children live in states of severe deprivation for a considerable part of their lives.[9] During the 1970s AFDC benefits fell far below inflation and, as the prices of necessities soared, the situation for these families was dire indeed.

Frustration in regard to the eradication of poverty is aggravated by failure to agree on how to define it. Measuring poverty as an absolute dollar amount, as with the annually computed poverty index, seems increasingly awkward. In 1959, median income was $5,417, and a family of four was counted poor at an income of $2,793. Life at the poverty line was, in a sense, $2,444 behind normal expectations. By 1980, however, economic and monetary growth resulted in a rise in median income to $21,023. The poverty line, adjusted only for general price changes and not for increased standards of living, stood at $8,414. The gap had grown to $12,069. The number of poor people had declined since 1959 but, in a relative sense, the severity of poverty had increased.

Virtually no redistribution of income has occurred in the United States since the end of World War II,[10] as shown in Table 8.1. This standstill has taken place despite economic growth, despite a seemingly progressive income tax system, despite a war on poverty, despite increases in income transfer programs, and despite an expansion of social services. Basic control of income in the United States remains unchanged. Rising regressive taxes—social security taxes on the federal level, and state and local sales taxes—have neutralized progressive income taxes. Indications are that were it not for income transfer programs, income distribution would be even more unequal.

Table 8.1 Distribution of Income

	PERCENTAGE OF NATIONAL INCOME	
INCOME CLASS	1947	1980
Lowest quintile	5.1%	5.1%
Second quintile	11.8	11.6
Third quintile	16.7	17.5
Fourth quintile	23.2	24.3
Highest quintile	43.3	41.5
Top 5 percent	17.5	15.3

The Balance of "Rights"

The state of the economy is only one factor likely to shape social welfare during the 1980s. The concern of the 1960s with the rights of oppressed groups, paced by the militancy of the black community, led to advances in rights to privacy, due process, and equal protection. The emergence of many groups—women, students, children, the aging, native Americans, prisoners, homosexuals, and others—demanding change resulted in their gaining at least some basic recognition. The historical value of individualism had broadened to a demand for group-determined rights.

Trends during the 1970s were conflicting. Successes in extending civil liberties were scored in affirmative action programs and in efforts to replace institutionalization with community-based programs. Judicial decisions required the payment of reparations to groups who had been shown to have suffered from discriminatory pay and promotion differentials. In July 1980, the Supreme Court, in *Fullilove* v. *Kultznick*, upheld the use of quotas for minority contractors when it decided that Congress could award federal funds on the basis of race in order to redress past racial discrimination.[11]

But—and there is a troublesome list of buts—the promise of the Gault decision of 1967, protecting the rights of children in trouble with the law, was compromised. There was visible return to giving priority to rehabilitation over justice in juvenile proceedings, despite the paucity of resources which undermined the quality of services. In 1972, the enactment of Title IV-D of the Social Security Act, the Child Support Enforcement Law, set off a search for putative fathers and for the support they might provide their children. Success was measured in amounts of AFDC payments reduced rather than in parental ties established. In the states, the intent of such a law as Pennsylvania's Act 148, designed to support deinstitutionalization and community/own-home planning for children, was countered by a lack of supportive community services and by active efforts to legally cut the tie between dependent children and their mothers. The Office of Child Development's thrust toward "permanency planning," though overtly intended to protect children from the uncertainties of long-time foster care placements, unnecessarily risked the permanent separation of some children from their natural parents. The notion of going "beyond the best interest of the child"[12] to forge new permanent ties could, in the 1980s, prove an updated version of "binding out." Certainly its potential for invading the rights of natural parents must be evaluated.

In the adult justice system, the boundaries of the *Gideon* decision of 1963, requiring the assignment of counsel to poor defendants, and of the *Miranda* decision of 1966, which required a clarifying statement of rights at the time of arrest, have been circumscribed. The interpretation of the right to counsel was weakened starting in 1972 with *Kirby* v. *Illinois*, which denied the right to counsel at lineup. In 1972, the *Schneckloth* v. *Bus-*

tamonte decision began the chipping away of the *Miranda* requirement that the defendent know his rights and only waive them intentionally. The Burger Court has continued, in successive opinions, to erode the rights of defendants and to balance concern for victims with the rights of the accused.[13]

For the most vulnerable of the poor, AFDC families, slippage of civil rights is most serious. Their right to privacy, to equal protection, and to due process eroded during the 1970s. Witness HEW's deletion from its regulations of the explicit prohibition of searches of homes made under false pretenses; New York State's subversion of the Supreme Court's ruling against residency requirements by refusing welfare to newcomers who had not managed to find standard housing; or the more coercive features with which Congress "strengthened" the WIN program in 1972.[14]

Perhaps the most serious retrogression of "rights" was the July 1, 1980, ruling of the Supreme Court that the states were not required to make Medicaid funds available for abortions for otherwise eligible women, except in pregnancies resulting from rape or directly threatening their health. Coming as it did after the Court had previously upheld women's control over their own bodies by supporting their right to abortion during the first trimester of pregnancy,[15] it was a disappointing "balancing" of rights for many women.

Expenditures for Social Welfare

Expenditures for social welfare continued to grow rapidly during the 1970s. This growth suggests basic support for social welfare purposes. Government expenditures for health, education, and welfare rose from $3.9 billion in the predepression year of 1929 to $145.8 billion in 1970, then almost doubled to $290 billion in 1975. By 1978, expenditures stood at $394.5 billion. The difference between 1970 and 1978 was almost $250 billion. Some of the increase was due to inflation and some to population growth. But, in 1978 prices, per capita welfare expenditures rose from $405 in 1950 to $1,142 in 1970, to $1,775 in 1978. Clearly there was a recognition of two results of the shift from a predominantly agricultural to a highly industrialized market society. First, the monetized economy had created new risks to family security, risks that the family could not meet on its own. Second, the economy had also provided the base for an ever-increasing standard of living. But although social welfare expenditures were going up, they were not rising as fast as gross national product. In 1976 the largest proportion of our resources went into public social welfare—20.4 percent. In 1977 welfare expenditures were 19.7 percent of gross national product, and in 1978 the figure was 19.3 percent. Although the belief that we could provide more for all had not been seriously challenged, the expansion rate had slowed significantly.[16]

The distribution of governmental welfare expenditures for 1978 indicates the areas of public concern. Functionally, about 45 percent of the $394.5 billion spent for social welfare purposes went for income security programs; 27 percent went for education; 19 percent for health; and 9 percent for public welfare services—including food stamps, child welfare services, veterans' welfare services, vocational rehabilitation, and economic opportunity and manpower programs. Programatically, more than $175 billion went for the various social insurances and for public employee and railroad retirement programs. About $60 billion went for public assistance, including Medicaid and food stamps and social service programs targeted toward the potential employability of public assistance recipients. More than $100 billion was expended for education. Roughly equal amounts, $22 billion and $20 billion, were spent for health programs and for veterans' programs, respectively. About $10 billion was spent on all "other social welfare services," including child welfare, child nutrition, and continuing special OEO programs. The priority given the social insurances suggests again the value placed on work-related programs and the opportunities for political influence lost when human service workers fail to recognize the strength of social values.

Of special interest is the reversal by which federal government expenditures became the dominant element in public social welfare. In 1929 the federal government contributed 21 percent of total governmental outlays for social welfare. By 1970 the federal share had risen to more than 50 percent. In 1978 the federal share was 61 percent. With expenditures for education excluded, the federal government's share of the cost of public social welfare in 1978 was 79 percent.

In large measure, the recent increases in federal expenditures for social welfare have been due to outlays that are not subject to administrative discretion. The bases of outlays for the social insurances, the public assistance programs, and others are mandated by law. Discouraging applications so as to reduce benefit take-up rates and curbing error rates can save some tax dollars. But basically, pending congressional action to amend the laws, expenditures are subject only to the limits of the readiness or ability of beneficiaries and the various levels of government to participate.

Nevertheless, there are indications of effective restraint in the expansion of expenditures for social welfare. After years of rising importance in governmental budgets, welfare expenditures as a percentage of all governmental outlays began to decline slightly after 1976. This was true at the federal and at the state and local levels. Candidate Reagan promised cuts in social programs as part of reaching a balanced federal budget. President Reagan, with congressional support, moved sharply in that direction in planning the budget for fiscal year 1982.

Yet actual cuts in social welfare budgeting are not entirely easy to come by as Presidents Nixon, Ford, and Carter all discovered. The efforts of Richard Nixon in the budgets of 1974 and 1975 to eliminate social welfare programs that he deemed unsuccessful and wasteful met with limited success.[17] The campaign to abolish the Office of Economic Opportunity symbolized his effort. OEO itself was abolished, but its major programs—the community action programs, community legal services, Head Start—were assigned to other agencies and continued with budgets essentially uncut. In the case of Head Start, the budget has even increased. Gerald Ford also discovered that executive pressure to cut programs is not easily executed. Notwithstanding the president's opposition, Congress refused to postpone salary increments for federal employees and resisted limiting the increase in veterans' benefits to the levels suggested by the Ford administration, even when these measures were touted as anti-inflationary. And President Carter found it necessary to yield to congressional pressures against withholding funds for a variety of local public works and to respond to the demands of black organizations and their leaders that funds for the employment of black youth be restored. The Reagan administration efforts to cut back on some social security benefits were unsuccessful. Constituencies for social welfare measures are organizing and learning to act effectively.

Not only are the politics of welfare increasingly effective in maintaining and even increasing expenditures for social welfare but the economy itself, in the early 1980s at any rate, operates in their behalf. President Carter's initial budget for the fiscal year 1981 for the first time in many years showed an increase in defense spending, relative to funds budgeted for social welfare.[18] As the 1980 presidential campaign heated up and calls for budget stringency increased, the president and the Congress explored possibilities of achieving a balanced budget by cutting an additional $16 billion from the initial proposal, almost all of which was to come from social welfare programming. Subsequently, both party candidates called for even further budget cuts. And, in fact, many individual programs were cut. But welfare expenditures, in total, rose nonetheless. The reasons were threefold: first, and of most importance, rising unemployment led to increases in outlays for unemployment insurance, Medicaid, food stamps, and energy assistance; second, increases in a number of programs resulted from natural disasters such as the eruption of Mount St. Helens; and third, there was an unexpected heavy influx in 1980 of Cuban and Haitian refugees. The budgets for 1980 and 1981 both ran to heavy deficits, despite political pressures for "balancing."

A discussion of social welfare expenditures must call attention to the rapid growth of the food stamp program. Starting with a relatively small appropriation of $550 million in 1970, it received $4.4 billion in 1975, and by 1981 expenditures are expected to reach $10 billion.[19] The program is funded totally by the federal government. Food stamps are available on the basis of income, and their value varies inversely with the size of family income. This program and the new energy assistance program are especially significant because they help the working as well as the nonworking poor and ease that major inequity. In addition, these in-kind programs ease the plight of the elderly in a decade of runaway inflation and help equalize the value of grants in AFDC across the nation, since states with the smallest cash grants give the largest in-kind benefits.

New Approaches to Income Security

In 1935, when provision was made in the Social Security Act for aid to dependent children, the conviction held that poor children should remain in their own homes with their mothers. The 1967 Amendments to the Social Security Act officially reversed that historic policy, reflecting the extent to which mothers of young children had moved, in public thinking, from unemployable to employable. Congress increased appropriations for day care programs and instituted the Work Incentive Program. The WIN program required that an assessment be made of the employability not only of unemployed fathers and out-of-school older children, but also of mothers. The transfer of administrative responsibility for OEO "work experience" programs from the Department of Health, Education, and Welfare to the Department of Labor further clarified the new congressional direction. The climax of policy change occurred in 1971, when the House Ways and Means Committee extolled as a primary virtue of day care its ability to free mothers for work:

> Your committee is convinced that . . . the child in a family eligible under these programs will benefit from the combination of quality child care and the example of an adult in the family taking financial responsibility for him.[20]

The Committee's thinking was translated into law by the compulsory work and supporting day care features of the Talmadge Amendments of December 1971.[21]

Thus, by the close of the 1960s, new definitions of employability and unemployability had come into being and public income transfer policy was in transition. Liberals and conservatives were agreed on the need for welfare reform, including more federal funding and more equitable standard setting and determination of terms of entitlement. State and local fiscal constraints, widely disparate state grants, and extensive discretionary and discriminatory practices made "federalization" attractive. The questions were of form and context.

Discussion during the 1960s had ranged across a number of possibilities for change in the country's assistance programs. First, suggestions for modification, rather than replacement, of existing programs were made. Then various forms of negative income tax proposals were publicized; and an extensive, closely followed "Negative Income Tax Experiment" was financed by the Office of Economic Opportunity. The National Association of Social Workers and the American Public Welfare Association urged a system of social "demogrants"—that is, allowances for children and families. A short-lived experiment with the provision of a children's allowance was also funded by OEO.* A proposal to pay a regular wage to mothers who chose to remain

---

*These particular "social experiments" were not the only ones that captured the imagination during the 1960s. Another proposal was for the use of vouchers for the purchase of education. The thought was that government-financed vouchers would make it possible for the poor to

at home to care for their children (rather than enter the labor market) received attention. The most important proposals were those put forth by President Johnson's Commission on Income Maintenance Programs and by President Nixon in the widely discussed Family Assistance Plan.

In a message to Congress on August 11, 1969, President Nixon publicized his administration's plan for reform of welfare.[22] His proposals were incorporated in a bill known as H.R.1 and were argued throughout 1970, 1971, and much of 1972, when some parts were finally adopted. The programs dealing with the adult categories of public assistance, Aid to the Aged, Aid to the Blind, and Aid to the Disabled, were to be combined in a new program, to be federally funded and federally administered. These groups of basically unemployable adult poor—the aged, the blind, and the disabled—were no problem. And on January 1, 1974, a new program, to be administered by the Social Security Administration and entitled "Supplemental Security Income," did come into being.

For those "American families who cannot care for themselves in whichever state they live," a new program, the Family Assistance Plan (FAP), was proposed as a substitute for AFDC. "Workfare" would replace welfare. A negative income tax mechanism was designed to set a floor on income while still encouraging people to work. A minimum guaranteed income—a subsidy—varying with family size, was set. Where working adults were involved, the subsidy was to be reduced as earned income went up, until a "breakeven point" in total income was reached. The program would, therefore, be available to the working as well as the nonworking poor. Mothers with very young children, originally under 6 years old later under 3 years of age, would be permitted to remain at home. In immediately employable families, however—that is, in two-parent families or in single-parent families with school-age children—financial aid would be conditioned upon the willingness of at least one adult to accept training or employment. In the president's words, FAP coupled "basic benefits to low-income families with children with incentives for employment and training to improve the capacity for employment of members of such families." In essence, "workfare" became the ideological base for different levels and plans of support for different groups of recipients. For poor families judged employable, inadequate grants were to be the incentive for work.

President Johnson's Commission on Income Maintenance Programs had been appointed in January 1968. Its report was released in November 1969,

---

choose among public and private school facilities. This freedom on the part of families to select a facility they deemed appropriate would, it was hoped, result in the upgrading of currently available facilities and the expansion of institutions to meet market demand.

The negative income tax is a plan to make a payment to poor families whose incomes are too low to require a tax payment to the government. The amount of payment (subsidy) would vary with family size and income. The basic intent is to guarantee a minimum income below which no one would fall. The children's allowance offered a grant to all families, hoping to help poor families with many children escape poverty.

only four months after President Nixon's message on reform in welfare had been delivered to Congress. Like the Nixon plan, the Commission's recommendations involved a negative income tax, although benefits were higher. The basic difference between FAP and the Commission's proposal stemmed from their different views of the poor and of the circumstances of the poor. The Commission wrote:

> It is often argued that the poor are to blame for their own circumstances and should be expected to lift themselves from poverty. The Commission has concluded that these assertions are incorrect. Our economic and social structure virtually guarantees poverty for millions of Americans. Unemployment and underemployment are basic facts of American life. The risks of poverty are common to millions more who depend on earnings for their income. . . . The simple fact is that most of the poor remain poor because access to income through work is currently beyond their reach.[23]

The Commission's report was ignored, and failure to obtain congressional approval for the Family Assistance Plan left unresolved many of the issues that had led to its proposal. The Nixon administration announced abandonment of plans to replace AFDC. President Ford's message to Congress on September 12, 1974, stating his legislative priorities, made no mention of welfare reform.

During the early 1970s a number of factors combined to lessen the pressure to replace or reform the family welfare system. One was the initiation of the federal government's Supplemental Security Income program for the elderly and disabled. Public interest in poor families could recede once these unemployable groups, the most favored of the poor, had been cared for. Pressures from the state for reform in welfare could lessen as the elimination of the Old Age Assistance, Aid to the Blind, and Aid to the Disabled categories of public assistance lowered demands on state treasuries. Pressures from the elderly and disabled could diminish with SSI's guarantee of income.

Other factors combined to lower the priority of welfare reform. In 1974, simultaneous with the waning of the civil rights movement, the AFDC welfare roll explosion came to a halt.[24] A serious criticism of the program, by recipients and the general public alike, was stilled by the amendments establishing "income disregards." Previously, all the money a recipient earned was subtracted from the grant, a 100 percent tax. Now the income disregard acted as a work incentive by allowing the retention of a part of earnings either for work expenses or as a "bonus" before grant reductions were made. Finally, expansions of the AFDC-UP and in-kind programs reduced inequities between the working and nonworking poor.

The climate changed again with the economic recession of 1974–1975. This economic crisis, with its rapid increase in the number of jobless, again highlighted the problems and costs of the welfare system. Much of the concern centered on the AFDC program, not only because of continuing costly outlays by the states but also because the program's focus had remained essentially unchanged since 1935, despite changes in familial patterns. Most recipients were single (female) parents. And, by the mid-1970s, these were generally divorced, separated, or never-married mothers, not the "worthy widows" of the 1930s. The public's attitude towards these mothers was, at best, ambivalent—and frequently hostile. Among many Americans, the Protestant/Puritan ethic continued to judge work as basically moral and extramarital sex as immoral. Women's proper place was in the home caring for children; but a father's proper place was at work supporting the family. In any case, public programs, it was felt, should support marriage and discourage its dissolution. The fear that AFDC might be doing the reverse of this opened the debate once more.

Several new suggestions for basic change in family welfare programs came to naught. They included presidential candidate George McGovern's 1972 proposal for a universal demogrant—a payment to be made to all persons—and the 1976 legislation introduced by Congresswoman Martha Griffith proposing a negative income tax that would favor married families.*

A more elaborate negative income tax plan was introduced by President Carter in 1978. The Better Jobs and Income Program, as it was named, was similar to that proposed earlier by Nixon. A federal guarantee of minimum income was provided; benefit scales provided work incentives; job training and child care were planned. The Carter proposal moved beyond the Nixon Family Assistance Plan in that its coverage would have included individuals as well as families, and in its provision of jobs. But, like the Nixon proposal and the Griffith legislation, Carter's plan failed to receive congressional approval.

The failure to reach consensus on welfare reform during the 1970s had been attributed to several factors. Arguments had ensued as to whether to pursue an incremental or comprehensive strategy. Incrementalism was meant to improve the current system without changing its categorical nature and its divided administrative structure. Proponents of incrementalism pointed not only to the reality of a system in place but also to the more likely chance that piecemeal change could be achieved. Proponents of comprehensive reform held the many criticisms of public welfare to mean that a new package of programs, integrated toward common purposes, had to be devised.

The Carter proposal had hoped to achieve reform at no increase in costs beyond those of current public welfare programs. This goal had almost immediately to be abandoned. The job proposal became a source of difficulty too. Some criticized the plan for establishing the federal government as a true "employer of the last resort"; others saw in the offing a threat to private industry. And as with the Nixon plan, there was sharp disagreement about the level of grants. Political agreement among interest groups was impossible to come by.[25]

---

*The legislation resulted from a three-year-long study by Congresswoman Griffith's Subcommittee on Fiscal Policy of the Joint Economic Committee.

By the close of the 1970s there was a growing realization that the welfare system had to be thought of broadly to include the social insurances, the means-tested cash transfer programs, in-kind subsidies, health plans, and public employment programs, which together comprise an income security system. Discussions of the Nixon and Carter plans had assumed the imminent passage of universal health insurance, but by 1980 this seemed much less probable. Although the push toward "workfare" was as persistent as ever, there was a continuing reluctance to provide public jobs. Social insurance funding was experiencing severe crises. The costs of old age insurance especially were escalating so rapidly that tax receipts were not keeping pace with charges against them. Discussions of funding mechanisms became the occasion for a new look at the program's intent and its place in a broadly based social security system. Throughout the 1950s and 1960s, the old age insurance program had become increasingly redistributive; now, with SSI in place, questions were being raised again about the relationship of individual contributions to the size of individual pensions.[26]

Changes in family life and in the labor force participation of women have raised questions about the social insurance program, just as it has about the AFDC program. The social insurance program—old age insurance—was designed for a nuclear family with two parents and one (male) wage earner. For nonemployed women, in an era of widespread marital instability, problems arose in a system where benefits derived from the income of the employed spouse and were not portable. Employed women, too, were dissatisfied with the way in which benefits were calculated, feeling that there were often inequities.[27]

Thus some new issues, particularly involving the relationship of the social insurance and public assistance programs, needed resolution. President Carter urged Congress to consider the establishment of a national minimum benefit level pegged at 65 percent of the federal poverty threshold as well as additional allocations for job development. Both were scheduled to begin during 1981.[28] President Reagan seems less inclined to broaden the role of the federal government and is moving toward the development of block grants with the states making the allocative decisions.

Income Transfer Programs: Summary and Issues for the 1980s

There are a tremendous number of public programs whose purpose is the redistribution of money and goods. The Institute for Social Economic Studies' *Inventory of Federal Income Transfer Programs* listed 182, each with its own level and degree of federal involvement, its own benefit standards, and its own eligibility criteria.[29] Each of the programs has its own history and, whatever its set of problems and issues, its own political constituency in Congress, in the executive branch of government, in the states' bureaucracies, and in the general citizenry. In addition to the Department of Health and Human Services, the Departments of Education,

Agriculture, Housing and Urban Development, Labor, Commerce, the Treasury, the Interior, and the Veterans Administration are involved.

The number of Senate and House committees and subcommittees with a stake in the funding and continuation of particular programs is similarly large. The number of lobby and special-interest groups is innumerable.[30] In connection with President Carter's Better Jobs and Income Program, for example, the writing of the original bill submitted for congressional consideration was described as having been "drafted by the bureaucracy." In order to have the bill actually reviewed by the House of Representatives during the 1978 session, Speaker of the House Thomas O'Neill "circumvented the problems of divided committee jurisdiction by creating a special panel" to serve as a subcommittee of the Committees on Ways and Means, Education and Labor, and Agriculture. Consideration by the Senate's Finance Committee could not even begin until the House had completed its deliberations.

Rather than a system, in the sense of a number of interacting and mutually reinforcing programs trying to achieve a clear-cut goal, what we have is a set of programs, that are frequently contradictory or at the least counterfunctional. The programs reflect national ideology and national ambivalences. Equity, the assurance of a return commensurate with contributions, vies with ideals of increased equality; the value of a mother remaining at home with her children is countered by the value ascribed to individual self-sufficiency and labor market participation. The programs are organized not by risk or need alone but also by the work force history and marital status of the claimant.

Changes in income security programs during the 1970s maintained the division of transfer program recipients into categorical groups, and change for the 1980s seems stalled awaiting clarification of program relationships. It does seem certain, however, that during the 1980s, predictably a period of inflation and continued unemployment, the design of change in income transfer policies will continue to be concerned with incentives and labor force participation. Some of the major issues involved can be considered by examining three groups at risk: aging, unemployed, and single parents.

The Aging

An increase in the number of people living to very old ages has meant an increase in the total amount of retirement benefits paid out and in the total costs of health care. In the context of inflation, rising unemployment, and falling birthrates this raises a host of questions for income and medical programs aimed at the aging population.

1. *The Financing of Social Security.* The 1979 Advisory Council on Social Security concluded that our social insurances are basically sound.

> The Council is unanimous in finding that the social security system is the government's most successful social program. It provides basic retirement, disability and survivorship protection which American workers can supplement

with their own savings and private pensions, and it will continue to provide this protection for as far ahead as anyone can see.

After reviewing the evidence, the Council is unanimously convinced that all current and future social security beneficiaries can count on receiving all the benefits to which they are entitled.[31]

Despite the long-run optimism, however, there are some immediate financing problems to be addressed. In June 1980 the Trustees pointed to an immediate cash flow crisis for the retirement system and recommended that the retirement trust fund be permitted to borrow from the other trust funds. For the longer run, the distribution of the payroll tax among the health funds, the disability fund, and the retirement system will have to be reassessed. Assuming that there is indeed some limit on total payroll taxes, then part of the system will have to be financed from general revenues if benefits are not to be cut below planned levels. The Advisory Council recommended that Health Insurance be financed from general revenues thus preserving for Old Age Insurance the image of "contributions" and "earned entitlements" to retirement income. Others have recommended a change to an older age for entitlement as a way out of perceived financing problems. In any case, it appears certain that the funding base of the social security system will be a primary concern for the 1980s.

2. *The Level of Benefits and the Benefit Formulas.* The Social Security Act, as originally legislated, provided work-related benefits much in the way such benefits would have been provided through private insurance. The notion of equity was the tie among wages, tax contributions, and benefits. Amendments to the Act have steadily altered this approach in order to reflect need and adequacy as well as equity. The passage of the Supplemental Security Income Program in 1972 provided a means-tested income transfer program that guarantees a minimum income for the elderly and disabled. Furthermore, SSI benefits, like OAI, are indexed to keep pace with inflation. This change has made it possible to rethink the extent to which the insurance programs should be used to redress inequities in wage and employment patterns. In fact, President Reagan's administration has already acted to eliminate minimum payments in the old age insurance program.

Concurrent with the debate about the balance of insurance and assistance programs in providing income for the aging is a debate about the level of income to be provided generally to the aged. In particular, questions are being raised about the current full indexing of pensions. Some are arguing for only 75 percent indexing on the grounds that wages generally are not keeping pace with the cost of living; others, notably the Advisory Council, argue for an increase in indexing to twice a year, in order that benefits stay closer to rising prices. Both programmatic structure and level of payments are at issue and both are open to possible change in the 1980s.

3. *The Structure of Benefits for Women.* The social insurance system was designed in an era of greater marital stability and in a period of much less labor market participation on the part of married women than we have today.

Many proposals to adjust the system for social change are under discussion. Some have argued for the paying of homemaker wages and for the maintenance of completely individualized retirement accounts. Others have pressed for full-scale earnings-sharing for couples. In any case, it is clear that changes in the structure of insurance benefits for women have potential for reducing poverty among older women and their need for SSI, food stamps, Medicaid, and other in-kind programs.

The Unemployed

1. *Job Provision.* For most American families, work is the antipoverty program of choice. Over the years many programs have been developed to spur opportunity for employment: the Manpower Development and Training Act, the Work Incentive Program, and the Comprehensive Employment Training Act. The inability of training opportunities to solve the job problem, especially in an era of rising unemployment rates, raises again the need for federal participation in job creation. President Carter's failed Better Jobs and Income Program moved in that direction, and the most recent amendments to the CETA provisions did make funds available for public service employment. But the right to a job and the full-employment issues of the Humphrey-Hawkins bill are unresolved as we enter the 1980s. President Reagan has moved to have CETA abolished. The future of governmental participation in job provision may be determined by the extent to which the private sector expands employment.

2. *Unemployment Insurance.* Unemployment has been most severe for young applicants entering the job market. Nationally, unemployment stood at 7.8 percent in May 1980. For teenagers it reached 19.2 percent, and for minority youth, two to three times that high.[32] Not having worked, this group of unemployed is not now eligible for insurance benefits; and one proposal is to reopen the issue of criteria for eligibility for this program. Because the program is state based and employer financed, an extension of coverage would require a new look at the financing base. One should note, however, that there is a precedent for federal participation in financing in past extensions of unemployment benefits during extended periods of high unemployment. The issue then is not only additional extensions during disastrous unemployment situations but the general extension of benefits to individuals who have not had a prior employment record but who are currently seeking work. Such a move would shift more of the responsibility for the unemployed to the federal government, and would therefore ease the costs of general relief for the states.

3. *General Assistance.* General Assistance is a state program with state administration and no federal financing. Pennsylvania is one of the states having such a program; and, as in other states, there are efforts to legislate the removal from the GA rolls all but the "chronically needy," those who are not considered employable. All other GA recipients, the "transitionally

needy," are to be eligible for only a single one-month assistance check—a job search subsidy—in a 12-month time period. Several questions emerge: First, what is meant by employable? Are those classified as "transitionally needy" truly capable of sustaining employment? Second, even if they are employable, is one month long enough for a job search? For those who are not immediately employable, what kind of training programs are to be provided and what are to be the criteria for admission to these programs?

Perhaps most basic of all is the issue of jobs. The economic situation hardly supports the view of a large number of jobs awaiting this population. This is even more true when one considers the geographic structure involved. In Pennsylvania, as in many industrial states, available jobs are distributed widely across the state, whereas the greatest proportions of the "transitionally needy" GA population are concentrated in the large urban areas. As a last resort—as a bow to the work effort—some states are resorting to new programs of work relief.

Single Parents

1. The Appropriate Recipient Group. Support for single parents started early in the twentieth century with the Mother's Pension movement and state programs of aid to widows with young children. The years have brought changes at many levels. With the introduction of the Social Security Act in 1935, Aid to Dependent Children—a combined federal, state, and local program—replaced the state programs. In the 1960s, a growing concern with marital instability and a wish to avoid incentives for marital disruption led to the AFDC-UP program—that is, to an extension of benefits in many states to two-parent families where the head of the household was unemployed. At the same time, rising recipient rolls led to more emphasis on work for women with young children. The Work Incentive Program (WIP or WIN) was legislated and implemented to encourage their labor force participation and to discourage program usage. But the WIN program, for all the rhetoric, failed to place all, or even most, of those AFDC adult recipients who were screened and were able or willing to work. The reason may be continued uncertainty about the purpose of public policy for poor families. We have moved toward a work orientation for the heads of poor families, but not entirely away from the original intent of Mother's Assistance and the Funds to Parents movements. Certainly, any success of the WIN program, of unemployment programs generally, has been compromised by the lack of public jobs and public day care facilities.

2. Level of Benefits. The view of AFDC recipients as less worthy than other Americans has made them "less eligible" for income support than other groups. Average benefit levels are well below the poverty level and falling, since the program is not indexed for inflation. The tripartite—federal, state, local—division of funding responsibility has meant, too, that payment levels vary widely from state to state.

Questions stemming from concerns with benefit levels are many: What level of government should fund benefits? Should there be a uniform national standard? Should benefits for single parents be tied to the cost of living, as for SSI and OASDI recipients? Should there be a two-tiered arrangement, with differential payments for employables and for those who are to remain at home with their children?

3. *Level of Administrative Responsibility.* Over the years the separate and different systems of administration of AFDC by the separate states have been seen to create administrative difficulties. Regardless of funding responsibility, questions arise about the working alignment among federal, state, and local governments. Should the states take on the responsibility for determining eligibility for income payments and designing social service support systems? How might state machinery and personnel, already in place in the various states, be best used? In a country as vast as the United States, are states the logical governmental units with whom to lodge the administration of income programs so that the differential needs of persons in particular geographic units can be met with reasonable efficiency?

One further note: Income transfer programs operate within the context of broader economic policy. Employment policy, growth policy, price policy, tax policy all impinge on income in more basic ways than do transfer payments. And, basically, our economic system operates toward the disadvantage of certain groups: blacks, Hispanics, women, the very young, and the very old, all suffer the penalty of unequal access to wealth and to income opportunities. The ways in which our income transfer programs—that is, our income security system—are organized perpetuate and extend these advantages and inequities. In the 1960s Americans still believed it possible to have more for everyone; in the 1980s this American dream seems less immediately achievable. Perhaps the increasing concern with the rights of women will force the issue.

Women

A staff report of the United States Commission on Civil Rights charged that federal and state welfare programs, federal job training programs, and social insurance and private pension plans all discriminate against women. AFDC and the WIN program were subject to special attack. Not only were low AFDC benefits keeping women and their families in poverty, but the WIN program, when it did succeed in placing women in jobs, had done so at discriminatory, low-entry wage levels in jobs that offered little chance for advancement. Significantly, a staff member of the United States Commission on Civil Rights had this to say about the Commission's first hearings on women's rights:

> The value of having low income women in these hearings is that they educate us and tell us problems. They also find . . . there are laws that cover them. . . . And these hearings get action . . . because they draw attention.[33]

That hearing took place in 1974. A Department of Justice Task Force on Sex Discrimination issued a report in 1979 with a broad overview of sexual discrimination in our pension system.[34]

A series of studies and reports on the changing position of women were issued in the late 1970s. The Department of Labor held a major conference analyzing "Women's Changing Roles at Home and on the Job" in 1977.[35] That same year the social security amendments legislated that the Secretary of Health, Education and Welfare, in consultation with the Task Force on Sex Discrimination in the Department of Justice, make a detailed study of unequal treatment of men and women under the Social Security Act, and started an exploration of ways of eliminating dependency as a factor in the determination of spouse's benefits.[36] A Task Force on the Treatment of Women was appointed and their report was issued early in 1978.[37] Secretary Califano also requested that the current Advisory Council on Social Security ". . . consider the criticism that the present benefit structure does not recognize the changing role of women in our society."[38] Reactions to the 1978 Task Force report and letters sent to the Advisory Council became basic data for the 1979 HEW Report, *Social Security and the Changing Roles of Men and Women.* Although the 1979 report itself analyzed options for change and did not make definite recommendations, it did serve a basic purpose: ". . . to focus public debate on concerns about the way social security relates to the present complex and diversified structure of American society. . . ."[39] and should provide a factual base for debate. Later in 1979 the Advisory Council stated the issue thus:

> Two new objectives [for social security] are commanding increasing attention. First, from the recognition that women are important contributors to the economic well being of the family, whether they work inside or outside the home, comes the desire that women be entitled to benefits in their own right, not simply or primarily as economic dependents of their spouses. Second, in addition to individual equity, equity is now also tested by whether couples with the same total earnings receive the same protection, regardless of which partner earned what share.[40]

The issues have been raised on many fronts: the courts, Congress, the administration, the women's movement, and the public generally. But change for women generally and for poor women in particular has not occurred with the predicted swiftness. Ambivalence about ways to help poor women has combined with a broader ambivalence about the proper role of all women in our society. The near miss at achieving ratification of the Equal Rights Amendment by the required approval of two-thirds of the states and the rescinding of approval by several states indicate the indecision of the 1970s. The time for attaining the necessary number of votes was extended, but 1980 saw no improvement in the situation. In fact, in a major test, the Illinois legislature failed to approve ERA, and the Republican Platform Committee, in support of the stance of the Republican presidential candidate, abandoned a 40-year tradition of including a plank in favor of such an amendment. But the ERA has received sufficiently widespread attention that issues are clarified for decision making during the 1980s.

Veterans

This coming together of women, black and white, "rich" and "poor," on problems of discrimination may result in common demand for change—change that may be reflected in the welfare of poor families. Twenty years ago some observers thought veterans would play such a catalytic role. The 1956 report of the President's Commission on Veterans' Pensions analyzed the meaning of the special status accorded veterans:

> Veterans and their families will eventually be a majority of the population of the United States. Veterans in modern times are better off economically than non-veterans in similar age groups.[41]

The 1956 Commission pointed to the extent to which basic needs of "all citizens, veterans and non-veterans alike, for economic security are being increasingly met through Federal, state and private programs." In summary, the Commission concluded: "Military service in time of war or peace is the obligation of citizenship and should not be considered inherently a basis for future Government benefits," and "all veterans' benefits should be meshed with the nation's general security system. . . ."

The Commission's report of 1956 wielded little influence. But the benefits awarded in 1966 to veterans of the Korean War (retroactively) and the Vietnam War suggested some policy shifts. Certainly, the educational benefits for these groups did not compare favorably with those provided for veterans in 1944. In 1980, however, at a time of high unemployment, the erosion of benefits appears unacceptable to veterans' organizations and to Congress. President Franklin D. Roosevelt, signing the G.I. Bill on June 22, 1944, stated: "This law gives emphatic notice to the men and women of our armed forces that the American people do not intend to let them down."[42] Americans still seem to agree that veterans are a group apart who deserve special consideration.

Unresolved Questions

The current state of social welfare policy formulation and program implementation reflects many issues of long standing. One such issue is the "universality" versus "selectivity" approach to making benefits available. Should benefits be for the entire population or just for those in financial need? In the area of income security, proponents of universal demogrants— children's allowances, for example—point to the psychological value of joining the poor and nonpoor in one stream. For many years the question appeared to have been generally resolved in favor of selectivity on the basis that any income transfer program that includes funds for the "haves" is not only expensive but also inherently unfair to the "have nots." The 1979 HEW Report opened the door somewhat to a universal demogrant in its consideration, as one of two alternatives, of a double-decker benefit structure for the social insurance program. Under this plan, a universal flat-dollar benefit would be provided to all retirees, survivors, or disabled U.S. residents, regardless of work history. A second tier of benefits would be earnings related. The Advisory Council rejected this plan, but the door may not be fully closed.

For services, too, the selectivity/universality issue is unresolved. Selectivity—namely, limiting services to the low-income population and creating programs for the poor only—has resulted in poor programs. Nevertheless, governmental provisions for medical care, mental health and mental retardation, foster care, legal aid, housing, and so on have fostered such a policy. In regard to the personal social services—homemaker service, child care services, counseling, and so on—the social service Amendments of 1974 (Title XX of the Social Security Act) made some public services available on a fee-for-service basis to a limited group above the poverty level. But overall, there would not seem to be an egalitarian force in the United States strong enough to move the country toward universality in social services.

In education, equality remains an accepted goal. However, as deterioration of the quality of public schools proceeds, the middle class has turned to private schools, leaving the public system to the poor and to further erosion of the quality of education. This process of deterioration may be accelerated by recent court decisions against the geographic broadening of the tax base for educational funding and against busing as a means toward racial integration.

Resolution of the selectivity/universality question may come as new approaches to social welfare needs are made possible by the restructuring of HEW. In May 1980 the Department of Education was created as an independent entity, and its head was given cabinet status. Health and Welfare were reconstituted as the Department of Health and Human Services.

A second unresolved question has to do with the provision of social welfare through cash grants or as in-kind programs. To give cash is to grant a degree of consumer choice. To provide commodities, on the other hand, channels the use of public funds more directly toward socially desired ends. Vouchers lie in between. The proposed use of vouchers to help meet educational and health needs suggests an increase in client freedom and more choice than existed in the direct assignment of service. Replacing surplus food distribution with food stamps was a move in that direction. But if the food stamp program, along with energy assistance and housing subsidies, become a substitute for cash income, then vouchers become a technique for social control. At this moment, a danger in the popularity of vouchers is that they may be used as an interesting gimmick, rather than as a tool for the consistent pursuit of social goals.

Also unresolved in social welfare are the issues of relationships between the federal and state governments and between the public and voluntary social welfare sectors. Revenue sharing, block grants, and the proposed return to the states of responsibility for job training, education, community development, and justice programs suggest a retreat from the long-time trend toward centralized—that is, federal—responsibility for social welfare. On the other hand, Supplemental Security Income moved responsibility for the adult poor to Washington; and all major proposals for change in the family welfare program (AFDC) look toward the federal government's assumption of basic responsibility. In part, the question is funding sufficiency, of course; but important too is accountability for the way funds are used. This matter is significant in view of a history that indicates that conservatism and restrictiveness increase as the level of government responsibility for program administration becomes more local. States' rights in social welfare have frequently been at variance with the rights of people to social benefits.

The federal-state relationship problem is complicated by the question of public-voluntary social welfare agency relationships. Disenchantment with governmental operation of social welfare programs led, in the 1970s, to a push for "reprivatization,"[43] a return to private voluntary enterprise. The return was hinted originally in the Public Welfare Amendments of 1962 and became viable when subsequent legislation made it possible for federal funds to pay voluntary agencies 75 percent of the cost of services provided public welfare recipients. During the 1970s the states moved rapidly toward purchasing services from voluntary agencies that were able to supply from their resources the 25 percent needed for fully funding the purchased services. With little or no outlay, the states were able to expand services and the use of personnel in behalf of public agency clientele.[44] The only limit to expansion was the cap placed on these purchases by Title XX of the Social Security Act. For fiscal year 1980, the cap was $2.7 billion. Additional limits may result from decisions to reorganize federal support for social programs through an expanded series of block grants, at the same time reducing the overall amount of funds authorized for each.

Unquestionably, the availability of public funds with which to purchase voluntary agency services revitalized the voluntary sector. Voluntary agencies, at the same time, are undergoing changing alignments with their traditional funding sources, the United Ways. Not only are United Ways encouraging agencies to seek public funds, but they are themselves starting to purchase services from their "member agencies." Some loss of voluntary agency autonomy would seem impossible to avoid, as governments struggle to retain ultimate responsibility for the public's general welfare. The long-held value of voluntarism and private enterprise in social welfare has been strengthened, but its meaning for both sectors of social welfare is yet to be seen. For clients, there is still more promise than service.

A continuing dilemma for social welfare and for social workers involves the conflict between client freedom and professional helping. The concept of client rights implies self-determination. Quality service, by definition, means that the one being helped must give over some degree of personal autonomy. When professional control joins with institutional control—as, for example, when social workers are employed in social agencies—the concern for client rights is heightened.[45] Professional social work's renewed interest in social action and social advocacy shows awareness of dangers. Social work's espousal of client/consumer participation will require more than that.

Epilogue

The history of social welfare has shown a broadening of public responses, both in terms of programs to meet needs and in terms of levels of governmental responsibility. As economic growth made it possible to meet pressing current needs, social values changed and required the acknowledgment of new problems. The cycle continued and responsibility for social welfare shifted from local governments to include state governments, and, finally, the federal government. Income security and social service programs moved from almshouse and workhouse care (indoor relief) to nationalized social insurance and to work-oriented public assistance programs. The system of apprenticeship for poor children evolved into state systems of public education. Institutional care of sick people developed into community-based health services and into the prospect of national health insurance. Despite shaky progress, there has been a move toward liberalization of benefits and entitlements, whether money transfers on services.*

Equalizing interventions have depended upon economic growth and the ability to pay. They have been essential to the maintenance of a democratic stance in the face of growing affluence. But they have followed slowly and reluctantly, reflecting two motifs in social welfare developments:

1. That few crimes are more reprehensible than the inability to pay one's way, to make a living
2. That the family is the unit basically responsible for family and social welfare and that the government is the provider of last resort.

These views still maintain considerable force in shaping social welfare policy and family welfare. Programs in aid of the poor continue to be judged by the view we hold of our society and of ourselves as we relate to that society. In that judgment, poor people still come off second best—scapegoats for circumstances beyond their control.

---

*Reaganomics and political conservatism threaten this progress. The 1981 Title XX amendments which provide block grants for social services not only shift planning responsibility back to the states, but also reduce required spending. Combined with severe budget cuts for other social programs this leaves the poor more vulnerable than at any time since the Depression.

DOCUMENTS
Social Change and Economic Stagnation

President Richard M. Nixon's *Message on Reform in Welfare* (1969) is one of two documents used to illustrate social welfare events during the first half of the 1970s. Although the message was written in 1969, it was operationalized as H.R. 1 in 1970. The debate that swirled around the message and the bill highlighted the major issues in public welfare.

The Family Assistance Plan (FAP) proposed in the message was the center of controversy. In the initial debate, attacks came from both liberals and conservatives. The merits of the negative income tax approach to helping poor families, the sufficiency of the guaranteed basic allowance, the work incentive features, the inclusion of benefits for the working poor, were all subject to scrutiny by proponents and opponents. Liberals generally approved the plan to federalize aid for poor families. They were dismayed, however, by the seemingly punitive "workfare" aspects of the message and by the low guaranteed basic allowance of $1,600 a year for a family of four. Conservatives were frightened by the possibility that an income transfer program that guaranteed benefits for the working poor would attract people to the welfare rolls and weaken their attachment to the labor force.

What comes through forcefully in the message is the switch from a service approach to welfare to an income-workfare approach. Moreover, the message makes clear that mothers are now to be considered employable—or potentially employable. The implication was of a reversal of the "own home" philosophy of child care proclaimed by President Theodore Roosevelt at the first National Conference on Children and Youth in 1909.

As criticisms of H.R. 1 become more volatile, the Nixon administration and Congress responded with changes in the original proposal. The basic guaranteed allowance was raised, but supplementation through food stamps was eliminated. Even more serious from the point of view of welfare recipients in the more generous North was the threat of a cutback in their grants. The plan, as originally devised, offered protection against such a loss by requiring the states to supplement the guaranteed allowance. This was also eliminated. Work requirements became more stringent, specifying that mothers with children over 3 years old be available for work. Three-quarters of the minimum wage was stipulated as acceptable pay.

On the one side were those who worried about the inadequacies and injustices of the program. On the other side was a group concerned with mounting costs. Analyses of multiple program benefits and their overlap increased the anxiety of those who feared the erosion of work incentives. Stalemate ensued and the proposal was quietly abandoned.

President Carter's Better Jobs and Income Program was, in its essential thrust, similar to the Family Assistance Proposal. The two plans differed in two major aspects: (1) the Carter plan provided universal coverage, whereas the Nixon proposal was for families only; and (2) the Carter proposal included job creation. Despite the differences, the Carter plan also failed to achieve approval.

The interest in the reform of welfare in the 1970s was paralleled by an interest in developing public personnel social services as an entity separate from income transfer programs. The failure of the 1962 social service amendments to bring about programs leading to reductions in the public assistance rolls resulted first in calls to separate the need for service from a need for financial assistance and finally to the establishment of social service programs whose raison d'être was self-contained. Public Law 93-647, providing grants to the states for services, was passed by the two houses of Congress during December 1974 and was signed into law on January 4, 1975, as Title XX of the Social Security Act. The new law's provisions became effective on October 1, 1975.

Title XX made $2.5 billion available to the states through a system of block grants. States were required to share the cost of services by putting up 25 percent of the funds. Each state's share could come from the state's welfare department, other state agencies, or through contributions from voluntary social agencies.

The goals of Title XX—that is, the goals for encouraging states to furnish social services—were broadly defined so as to make it possible for each state to implement such services as seemed best to meet each individual state's need. The requirement that each state submit an annual plan for services to be offered was meant to stimulate planning and to ensure integrity. The ability to provide some services on a fee-paying basis meant that the provision of services was not completely restricted to recipients of income transfer payments. Encouragement to purchase services made possible a strengthening of the voluntary sector of social welfare.

REFORM IN WELFARE
MESSAGE FROM PRESIDENT RICHARD M. NIXON

August 11, 1969

TO THE CONGRESS OF THE UNITED STATES:

A measure of the greatness of a powerful nation is the character of the life it creates for those who are powerless to make ends meet.

If we do not find the way to become a working nation that properly cares for the dependent, we shall become a Welfare State that undermines the incentive of the working man.

The present welfare system has failed us—it has fostered family breakup, has provided very little help in many States and has even deepened dependency by all too often making it more attractive to go on welfare than to go to work.

I propose a new approach that will make it more attractive to go to work than to go on welfare, and will establish a nationwide minimum payment to dependent families with children.

I propose that the Federal government pay a basic income to those American families who cannot care for themselves in whichever State they live.

I propose that dependent families receiving such income be given good reason to go to work *by making the first sixty dollars a month they earn completely their own, with no deductions from their benefits.*

I propose that we *make available an addition to the incomes of the "working poor,"* to encourage them to go on working and to eliminate the possibility of making more from welfare than from wages.

I propose that these payments be made upon certification of income, with demeaning and costly investigations replaced by simplified reviews and spot checks and with *no eligibility requirements that the household be without a father.* That present requirement in many States has the effect of breaking up families and contributes to delinquency and violence.

I propose that all employable persons who choose to accept these payments be required to register for work or job training and *be required to accept that work or training,* provided suitable jobs are available either locally or if transportation is provided. Adequate and convenient day care would be provided children wherever necessary to enable a parent to train or work. The only exception to this work requirement would be mothers of pre-school children.

I propose *a major expansion of job training and day care facilities,* so that current welfare recipients able to work can be set on the road to self-reliance.

I propose that we also *provide uniform Federal payment minimums for the present three categories of welfare aid to adults*—the aged, the blind and the disabled.

This would be total welfare reform—the transformation of a system frozen in failure and frustration into a system that would work and would encourage people to work.

Accordingly, we have stopped considering human welfare in isolation. The new plan is part of an overall approach which includes a comprehensive new Manpower Training Act, and a plan for a system of revenue sharing with the State to help provide all of them with necessary budget relief. Messages on manpower training and revenue sharing will follow this message tomorrow and the next day, and the three should be considered as parts of a whole approach to what is clearly a national problem.

Need for New Departures

A welfare system is a success when it takes care of people who cannot take care of themselves and when it helps employable people climb toward independence.

A welfare system is a failure when it takes care of those who *can* take care of themselves, when it drastically varies payments in different areas, when it breaks up families, when it perpetuates a vicious cycle of dependency, when it strips human beings of their dignity.

America's welfare system is a failure that grows worse every day.

First, it fails the recipient: In many areas, benefits are so low that we have hardly begun to take care of the dependent. And there has been no light at the end of poverty's tunnel. After four years of inflation, the poor have generally become poorer.

Second, it fails the taxpayer: Since 1960, welfare costs have doubled and the number on the rolls has risen from 5.8 million to over 9 million, all in a time when unemployment was low. The taxpayer is entitled to expect government to devise a system that will help people lift themselves out of poverty.

Finally, it fails American society: By breaking up homes, the present welfare system has added to social unrest and robbed millions of children of the joy of childhood; by widely varying payments among regions, it has helped to draw millions into the slums of our cities.

The situation has become intolerable. Let us examine the alternatives available:

—We could permit the welfare momentum to continue to gather speed by our inertia; by 1975 this would result in 4 million more Americans on welfare rolls at a cost of close to 11 billion dollars a year, with both recipients and taxpayers shortchanged.

—We could tinker with the system as it is, adding to the patchwork of modifications and exceptions. That has been the approach of the past, and it has failed.

—We could adopt a "guaranteed minimum income for everyone," which would appear to wipe out poverty overnight. It would also wipe out the basic economic motivation for work, and place an enormous strain on the industrious to pay for the leisure of the lazy.

—Or, we could adopt a totally new approach to welfare, designed to assist those left far behind the national norm, and provide all with the motivation to work and a fair share of the opportunity to train.

This administration, after a careful analysis of all the alternatives, is committed to a new departure that will find a solution for the welfare problem. The time for denouncing the old is over; the time for devising the new is now.

Recognizing the Practicalities

People usually follow their self-interest.

This stark fact is distressing to many social planners who like to look at problems from the top down. Let us abandon the ivory towers and consider the real world in all we do.

In most States, welfare is provided only when there is no father at home to provide support. If a man's children would be better off on welfare than with the low wage he is able to bring home, wouldn't he be tempted to leave home?

If a person spent a great deal of time and effort to get on the welfare rolls, wouldn't he think twice about risking his eligibility by taking a job that might not last long?

In each case, welfare policy was intended to limit the spread of dependency; in practice, however, the effect has been to increase dependency and remove the incentive to work.

We fully expect people to follow their self-interest in their business dealings; why should we be surprised when people follow their self-interest in their welfare dealings? That is why we propose a plan in which it is in the interest of every employable person to do his fair share of work.

The Operation of the New Approach

1. *We would assure an income foundation throughout every section of America for all parents who cannot adequately support themselves and their children.* For a family of four with less than $1,000 income, this payment would be $1,600 a year; for a family of four with $2,000 income, this payment would supplement that income by $960 a year.

Under the present welfare system, each State provides "Aid to Families with Dependent Children," a program we propose to replace. The Federal government shares the cost, but each State establishes key eligibility rules and determines how much income support will be provided to poor families. The result has been an uneven and unequal system. The 1969 benefits average for a family of four is $171 a month across the nation, but individual State averages range from $263 down to $39 a month.

A new Federal minimum of $1,600 a year cannot claim to provide comfort to a family of four, but the present low of $468 a year cannot claim to provide even the basic necessities.

The new system would do away with the inequity of very low benefits levels in some States, and of State-by-State variations in eligibility tests, by establishing a Federally-financed income floor with a national definition of basic eligibility.

States will continue to carry an important responsibility. In 30 States, the Federal basic payment will be less than the present levels of combined Federal and State payments. These States will be required to maintain the current level of benefits, but in no case will a State be required to spend more than 90% of its present welfare cost. The Federal government will not only provide the "floor," but it will assume 10% of the benefits now being paid by the States as their part of welfare costs.

In 20 States, the new payment would exceed the present average benefit payments, in some cases by a wide margin. In these States, where benefits are lowest and poverty often the most severe, the payments will raise benefit levels substantially. For 5 years, every State will be required to continue to spend at least half of what they are now spending on welfare, to supplement the Federal base.

For the *typical "welfare family"*—a mother with dependent children and no outside income—the new system would provide a basic national minimum payment. A mother with three small children would be assured an annual income of at least $1,600.

For the family headed by an employed father or working mother, the same basic benefits would be received, but $60 per month of earnings would be "disregarded" in order to make up the costs of working and provide a strong advantage in holding a job. The wage earner could also keep 50% of his benefits as his earnings rise above that $60 per month. A family of four, in which the father earns $2,000 in a year, would receive payments of $960, for a total income of $2,960.

For *the aged, the blind* and *the disabled,* the present system varies benefit levels from $40 per month for an aged person in one State to $145 per month for the blind in another. The new system would establish a minimum payment of $65 per month for all three of these adult categories, with the Federal government contributing the first $50 and sharing in payments above the amount. This will raise the share of the financial burden borne by the Federal government for payments to these adults who cannot support themselves, and should pave the way for benefit increases in many States.

For the *single adult* who is not handicapped or aged, or for the *married couple without children*, the new system would not apply. Food stamps would continue to be available up to $300 per year per person, according to the plan I outlined last May in my message to the Congress on the food and nutrition needs of the population in poverty. For dependent families there will be an orderly substitution of food stamps by the new direct monetary payments.

2. *The new approach would end the blatant unfairness of the welfare system.*

In over half the States, families headed by unemployed men do not qualify for public assistance. In no State does a family headed by a father working full-time receive help in the current welfare system, no matter how little he earns. As we have seen, this approach to dependency has itself been a cause of dependency. It results in a policy that tends to force the father out of the home.

The new plan rejects a policy that undermines family life. It would end the substantial financial incentives to desertion. It would extend eligibility to *all* dependent families with children, without regard to whether the family is headed by a man or woman. The effects of these changes upon human behavior would be an increased will to work, the survival of more marriages, the greater stability of families. We are determined to stop passing the cycle of dependency from generation to generation.

The most glaring inequity in the old welfare system is the exclusion of families who are working to pull themselves out of poverty. Families headed by a non-worker often receive more from welfare than families headed by a husband working full-time at very low wages. This has been rightly resented by the working poor, for the rewards are just the opposite of what they should be.

3. *The new plan would create a much stronger incentive to work.*

For people now on the welfare rolls, the present system discourages the move from welfare to work by cutting benefits too fast and too much as earnings begin. *The new system would encourage work by allowing the new worker to retain the first $720 of his yearly earnings without any benefit reduction.*

For people already working, but at poverty wages, the present system often encourages nothing but resentment and an incentive to quit and go on relief where that would pay more than work. The new plan, on the contrary, would provide a supplement that will help a low-wage worker—struggling to make ends meet—achieve a higher standard of living.

For an employable person who just chooses not to work, neither the present system nor the one we propose would support him, though both would continue to support other dependent members in his family.

However, a welfare mother with pre-school children should not face benefit reductions if she decides to stay home. It is not our intent that mothers of pre-school children must accept work. Those who can work and desire to do so, however, should have the opportunity for jobs and job training and access to day care centers for their children: this will enable them to support themselves after their children are grown.

A family with a member who gets a job would be permitted to retain all of the *first $60 monthly income*, amounting to $720 per year for a regular worker, *with no reduction of Federal payments*. The incentive to work in this provision is obvious. But there is another practical reason: Going to work costs money. Expenses such as clothes, transportation, personal care, Social Security taxes and loss of income from odd jobs amount to substantial costs for the average family. Since a family does not begin to *add* to its net income until it surpasses the cost of working, in fairness this amount should not be subtracted from the new payment.

After the first $720 of income, the *rest* of the earnings will result in a systematic reduction in payments.

I believe the vast majority of poor people in the United States prefer to work rather than have the government support their families. In 1968, 600,000 families left the welfare rolls out of an average caseload of 1,400,000 during the year, showing a considerable turnover, much of it voluntary.

However, there may be some who fail to seek or accept work, even with the strong incentives and training opportunities that will be provided. It would not be fair to those who willingly work, or to all taxpayers, to allow others to choose idleness when opportunity is available. Thus, they must accept training opportunities and jobs when offered, or give up their right to the new payments for themselves. No able-bodied person will have a "free ride" in a nation that provides opportunity for training and work.

4. *The bridge from welfare to work should be buttressed by training and child care programs.* For many, the incentives to work in this plan would be all that is necessary. However, there are other situations where these incentives need to be supported by measures that will overcome other barriers to employment.

I propose that *funds be provided for expanded training and job development programs* so that an additional 150,000 welfare recipients can become job worthy during the first year.

Manpower training is a basic bridge to work for poor people, especially people with limited education, low skills and limited job experience. Manpower training programs can provide this bridge for many of our poor. In the new Manpower Training proposal to be sent to the Congress this week, the interrelationship with this new approach to welfare will be apparent.

I am also requesting authority, as a part of the new system, to provide child care for the 450,000 children of the 150,000 current welfare recipients to be trained.

The child care I propose is more than custodial. This Administration is committed to a new emphasis on child development in the first five years of life. The day care that would be part of this plan would be of a quality that will help in the development of the child and provide for its health and safety, and would break the poverty cycle for this new generation.

The expanded child care program would bring new opportunities along several lines: opportunities for the further involvement of private enterprise in providing high quality child care service; opportunities for volunteers; and opportunity for *training and employment in child care centers of many of the welfare mothers themselves*. I am requesting a total of $600 million additional to fund these expanded training programs and child care centers.

5. *The new system will lessen welfare red tape and provide administrative cost savings.* To cut out the costly investigations so bitterly resented as "welfare snooping," the Federal payment will be based upon a certification of income, with spot checks sufficient to prevent abuses. The program will be administered on an automated basis, using the information and technical experience of the Social Security Administration, but, of course, will be entirely separate from the administration of the Social Security trust fund.

The States would be given the option of having the Federal government handle the payment of the State supplemental benefits on a reimbursable basis, so that they would be spared their present administrative burdens and so a single check could be sent to the recipient. These simplifications will save money and eliminate indignities; at the same time, welfare fraud will be detected and lawbreakers prosecuted.

6. *This new departure would require a substantial initial investment, but will yield future returns to the Nation.* This transformation of the welfare system will set in motion forces that will lessen dependency rather than perpetuate and enlarge it. A more productive population adds to real economic growth without inflation. The initial investment is needed now to stop the momentum of work-to-welfare, and to start a new momentum in the opposite direction.

The costs of welfare benefits for families with dependent children have been rising alarmingly the past several years, increasing from $1 billion in 1960 to an estimated $3.3 billion in 1969, of which $1.8 billion is paid by the Federal government, and $1.5 billion is paid by the States. Based on current population and income data, the proposals I am making today will increase Federal costs during the first year by an estimated $4 billion, which includes $600 million for job training and child care centers.

The "start-up costs" of lifting many people out of dependency will ultimately cost the taxpayers far less than the chronic costs—in dollars and in national values—of creating a permanent underclass in America.

From Welfare to Work

Since this Administration took office, members of the Urban Affairs Council, including officials of the Department of Health, Education and Welfare, the Department of Labor, the Office of Economic Opportunity, the Bureau of the Budget, and other key advisers, have been working to develop a coherent, fresh approach to welfare, manpower training and revenue sharing.

I have outlined our conclusions about an important component of this approach in this message; the Secretary of HEW will transmit to the Congress the proposed legislation after the summer recess.

I urge the Congress to begin its study of these proposals promptly so that laws can be enacted and funds authorized to begin the new system as soon as possible. Sound budgetary policy must be maintained in order to put this plan into effect—especially the portion supplementing the wages of the working poor.

With the establishment of the new approach, the Office of Economic Opportunity will concentrate on the important task of finding new ways of opening economic opportunity for those who are able to work. Rather than focusing on income support activities, it must find means of providing opportunities for individuals to contribute to the full extent of their capabilities, and of developing and improving those capabilities.

This would be the effect of the transformation of welfare into "workfare," a new work-rewarding system:

For the first time, all dependent families with children in America, regardless of where they live, would be assured of minimum standard payments based upon uniform and single eligibility standards.

For the first time, the more than two million families who make up the "working poor" would be helped toward self-sufficiency and away from future welfare dependency.

For the first time, training and work opportunity with effective incentives would be given millions of families who would otherwise be locked into a welfare system for generations.

For the first time, the Federal government would make a strong contribution toward relieving the financial burden of welfare payments from State governments.

For the first time, every dependent family in America would be encouraged to stay together, free from economic pressure to split apart.

These are far-reaching effects. They cannot be purchased cheaply, or by piecemeal efforts. This total reform looks in a new direction; it requires new thinking, a new spirit and a fresh dedication to reverse the downhill course of welfare. In its first year, more than half the families participating in the program will have one member working or training.

We have it in our power to raise the standard of living and the realizable hopes of millions of our fellow citizens. By providing an equal chance at the starting line, we can reinforce the traditional American spirit of self-reliance and self-respect.

• • •

TITLE XX—GRANTS TO STATES FOR SERVICES

Appropriation Authorized

Sec. 2001. For the purpose of encouraging each State, as far as practicable under the conditions in that State, to furnish services directed at the goal of—

(1) achieving or maintaining economic self-support to prevent, reduce, or eliminate dependency,

(2) achieving or maintaining self-sufficiency, including reduction or prevention of dependency,

(3) preventing or remedying neglect, abuse, or exploitation of children and adults unable to protect their own interests, or preserving, rehabilitating or reuniting families,

(4) preventing or reducing inappropriate institutional care by providing for community-based care, home-based care, or other forms of less intensive care, or

(5) securing referral or admission for institutional care when other forms of care are not appropriate, or providing services to individuals in institutions,

there is authorized to be appropriated for each fiscal year a sum sufficient to carry out the purposes of this title. The sums made available under this section shall be used for making payments to States under section 2002.

Payments To States

Sec. 2002. (a) (1) From the sums appropriated therefore, the Secretary shall, subject to the provisions of this section and section 2003, pay to each State, for each quarter, an amount equal to 90 per centum of the total expenditures during that quarter for the provision of family planning services and 75 per centum of the total expenditures . . . including expenditures for administration (including planning and evaluation) and personnel training and retraining directly related to the provision of those services (including both short- and long-term training at educational institutions through grants to such institutions or by direct financial assistance to students enrolled in such institutions). Services that are directed at these goals include, but are not limited to, child care services, protective services for children and adults, services for children and adults in foster care, services related to the management and maintenance of the home, day care services for adults, transportation services, training and related services, employment services, information, referral, and counseling services, the preparation and delivery of meals, health support services, and appropriate combinations of services designed to meet the special needs of children, the aged, the mentally retarded, the blind, the emotionally disturbed, the physically handicapped, and alcoholics and drug addicts.

(2) (A). No payment with respect to any expenditures other than expenditures for personnel training or retraining directly related to the provision of services may be made under this section to any State for any fiscal year in excess of an amount which bears the same ratio to $2,500,000,000 as the population of that State bears to the population of the fifty States and the District of Columbia. The Secretary shall promulgate the limitation applicable to each State for each fiscal year under this paragraph prior to the first day of the third month of the preceding fiscal year, as determined on the basis of the most recent satisfactory data available from the Department of Commerce.

(3) No payment may be made under this section to any State with respect to any expenditure for the provision of any service to any individual unless—

(A) the State's services program planning meets the requirements of section 2004, and

(B) the final comprehensive annual services plan in effect when the service is provided to the individual includes the provision of that service to a category of individuals which includes that individual in the descriptions required by section 2004(2)(B) and (C) of the services to be provided under the plan and the categories of individuals to whom the services are to be provided.

The Secretary may not deny payment under this section to any State with respect to any expenditure on the ground that it is not an expenditure for the provision of a service or is not an expenditure for the provision of a service directed at a goal described in paragraph (1) of this subsection.

(4) So much of the aggregate expenditures with respect to which payment is made under this section to any State for any fiscal year as equals 50 per centum of the payment made under this section to the State for that fiscal year must be expended for the provision of services to individuals—

(A) who are receiving aid under the plan of the State approved under part A of title IV or who are eligible to receive such aid, or

(B) whose needs are taken into account in determining the needs of an individual who is receiving aid under the plan of the State approved under part A of title IV, or who are eligible to have their needs taken into account in determining the needs of an individual who is receiving or is eligible to receive such aid, or

(C) with respect to whom supplemental security income benefits under title XVI or State supplementary payments, as defined in section 2007(1), are being paid, or who are eligible to have such benefits or payments paid with respect to them, or

(D) whose income and resources are taken into account in determining the amount of supplemental security income benefits or State supplementary payments, as defined in section 2007(1), being paid with respect to an individual, or whose income and resources would be taken into account in determining the amount of such benefits or payments to be paid with respect to an individual who is eligible to have such benefits or payments paid with respect to him, or

(E) who are eligible for medical assistance under the plan of the State aproved under title XIX.

(5) No payment may be made under this section to any State with respect to any expenditure for the provision of any service to any individual—

(A) who is receiving, or whose needs are taken into account in determining the needs of an individual who is receiving, aid under the plan of the State approved under part A of title IV, or with respect to whom supplemental security income benefits under title XVI or State supplementary payments, as defined in section 2007(1), are being paid, or

(B) who is a member of a family the monthly gross income of which is less than the lower of—

(i) 80 per centum of the median income of a family of four in the State, or

(ii) the median income of a family of four in the fifty States and the District of Columbia,

adjusted, in accordance with regulations prescribed by the Secretary, to take into account the size of the family,

if any fee or other charge (other than a voluntary contribution) imposed on the individual for the provision of that service is not consistent with such requirements (including requirements prohibiting the imposition of any such fee or charge) as the Secretary shall prescribe.

(6) No payment may be made under this section to any State with respect to any expenditure for the provision of any service, other than an information or referral service or a service directed at the goal of preventing or remedying neglect, abuse, or exploitation of children and adults unable to protect their own interests, to any individual who is not an individual described in paragraph (5), and—

(A) who is a member of a family the monthly gross income of which exceeds 115 per centum of the median income of a family of four in the State, adjusted, in accordance with regulations prescribed by the Secretary, to take into account the size of the family, or

(B) who is a member of a family the monthly gross income of which—

(i) exceeds the lower of—

(I) 80 per centum of the median income of a family of four in the State, or

(II) the median income of a family of four in the fifty States and the District of Columbia.

adjusted, in accordance with regulations prescribed by the Secretary, to take into account the size of the family, and

(ii) does not exceed 115 per centum of the median income of a family of four in the State, adjusted, in accordance with regulations prescribed by the Secretary, to take into account the size of the family.

unless a fee or other charge reasonably related to income is imposed on the individual for the provision of the service.

The Secretary shall promulgate the median income of a family of four in each State and the fifty States and the District of Columbia applicable to payments with respect to expenditures in each fiscal year prior to the first day of the third month of the preceding fiscal year.

• • •

(9)(A) No payment may be made under this section with respect to any expenditure in connection with the provision of any child day care service, unless—

(i) in the case of care provided in the child's home, the care meets standards established by the State which are reasonably in accord with recommended standards of national standard-setting organizations concerned with the home care of children. . . .

(B) The Secretary shall submit to the President of the Senate and the Speaker of the House of Representatives, after December 31, 1976, and prior to July 1, 1977, an evaluation of the appropriateness of the requirements imposed by subparagraph (A), together with any recommendations he may have for modification of those requirements. No earlier than ninety days after the submission of the report, the Secretary may, by regulation, make such modifications in the requirements imposed by subparagraph (A) as he determines are appropriate.

(C) The requirements imposed by this paragraph are in lieu of any requirements that would otherwise be applicable under section 522(d) of the Economic Opportunity Act of 1964 to child day care services with respect to which payment is made under this section.

(10) No payment may be made under this section with respect to any expenditure for the provision of any educational service which the State makes generally available to its residents without cost and without regard to their income.

(11) No payment may be made under this section with respect to any expenditure for the provision of any service to any individual living in any hospital, skilled nursing facility, or intermediate care facility (including any such hospital or facility for mental diseases or for the mentally retarded), any prison, or any foster family home . . .

• • •

(12) No payment may be made under this section with respect to any expenditure for the provision of cash payments as a service.

(13) No payment may be made under this section with respect to any expenditure for the provision of any service to any individual to the extent that the provider of the service or the individual receiving the service is eligible to receive payment under title XVIII with respect to the provision of the service.

• • •

Program Reporting

Sec. 2003. (a) Each State which participates in the program established by this title shall make such reports concerning its use of Federal social services funds as the Secretary may by regulation provide.

• • •

Services Program Planning

Sec. 2004. A State's services program planning meets the requirements of this section if, for the purpose of assuring public participation in the development of the program for the provision of the services described in section 2002 (a) (1) within the State—

(1) the beginning of the fiscal year of either the Federal Government or the State government is established as the beginning of the State's services program year; and

(2) at least ninety days prior to the beginning of the State's services program year, the chief executive officer of the State, or such other official as the laws of the State provide, publishes and makes generally available

(as defined in regulations prescribed by the Secretary after consideration of State laws governing notice of actions by public officials) to the public a proposed comprehensive annual services program plan prepared by the agency designated pursuant to the requirements of section 2003 (d) (1) (C) and, unless the laws of the State provide otherwise, approved by the chief executive officer, which sets forth the State's plan for the provision of the services described in section 2002 (a) (1) during that year, including—

(A) the objectives to be achieved under the program,

(B) the services to be provided under the program, including at least one service directed at at least one of the goals in each of the five categories of goals set forth in section 2002 (a) (1) (as determined by the State) and including at least three types of services (selected by the State) for individuals who are recipients of supplemental security income benefits under title XVI and who are in need of such services, together with a definition of those services and a description of their relationship to the objectives to be achieved under the program and the goals described in section 2002 (a) (1),

(C) the categories of individuals to whom those services are to be provided, including any categories based on the income of individuals or their families,

(D) the geographic areas in which those services are to be provided, and the nature and amount of the services to be provided in each area,

(E) a description of the planning, evaluation, and reporting activities to be carried out under the program,

(F) the sources of the resources to be used to carry out the program,

(G) a description of the organizational structure through which the program will be administered, including the extent to which public and private agencies and volunteers will be utilized in the provision of services,

(H) a description of how the provision of services under the program will be coordinated with the plan of the State approved under part A of title IV, the plan of the State developed under part B of that title, the supplemental security income program established by title XVI, the plan of the State approved under title XIX, and other programs for the provision of related human services within the State, including the steps taken to assure maximum feasible utilization of services under these programs to meet the needs of the low income population.

(I) the estimated expenditures under the program, including estimated expenditures with respect to each of the services to be provided, each of the categories of individuals to whom those services are to be provided, and each of the geographic areas in which those services are to be provided, and a comparison between estimated non-Federal expenditures under the program and non-Federal expenditures for the provision of the services described in section 2002 (a) (1) in the State during the preceding services program year, and

(J) a description of the steps taken, or to be taken, to assure that the needs of all residents of, and all geographic areas in, the State were taken into account in the development of the plan; and

(3) public comment on the proposed plan is accepted for a period of at least forty-five days; and

(4) at least forty-five days after publication of the proposed plan and prior to the beginning of the State's services program year, the chief executive officer of the State, or such other official as the laws of the State provide, publishes a final comprehensive annual services program plan prepared by the agency designed pursuant to the requirements of section 2003 (d) (1) (C) and, unless the laws of the State provide otherwise, approved by the chief executive officer, which sets forth the same information required to be included in the proposed plan, together with an explanation of the differences between the proposed and final plan and the reasons therefor; and

(5) any amendment to a final comprehensive services program plan is prepared by the agency designated pursuant to section 2003 (d) (1) (C), approved by the chief executive officer of the State unless the laws of the State provide otherwise, and published by the chief executive officer of the State, or such other official as the laws of the State provide, as a proposed amendment on which public comment is accepted for a period of at least thirty days, and then prepared by the agency designated pursuant to section 2003 (d) (1) (C), approved by the chief executive officer of the State unless the laws of the State provide otherwise, and published by the chief executive officer of the State, or such other official as the laws of the State provide, as a final amendment, together with an explanation of the differences between the proposed and final amendment and the reasons therefor.

Evaluation; Program Assistance

Sec. 2006. (a) The Secretary shall provide for the continuing evaluation of State programs for the provision of the services described in section 2002 (a) (1).

(b) The Secretary shall make available to the States assistance with respect to the content of their services program, and their services program planning, reporting, administration, and evaluation.

(c) Within six months after the close of each fiscal year, the Secretary shall submit to the Congress a report on the operation of the program established by this title during that year, including—

(1) the evaluations carried out under subsection (a) and the results obtained therefrom, and

(2) the assistance provided under subsection (b) during that year.

• • •

References

Chapter 2

1. *Records of the Colony of Rhode Island and Providence Plantations in New England*, vol. 1, 1636–1663 (Providence: A. Crawford Greene and Brother, State Printers, 1856), 1:184–185.
2. Danby Pickering, ed., *The Statutes at Large from the Thirty-Ninth Year of Q. Elizabeth to the Twelfth Year of K. Charles II, Inclusive* (Cambridge: Bentham & Bathhurst, 1763), 7:30–37.
3. *An Acte for the Better Reliefe of the Poor of the Kingdom. The Statutes at Large from the First Year of King James the First to the Tenth Year of the Reign of King William the Third* (London: Basket, Woodfall and Straham, 1763), 3:243–247.
4. Katherine D. Hardwick, *As Long As Charity Shall Be a Virtue* (Boston: 1964,) p. 5. John Adams by Page Smith. Copyright © 1962 by Page Smith. Reprinted by permission of Doubleday & Company, Inc., 1964.
5. Thomas J. Scharf and Westcott Thompson, *History of Philadelphia, 1609–1884* (Philadelphia: L. H. Everts & Co., 1884), pp. 1452–1453.
6. Hardwick, op. cit., p. 8.
7. Raymond A. Mohl, "Poverty in Early America, A Reappraisal: The Case of Eighteenth-Century New York," *New York History*, Vol. L, January 1969, p. 19.
8. Edith Abbott, *Women in Industry: A Study in American Economic History.* (New York: D. Appleton & Company, 1909), p. 21.
9. *Province Laws* (Mass.), 1753–1754.
10. Quoted in Abbott, op. cit., p. 33.
11. Milton T. Rolla, *Household Manufacturers in the United States, 1640–1860.* (Chicago: University of Chicago Press, 1919), p. 6.

12. Act XXVII, October, 1646, in *The Statutes at Large: Being a Collection of All the Laws of Virginia from the First Session of the Legislature in the Year 1619,* William Waller Henning, ed. (New York: 1823), 1:336.

13. *Records of the Governor and Company of the Massachusetts Bay in New England,* vol. 2, 1624–1629, 2:6.

14. *Acts and Resolves, An Act of Supplement to the Acts Referring to the Poor,* Province of the Massachusetts Bay, 1703.

15. William Brigam, ed., *The Compact with the Charter and Laws of the Colony of New Plymouth,* and so on. This contains *The Book the General Laws of the Inhabitants of the Jurisdiction of New Plymouth,* and so on. To be found in Marcus Wilson Jernegan, *Labouring and Dependent Classes in Colonial America, 1607–1783* (Chicago: University of Chicago Press, 1931), pp. 98–99.

16. *Acts and Resolves,* Province of Massachusetts Bay, 1692.

17. Scharf and Thompson, op. cit., p. 1450.

18. Gary B. Nash, "Poverty and Poor Relief in Pre-Revolutionary Philadelphia," *William and Mary Quarterly,* Third Series, Vol. XXXIII, January 1976, pp. 12–13.

19. *Statutes at Large of Pennsylvania, 1682–1801,* Vol. 3, chap. 238.

20. Mohl, op. cit., pp. 8–9.

21. *Statutes at Large of Pennsylvania, 1682–1801,* Vol. 2, chap. 154.

22. Ibid.

23. Schneider, David M., *The History of Public Welfare in New York State, 1609–1866* (Chicago: University of Chicago Press, 1938), pp. 9–44.

24. Cotton Mather, A Letter [An Horrid Snow], 10d. X m. 1717. To be found in Norman Foerster, ed., *American Poetry and Prose* (New York: Houghton Mifflin, 1934), pp. 79–80.

25. Jeannette P. Nichols and Roy F. Nichols, *The Growth of American Democracy* (New York: Appleton-Century, 1939), p. 16.

26. U.S. Department of Commerce, Bureau of the Census, *Historical Statistics of the United States: Colonial Times to 1957* (Washington, D.C.: Government Printing Office, 1960), p. 756.

27. Merrill Jensen, ed., *English Historical Documents: American Colonial Documents to 1776* (London: Eyre and Spottiswoode, 1955), p. 480.

28. Schneider, op. cit., p. 87.

29. William Byrd, *The History of the Dividing Line* [Life in North Carolina], [March] 25 [1728]. To be found in Norman Foerster, op. cit., pp. 87–92.

30. Letter to Richard Jackson, May 5, 1753, in *The Writings of Benjamin Franklin,* Vol. III, 1750–1759, Albert Henry Smith, ed. (New York: Macmillan, 1907), pp. 134–135, 137.

31. Ibid., "Essay on the Labouring Poor," Vol. V, pp. 124–125.

32. Joseph Townsend, "A Dissertation on the Poor Laws By a Well-Wisher to Mankind," in *A Select Collection of Scarce and Valuable Economic Tracts,* J. R. McCulloch, ed. (London: Lord Overstone, 1859), pp. 397–449.

33. U.S. Congress, House Committee Print No. 4, *Medical Care of Veterans,* 90th Cong., 1st sess., April 17, 1967, p. 21. Printed for the use of the Committee on Veterans' Affairs.

34. Ibid., p. 28.

Chapter 3

1. James Madison, "Vices of the Political System of the United States," April, 1787, *The Papers of James Madison*, Vol. 9 (Chicago: University of Chicago Press, 1975), p. 351.
2. U.S. Department of Commerce, Bureau of the Census, *Historical Statistics of the United States: Colonial Times to 1957* (Washington, D.C.: Government Printing Office, 1960) (hereafter cited as *Historical Statistics*).
3. Edward C. Kirkland, *A History of American Economic Life* (New York: F. S. Crofts, 1941), p. 144.
4. *Historical Statistics*, p. 302.
5. Walter W. Jennings, *A History of Economic Progress in the United States* (New York: Thomas Y. Crowell, 1926), Appendix, Table 7, "Development of Typical Manufactures," p. 759.
6. Vernon Louis Parrington, *Main Currents in American Thought* (New York: Harcourt, Brace, 1930), vol. 2, *The Romantic Revolution in America*, p. 104. Quoted from William J. Grayson, *The Hireling and the Slave*, Preface, pp. XIV–XV.
7. Ibid.
8. Jennings, op. cit., p. 153. Quoted from *American State Papers, Series Finance*, Vol. 1, pp. 123–141.
9. Ibid., p. 166.
10. For a detailed description of the boarding house system, see Vera Shlakman, *Economic History of a Factory Town*, Smith College Studies in History, Vol. 20, Nos. 1–4 (Northampton, Mass.: Smith College, Department of History, Oct. 1934–July 1935).
11. Harriet Martineau, *Society in America* (London: 1837), 2:247–248. Quoted in Jennings, op. cit., p. 303.
12. For an interesting discussion of this point, see Thomas Dublin, *Women at Work* (New York: Columbia University Press, 1979).
13. *Historical Statistics*, p. 14.
14. S. E. Forman, *The Rise of American Commerce and Industry* (New York: The Century, 1927), pp. 195, 471.
15. Jennings, op. cit., pp. 295–297.
16. Ibid., pp. 300–310. See also Philip S. Foner, *History of the Labor Movement in the United States* (New York: International Publishers, 1947), pp. 143–166.
17. Horace Mann, *Education and Prosperity*, Old South Leaflet No. 144 (Boston: Directors of Old South Work, Old South Meeting House, 1848), p. 6.
18. Ibid., p. 7.
19. Jeannette P. Nichols and Roy F. Nichols, *The Growth of American Democracy* (New York: Appleton-Century, 1939), p. 182.
20. "Pastoral Letter of the General Association of Massachusetts to the Congressional Churches under Their Care," reprinted in *The Liberator*, August 11, 1837.
21. For an in-depth study of drinking in the United States during the early decades of the nineteenth century, see W. J. Rorabaugh, *The Alcoholic Republic* (New York: Oxford University Press, 1979).
22. Ibid., pp. 8–9.

23. Judith Papachristou, *Women Together*, A Ms. Book (New York: Knopf, 1976), p. 19.

24. *The Lily*, January 1, 1848. Reprinted in Papachristou, op. cit., p. 20.

25. Dorothea L. Dix, Memorial, *Praying A Grant of Land for the Relief and Support of the Indigent Curable and Incurable Insane in the United States*, Miscellaneous Senate Document No. 150, 30th Cong., 1st sess, June 27, 1848, p. 213. Reprinted in *Poverty, U.S.A., On Behalf of the Insane Poor* (New York: Arno Press and *New York Times*, 1971).

26. Ibid., p. 25.

27. President Franklin Pierce, "Veto Message—An Act Making a Grant of Public Lands to the Several States for the Benefit of Indigent Insane Persons," May 3, 1854.

28. John V. I. Yates, *Report of the Secretary of State on the Relief and Settlement of the Poor*, p. 942. Reprinted in *Poverty, U.S.A., The Almshouse Experience* (New York: Arno Press and *New York Times*, 1971).

29. B. J. Klebaner, "Public Poor Relief in America 1790–1860" (Ph.D. diss., Columbia University, 1952), p. 329.

30. Thomas Paine, *The Rights of Man*, part 2. Reprinted in *Basic Writings of Thomas Paine* (New York: Wiley, 1942), p. 253.

31. Mathew Carey, *Appeal to the Wealthy of the Land, Ladies as Well As Gentlemen, on Character, Conduct, Situation and Prospects of Those Whose Sole Dependence for Subsistence Is on the Labour of Their Hands* (Philadelphia: Sterotyped by L. Johnson, No. 6 George Street, August 15, 1833), pp. 3–34.

32. Ibid.

33. Josiah Quincy, *Report of the Committee to Whom Was Referred the Consideration of the Pauper Laws of This Commonwealth*, p. 7. Reprinted in *Poverty, U.S.A., The Almshouse Experience*, op. cit.

34. The Society for the Prevention of Pauperism in the City of New York, *The First Annual Report, to which is added A Report on the Subject of Pauperism* (New York: J. Seymour, 1818), p. 3.

35. Ibid., p. 16.

36. Ibid., p. 18.

37. Ibid., p. 12.

38. Ibid., p. 5.

39. Quincy, op. cit., p. 9.

40. Ibid., p. 10.

41. Yates, op. cit., pp. 941–942.

42. Ibid., p. 955.

43. Report of *Select Senate Committee to Visit Charitable and Penal Institutions*, 1857, New York Senate Document No. 8, 1857. Reprinted in Sophonisba P. Breckinridge, *Public Welfare Administration in the United States* (Chicago: University of Chicago Press, 1927), p. 149.

44. Klebaner, op. cit., pp. 73–74, 86, 89. For a discussion of the extension of the use of almshouses, see David J. Rothman, *The Discovery of the Asylum* (Boston: Little, Brown, 1971), pp. 180–205.

45. Grace Abbott, *The Child and the State* (Chicago: University of Chicago Press, 1938), 2:29.

46. Homer Folks, *The Care of Destitute, Neglected and Delinquent Children* (New York: Macmillan, 1911), pp. 52–55.

47. New York House of Refuge, *Second Annual Report.* Quoted in Rothman, op. cit., p. 215.
48. Report of the committee appointed to Visit and Examine into the Affairs and Management of the [Philadelphia] House of Refuge. *Hazard's Register of Pennsylvania, Devoted to the Preservation of Facts and Documents and Every Kind of Useful Information Respecting the State of Pennsylvania,* vol. 15 (January–July 1835), ed. Samuel Hazard. Also to be found in Grace Abbott, op. cit., 2:357–361.
49. Robert A. Bremner, *From the Depths: The Discovery of Poverty in the United States* (New York: New York University Press, 1956), p. 39.
50. Folks, op. cit., p. 41.
51. Edith Abbott, *Some American Pioneers in Social Welfare: Select Documents with Editorial Notes* (Chicago: University of Chicago Press, 1937), p. 132.
52. Charles Loring Brace, *The Dangerous Classes in New York* (New York: Wynkoop and Hallenbeck, 1880), pp. 224–266.
53. Ibid.
54. Henry W. Thurston, *The Dependent Child* (New York: Columbia University Press, 1930), p. 121.
55. *Report of Select Senate Committee,* 1857, op. cit., p. 149.
56. Ibid., p. 150.
57. Ibid., p. 154.
58. Ibid., pp. 153–154.
59. Ibid., p. 152.
60. Ibid., pp. 154, 155.
61. Breckinridge, op. cit., p. 142.
62. Klebaner, op. cit., passim; Rothman, op. cit., pp. 287–295.

Chapter 4

1. U.S. Department of Commerce, Bureau of the Census, *Historical Statistics of the United States: Colonial Times to 1957* (Washington, D.C.: Government Printing Office, 1960), pp. 7, 143 (hereafter cited as *Historical Statistics*).
2. S. E. Forman, *The Rise of American Commerce and Industry* (New York: Century, 1927), p. 317.
3. *Historical Statistics,* p. 7.
4. Ibid., pp. 56–57.
5. Theodore Hershberg, "Free Blacks in Antebellum Philadelphia: A Study of Ex-Slaves, Freeborn, and Socio-economic Decline," *Journal of Social History* 5 (Winter 1971–1972): 190.
6. Walter W. Jennings, *A History of Economic Progress in the United States* (New York: Thomas Y. Crowell, 1926), p. 380; *Historical Statistics,* p. 8.
7. Forman, op. cit., p. 471.
8. *Historical Statistics,* p. 14.
9. Jennings, op. cit., p. 409.
10. Ibid., p. 412.
11. *Historical Statistics,* p. 302.
12. Ibid., p. 297.
13. Ibid., p. 546.
14. Ibid., p. 139.

15. Forman, op. cit., p. 481.
16. *Historical Statistics*, p. 139.
17. Jennings, op. cit., p. 447.
18. U.S. Congress, House Committee Print No. 4, *Medical Care of Veterans*, 90th Cong., 1st sess., April 17, 1967, p. 49. Printed for the use of the Committee on Veterans' Affairs.
19. Ibid., p. 52.
20. U.S. Sanitary Commission, Document No. 49, October 1862.
21. Charles J. Stille, *History of the United States Sanitary Commission* (Philadelphia: Lippincott, 1866), p. 524.
22. U.S. Sanitary Commission, *The Sanitary Commission of the United States Army: A Succinct Narrative of the Works and Purposes*. New York: Published for the benefit of the Commission, 1864.
23. Stille, op. cit., p. 82.
24. U.S. Sanitary Commission, Document 4042, May 1865.
25. U.S. Congress, House of Representatives, Report No. 45, 41st Cong., 3rd sess., 1871.
26. Knowlton Durham, *Billions for Veterans* (New York: Brewer, Warren and Putnam, 1932), pp. 25–26.
27. The President's Commission on Veterans' Pensions, *The Historical Development of Veterans' Benefits in the United States*, A Report on Veterans' Benefits in the United States, 84th Congress, 2nd sess., House Committee Print No. 244, May 9, 1956, pp. 17–18.
28. Laws of the State of New York, An act to provide for the relief of indigent soldiers, sailors and marines, and the families of those deceased, June 25, 1887.
29. William Miller, *A New History of the United States* (New York: Braziller, 1958), p. 219.
30. Elizabeth Wisner, *Social Welfare in the South* (Baton Rouge: Louisiana State University Press, 1970), p. 107.
31. George R. Bentley, *A History of the Freedmen's Bureau* (New York: Octagon, 1970).
32. New York A.I.C.P., *Thirty-second Annual Report 1875* (New York, 1875), p. 367. Also to be found in Albert Deutsch, "American Labor and Social Work," *Science and Society*, Vol. VIII (Fall 1944), p. 294.
33. Jeannette P. Nichols and Roy F. Nichols, *The Growth of American Democracy* (New York: Appleton-Century, 1939), p. 450.
34. Ewan Clague, *The Bureau of Labor Statistics* (New York: Praeger, 1968), p. 8.
35. Forman, op. cit., p. 292.
36. Ibid., p. 337.
37. Terence V. Powderly, *Proceedings of the General Assembly, 1882*, p. 278. Quoted in Philip S. Foner, *History of the Labor Movement in the United States* (New York: International Publishers, 1947), 1:508.
38. Charles A. Beard and Mary R. Beard, *The Rise of American Civilization* (New York: Macmillan, 1930), 2:416.
39. Russell H. Conwell, *Acres of Diamonds* (Philadelphia: Temple University Press), pp. 18, 19.
40. "Pauperism in the City of New York," A Report from the Department of Social Economy, *Proceedings, NCCC: 1874*, pp. 18–28.

41. Mrs. Charles Russell Lowell, "The Economic and Moral Effects of Public Outdoor Relief," *Proceedings, NCCC: 1890*, pp. 81–91.
42. Community Service Society of New York, *Frontiers in Human Welfare: The Story of a Hundred Years of Service to the Community of New York, 1848–1948* (New York: 1948), p. 35.
43. Reverend Oscar C. McCulloch, "The Tribe of Ishmael, A Study in Social Degradation," *Proceedings, NCCC: 1888*, pp. 154–159.
44. Amos Griswold Warner, *American Charities* (New York: Thomas Y. Crowell, 1894), pp. 36–63.
45. Fred H. Wines, "Causes of Pauperism and Crime," *Proceedings, NCCC: 1886*, pp. 207–214.
46. Franklin B. Sanborn, "Indoor and Outdoor Relief," *Proceedings, NCCC: 1890*, pp. 73–80.
47. Charles D. Kellogg, "Charity Organization in the United States: A Report of the Committee on History of Charity Organization", *Proceedings, NCCC: 1893*, p. 72.
48. Ibid., 82.
48. Ibid., p. 93.
50. John Boyle O'Reilly, "In Bohemia" (1886), quoted in Jane Addams et al., *Philanthropy and Social Progress* (New York: 1845), p. 135.
51. Leah Hanna Feder, *Unemployment Relief in Periods of Depression* (New York: Russell Sage Foundation, 1936), p. 133. See also, Charles D. Kellogg, "The Situation in New York City during the Winter of 1893–1894," *Proceedings, NCCC: 1894*, p. 24. Kellogg ascribes to organized labor the belief that charitable agencies are "an aristocratic concession to poverty."
52. Frank D. Watson, *The Charity Organization Movement in the United States* (New York: Macmillan, 1922), pp. 215, 225–226.
53. See letter "To the Editor of the *Times–Democrat*" of New Orleans, March 18, 1903. The letter is signed by NAWSA's officers, including Susan B. Anthony and Carrie Chapman Catt. Reprinted in Papachristou, op. cit., pp. 143–144.
54. Andrew Sinclair, *The Better Half: The Emancipation of the American Woman* (New York: Harper & Row, 1965), p. 194.
55. *Historical Statistics*, p. 49.
56. Ibid., p. 22. Also: Ernest R. Groves, *The American Woman: The Feminine Side of a Masculine Civilization* (New York: Arno Press, 1972), p. 112.
57. Papachristou, op. cit., p. 90.
58. Frances E. Willard, *Woman and Temperance, or Work of the Women's Christian Temperance Union* (Hartford: Park Publishing Co., 1884), pp. 457–459.
59. Ibid.
60. For an interesting review of higher education for women during the post-Civil War and Progressive eras, see Sheila M. Rothman, *Woman's Proper Place* (New York: Basic Books, Inc., 1978), pp. 26–42, 97–132.
61. Willard, op. cit. For a discussion of the connection between the temperance and suffrage movements, see Papachristou, op. cit., pp. 88–97.
62. U.S. Labor Commissioner Wright reported "that by 1890 only nine out of 360 general groups to which the country's industries had been assigned did not employ women." Sharlene J. Hesse, *Working Women and Families* (Beverly Hills: Sage Publications, 1979), p. 42.

63. Joan D. Mandle, *Women and Social Change in America* (Princeton: Princeton Book Company, Publishers, 1979), p. 23.

64. U.S. Department of Labor, Women's Bureau, *1969 Handbook on Women Workers*, Bulletin No. 294 (Washington, D.C.: Government Printing Office, 1969); and *Historical Statistics*, op. cit., pp. 132−133.

65. Edith Abbott, *Women in Industry: A Study in American Economic History* (New York: D. Appleton Company, 1909), p. 123.

66. "Discussion on Charity Organization," *Proceedings, NCCC: 1888*, p. 420.

67. Laws of the State of Illinois, 1899, An Act to Regulate the Treatment and Control of Dependent, Neglected, and Delinquent Children.

68. State Board of Charities of the State of New York, *Eighth Annual Report*, 1875.

69. Laws of the State of New York, An Act to Provide Better Care of Pauper and Destitute Children, April 24, 1875.

70. Anne B. Richardson, "Massachusetts Institutions: Supplementary Work in the Care of Dependent and Delinquent Children," *Proceedings, NCCC: 1886*, pp. 131−138.

71. Warner, op. cit., p. 99.

72. Commonwealth of Pennsylvania, *Report of the Commissioners of Public Charities for the Year 1882*, Legislative Document No. 5.

73. Welfare Laws of the State of Pennsylvania, 1883 Laws, p. 1074, sec. 904.

74. Charles S. Hoyt, "The Causes of Pauperism," *Tenth Annual Report of the New York State Board of Charities*, 1877, pp. 97−292.

75. Board of Commissioners of Public Charities of the State of Pennsylvania, *Fourteenth Annual Report*, 1883, p. 2.

76. *Twenty-fourth Annual Report* (Boston: Boston Children's Aid Society, 1888), p. 16. The Report is quoted extensively in Henry W. Thurston, *The Dependent Child* (New York: Columbia University Press), 1930.

77. *Twenty-eighth and Twenty-ninth Annual Reports* (Boston: Boston Children's Aid Society, 1893), p. 10. This two-year report is quoted extensively in Thurston, op. cit., pp. 191−192.

78. Homer Folks, *The Care of Destitute, Neglected and Delinquent Children* (New York: Macmillan, 1911), p. 80.

79. Zilpha D. Smith, "Report of the Committee on the Organization of Charity," *Proceedings, NCCC: 1888*, pp. 120−130.

80. Charles D. Kellogg, "Report of the Committee on History of Charity Organization," *Proceedings, NCCC: 1893*, pp. 52−93.

81. Allen F. Davis, *Spearheads for Reform: The Social Settlements and the Progressive Movement, 1890−1914* (New York: Oxford University Press, 1967).

82. Humphreys S. Gurteen, *A Handbook of Charity Organization* (Buffalo: Courier, 1882), pp. 120−123.

83. Jane Addams, "Social Settlements," *Proceedings, NCCC: 1897*, p. 339.

Chapter 5

1. Herbert Hoover, *The New Day* (Stanford, Calif.: Stanford University Press, 1928), p. 16.

2. S. E. Forman, *The Rise of American Commerce and Industry* (New York: Century, 1927), p. 369.

3. U.S. Department of Commerce, Bureau of the Census, *Historical Statistics of the United States: Colonial Times to 1957* (Washington, D.C.: Government Printing Office, 1960), p. 414 (hereafter cited as *Historical Statistics*).

4. Forman, op. cit., p. 442.

5. *Historical Statistics*, p. 139.

6. Ibid., p. 14.

7. U.S., Bureau of the Census, *Fourteenth Census of the United States: 1920*, vol. 3, p. 15, and *Fifteenth Census of the United States: 1930*, vol. 2, p. 27.

8. Forman, op. cit., p. 439.

9. *Historical Statistics*, p. 14.

10. An excellent survey and analysis of the growth of concentration in American industry may be found in Arthur R. Burns, *The Decline of Competition* (New York: McGraw-Hill, 1936).

11. U.S. Commission on Industrial Relations, *Final Report* (Washington, D.C.: Government Printing Office, 1915), p. 8.

12. U.S. Bureau of the Census, *Sixteenth Census of the United States: 1940, Comparative Occupation Statistics for the United States, 1870 to 1940*, p. 93.

13. Robert Hunter, *Poverty* (New York: Grossett & Dunlap, 1904), pp. 2–7, 56–65, 76–88, 96–97, 350–351. Reprinted in Roy Lubove, ed., *Poverty and Social Welfare in the United States* (New York: Holt, Rinehart & Winston, 1972), pp. 7–18.

14. John A. Ryan, *A Living Wage: Its Ethical and Economic Aspects* (New York: Macmillan, 1910), pp. 123–177. Father Ryan estimated the minimum "living wage" at over $900 for the large Eastern cities.

15. *Historical Statistics*, p. 278.

16. Justice Miller, Supreme Court Decision, 16 Wallace 36, 1873.

17. G. W. Cable, "The Freedman's Case in Equity," *The Century Magazine*, January 1885. Quoted in Samuel Eliot Morrison and Henry Steele Commanger, *The Growth of the American Republic* (New York: Oxford University Press, 1962), p. 90.

18. *Plessy* v. *Ferguson*, 163 U.S. 537 (1896).

19. Imperial Wizard Hiram W. Evans, "The Klan of Tomorrow." Quoted in William Miller, *A New History of the United States* (New York: Braziller, 1958), pp. 355–356.

20. Booker T. Washington, "The Atlanta Cotton Exposition Address of 1895." Quoted in *Up From Slavery*, in *The Booker T. Washington Papers*, ed. Louis R. Harlan (Urbana: University of Illinois Press, 1972) 1:333.

21. Lillian Brandt, "The Make-up of Negro City Groups," *Charities and the Commons* 15 (October 7, 1905): 7.

22. *Historical Statistics*, p. 46. New York, Pennsylvania, Ohio, Illinois, and Michigan accounted for 78 percent of this.

23. Ibid., pp. 409, 73.

24. Sidney Lens, *Poverty: America's Enduring Paradox* (New York: Thomas Y. Crowell, 1969), pp. 209–210.

25. See, for example, Ida M. Tarbell, *The History of the Standard Oil Company* (New York: McClure, Phillips, 1904); Ray Stannard Baker, "The Right to Work," *McClure's Magazine*, 20 (January 1903): 323–326; Samuel Hopkins Adams, "Fraud Medicines Own Up," *Collier's* 48 (January 20, 1912).

26. See, for example, Lincoln Steffens, *The Shame of the Cities* (New York:

McClure, Phillips, 1904); David Graham Phillips, "The Treason of the Senate," *Cosmopolitan* 40 (March 1906): 603–610.

27. Arthur P. Miles, *An Introduction to Public Welfare* (Washington, D.C.: Heath, 1947), p. 124.

28. Theodore Roosevelt, "Reform Through Social Work," *McClure's Magazine* 26 (March 1901): 448–454.

29. Arthur S. Link, *American Epoch: A History of the United States Since the 1890's* (New York: Knopf, 1955), p. 68.

30. Lens, op. cit., p. 212.

31. Charles Faulkner, "Twentieth Century Alignments for the Promotion of Social Order," *Proceedings, NCCC: 1900*, pp. 2–6.

32. Mary E. Richmond, "The Family and the Social Worker," *Proceedings, NCCC: 1908*, pp. 76–79.

33. *Sixteenth Census: 1940*, pp. 93, 100.

34. *The Child Labor Bulletin*, vol. 3, no. 1, May 1914 (New York: National Child Labor Committee).

35. Owen R. Lovejoy, "Report of the Committee on Standards of Living and Labor," *Proceedings, NCCC: 1912*, p. 386.

36. U.S. 37 stat. 79. The Act establishing the Children's Bureau, approved April 7, 1912.

37. *Hammer v. Dagenhart* 247 U.S. Reports 251, 268 (June 1918). To be found in Grace Abbott, *The Child and the State* (Chicago: University of Chicago Press, 1938), pp. 495–506.

38. "State Child-Labor Standards, January 1, 1930," a chart prepared by the U.S. Department of Labor, Children's Bureau, and reprinted by permission of the Federal Board for Vocational Education (Washington, D.C.: Government Printing Office, 1930), chart no. 2.

39. *Fifteenth Census: 1930*, vol. 2, pp. 1180–1196.

40. Lovejoy, op. cit., p. 383.

41. Edward C. Kirkland, *A History of American Economic Life* (New York: Appleton-Century-Crofts, 1969), p. 409.

42. Paul H. Douglas, *Real Wages in the United States, 1890–1926* (Boston: Houghton Mifflin, 1930), p. 208.

43. George Soule, *American Economic History* (New York: Dryden Press, 1957), p. 277.

44. Douglas, op. cit., pp. 112, 114.

45. "Discussion on Charity Organization," *Proceedings, NCCC: 1888*, p. 420.

46. Alice Stone Blackwell, "Editorial," *The Woman's Journal*, April 11, 1911.

47. U.S. Department of Labor, Women's Bureau, *Handbook on Women Workers*, Bulletin No. 294, (Washington D.C.: Government Printing Office, 1969); and *Historical Statistics*, op. cit., pp. 132–133.

48. Annie Marion Mac Lean, *Wage-Earning Women* (New York: Macmillan, 1919), p. 178.

49. Even a small number of references to the literature of the Progressive Era confirm the nature of special concern for women. See John A. Ryan, "A Minimum Wage and Minimum Wage Boards: With Special Reference to Immigrant Labor and Woman Labor," *Proceedings, NCCC: 1910*, pp. 457–475; Ann Garton Spencer, "What Machine Dominated Industry Means in Relation to Woman's Work: The Need for New Training and Apprenticeship for Girls," *Proceedings, NCCC: 1910*, pp. 202–211; Florence Kelley, "The Family and the

Woman's Wage," *Proceedings, NCCC: 1909*, pp. 118–121; Mary Anderson, "Women's Work and Wages: The Women's Bureau and Standards of Work," *Proceedings, NCCC: 1921*, pp. 285–287.

50. Douglas, op. cit., p. 384.
51. Ibid.
52. An excellent review of this history may be found in Clarke A. Chambers, *Seedtime of Reform* (Minneapolis: University of Minnesota Press, 1963), pp. 151–182.
53. Abbott, op. cit., 2:395.
54. Ibid., 2:332.
55. Clarke A. Chambers, *Paul U. Kellogg and the Survey* (Minneapolis: University of Minnesota Press, 1971), p. 36.
56. Ibid.
57. Special message by the president of the United States to the Senate and House of Representatives at the conclusion of the White House Conference Meeting of 1909. Reprinted in *Dependent and Neglected Children*, Report of the Committee on Socially Handicapped—Dependency and Neglect—of the White House Conference on Child Health and Protection (New York: Appleton-Century, 1933), p. 56.
58. Alice Higgins, "Helping Widows To Bring Up Citizens," *Proceedings, NCCC: 1910*, p. 140.
59. Mary E. Richmond, "Public Pensions to Widows—Discussion," *Proceedings, NCCC: 1912*, pp. 492–493.
60. Ibid.
61. Frederic Almy, "Public Pensions to Widows: Experiences and Observations Which Lead Me to Oppose Such a Law," *Proceedings, NCCC: 1912*, p. 482.
62. Ibid.
63. Abbott, op. cit., 2:229.
64. U.S. Department of Labor, Children's Bureau, *Administration of Mother's Aid in Ten Localities*, prepared by Mary F. Bogue in Children's Bureau Publication No. 184 (Washington, D.C.: Government Printing Office, 1928), p. 4.
65. Ibid., pp. 25–26.
66. C. C. Carstens, "Discussion" of Emma O. Lundberg's "The Present Status of Mother's Pension Administration," *Proceedings, NCSW: 1921*, pp. 230–240. Mr. Carsten's remarks are to be found on p. 240.
67. Mary F. Bogue, *Administration of Mother's Aid in Ten Localities: With Special Reference to Health, Housing, Education and Recreation.* Children's Bureau Publication No. 184, (Washington, D.C.: Government Printing Office, 1928), p. 5.
68. Ibid., p. 20.
69. J. S. Parker, *Social Security Reserves* (Washington, D.C.: American Council on Public Affairs, 1942).
70. *Historical Statistics*, pp. 139, 723.
71. "The Negroes in the Cities of the North," *Charities and the Commons* 15 (October 7, 1905).
72. W. E. Burghardt Du Bois, "National Committee on the Negro," *The Survey* 22 (June 12, 1909): 407–408, and "National Negro Conference," *The Survey*, 24 (April 23, 1910): 124.
73. *The Survey* 29 (February 1, 1913): 567–581.
74. Franz Boas, "The Negro and the Demands of Modern Life: Ethnic and

Anatomical Considerations," *Charities and the Commons* 15 (October 7, 1905): 2.

75. Steven Diner, "Chicago Social Workers and Blacks in the Progressive Era," *Social Service Review* 44 (December 1970): 393–410.
76. Herbert Hoover, op. cit., p. 16.
77. Jane Addams, *The Second Twenty Years at Hull House* (New York: Macmillan, 1930), pp. 10–48.
78. Emil Frankel, *Poor Relief in Pennsylvania: A State-Wide Survey of Pennsylvania* (Commonwealth of Pennsylvania: By the Public Board of Welfare, 1925), pp. 65–66.
79. Josephine Shaw Lowell, "The Economic and Moral Effects of Public Outdoor Relief," *Proceedings, NCCC: 1890*, p. 82.
80. Margaret E. Rich, *A Belief in People: A History of Family Social Work* (New York: Family Service Association of America, 1956), p. 74.
81. All material dealing with the expansion of benefits to veterans in the Progressive and predepression eras is based on information to be found in U.S. Congress, House Committee Print No. 4. *Medical Care of Veterans*, 90th Cong., 1st sess., April 17, 1967. Printed for the use of the Committee on Veterans' Affairs.
82. Roy Lubove, *The Professional Altruist: The Emergence of Social Work as a Career, 1880–1930* (New York: Atheneum, 1969).
83. George A. Bellamy, "The Culture of the Family from the Standpoint of Recreation," *Proceedings, NCCC: 1914*, pp. 104–105.
84. Arthur Kennedy, ed., *Settlement Goals for the Next Third of a Century: A Symposium* (Boston: National Federation of Settlements, 1926), p. 45.
85. Porter R. Lee, "Social Work: Cause and Function," *Proceedings, NCSW: 1929*, p. 20.

Chapter 6

1. Maurice Leven, Harold G. Moulton, and Clark Warburton, *America's Capacity to Consume* (Washington, D.C.: The Brookings Institution, 1934).
2. Frederick Lewis Allen, *Only Yesterday* (New York: Bantam, 1959), p. 241.
3. U.S. Department of Commerce, Office of Business Economics, *The National Income and Product Accounts of the United States, 1929–1965—Statistical Tables* (Washington, D.C.: Government Printing Office, 1966).
4. U.S. Department of Commerce, Bureau of the Census, *Historical Statistics of the United States: Colonial Times to 1957* (Washington, D.C.: Government Printing Office, 1960), p. 73 (hereafter cited as *Historical Statistics*).
5. William H. Matthews, "Breaking the Poverty Circle," *Survey* 52 (April 15, 1924): 96–98.
6. Lucille Eaves, "Studies of Breakdowns in Family Income," *The Family* 10 (December 1929): 228.
7. Ibid., p. 227.
8. Marion Elderton, ed., *Case Studies of Unemployment* (Philadelphia: University of Pennsylvania Press, 1931), p. XXIV.
9. Ibid., pp. XXIII–XXIV.
10. U.S. 72nd Cong., 1st sess., Public Law No. 2, January 22, 1932.
11. 47 Stat. 1932, p. 709.
12. Elderton, op. cit., p. XLIX.

13. U.S. Congress, House, *Platforms of the Two Great Political Parties, 1932* (Washington, D.C.: Government Printing Office, 1945), p. 340.
14. Ibid., p. 335.
15. Ibid., p. 343.
16. Franklin D. Roosevelt, Speeches at Sioux City, Iowa, September 1932, and Pittsburgh, Pennsylvania, October 1932. Quoted in William Leuchtenberg, *Franklin D. Roosevelt & the New Deal* (New York: Harper & Row, 1963), p. 11.
17. Anne O'Hare McCormick, "Vast Tides That Stir the Capital," *The New York Times Magazine*, May 7, 1933. Also to be found in Frank Freidel, ed., *The New Deal and the American People* (Englewood Cliffs, N.J.: Prentice-Hall, 1964), p. 5.
18. *Historical Statistics*, pp. 409, 473.
19. Ibid., p. 141.
20. Ibid., p. 283.
21. Ibid.
22. U.S., Department of Agriculture, Economic Research Service, *The Farm Income Situation*, July 1958.
23. *Historical Statistics*, p. 7, 47.
24. Ibid., p. 278.
25. Ibid.
26. Ibid.
27. U.S., Department of Commerce, Bureau of the Census, *Statistical Abstract of the United States* (Washington, D.C.: Government Printing Office, 1969), Table 892, p. 590.
28. *Historical Statistics*, p. 283.
29. Ibid., p. 286.
30. Ibid., p. 278.
31. Ibid., pp. 73, 409; and *The National Income and Product Accounts*, op. cit.
32. Arthur S. Link, *American Epoch: A History of the United States Since the 1890's* (New York: Knopf, 1935), p. 347.
33. Ibid., p. 395.
34. U.S., Congress, Senate, Committee on Education and Labor, 74th Cong., 1st sess., *Hearings on Senate Resolution 266*; and 75th Cong., 1st sess., *Hearings on Senate Resolution 60*.
35. Link, op. cit., pp. 431–432.
36. Public Law 718, 75th Cong.
37. Dixon Wecter, *The Age of the Great Depression: 1929–1941*, vol. 13 of Arthur M. Schlesinger and Dixon Ryan Fox, ed., *A History of American Life* (New York: Macmillan, 1948), pp. 119–120.
38. National Urban League, "The Negro in the Industrial Depression: Negroes Out of Work," *Nation* (April 22, 1931): 441–442.
39. Bruce Minton and John Stuart, *Men Who Lead Labor* (New York: Modern Age, 1937), p. 167.
40. *Historical Statistics*, p. 71.
41. Quoted in William H. Chafe, *The American Woman* (New York: Oxford University Press, 1972), p. 107.
42. The National Economy Act, 1932, Sec. 213. For extensive documentation in regard to federal and state restrictions on the employment of married women, see Chafe, op. cit., p. 283.

43. *Historical Statistics*, p. 72.
44. U.S. Congress, House Committee Print No. 4, *Medical Care of Veterans*, 90th Congress, 1st sess., April 17, 1967, pp. 154–155. Printed for use of the Committee on Veterans' Affairs.
45. Joanna C. Colcord, "The Challenge of the Continuing Depression," *The Annals* 176 (November 1934): 17.
46. Gordon Hamilton, "Refocusing Family Casework," *Proceedings: NCSW, 1931*, p. 176.
47. Ibid., p. 178.
48. Wendell F. Johnson, "How Caseworking Agencies Have Met Unemployment," *Proceedings: NCSW, 1931*, pp. 189–200.
49. Ibid., p. 197.
50. Joanna C. Colcord, "Unemployment Relief, 1929–32," *The Family* 13 (December 1932): 270–274.
51. U.S. Federal Emergency Relief Administration, *Monthly Report*, May 22–June 30, 1933, pp. 1–2.
52. U.S. Federal Emergency Relief Administration, *Final Statistical Report* (Washington, D.C.: Government Printing Office, 1942).
53. A. F. Kifer, "The Negro Under the New Deal: 1933–1941" (Ph.D. diss., University of Wisconsin, 1961).
54. Harry L. Hopkins, "The Developing National Program of Relief," *Proceedings: NCSW, 1933*, pp. 65–67, 71.
55. President Franklin D. Roosevelt, Annual Message to Congress, January 4, 1935.
56. President Franklin D. Roosevelt, Message of the President Recommending Legislation on Economic Security, January 17, 1935.
57. Roosevelt, Annual Message to Congress, January 4, 1935.
58. Ibid.
59. Ibid.
60. Ibid.
61. Ibid.
62. William Hodson, "Unemployment Relief," *Social Work Year Book: 1937* (New York: Russell Sage Foundation, 1937), p. 522. A good review of WPA may be found in Wecter, op. cit.
63. Helen Seymour, *When Clients Organize* (Chicago: American Public Welfare Association, 1937), pp. 16–17.
64. U.S. Federal Emergency Relief Administration, *Monthly Report*, May 22–June 30, 1933, *Rules and Regulations*, p. 7.
65. "External and Internal Forces in Family and Child Welfare Work," Report of the Committee on Family and Child Welfare, Blue Ridge Institute, 1932, *The Family* 13 (November, 1932): 240.
66. Ibid.
67. U.S. Federal Emergency Relief Administration, *Monthly Report*, May 22–June 30, 1933, *Rules and Regulations*, p. 10.
68. Hopkins, op. cit., p. 68.
69. Ibid., p. 69.
70. Franklin D. Roosevelt, Acceptance of the Nomination for the Presidency, Chicago, Illinois, July 2, 1932.
71. *The Report of the Committee on Economic Security* (Washington, D.C., January 15, 1935), p. 3.

72. Ibid., p. 44.
73. President Franklin D. Roosevelt, Message of the President Recommending Legislation on Economic Security, January 17, 1935.
74. U.S., 74th Cong., 1st sess., Public Law No. 271.
75. *The Report of the Committee on Economic Security*, op. cit., p. 36.
76. U.S. Congress, Senate, Committee on Finance, Statement of Miss Katherine F. Lenroot, *Hearings on S. 1130, The Economic Security Act, January 22 to February 20, 1935, revised*, pp. 337–341.
77. U.S. Congress, House, Committee on Ways and Means, Statement of Mr. Jacob Kepecs, *Hearings on H.R. 4120, The Economic Security Act*, January 1935, pp. 500–503.
78. Edwin Witte, *The Development of the Social Security Act*, A Memorandum on the History of the Committee on Economic Security and Drafting and Legislative History of the Social Security Act (Madison: University of Wisconsin Press, 1962), p. 164.
79. Committee on Economic Security, *Social Security in America*, The Factual Background of the Social Act as summarized from staff reports for the Committee (Washington, D.C.: Government Printing Office, 1937), p. 229.
80. S. P. Breckinridge, "The Activities of Women Outside the Home," *Recent Social Trends in the United States, Report of the President's Research Committee on Social Trends* (New York: McGraw-Hill, 1933), 1:711.
81. Ibid., p. 712.
82. Ibid., p. 715.
83. Ibid., p. 712.
84. Ibid., p. 717.
85. *Historical Statistics*, p. 30.
86. Ibid., p. 23.
87. Ibid., p. 30.
88. Caroline Bird, *The Invisible Scar* (New York: David McKay, 1966), pp. 41–70.
89. American Association of Social Workers, *This Business of Relief*, Proceedings of the Delegate Conference, Washington, D.C., February 14–16, 1936 (New York: AASW, 1936).
90. Aubrey Williams, "The Works Progress Administration," ibid., pp. 128, 137.
91. Ewan Clague, "The Social Security Act as a Relief Measure," ibid., pp. 78–82.
92. Dorothy C. Kahn, "The Use of Cash, Orders for Goods, or Relief in Kind, in a Mass Program," *Proceedings: NCSW, 1933*, p. 273.
93. Harry L. Hopkins, *Spending to Save* (New York: W. W. Norton, 1936), p. 81.
94. *The Report of the Committee on Economic Security*, op. cit., p. 30.
95. Committee on Economic Security, *Social Security in America*, op. cit., p. 239.
96. Family Welfare Association of America, *The Crisis in Community Programs*, a detailed report on responses of member agency boards to propositions submitted by the Association board, March 1936. Multigraph.
97. Ibid.
98. Ibid.
99. Ibid.
100. Family Welfare Association of America, Committee on Relationship between Family and Children's Work, *Preliminary Report*, November 1937. Multigraph.
101. Frank J. Hertel, "Family Social Work," *Social Work Year Book, 1951* (New York: American Association of Social Workers, 1951), p. 187.
102. In the matter of *Helvering* v. *Davis*, the Opinion of the Supreme Court, *U.S.*

Reports, October Term, 1936 (Washington, D.C.: Government Printing Office).

103. National Conference on Social Welfare, *Proceedings, 1934* and *Proceedings, 1936* (Chicago: University of Chicago Press, 1934 and 1936, respectively), tables of contents.

Chapter 7

1. *Economic Report of the President: 1974,* Together with the Annual Report of the Council of Economic Advisors (Washington, D.C.: Government Printing Office, 1974), pp. 249, 259.
2. Ibid.
3. U.S. Bureau of the Census, *Statistical Abstract of the United States: 1973,* 94th ed. (Washington, D.C.: Government Printing Office 1973), p. 328.
4. U.S. Bureau of the Census, *Current Population Reports,* Series P 60, No. 77, May 7, 1971.
5. *Economic Report of the President: 1974,* op. cit., p. 276.
6. For a good discussion see *Economic Report of the President: 1973,* (Washington, D.C.: Government Printing Office, 1973), pp. 89–112.
7. U.S. Bureau of Labor Statistics, *Employment and Earnings,* monthly in *Monthly Labor Review.*
8. *Economic Report of the President: 1974,* op. cit., p. 219.
9. *Statistical Abstract: 1973,* op. cit., p. 51 and U.S., Department of Commerce, Bureau of the Census, *Historical Statistics of the United States: Colonial Times to 1957* (Washington, D.C.: Government Printing Office, 1960), p. 23 (hereafter cited as *Historical Statistics*). Data from U.S. National Center for Health Statistics, *Vital Statistics of the United States,* annual.
10. *Statistical Abstract: 1973,* op. cit., pp. 58–59.
11. Ibid., pp. 30, 31.
12. U.S. Bureau of the Census, *Current Population Reports,* Series P 23, No. 29, February, 1970.
13. Ibid.
14. U.S. Bureau of Economic Analysis, *Long Term Economic Growth, 1860–1970* (Washington, D.C.: U.S. Government Printing Office, 1973), p. 76.
15. Ibid., p. 185.
16. *Statistical Abstract: 1973,* op. cit., p. 585.
17. *Vital Statistics of the United States,* annual.
18. *Statistical Abstract: 1973,* op. cit., p. 54. Data from U.S. National Center for Health Statistics.
19. Nathan E. Cohen, *Social Work in the American Tradition* (New York: Dryden Press, 1958), p. 226.
20. Ibid.
21. National Commission on Productivity, *Second Annual Report* (Washington, D.C.: Government Printing Office, 1973), p. 8.
22. *Long Term Economic Growth, 1960–1970,* op. cit., p. 76.
23. *Statistical Abstract: 1973,* op. cit., p. 250.
24. Ibid., p. 319.
25. *Economic Report of the President: 1949,* Together with the Annual Economic Review, January 1949, by the Council of Economic Advisers (Washington, D.C.:

Government Printing Office, 1949), pp. 13–15.

26. *Historical Statistics*, p. 167.

27. *Economic Report of the President: 1974*, op. cit., p. 272.

28. Executive Order 8802 of June 25, 1941, vol. 6, *Federal Register*, p. 3109.

29. For an excellent review of this period, see John Hope Franklin, *From Slavery to Freedom* (New York: Vintage, 1969), pp. 573–607; and Geoffrey Perrett, *Days of Sadness, Years of Triumph: The American People, 1939–1945* (New York: Coward, McCann and Geoghegan, 1973), pp. 143–154, 310–324.

30. National Association of Social Workers, *Encyclopedia of Social Work* (New York: NASW, 1971), p. 554.

31. U.S., Congress, House Committee Print No. 4, *Medical Care of Veterans*, 90th Cong., 1st sess., April 17, 1967, p. 168. Prepared for the use of the House Committee on Veterans' Affairs.

32. *The Budget of the United States Government* (Washington, D.C.: Government Printing Office), fiscal years, annually.

33. *Social Work Year Book: 1945* (New York: Russell Sage Foundation, 1945), pp. 84–92, 163, 479–485, 502, 505.

34. U.S., 77th Cong., 2nd sess., Public Law No. 625, June 23, 1942.

35. *Social Work Year Book: 1947* (New York: Russell Sage Foundation, 1947), p. 414.

36. U.S., 76th Cong., 3rd sess., Public Law No. 801, October 8, 1940.

37. The President's Commission on Veterans' Pensions, *The Historical Development of Veterans' Benefits in the United States*, A Report on Veterans' Benefits in the United States, 84th Cong., 2nd sess., House Committee Print No. 244, May 9, 1956, p. 57.

38. Ibid., p. 52.

39. Public Law 346, 78th Congress, 2nd Session, June 22, 1944.

40. U.S. Senate, 78th Congress, Finance Committee, Report 755. Cited in The President's Commission on Veterans' Benefits, op. cit., p. 53.

41. The President's Commission on Veterans' Benefits, op. cit., p. 55.

42. *Historical Statistics*, p. 740.

43. *Brown* v. *Board of Education of Topeka*, 347, U.S. 483 (1954).

44. U.S. Department of Health, Education, and Welfare, *Social Security Bulletin*, monthly.

45. Winifred Bell, *Aid to Dependent Children* (New York: Columbia University Press, 1965).

46. *Benny Max Parrish* v. *The Civil Service Commission of the County of Alameda*, S.F. 22429, Supreme Court of California in Bank, March 27, 1967.

47. Michael Harrington, *The Other America: Poverty in the United States* (New York: Macmillan, 1962); Dwight MacDonald, "Our Invisible Poor," *The New Yorker* (January 19, 1963): 37.

48. Ibid.

49. *Economic Report of the President, 1964*, Together with the Annual Report of the Council of Economic Advisers (Washington, D.C.: Government Printing Office, 1964), pp. 55–83.

50. The Civil Rights Act of 1964, Public Law 83-352, 78 Stat. 241, Title VII.

51. U.S. Bureau of the Census, *Statistical Abstract of the United States: 1964*, 85th ed. (Washington, D.C.: U.S. Government Printing Office, 1964) and U.S. Bureau of the Census, *Statistical Abstract of the United States: 1971*, 92nd ed. (Washington, D.C.: Government Printing Office, 1971).

52. Office Memorandum, U.S. Government, Abraham Ribicoff to Mr. W. L. Mitchell, commissioner of Social Security, December 6, 1961. To be found in U.S. Congress, House Committee on Ways and Means, *Hearings on H.R. 10032, Public Welfare Amendments of 1962*, 87th Cong., 2nd sess. February 7, 9, and 13, 1962, pp. 158–162.

53. *Hearings on H.R. 10032*, op. cit., p. 64.

54. George K. Wyman, "A Reporter for the Secretary of Health, Education, and Welfare," August 1961. To be found in *Hearings on H.R. 10032*, op. cit., p. 108.

55. Report of the Ad Hoc Committee on Public Welfare to the Secretary of Health, Education, and Welfare, September 1961. To be found in *Hearings on H.R. 10032*, op. cit., p. 78.

56. *Hearings on H.R. 10032*, op. cit., p. 430.

57. Report of the Ad Hoc Committee, op. cit., p. 73.

58. Ibid., pp. 81–100.

59. Ibid., p. 74.

60. Office Memorandum, U.S. Government, op. cit., p. 158–162.

61. President John F. Kennedy, Message to Congress on Public Welfare, February 1962.

62. Public Law 87-543 had been considered as H.R. 10032 in public hearings held by the House Committee on Ways and Means, February 7, 9, and 13, 1962. It was introduced on March 8, 1962 in the House of Representatives as H.R. 10606 by Congressman Wilbur D. Mills.

63. U.S. Congress, House of Representatives, *Compilation of the Social Security Laws, including the Social Security Act, as Amended, and Related Enactments through December 31, 1962*, House Document No. 616, 87th Cong., 2nd sess., p. 132.

64. Ibid., Title IV, Sec. 407, p. 142.

65. Ibid., Sec. 409, pp. 144–146.

66. Ibid., Sec. 528, p. 158.

67. Gilbert Steiner, *Social Insecurity* (Chicago: Rand McNally, 1966), pp. 142–147, Steiner reviews the reasoning of professional social workers during this period.

68. American Public Welfare Association, Statement Submitted to the Advisory Council on Public Welfare, San Francisco, California, August 12, 1965, p. 6.

69. See, for example, Herman Levin, "The Essential Voluntary Agency," *Social Work* 11 (January 1966): 98–106. See also Ellen Winston, "A New Era of Partnership in Services for Children," *Child Welfare* 43 (May 1964): 221–225; and in the same issue, Leonard W. Mayo, "Discussion of a New Era of Partnership for Children," 225–228.

70. *Compilation of the Social Security Laws*, op. cit., Title IV, Sec. 403, p. 136.

71. U.S., Department of Health, Education and Welfare, Social Security Administration, Bureau of Family Services, Press Release, January 6, 1963.

72. President Lyndon B. Johnson, Message on Poverty, March 16, 1964.

73. U.S. 88th Cong., 2nd sess., Public Law 88-452, Sec. 2.

74. Congressional Presentation, March 17, 1964, prepared under the direction of Sargent Shriver. To be found in *The War on Poverty: The Economic Act of 1964*, A Compilation of Materials Relevant to S. 2642, prepared for the Select Subcommittee on Poverty of the U.S. Senate Committee on Labor and Public Welfare, 88th Cong., 2nd sess., Document No. 86, July 23, 1964, p. 65.

75. U.S., Department of Health, Education, and Welfare, Welfare Administration, *Having the Power, We Have the Duty*, Report of the Advisory Council on Public Welfare to the Secretary of H.E.W., June 29, 1966.
76. Gilbert Steiner, *The State of Welfare* (Washington, D.C.: The Brookings Institution, 1971), p. 109.
77. U.S. Department of Health, Education, and Welfare, "Report of the Task Force in Social Services," Submitted to Assistant Secretary Lisle Carter, September 1, 1966, in the files of the department.
78. Quoted in National Association of Social Workers, *Washington Memorandum*, No. 90-1-9, August 30, 1967.
79. National Association of Social Workers, *Policy Statement on Separation of Social Services and Income Security Programs*. Approved by the Board of Directors, June 29, 1967.
80. U.S. Supreme Court, *In re: Gault et al.*, No. 116, May 15, 1967.

Chapter 8

1. For a discussion of this point, see Aris T. Allen, *The New York Times*, July 13, 1980, p. E 21.
2. David Cohen, President of Common Cause, membership letter, June 1980.
3. For an interesting discussion of family policy concepts, see Allan C. Carlson, "Families, Sex, and the Liberal Agenda," *The Public Interest*, No. 58 (Winter 1980): 62–79.
4. U.S. Department of Commerce, Bureau of the Census, *Current Population Reports*, Series P-25, and *Historical Statistics of the United States: Colonial Times to 1970*.
5. An early discussion of some of the issues involved may be found in Juanita M. Kreps, "Social Security in the Coming Decade: Questions For A Mature System", *Social Security Bulletin* 39 (March 1976): 21–29.
6. U.S. Department of Labor, Bureau of Labor Statistics. *Employment in Perspective: Working Women*, monthly; and *Historical Statistics of the United States: Colonial Times to 1970*.
7. U.S. Bureau of the Census, *Current Population Reports*, Series P-60, No. 125, "Money Income and Poverty Status of Families and Persons in the United States, 1979," (Advance Report). (Washington, D.C.: Government Printing Office, 1980).
8. Robert J. Lampman, "Changing Patterns of Income, 1960–1974," in David Warner, ed., *Toward New Human Rights: The Social Policies of the Kennedy and Johnson Administrations* (Austin: The University of Texas, 1977), p. 122.
9. Kenneth Keniston, *All Our Children: The American Family Under Pressure* (New York: Harcourt Brace Jovanovich, 1977), p. 26.
10. U.S. Bureau of the Census, op. cit., Table 5, p. 14.
11. *Fullilove* v. *Kulznick*, Bureau of National Affairs, *U.S. Law Week, Supreme Court* 48 (July 2, 1980): 4979–5008.
12. Joseph Goldstein, Anna Freud, and Albert J. Solnit, *Beyond the Best Interest of the Child* (New York: Free Press, 1979).
13. For an excellent review of this history, see Edward Chase, "The Burger Court, The Individual and Criminal Process: Directions and Misdirections," *New York*

University Law Review 52:518−597; and "The 9th Annual Review of Criminal Procedure," *Georgetown Law Journal* 68(2): 384−390; 487−506.

14. Frances Piven and Richard Cloward, "Eroding Welfare Rights," *Civil Liberties Review* (Winter−Spring 1974):41−51.

15. *Harris* v. *McRae,* Bureau of National Affairs, op. cit., June 30, 1980, pp. 4941−4957.

16. Alma W. McMillan and Ann Kallman Bixby, "Social Welfare Expenditures, Fiscal Year, 1978," *Social Security Bulletin,* 43 (May 1980):3−17.

17. Edward R. Fried et al., *Setting National Priorities: The 1974 Budget* (Washington, D.C.: The Brookings Institution, 1973), pp. 170−232; Barry M. Blechman et al., *Setting National Priorities: The 1975 Budget* (Washington, D.C.: The Brookings Institution, 1974), pp. 18−42, 166−206.

18. Executive Office of the President, *The Budget of the United States Government, 1981* (Washington, D.C.: Government Printing Office, 1980).

19. Ibid.

20. *Report on H.R. 1,* U.S. Congress, House Committee on Ways and Means, 92nd Cong., 1st sess., 1971, p. 163.

21. U.S. 92nd Cong., 2nd sess., Public Law 92-223, December 28, 1971.

22. President Richard M. Nixon, Message on Reform in Welfare, August 11, 1969.

23. U.S. Department of Health, Education, and Welfare, *Poverty Amid Plenty: The American Paradox,* Report of the President's Commission on Income Maintenance, November 1969.

24. Social Security Administration, Annual Statistical Supplement to the *Social Security Bulletin;* monthly.

25. For a detailed description of discussions of welfare reform see Gordon L. Weil, *The Welfare Debate of 1978* (White Plains, N.Y.: Institute for Socioeconomic Studies, 1978); and Irving Garfinkel, "Welfare Reform: Two Views," *Journal/The Institute for Socioeconomic Studies* 4(4, 1979): p. 58−72.

26. See, for example, U.S. Department of Health, Education, and Welfare, *Social Security Financing and Benefits,* Reports of the 1979 Advisory Council on Social Security, December 1979.

27. U.S. Department of Health, Education, and Welfare, *Social Security and the Changing Roles of Men and Women,* February 1979.

28. Institute for Socioeconomic Studies, *The Socioeconomic Newsletter* (May 1980):1 (White Plains: ISS).

29. *Inventory of Federal Income Transfer Programs* (White Plains, N.Y.: ISS, 1979), p. 10.

30. Weil, op. cit., p. 98.

31. Reports of the 1979 Advisory Council on Social Security, p. 1.

32. U.S. Department of Labor, Bureau of Labor Statistics, *News,* "The Employment Situation," May 1980.

33. Lucy Edwards, Assistant General Counsel, U.S. Commission on Civil Rights. Quoted in the *New York Times,* June 20, 1974, p. 44.

34. U.S. Department of Justice, Task Force on Sex Discrimination. *The Pension Game: American Pension System From the Viewpoint of the American Woman* (Washington, D.C.: Government Printing Office, 1979).

35. U.S. Department of Labor, National Commission for Manpower Policy, *Women's Changing Roles at Home and On the Job,* Special Report No. 26, September 1978.

36. Sec. 341 of PL 95-216.
37. U.S. Department of Health, Education, and Welfare, *Social Security and the Changing Roles of Men and Women*, February 1979.
38. Ibid., p. 4.
39. Ibid., p. 7.
40. Advisory Council, p. 91.
41. To be found in U.S. Congress, House Committee Print No. 4, *Medical Care of Veterans*, 90th Cong., 1st sess., April 17, 1967, p. 255. Prepared for the use of the Committee on Veterans' Affairs.
42. U.S. Congress, *Congressional Record*, 78th Cong., 2nd sess., 1944, 90 pt. 5:6588.
43. Peter F. Drucker, "The Sickness of Government," *The Public Interest* 14 (Winter 1969): 3–23.
44. For a discussion of the issues in purchase of service by the states see "The Politics and Organization of Services," *Public Welfare*, 36 (Summer 1978): 13–55.
45. Ira Glasser, "Life Under the New Feudalism," *Civil Liberties Review* (Winter–Spring, 1974): 27–40.

Index